R THE ADMINISTRATION O

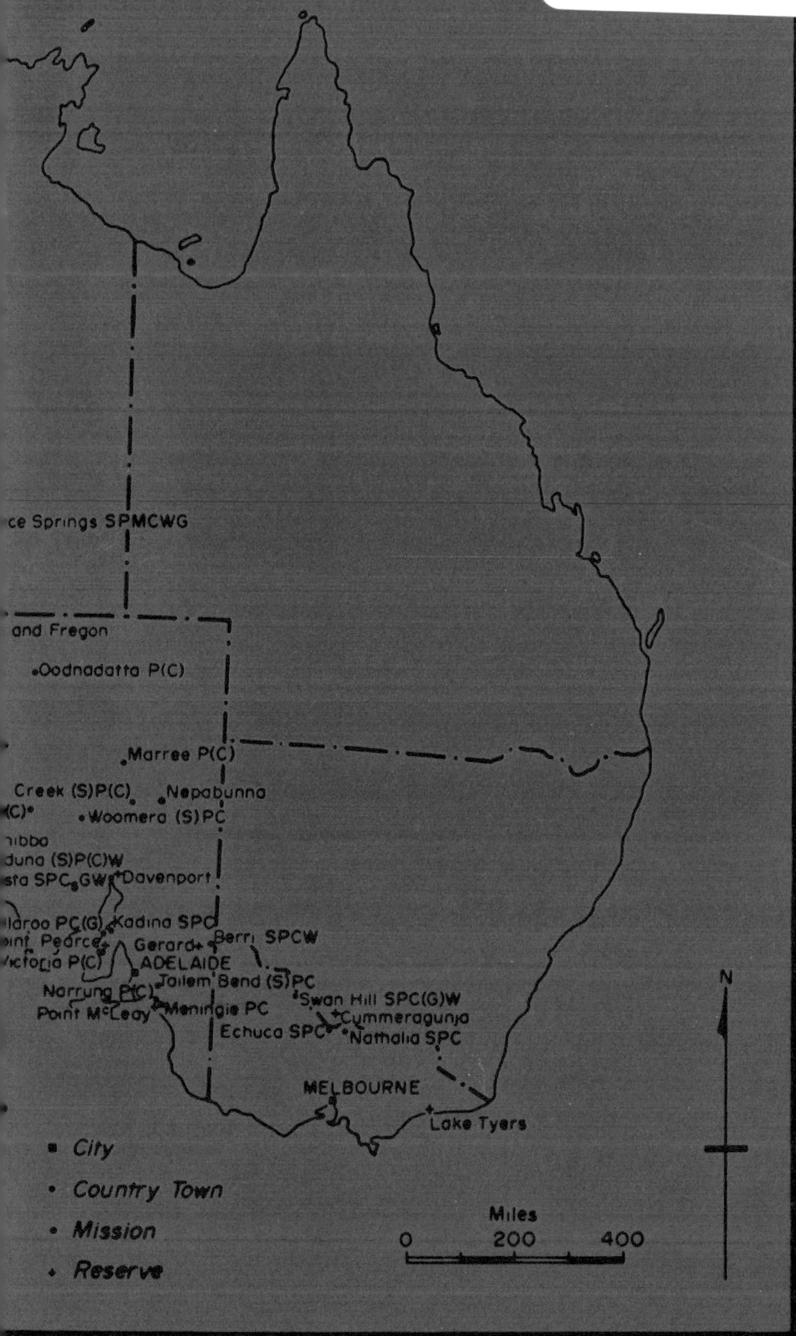

FEAR, FAVOUR OR AFFECTION

Aborigines in Australian Society 13

A series sponsored by
The Academy of the Social Sciences in Australia

FEAR, FAVOUR OR AFFECTION

ABORIGINES AND THE CRIMINAL LAW IN VICTORIA, SOUTH AUSTRALIA AND WESTERN AUSTRALIA

Elizabeth Eggleston

AUSTRALIAN NATIONAL UNIVERSITY PRESS, CANBERRA 1976

First published in Australia 1976

Printed in Australia for the Australian National University Press, Canberra

National Library of Australia Cataloguing-in-Publication entry

---

Eggleston, Elizabeth Moulton.
Fear, favour or affection: Aborigines and the criminal law in Victoria, South Australia and Western Australia/ [by] Elizabeth Eggleston.—Canberra: Australian National University Press, 1976.—(Aborigines in Australian society; 13).
Index.
Based on the author's thesis 'Aborigines and the administration of justice: a critical analysis of the application of the criminal law to Aborigines'—Monash University, 1970.
Bibliography.
ISBN 0 7081 0191 7.

1. Criminal justice, Administration of—Australia.
[2]. Aborigines, Australian—Crime. I. Title (Series).

345.94

North, South, and Central America: International Scholarly Book Services, Inc., Portland, Oregon.
Southeast Asia: Angus & Robertson (S.E. Asia) Pty Ltd, Singapore.
Japan: United Publishers Services Ltd, Tokyo.

A justice swears to 'do equal justice to the poor and the rich and discharge the duties of my office . . . without fear, favour or affection'—

Justices Act, 1902 (W.A.).

FEAR, FAVOUR OR AFFECTION

NOTE ON THE SERIES

The Social Science Research Council of Australia (now The Academy of the Social Sciences in Australia), which was founded in its present form in 1952, is the national organisation of social scientists. Some of its major functions are:

to encourage the advancement of the social sciences in Australia;
to act as a co-ordinating group for the promotion of research and teaching in the social sciences;
to foster research and to subsidise the publication of studies in the social sciences.

To these ends the Council has sponsored a number of major research projects. The first related to the role of women in public and professional life in Australia and was carried out by Mr Norman MacKenzie. His report, together with the associated study of the legal status of women in Australia by Dr Enid Campbell, was published in 1962 in a book, *Women in Australia* (F.W. Cheshire Pty Ltd, Melbourne).

The second major project, carried out by a group of economists, was concerned with the Australian taxation structure and under the authorship of R.I. Downing, H.W. Arndt, A.H. Boxer, and R.L. Mathews, the results were published in 1964 in *Taxation in Australia: Agenda for Reform* (Melbourne University Press, Melbourne).

In 1963 the Council approved its third and most ambitious major project, Aborigines in Australian Society, with the broad objectives of:

elucidating the problems arising from contacts between Aborigines and non-Aborigines and formulating policy implications from these;
drawing together existing knowledge in various parts of Australia

and undertaking such further original research as can be carried out over a period of three years.

In May 1964, Mr C.D. Rowley, formerly Principal of the Australian School of Pacific Administration in Sydney, was appointed Director of the Project, to work under the general guidance of a Project Committee appointed by the Council. The volumes now being published represent a major research enterprise in which many social scientists collaborated over the length and breadth of Australia.

However, the whole enterprise depended in very large measure on the magnificent support received, from the outset, from the Myer Foundation of Australia and the Sidney Myer Charity Trust. The Council wishes to acknowledge its gratitude for their generosity.

W.D. Borrie

PREFACE

Until recently the outstanding feature of the literature on Aborigines was the paucity of material on current socio-economic, political and legal aspects of Aboriginal life (Tatz 1967:53). More attention is now being paid to these topics but few studies on the relationship between Aborigines and the law have yet been published.

Campbell and Whitmore discuss current legislation relating to Aborigines but go on to point out that 'an entire volume would be required to even sketch the practical administration of the law' (Campbell and Whitmore 1966:248). The present volume is an attempt to supply in part this deficiency. It was decided to study not only the administration of special legislation relating to Aborigines but also the administration of the general law as it affected them.

Even a cursory examination of official statistics reveals heavy involvement of Aborigines with the criminal law. Welfare agencies must be aware of such involvement, yet little has been heard about it in current discussions of the problems of Aborigines. A few excellent articles by anthropologists have appeared about Aborigines and the law, chiefly relating to Aboriginal evidence and its value, but lawyers have rarely written on the subject.

It was originally intended to study both criminal and civil law, but as research proceeded it became apparent that, in practice, Aborigines' involvement with the criminal law completely overshadowed their contact with the civil law. The fact that Aborigines do not often participate in civil proceedings, particularly as plaintiffs, is in itself significant. Precise information on the extent of their participation (or rather non-participation) was difficult to obtain and for this reason, civil law has been omitted.

The study examines the administration of the criminal law in its application to Aborigines in Victoria, South Australia and Western Australia. First, background material is presented on the general situation of Aborigines in the Australian community, on the framework of legal institutions in the three States and on the pattern of Aboriginal involvement with the criminal law.

Chapters 3-6 then examine the treatment of Aborigines under the general law at all stages of the criminal justice process from the initiation of prosecution to sentencing. Chapters 7 and 8 look at special laws and institutions established for Aborigines as a separate group and Chapter 9 deals with what I have called the 'indigenous legal system', that is, the remnants of tribal law and custom, and examines the question whether these survivals may be used in future administration of the law affecting Aborigines. Finally an attempt is made to draw conclusions about the nature of the administration of criminal justice and to make suggestions about principles to be adopted in the reform of law and practice.

Fieldwork for the doctoral thesis on which this book is based began with two months' work on records at the headquarters of the Victoria Police in Melbourne in 1965. The year from March 1966 to March 1967 was spent on fieldwork in South Australia and Western Australia.

In rewriting for publication, I have not attempted a comprehensive revision to bring the study up to date. It remains a description of the situation existing during the fieldwork period (1965-7). Legislation discussed is mainly that operative at the time, though at some points reference has been made to later developments in the law.

The statistical tables in the original work were more complex than those reproduced here, as they included chi-square values in addition to percentages. Anyone interested in this more detailed statistical presentation should consult the original thesis.

Though there have been considerable changes in Aboriginal affairs since this study was carried out, it still has contemporary relevance. The most significant development has been the growth of the Aboriginal Legal Services. The availability of legal assistance specifically for Aborigines has already had some impact on the situation described here and will have more in the future. But there are still too many Aborigines being arrested and detained in Australian prisons.

E.E.

ACKNOWLEDGMENTS

So many people assisted me in the course of this research that it is impossible to name them all individually. But I am grateful to all named and unnamed assistants and informants.

I would particularly like to thank those Ministers and Police Commissioners who gave me permission to read police and court records; mission authorities and missionaries who enabled me to enjoy visiting missions; and government officers who helped in innumerable ways. The Commonwealth Bureau of Census and Statistics in Perth was particularly helpful in providing statistical information.

Professor Charles Rowley, as Director Aborigines Project of the Academy of Social Sciences in Australia, helped me to obtain access to records during fieldwork. I wish to thank him and the Academy.

As a newcomer to the strange world of computers I thank Mr B. Neil and Mr Kim Wyman for writing the computer programs that were used in this research; the students and others who assisted with the coding for the punched cards; and particularly Mr Oscar Roberts, who encouraged me to persist with the statistical treatment of the cases.

Monash University provided a Graduate Scholarship and a grant which made the fieldwork possible. My deepest debt of gratitude is to Professor D.P. Derham, who offered considerable encouragement and support as my thesis supervisor; to Professor P.L. Waller, who took over the task of supervision when Professor Derham left Monash, and to Professor Colin Tatz, who initially suggested the project and has helped in every way since I first started to work on it.

Professor G. Sawer offered helpful suggestions on how the thesis should be rewritten for publication. Finally I wish to acknowledge the assistance of the Australian Research Grants Committee, which provided a grant for, amongst other things, checking and supplementing the statistical data which had originally been compiled for the thesis.

Thanks are due to the Geography Department at Monash University for work in preparing the maps. I am particularly grateful to Mr Bruce Petty, cartoonist with *The Australian*, Sydney, for drawing the illustration on p. xx. I should also like to thank Mr Dougie Young for permission to quote from a song he wrote and Ms Edith Pearse, Ms Cheryl Buchanan and the Battye Library for assistance with plates.

CONTENTS

ILLUSTRATIONS

APPENDIXES

They are not ready for justice yet.
ABORIGINALS
WHITE COURTS
LAW
BAIL ETC
Petty

INTRODUCTION

METHODS OF RESEARCH

At the beginning of the study it was expected that Aborigines would show a high rate of involvement with legal institutions. This was readily confirmed by examination of official statistics for Western Australia, which showed, for example, that the percentage of the Aboriginal population in prison is much higher than that of the white population. One objective of the study was simply to discover whether a similar pattern occurred in the other States.

A further and more important objective was to find explanations for the imbalance found. On one hand overrepresentation in the prison population may be due to greater criminality in the Aboriginal population when compared with the white population; alternatively, it may be due to discrimination in the administration of justice. If the latter explanation is correct, the greater number of Aborigines in prison is due to 'career contingencies', in Goffman's phrase (1968: 126), rather than to actual criminality. The study attempts to test which of these explanations is closer to the truth by ascertaining whether there is any discrimination in the way criminal law is administered for Aboriginal and white defendants.

Discrimination in the administration of justice may operate in different ways. First, officials of the legal system may not be impartial and may express prejudiced attitudes in discriminatory acts against Aborigines. Such discrimination is not justified by existing legal rules. On the other hand, there may be discrimination built into the legal system itself. Some legislation applies only to Aborigines and law officers who enforce that legislation are then acting in accordance with law even though they thereby discriminate against Aborigines.

To establish the framework within which the administration of law functions, orthodox legal materials were collected, including legislation, delegated legislation and reported cases. It soon became clear, however, that to obtain a picture of the law in action it would be necessary to undertake fieldwork and collect other types of data, including unreported cases.

More extensive fieldwork was undertaken in South Australia and Western Australia than in Victoria. In the former two States some time was spent in the capital cities and many country towns and the missions and Aboriginal reserves as shown on the front endpaper map were visited.

The choice of places to visit was determined by two factors: the concentration of Aboriginal population and the location of courts and police stations. Most country towns were selected because it was known that they had a substantial Aboriginal population but others were visited because, for example, they were police district headquarters, even if there was not a large Aboriginal population. The map shows where facilities for the administration of justice exist.

It cannot be claimed that the country towns visited constitute a representative sample of all towns in South Australia and Western Australia, but they may reasonably be considered to represent a sample of towns having a relatively large Aboriginal population.

The main method of obtaining information was to search police and court records. Interviews were also held with magistrates and judges, justices of the peace, police officers, solicitors, crown prosecutors, officers of Aboriginal welfare departments, prison officers, Aborigines, members of Aboriginal advancement organisations and other interested people.

Direct observation provided information about the conduct of court hearings, police actions, and the physical surroundings and actual operation of reserves, missions and prisons.

The collection of information was directed to establishing whether Aborigines were treated differently from whites in the process of administering the criminal law. Differential treatment may be either disadvantageous or favourable to a particular group. Merely to find different treatment does not establish that the Aboriginal group is being subjected to racial discrimination.

In some instances it is clear that different treatment is unfavourable and that there is discrimination against members of the minority group. In other cases, an attempt may be made to justify different treatment on the ground that it is beneficial or protective of the Aborigines. Such claims are sometimes difficult to assess. 'Discrimination' is a somewhat slippery concept. The final chapter discusses the idea of equality, the underlying value sought by those who want to do away with racial discrimination. It is hoped that this study will show how in some contexts the pursuit of equality should lead to similar treatment for Aborigines and whites, while in other circumstances differential (preferential) treatment may be justified.

Two main approaches were adopted in treating the data collected during fieldwork. First, quantitative analysis was applied to a sample of criminal cases heard by the courts. The sample consists of almost all the 1965 cases collected from ten Western Australian country towns (all cases from seven towns; from the other three cases were collected for varying periods, none less than six months). The 4002 cases so derived are referred to as the 'Ten Towns Sample'. The statistical tables relating to the Ten Towns Sample have been included together in Appendix 2 for ease of reference. Comments on them are included where relevant throughout the book.

Quantitative methods are intended to provide objective measurements against which to test subjective impressions gained from interviews and direct observation. They also enable a picture of the average, standard practice to be drawn. Provided that the Ten Towns Sample is sufficiently representative, it also enables predictions to be made about what would be found if cases in other country towns were examined and if cases heard in other years in these towns were analysed.

The second, equally important, method of treatment of data collected is non-quantitative. Individual cases have been selected for comment or criticism if they point to any discrimination, anomaly or malfunctioning of the system of administration of justice. The illustrative material used in this way covers all case records collected during fieldwork in all three States and also information obtained from interviews and direct observation. Most of these cases are not reported in official law reports.

It can not be claimed that individual cases used to illustrate particular points are necessarily representative of the general operation of the criminal justice system. At times the most extreme examples are cited but this should be clear from the context. The justification for using this material rather than confining attention to the average pattern as revealed in the statistics is twofold. First, discussion of individual cases gives life to dry statistics; it becomes apparent that human beings are involved, both as defendants and as officials of the criminal justice system. Secondly, lawyers are concerned with injustice wherever it occurs. An individual unjustly treated is important whether or not he represents a significant statistic.

The value of a dual approach has been stated by Mitchell (1966: 42): 'In this interaction between intensive and quantitative research it is likely that fruitful hypotheses will arise most frequently out of the insights acquired in intensive studies. The appropriate role for quantitative research is to test and refine these hypotheses rather than to generate them.'

TERMINOLOGY

Unless otherwise stated an 'Aboriginal' is defined as a person of Aboriginal descent who identifies as an Aboriginal and is accepted as such by the community with which he is associated. This definition is now used by the federal government. The wide definition is preferred because it overcomes the marked inconsistencies of definitions embodied in legislation of the various States and because it substitutes a cultural test for a racial one.

'Full-blood' refers to a person whose ancestry is solely Aboriginal; 'part-Aboriginal' refers to a person of mixed descent. 'Native' was the former Western Australian term for 'Aboriginal', as defined in the State legislation.

The term 'white' is used to refer to the majority group in the Australian population, those of European origin.

1 THE BACKGROUND

ABORIGINES TODAY

POPULATION AND GEOGRAPHICAL DISTRIBUTION

It has been estimated that the population of Aborigines in Australia at the date of European occupation (1788) was about 300,000 (Mulvaney 1969: 40). Since that time a substantial reduction in the Aboriginal population has occurred, though the numbers are now increasing again. Estimates current at the time of fieldwork put the total population at approximately 130,100, comprising both full-bloods and part-Aborigines (Dunn and Tatz 1969: 60-1; Commonwealth. Department of Territories 1967: 50-1, 61-2). This figure is an estimate of the total population of 'Aborigines' as defined earlier, namely those persons who identify themselves as being of Aboriginal descent.

Other population estimates differ from this figure, chiefly owing to different concepts of the meaning of 'Aboriginal'. The 1966 Commonwealth Census showed a total Aboriginal population of 80,207 but included only persons of 50 per cent or more Aboriginal blood (Commonwealth. Bureau of Census and Statistics 1968: 150). Aborigines have been enumerated in all Commonwealth censuses but the degree of coverage and information obtained has varied substantially over the years. At the 1966 Census efforts were made to obtain complete coverage.

Although some had been counted in previous censuses, full-blood Aborigines were excluded from published census tables, because it was considered that section 127 of the Commonwealth Constitution prevented their inclusion. Sawer has shown that this was a misinterpretation of the section, which actually operated only to prevent Aborigines from being taken into account in the distribution of federal electorates (Sawer 1966; 1969). In 1967 section 127 was repealed following a referendum, so that Aborigines are now counted for all electoral purposes.[1] The repeal also removed the basis for the misapprehension about the census and Aborigines are now included in Commonwealth demographic tables.

Out of the total of 130,100 the estimated Aboriginal population of the three States visited on fieldwork was as shown in the following table (Dunn and Tatz 1969: 60-1; Commonwealth. Department of Territories 1967: 62):

	Victoria	South Australia	Western Australia
Full-blood Aborigines	—	3128	9905
Part-Aborigines	3500	4632	11985
Totals	3500	7760	21890

The estimated total population of these three States as at 31 December 1966 (Commonwealth. Bureau of Census and Statistics 1968: 122) and the percentage of Aborigines thus represented in those populations was: Victoria 3,249,870 (0·1 per cent), South Australia 1,104,590 (0·7 per cent) and Western Australia 862,685 (2·5 per cent).

The decline in the Aboriginal population after the advent of white settlers was accompanied by a shift in geographical distribution. In 1788 the Aboriginal 'population was spread thinly over the continent' (Mulvaney 1969: 40). The back endpaper map illustrates the estimated population distribution in 1966. It can be seen that the heaviest concentrations of Aboriginal population are outside the metropolitan area. This pattern contrasts sharply with that of the white population.

The percentage distribution of population between urban and rural areas in the three States at 30 June 1966 is shown in the following table:[2]

[1] Constitution Alteration (Aboriginals) Act 1967 (Cwlth).

[2] Commonwealth Bureau of Census and Statistics 1968: 123. A detailed explanation of terms 'urban', 'rural', etc. is set out there. 'Migratory' means persons travelling on the census night, not migrating workers, as might be expected.

	Victoria	South Australia	Western Australia
Urban—			
Metropolitan	65·54	66·67	59·76
Other	19·97	15·92	16·76
Rural	14·39	17·27	23·12
Migratory	0·09	0·14	0·36
Total	100·00	100·00	100·00

Full-blood Aborigines are excluded but other Aborigines are included. It is clear that a substantial majority of the white population is to be found in the capital cities.

The map shows heavy concentrations of Aboriginal population at some of the places visited on fieldwork, including Lake Tyers and Swan Hill in Victoria; Point Pearce, Point McLeay and Ernabella in South Australia; Broome, Derby, Port Hedland, Onslow and the Warburton Ranges in Western Australia. In Western Australia it is particularly noticeable that Aborigines are concentrated in areas remote from Perth and where there are few lawyers (see front endpaper map).

The regional distribution of the Western Australian and South Australian Aboriginal population is shown in Appendix 3.

LIVING CONDITIONS

The majority of Aborigines live in poverty. Stubbs (1966: 7-8) estimated that 'probably 90 per cent of the people of Aboriginal descent in Australia are living in poverty, some to a degree matched only in the most backward of the poverty-stricken areas of Asia, Africa and Latin America'. The fact of poverty is obvious to anyone who visits Aborigines on reserves, missions and in shanties on the fringes of country towns.

The dimensions of their poverty have been documented in recent studies. Rowley's survey of non-metropolitan areas in New South Wales and South Australia shows the high proportion of Aborigines who live in shack dwellings. In South Australia it was 28·3 per cent of the people surveyed. By contrast the proportion of the Australian rural population as a whole living in such dwellings was only 4·2 per cent (Rowley 1971: 317).

Closely linked with poverty (both as cause and effect) are limited education and low occupational status. Rowley (1971: 309) sets out school attainments of Aborigines who had left school and for whom the information could be obtained. Of this group in South Australia, 49·6 per cent had incomplete primary schooling; 36 per cent had primary only; 10·8 per cent had secondary, below Intermediate; 3·6 per cent had Intermediate, and none had any higher educational qualifications.

There is no reason to suppose that the position is much better in Victoria or Western Australia. Broom's analysis of the 1966 Census figures demonstrates that, though Aboriginal educational attainment varies from State to State, it is inadequate everywhere (Broom 1970: 152; see also Dunn and Tatz 1969). Many Aborigines are completely or functionally illiterate.

With the handicap of inadequate education it is not surprising that many Aborigines find only unskilled or casual employment or are frequently unemployed.[3] Poor education handicaps Aborigines in many ways other than employment (Broom 1970: 155). Aboriginal poverty is also reflected in poor health, including a high infant mortality rate (see, for example, Kalokerinos 1969).

It is apparent that Aborigines as a group have the lowest socio-economic status of any in the community. To some extent the adoption of a cultural definition of 'Aboriginal' rather than a racial one probably distorts the overall picture. There are, no doubt, a number of people with some Aboriginal ancestry who do not identify as 'Aborigines' and thus are not included in the population studied here. Other people of similar racial origin who have remained on reserves or as 'fringe-dwellers' (that is, in the poorest conditions) are identified as Aborigines.

ABORIGINAL ADMINISTRATION

Originally the Commonwealth Constitution gave no power to the federal Parliament to legislate for Aborigines, except in the Northern Territory and other federal territories. The referendum of 1967 produced an overwhelming vote in favour of an amendment of section 51(xxvi) of the Constitution (Sawer 1966; 1969: 1-2). As a result the Commonwealth Parliament may now treat the Aborigines as a 'race for whom it is deemed necessary to make special laws'.

A federal Department of Aboriginal Affairs has now been established. During the fieldwork period, however, the States had exclusive legislative power over Aborigines within their respective boundaries. The following authorities administered Aboriginal affairs in the three fieldwork States:

[3] For the pattern of Aboriginal employment see *Annual Report for the year ended 30th June, 1966. Commissioner of Native Welfare* (1966), p. 64. Perth: Government Printer.

in South Australia, the Department of Aboriginal Affairs and the Aboriginal Affairs Board; in Western Australia, the Department of Native Welfare; and in Victoria, the Aborigines Welfare Board.[4] Welfare officers referred to in this study are officials of these authorities.

Before 1967 there was little co-ordination of Aboriginal policies between the different States. Commonwealth and State Ministers did hold a conference in 1937 to discuss Aboriginal policies (Commonwealth. Department of Territories 1967: 38). Similar conferences have been held at intervals since then.

The 1965 conference adopted the definition of the policy of assimilation which was then accepted by all Australian governments:

> The policy of assimilation seeks that all persons of Aboriginal descent will choose to attain a similar manner and standard of living to that of other Australians and live as members of a single Australian community—enjoying the same rights and privileges, accepting the same responsibilities and influenced by the same hopes and loyalties as other Australians. Any special measures taken are regarded as temporary measures, not based on race, but intended to meet their need for special care and assistance and to make the transition from one stage to another in such a way as will be favourable to their social, economic and political advancement. (Commonwealth. Department of Territories 1967: 44)

Aborigines resisted the idea of assimilation, as most prefer to keep a separate identity. The federal Department of Aboriginal Affairs has now abandoned the assimilation policy and lays stress instead on Aboriginal self-determination, recognition of Aboriginal culture and accommodation to Aboriginal concepts (Dexter 1974).

These ideas had not gained currency in government circles during the fieldwork period. Unfortunately ideas of assimilation ('to make them more like us') die hard and they are still widespread in the general community, in some State administrations and even amongst some federal administrators, though the policy has officially changed.

ABORIGINES AND THE PAST

The roots of poverty and of many of the problems facing Aborigines in present-day society are to be found in the past. Elkin has described the process of culture conflict between Aborigines and whites, in general

[4] Aboriginal Affairs Act, 1962 (S.A.) (No. 45 of 1962); Native Welfare Act, 1963 (W.A.) (No. 79 of 1963); Aborigines Act 1958 (Vic.) (Act No. 6190).

(1951) and as background to the specific problem of Aboriginal evidence in legal proceedings (1947: 173-6). Aborigines are the remnants of an invaded people, whose land and sources of food have been almost entirely expropriated by the whites. Though the land and its resources were not exploited by the indigenous inhabitants in the same manner as they are now, their loss represents the deprivation of an economic asset and means the pauperisation of modern Aborigines.

Rowley (1966: 346-50) emphasises the main features of the historical situation still significant today. Among these are conquest (in spite of Aboriginal resistance) and the deprivation of resources and 'the long period of domination by the gun and the threat of the gun and the whip' (Rowley 1966: 348). The police were not alone in using violence or coercion, but the role of the police is particularly important in a study concerned with the administration of justice. Elements of brutality in the history of police-Aboriginal relations must have left a mark on current attitudes, particularly amongst Aborigines who remember ill-treatment of members of their tribe. The Roth Report (*Report of the Royal Commission on the Condition of the Natives*) in 1905 was an indictment of aspects of police treatment of Aboriginal prisoners arrested for cattle-killing. In 1927 a Royal Commission was appointed to investigate the alleged killing and burning of bodies of Aborigines in East Kimberley and police methods when effecting arrests.[5] One of the findings of the Royal Commissioner was that four Aborigines met their death and were burned while in the custody of two police constables and that the only persons responsible for those deaths were the constables (p. xv). This was the last example of a police reprisal party in Western Australia.

Another major historical factor, which is still important is institutionalisation, in that many Aborigines have lived on supervised missions and reserves or in child welfare homes (see Chapter 8). Finally, there are 'conditions promoting doubt, insecurity and tension over long periods of time' (Rowley 1966: 350). These have led to an all-pervading mistrust of authority.

It appears that another factor producing rather than resolving Aboriginal problems may have been discriminatory legislation. Some of the legislation had the avowedly benevolent intention of smoothing the

[5] *Report of the Royal Commission of inquiry into alleged killing and burning of bodies of Aborigines in East Kimberley and into police methods when effecting arrests* (1927). Perth: Government Printer.

transition of Aborigines from one culture to another. The extent to which it actually aggravated their difficulties is examined in Chapter 7.

THE LEGAL SYSTEM

In Australia the States have power to enact general penal legislation.[6] Each State has its own system of criminal law. The Commonwealth has criminal jurisdiction in federal territories, including the Northern Territory.[7]

The three States with which this study is concerned came into existence in the nineteenth century as separate British colonies. They all became States of the new Commonwealth of Australia in 1901.

Each State has its hierarchy of criminal courts. In Victoria summary trials are held in Magistrates Courts. These courts are constituted by a stipendiary magistrate or by honorary justices of the peace. Indictable offences are tried by the County Court[8] or in the Supreme Court. The County Court and the Supreme Court also hear appeals and, in certain circumstances, an appeal may lie to the High Court of Australia or to the Privy Council.

Preliminary inquiries in indictable offences are held in Magistrates Courts; a Coroner's Court may also commit a person for trial on a charge of murder or manslaughter where there is sufficient evidence to warrant it.

In Western Australia there is also a three-tier hierarchy, in which Police Courts exercise functions similar to those of Magistrates Courts in Victoria. Courts of Session differ from the Victorian County Court, however, in that they sit only outside the metropolitan area at the principal court house of each of the fourteen session divisions.[9] Several of the towns visited during fieldwork are the sites of Courts of Session. The Court sits four times a year at Kalgoorlie and Geraldton, and as

[6] Morris and Howard 1964: Introduction by Sir John Barry, xvi-xix, xxxiv. This contains a brief background of the legal framework of the criminal justice system and is the source of most of the material in this section. See also Barry, Paton and Sawer 1948: 1-12.

[7] Crimes Act, 1914-1966 (Cwlth), which is not confined to federal territories, covers limited subject matter which has no particular relevance to Aborigines.

[8] During the fieldwork period Magistrates Courts were called Courts of Petty Sessions. At that time the criminal jurisdiction of the County Court was exercised by Courts of General Sessions: Justices Act, 1958 (Vic.); County Court (Jurisdiction) Act, 1968 (Vic.).

[9] Courts of Session Act, 1921 (W.A.) (No. 24 of 1921).

required at Wyndham, Derby, Broome, Roebourne, Port Hedland, Onslow and Carnarvon. Either a judge of the Supreme Court or a chairman of the Court of Sessions may preside. The chairman of a Court of Session is the stipendiary magistrate stationed at the centre at which the court is held. Only criminal cases are tried.[10] The Supreme Court is at the peak of the State hierarchy and exercises functions similar to those of the Supreme Court of Victoria.

Inferior criminal courts in South Australia are known as Courts of Summary Jurisdiction.[11] During the fieldwork period there were no intermediate criminal courts. The Supreme Court, the highest State court, holds circuit sessions at Port Augusta and Mount Gambier three times a year.

The location of courts and other facilities for the administration of justice is shown on the front endpaper map. It does not show all courts in the three States but shows the facilities which exist at the named fieldwork locations. The capital cities in each State have all facilities. Some of the symbols require explanation. 'Cs' ('superior court') means the Supreme Court or County Court on circuit or a Court of Session. 'C' means all other criminal courts, that is, inferior courts. 'S' means a resident solicitor; '(S)' means that a solicitor visits the town regularly but does not reside there.

The map clearly demonstrates the lack of criminal justice facilities in the remote areas of Western Australia and South Australia; these are areas where many Aborigines live. Even though some towns in these areas are designated as 'superior court' towns, such courts are held infrequently in country areas.

Since each State administers the criminal law separately the law is by no means uniform. Western Australia has a Criminal Code, enacted in 1902, supplemented by other statutes creating offences. South Australia and Victoria are known as 'common law' States because the criminal law has not been codified and many important rules of the criminal law are found in judicial decisions. In these States the sources of law are the common law (reported cases), State statutes, and as much of English law, made applicable in 1828, as still survives (Morris and Howard 1964: xviii).

[10] *Western Australian Year Book 1968* (1968), p. 205. Perth: Commonwealth Bureau of Census and Statistics; *Law Almanac* (1966), p. 16. Perth: Government Printer.

[11] Justices Act, 1921 (S.A.), sections 42 to 48. See also section 4 for interpretations of 'court of summary jurisdiction', 'justice' and 'justices'. These courts are popularly known as Magistrates Courts when presided over by a magistrate.

The distinction between the code States and the common law States has been emphasised in other works on Australian criminal law, but is of little importance in this study. More attention is paid here to petty offences than to major crimes; so the Western Australian Code is less important than other legislation.

ABORIGINES AND THE CRIMINAL LAW: A PATTERN

The offences with which Aborigines are charged, and of which they are convicted, fall into a distinct pattern which contrasts sharply with the white one. Appendix 4.1 shows offences charged against Aborigines and whites respectively in Western Australia in 1965. The table shows that, though Aborigines constituted only 2·5 per cent of the total population of the State, they were defendants to 11 per cent of the charges laid. Aboriginal convictions for all offences totalled 7357; white convictions totalled 57,128; thus Aboriginal convictions were 11 per cent of all convictions. One hundred and thirty-four charges against Aborigines were dismissed or otherwise disposed of without conviction. The comparable figure for whites was 2625, a total of 2759 dismissals. The Aboriginal figure represented only 4·8 per cent of the total dismissals. The comparison between the outcome of criminal proceedings against Aborigines and whites is discussed in Chapter 6.

Appendix 4.2 demonstrates clearly that Aborigines are charged with particular types of offences. Taking first the sub-totals for the five classes of offences used by the Commonwealth Statistician: Aborigines were charged with 30 per cent of offences against the person and whites with the remaining 70 per cent; Aborigines were charged with 10 per cent of the offences against property and whites with the remaining 90 per cent; Aborigines were charged with no offences of forgery or uttering, all such charges were laid against whites; Aborigines were charged with 42 per cent of the offences against good order and whites with 58 per cent; finally, Aborigines were charged with 3 per cent of the other offences (which include traffic offences) and whites with 97 per cent.

The figures are even more meaningful when looked at as percentages of total offences committed by members of the particular racial group (see Appendix 4.2): offences against the person represent 4 per cent of the total Aboriginal offences but only 1 per cent of the white total; offences against property represent 12 per cent of total Aboriginal offences and 12 per cent of the white total; forgery and uttering do not figure in the Aboriginal list at all, and formed only 0·1 per cent of offences charged against whites; offences against good order represented 68 per cent of charges against Aborigines and only 12 per cent of those against whites; other offences were responsible for 16 per cent of charges against Aborigines and 74·9 per cent of those against whites.

The five offences with which Aborigines were most frequently charged were drunkenness, disorderly conduct, traffic offences, stealing and Native Welfare offences, in that order (Appendix 4.1). On the other hand, white offences similarly ranked show traffic offences leading the field, followed by offences under other Acts, drunkenness, stealing and offences under the Licensing Act (Appendix 4.1). This contrasting pattern is extremely significant. The Aboriginal offence *par excellence* is drunkenness, with charges constituting 48 per cent of all charges against Aborigines. The same role is filled in relation to whites by traffic offences, which represent 57 per cent of all charges against whites.

Appendix 2.1, showing offences charged against Aborigines and whites in the Ten Towns Sample, confirms the primacy of drunkenness and traffic offences respectively. This table, unlike Appendix 4.1, excludes Children's Court cases and, of course, is confined to the selected ten towns. All offences have been divided into ten categories. In rank order Aboriginal offences are: drunkenness, Native Welfare offences, disorderly conduct, traffic, other minor offences, assault, offences against the police, stealing, major offences and unlawfully using motor vehicles (see Appendix 1 for explanation of offence categories). The corresponding ranking of white offences is: traffic, drunkenness, other minor offences, disorderly conduct, stealing, Native Welfare offences, major offences, offences against the police, assault and unlawfully using motor vehicles. There is a highly significant relationship between race and type of offence.

Thus the detailed pattern of offences is not precisely the same in the selected ten towns as it is in Western Australia as a whole. But the important point is that the 630 charges of drunkenness laid against Aborigines represent 32·9 per cent of all charges against Aborigines; 1001 traffic charges against whites represent 48·9 per cent of all charges against whites. The rank order of the remaining offences is less significant.

Aborigines were charged with a total of 1913 offences in the ten towns in 1965, 48 per cent of all charges laid. Whites were defendants to the remaining 52 per cent of charges. These percentages should be compared with those for the entire State of Western Australia: 11 per cent for Aborigines and 89 per cent for Whites.

The difference must be largely attributable to the proportionately larger Aboriginal population in the fieldwork towns. Appendix 5 sets out the racial composition of fieldwork areas in Western Australia. The population figures are approximate because of the difficulties of rationalising statistics produced by the Native Welfare Department and the Commonwealth Statistician using different definitions of 'Aborigines' and different administrative boundaries. But it is clear that Aborigines form a much greater proportion of the population in these areas than their 2·5 per cent in the State as a whole. So their larger share of offences in the Ten Towns Sample than in the State as a whole is not unexpected.

Similar statistics for Aboriginal and white offences in South Australia and Victoria are not yet available. The information which has been collected, though not yet reduced to quantitative form, suggests that at least the main outlines of the pattern of offences are similar in these two States; that is, that Aborigines are charged largely with liquor and disorderly offences, while whites most frequently face traffic charges.[12]

Imprisonment is another major aspect of criminal justice in which a contrasting pattern emerges for Aborigines and whites. In Western Australia the daily average prison population for the year ended 30 June 1965 was 876·93.[13] This included a daily average Aboriginal prison population of 214·78. Thus, Aborigines, forming 2·5 per cent of the population of Western Australia and being convicted of 11 per cent of offences, made up 24 per cent of the prison population of the State.[14]

[12] An unpublished study of one South Australian town confirms that drunkenness leads the field of Aboriginal offences, while traffic offences are most frequent for whites (Graves and Collett 1972: Table V).

[13] *Annual Report of the Prisons Department from 1st July, 1964 to 30th June, 1965* (1966), pp. 3, 8. Perth: Government Printer.

[14] The percentages are not strictly comparable because prison statistics are for the financial year to 30 June 1965; the population figures are based partly on the Census of 30 June 1966 and partly on Department of Native Welfare estimates; while the statistics of convictions are for the calendar year 1965. Prison statistics for the next year (ending 30 June 1966) are: daily average prison population, 862·83; daily average Aboriginal prison population, 228·33 or 26 per cent of the total (*Annual Report of the Prisons Department from 1st July, 1965 to 30th June, 1966* (1967), pp. 3, 10. Perth: Government Printer).
The proportion of Aborigines in the prison population thus showed an increase in these two years, but in both cases was approximately a quarter of the total prison population. Since then the Aboriginal proportion has increased. Aborigines were 32 per cent of the prison population for the year ending 30 June 1971 (*Annual*

The other noticeable feature is the imbalance of female Aboriginal prisoners. The above daily average of 876·93 is made up of 837·31 males (including 189·78 Aborigines) and 39·62 females (including 25·00 Aborigines).[15] Aborigines comprise 22 per cent of the male prison population but 64 per cent of the female prison population.

A similar pattern may be observed in South Australia. The total number of prisoners admitted for the year ended 30 June 1965 was 7060, including 1043 Aborigines.[16] The total was made up of 6735 males (including 941 Aborigines) and 325 females (including 102 Aborigines). Aborigines constitute 14 per cent of the prison population; male Aborigines form 13 per cent of the male prison population and female Aborigines 31 per cent of the female prison population.[17] Aborigines form only 0·7 per cent of the total population of South Australia, so they are vastly overrepresented in the prisons.

A number of writers have observed this phenomenon and examined it from different viewpoints: a geographer (Gale 1966: 35); an anthropologist (Robinson 1969: 14-19); and a psychiatrist (Rollo n.d.). Chapters 1-6 of this book are largely directed to examining the excessive representation of Aborigines in the prison population from a lawyer's standpoint. The aim is to assess the extent to which the disproportion is due to the workings of the legal system rather than to the criminality of Aborigines.

Report of the Department of Corrections from 1st July 1970 to 30th June 1971 (1972). Perth: Government Printer.

15 *Annual Report of the Prisons Department from 1st July, 1964 to 30th June, 1965* (1966), pp. 3, 8. Perth: Government Printer.

16 *Annual Report of the Gaols and Prisons, 1964-65* (1966), pp. 3, 15. Adelaide: Government Printer.

17 Figures for the following year (1965/66) are: total initial admissions to all prisons, 8353; Aboriginal admissions to all prisons, 1638 (19 per cent); total admissions made up of 7871 males, 482 females; Aboriginal admissions made up of 1364 males (17 per cent), 274 females (56 per cent) (*Prisons Department Annual Report 1965-66* (1967), p. 3. Adelaide: Government Printer).
Note that South Australian statistics are for admissions to prisons, *not* daily averages. Compare Western Australian figures, above. The daily average prison population is a more meaningful measure because it takes account of the period for which each person is confined. The racial breakdown of the daily average prison population is not available for South Australia.

2 THE INITIATION OF CRIMINAL PROSECUTIONS

The relationship between police and Aborigines is a major facet of the whole topic of the administration of justice to Aborigines. In many areas the police officer and the local justice of the peace are the only representatives of the legal system with whom the Aborigines have any contact. Often contact with the police is intense and prolonged.

In addition to normal police duties, policemen frequently perform other functions. In many cases they act as prosecutors in court. Formerly they were appointed as Protectors and were supposed to represent Aboriginal defendants in court. They act as process servers in civil actions and as bailiffs in debt cases. Policewomen sometimes initiate neglected children cases. In some country towns police also act as gaolers and as clerks of courts. They also play an important role in relation to the granting or refusal of bail.

Attention is concentrated here on the usual police functions: the detection of offences and initiation of prosecutions against offenders. Reference will be made later to the police in other roles, many of which would be carried out by other officers in a more closely settled country.

The fact that the police combine such a multiplicity of functions is itself highly significant. First, it is one reason why their contact with many Aborigines is frequent and prolonged. Second, as might be expected, the exercise of different—sometimes conflicting—functions by the one officer, leads to abuse and injustice in certain cases.

ATTITUDES OF POLICE TO ABORIGINES

The attitudes of individual police officers range from one who was honoured by an invitation to an Aboriginal initiation ceremony to one who wrote in a police antecedents report about 'a *typical* aboriginal who rarely works but gets drunk very often and gets himself and others into trouble' (my emphasis).

Although no full-scale attitude survey was carried out as part of this investigation, it appears that the majority of policemen share this attitude to Aborigines and would agree with the quoted statement. This conclusion is based on my interviews with more than fifty-five policemen, observations of police behaviour and perusal of innumerable police documents.

Many policemen tend to generalise about the Aborigines as a group and to ascribe to its members inferior standards of intelligence, morality and behaviour. They are prejudiced against the race. 'Prejudice' here is used in the sense defined by Simpson and Yinger (1965: 10): 'a rigid, emotional attitude toward a human group'. Prejudice involves prejudgment and misjudgment of the members of a supposed human group. This attitude appeared to be more common amongst police in country and outback towns than in the cities.

Reasons for this police prejudice towards Aborigines may be suggested. First, there are traditional attitudes carried over from an earlier period when frontier conditions produced direct conflict between the two races and most restrictive legislation embodied notions of Aboriginal inferiority. The surviving relics of this legislation still produce a lower status for Aborigines, and to that extent police may find a justification for their attitude within the law itself (for a short account of the history of police-Aboriginal relations see Chapter 1; for further discussion of restrictive legislation see Chapter 7).

Second, general attitudes in the community in which the policeman works may reinforce or even produce prejudiced attitudes. Social pressures on a policeman in a small country town can be very strong. He is almost certain to find friends amongst white citizens rather than amongst the Aborigines who, in general, have the lowest social and economic status. Unless he is firmly committed to the principle of racial tolerance himself, he is likely to adopt the views of the local townspeople, who are often very intolerant (Taft 1970: 49).

Third, police attitudes may, to a limited extent, be based on objective fact and on their observation of the actual behaviour of Aborigines. For example, it may be true that more Aborigines in a particular town do get drunk more often than whites in the same town (Taft 1970: 39). But the police who express contempt for Aborigines on the basis of this type of observation rarely consider the extent to which their observation depends on the high 'visibility' of Aborigines. This visibility arises not only from skin colour, which makes them easy to identify, but also from the conditions under which they live on the fringes of country towns. Reserves and fringe-dwellers' camps provide very little privacy. Drunkenness is far more obvious here than it would be amongst whites living in ordinary homes, even if the actual extent of the drunkenness is the same. These police officers rarely demonstrate any understanding of factors causing this type of behaviour. Heavy drinking may be an expression of feelings of despair in the face of poor living conditions and racial discrimination, yet it is viewed rather as an innate characteristic of the race as a whole (see further Chapter 7).

It is important to realise that prejudice does not necessarily bring with it discrimination, that is, it need not have any result in action. Discrimination is, in the words of Robin Williams, 'the differential treatment of individuals considered to belong to a particular social group' (cited in Simpson and Yinger 1965: 13). Prejudice may never be expressed in open hostility because of other counteracting attitudes within the individual. Similarly, discrimination can occur without prejudice. A shopkeeper may discriminate against Aborigines because he believes that other people are prejudiced rather than because he is prejudiced himself. A policeman may feel obliged to enforce a discriminatory law as part of his official duty, although he himself has no prejudice. Nevertheless, it seems reasonable to expect that in most cases prejudice and discrimination will co-exist. For this reason the existence of many prejudiced individuals within the police force is important and would be expected to lead to discriminatory behaviour against Aborigines. An attempt to assess the extent of this discrimination is made later in this chapter.

ATTITUDES OF ABORIGINES TO POLICE

In interviews with Aborigines, surprisingly few express statements of general hostility against the police were made.[1] Although Ben Whitaker

[1] This may have been partly due to the brevity of most of these interviews and consequent inhibitions about speaking freely. Since the fieldwork period young urban Aborigines have been outspoken about police discrimination.

(1964: 163) suggests that the police are another minority group who suffer the fate of stereotyping, most Aborigines seemed well able to distinguish between policemen who treated them fairly and those who harassed them. As with police, attitudes differed from one individual Aboriginal to another.

Interviews are not the only source of information on Aboriginal attitudes. Where there is difficulty in verbal communication with Aborigines, 'there is still recourse to physical observation of Aboriginal reactions to the actions of whites' (Tatz 1965: 11). The inference can be drawn from some Aboriginal behaviour that the local police are respected and trusted. One woman, after killing her husband and taking an overdose of sleeping tablets, went to the local police station with a note asking the police to look after her children (fieldwork notes).

On the other hand, Aboriginal assaults on police and similar offences may perhaps be interpreted as expressions of resentment against the police generally. In the Ten Towns Sample Aborigines were charged with more offences against the police (resisting arrest and so on) than whites were (see Appendix 2.1). In addition Aborigines were charged with fifteen assaults on the police and whites with only four such offences. These figures appear to support the view that Aborigines are hostile to the police. But it should be noted that Aborigines were also charged with more assaults on other Aborigines than whites were (see Appendix 2.2). The figures may reflect Aboriginal liability to assault charges rather than aggression directed specifically at the police. Further research on Aboriginal attitudes is needed before firm conclusions can be drawn.

It is meaningful to speak of Aborigines and the police as two separate groups, because only a few Aborigines are employed in the police force. Most are employed as trackers on a casual rather than on a permanent basis.[2]

[2] One Aboriginal was employed permanently as a tracker by the Victoria Police (*Annual Report of the Chief Commissioner of Police for the year 1959* (1960), p. 24. Melbourne: Government Printer). In South Australia and Western Australia local Aborigines are called into service as trackers when required. An Aboriginal police cadet graduated in the South Australian Police Force in 1968. The press reported that he was the first Aboriginal police cadet in Australia (Melbourne *Herald* 26/6/68: 11).

POLICE DISCRETION

A commonplace view among criminologists is that 'statistics of criminal convictions . . . cannot be taken as anything like accurate measures of actual criminality' (Wootton 1959: 22).

A major source of the discrepancy between the actual number of actions which offend against the criminal law and the number which find their way into the statistics as 'convictions' or even as charges, is the amount of discretion which the police exercise. 'Full enforcement of our present laws is physically impossible; consequently the police have developed a discretion in prosecuting which has expanded with the amount of legislation' (Whitaker 1964: 170). This is the first area of police discretion needing examination.

THE INITIATION OF A PROSECUTION

This discretion operates in two main ways. First, the police may have a general policy of not enforcing particular legislation or of enforcing it only in exceptional circumstances. For example, a South Australian Royal Commission heard evidence that police had for years been tolerant of the illegal sale and supply of liquor by R.S.L. sub-branches and sporting clubs. The Royal Commissioner 'was appalled by the nature and extent of the illegal practices actively or tacitly allowed to grow up and thrive in our community'.[3] Another law which was rarely enforced was the Commonwealth Electoral Act's provision limiting campaign expenditure.

The police may claim that the attitude of the public influences them in the degree of enforcement of any particular law. When this approach is applied to laws that are clearly obsolete it is quite reasonable. All too often, however, the 'public' really means those members of the public who have power and influence. The obverse of this approach is the enthusiasm and zeal with which the police proceed against other offences, for example, the offence of a 'Native receiving liquor' under section 150 of the Licensing Act, 1911 (W.A.). It can hardly be claimed that this offence is a source of great danger to the community yet offenders are

[3] *Report of the Royal Commission into the Law relating to the Sale, Supply and Consumption of Intoxicating Liquors and Other Matters (including Matters dealt with by the Licensing Act, 1932-1966)* (1966), p. 7. Adelaide: Government Printer. Standards of accommodation laid down by the Wards Employment Regulation for Aboriginal employees were not observed on Northern Territory cattle stations, yet no prosecutions were instituted against the employers (Stevens 1974: 98).

pursued with a vigour revealed partly by the number of convictions obtained and partly by an examination of the actual circumstances in which many of these offenders were arrested (see Chapter 7 for some cases). These figures can be read as an index of police harassment rather than of police efficiency. On the other hand, although it is well known that hotel licensees in many Western Australian towns refuse to serve Aborigines with liquor, thus committing a breach of section 118 of the Licensing Act, 1911 (W.A.), no prosecutions have been launched by the police under section 118 on this ground.[4]

Offences may come to the notice of the police as the result of a report by a member of the public or through observation in the course of routine patrolling or through police investigative work. The police may have to decide whether behaviour which comes to their attention constitutes an offence at all and whether any charge should be laid. The class of 'offences against good order', for example drunkenness in a public place, usually constitutes no problem to the police officer in this respect. His own observation supplies the evidence he needs that an offence has been committed and he finds it easy to decide whether to lay a charge or not. The high visibility of the type of offence they commit is one source of the high rate of charges against Aborigines.

When this type of offence, which is obvious to a policeman on patrol, is compared with other offences, which require actual detective work, it is clear that he will find it much easier to identify the offender and obtain a conviction in the former. Clearance rates of different types of offences in Victoria and South Australia are given in Appendix 6. Even if the police were allocating equal amounts of time and manpower to the detection of all classes of offence, it would be expected that the clearance rate would be higher in the 'offences against good order' class. However, there is undoubtedly the temptation—particularly where the police are understaffed and probably more so at one-man police stations in country areas—to allocate police time to offences committed in public. One country policeman said in an interview that if he had an assistant available he could prosecute many more white crimes while the number of offences by Aborigines would remain stable at about the existing rate.

The police also make decisions about what places to visit on routine patrols. Patrols normally cover public places not private houses. If the

[4] The police have, however, taken proceedings against licensees under this section on behalf of white complainants. *Barbour* v. *Donaldson* (1960) 1 Western Australian Case Notes 23 (in *U. Western Aust. L. Rev.* **5**).

police decide to patrol an Aboriginal reserve, their decision is discriminatory in effect. A reserve is not a 'public place', so if the police regularly patrol reserves they are subjecting Aboriginal residents to more surveillance than is exercised over the rest of the community (cf. Beckett 1964: 39-40).

The Native Welfare Act Regulations, 1964 (W.A.) specifically defined the conditions under which police officers might enter reserves. Regulation 20 provided:

> Members of the police force . . . are persons authorised under these regulations to enter or remain within the boundaries of a reserve, if and so long as any such authorised person so enters and remains for the purpose of the lawful exercise and performance of the functions and duties appertaining to his office to the degree permitted in the community in general.

There might be some argument about exactly where the boundary should be drawn between a proper exercise of this authority to enter a reserve and an action in excess of the power conferred. In some cases police officers have clearly exceeded their powers. Aborigines have complained that police patrol a reserve frequently during the day and late at night, shining spotlights and disturbing the residents. There have also been complaints that the police enter houses on reserves without warrants. An interview with a police constable indicates that most of these complaints appear to be justified. One magistrate held that Aboriginal houses on reserves were in the same position as houses in the general community. The decision was not reported or taken on appeal and it is not known to what extent this view has been adopted by other magistrates or by the police. The decision seems clearly correct in view of the terms of Regulation 20.

Police practice regarding the patrolling of reserves varies from place to place. In some towns they do not carry out any such regular patrols and instead wait to be called in by a member of the Aboriginal community or a welfare officer. The complaints against police practice were made in only a few towns.

Even within an overall policy of enforcement of a particular law, the police may exercise discretion in relation to charging in individual cases. There is clearly a general policy that laws against drunkenness will be enforced, but in individual cases persons found drunk in a public place may be sent home rather than arrested. No statistics are compiled of the frequency of this practice, so it is impossible to state definitely the number of times that whites and Aborigines are the beneficiaries of this kind of generosity. However, it is clear that considerations which should be irrelevant to the proper exercise of this discretion are taken into account at times.[5]

There is also clear evidence of discrimination against Aborigines in some areas. One policeman stated that it was his invariable practice to arrest a drunk Aboriginal and not to let him go home to the reserve. The rate of charges against Aborigines in this town was extremely high considering the population and seems to have been largely due to police policy. The police usually claim that the number of convictions obtained has no bearing on promotion. However, the promotion and transfer of this officer—which subsequently occurred—while not proving that a large number of convictions is necessary for promotion, does nothing to dispel the belief that zeal is rewarded.

Another class of offences in which offenders are often warned rather than prosecuted is that of minor traffic offences. This policy has been explicitly adopted in South Australia.[6] It, too, seems to favour white offenders. Information is not available on the race of the offenders warned in this way. But since there are far more whites convicted of traffic offences than Aborigines, it is reasonable to assume that those given warnings are also predominantly white.

Juvenile offenders are also often warned rather than charged. Again this policy seems to operate in a differential way against Aborigines. Aboriginal children have been charged with trivial offences, such as the theft of three oranges or of a bottle of milk or soft drink. The effect of having criminal convictions recorded against one at an early age can be serious, in terms of employment opportunities and the length of the record of prior convictions that can be produced to a court at a later date. As Mary Durack says of the young Aboriginal artists she knew: 'From first offences that, in the case of white boys and girls, would have been dismissed as mere peccadilloes, it became very difficult for them to avoid being returned to jail.'[7] It was put to me that the reason for this differential treatment of white and Aboriginal juveniles was not primarily

[5] Cf. R.W.H., Book review of Campbell and Whitmore, *Freedom in Australia* (*U. Western Aust. L. Rev.* **7**, pp. 606-7).

[6] *Annual Report of the Commissioner of Police 1963-64* (1965), p. 3. Adelaide: Government Printer.

[7] In her Foreword to Johnson (1966: 9).

that the local policeman was friendly with the parents of the white children but was rather that he could not regard Aboriginal parents as reliable supervisors of their children if he let them off with a warning. To the extent that some of the Aboriginal parents are themselves in and out of gaol and are 'anti-police', there may be some logic in the policeman's view. But magistrates frequently release convicted Aboriginal children into the custody of their parents—which goes a long way towards disposing of this argument. Even if it had some weight in connection with serious offences, there can surely never be any justification for taking children to court for extremely trivial offences.

Adult Aborigines have also been charged with trivial offences in circumstances where it is difficult to believe that any white person, other than perhaps a vagrant white, would have been. It is unlikely that many white people would find themselves charged with stealing a bunch of grapes (from a policeman), or unlawfully wearing an R.S.L. badge, yet Aborigines were so charged.[8] The basis for this harassment seemed to be a general policy directed against persons of low socio-economic status. The policeman involved in both these cases made the class basis of his policy quite explicit in stating that he always 'chatted' hitch-hikers, most of whom were white vagrants. ('Chatting' apparently means warning them that they will be charged with vagrancy if they stay around the town.) However, he said that some hitch-hikers are university students, who are in a different class, and he lets them stay in the single men's quarters.

Contrasted with this approach to trivial offences committed by Aborigines is the 'velvet glove' technique applied to many offenders against Aborigines. There are cases where an offence has clearly been committed but the white offender has not been charged. A member of staff at a remote mission in Western Australia caned Aboriginal children severely on the backs of their legs. The caning was certainly severe enough for the staff member concerned to have been charged with assault, but no such action was taken. Instead, the mission authorities were given a 'stern warning' by the Minister for Native Welfare.[9]

[8] Fieldwork notes. But see a newspaper report of a defendant in Adelaide pleading guilty to stealing a flower from the garden of a police sergeant (*Age* 23/5/67).

[9] *West Australian*, *Daily News*, *Age* and *Australian* reports, 7/2/67-18/2/67 and information from Department of Native Welfare.

THE KIND OF CHARGE LAID

Once the police officer has decided to take some action against a person he believes to be guilty of an offence he has a certain amount of choice as to precisely what offence to charge.

Occasionally he may lay a more serious charge than the facts seem to warrant. This exercise of his discretion may have an intimidatory effect on the defendant. One Aboriginal was charged by the police with 'assault with intent to rape'. There was absolutely no evidence that he had any such intent and the charge was subsequently reduced to 'common assault'.[10]

However, it appears that the reverse situation is more often the case. The police frequently lay a charge of common assault rather than assault occasioning actual bodily harm or stealing rather than breaking and entering. Although this might appear to be a sign of tenderness for the defendant, the real motive is to enable the local inferior court to deal with it without all the time and trouble entailed in a superior court trial. One policeman stated that he tried to avoid having Aborigines committed to the Supreme Court. He believed it best to get the hearing over quickly while the matter was still fresh in their minds. Moreover, when brought before justices of the peace, they would usually be sentenced to imprisonment for an assault. If sent to the Supreme Court, they would be given bonds, which he considered useless.

Another area of police discretion is that the officer often has a choice as to whether he lays one charge or more against the defendant. It is quite common to find, for example, that one defendant is charged at the same time with resisting arrest, assaulting the police, indecent language and drunkenness. This is perfectly legal, provided that the different offences charged require different evidence to support them even though they arose out of the same incident. However, the opportunity to 'throw the book' at an unpopular defendant can be a powerful weapon in the hands of the police. Appendix 2.3 shows the number of Aboriginal and white defendants in the Ten Towns Sample charged on multiple counts compared with those charged on a single count at a time. Aborigines are more often charged with multiple counts. Before it could be definitely concluded that this fact results from discrimination it would be necessary to examine the circumstances of the cases in some detail. But at least a *prima facie* case of discrimination has been raised.

[10] Supreme Court, Adelaide, File No. 40, May 1965.

ARREST OR SUMMONS

Another area of choice available to a police officer is in the mode of initiation of prosecutions. He may proceed by way of arrest or summons. In general, if he believes that the defendant would appear in court in answer to a summons it is open to him to proceed in that way instead of by arrest (Campbell and Whitmore 1966: 33).

Appendix 2.4 shows the number of Aborigines and whites in the Ten Towns Sample who were proceeded against by way of arrest and summons respectively. No distinction is made in the table between an arrest under warrant and an arrest without warrant, but almost all the arrests were made without a warrant. The table shows that a much higher proportion of Aborigines than whites are proceeded against by way of arrest.

However, this difference can not primarily be explained in terms of the exercise of police discretion. Appendix 2.5, in which the information in 2.4 is broken down into offence categories, shows that the difference in procedure can mainly be explained in terms of the offence charged. Aborigines are charged proportionately with many more drunkenness offences and whites with more traffic offences. In the case of many offences under the Traffic Act, 1919 (W.A.) the only procedure available to the police officer or the traffic inspector is that by way of summons. Specific powers of arrest are given only under a few sections of the Traffic Act.[11] In the absence of specific powers in connection with other offences, proceedings could only be by way of summons. On the other hand, section 43 of the Police Act, 1892 (W.A.) provides that any police officer or constable may arrest without warrant 'any person whom he may find drunk, or disorderly, or using . . . obscene language . . . in any street' (by section 2, 'street' includes 'public place'). Thus, the general practice of the police in cases of offences against good order is to proceed by way of arrest.

Since an arrest constitutes a greater interference with individual liberty than a prosecution by way of summons, powers of arrest should be scrutinised carefully by those who are concerned about individual rights. The issue can be posed in this form: does an arrested person have an action for wrongful arrest where a policeman has used the arrest procedure and it would have been reasonable to expect the individual concerned to appear in response to a summons? It is difficult to give a dogmatic

[11] For example, section 25(2) and section 32(2). In Western Australia many traffic prosecutions are brought by traffic inspectors, not by the police. Summonses in the tables in Appendix 2 include those laid by traffic inspectors.

answer. The Commonwealth Crimes Act and the Tasmanian Police Offences Act contain provisions that the power of arrest exists only where the police officer reasonably believes that a summons would not be effective. Campbell and Whitmore (1966: 34) express the view that if there is reasonable cause to believe that the alleged offender would answer a summons, his arrest would be illegal. In the other States, where there is no such statutory provision, it is difficult to imagine that a defendant would be successful in an action against a policeman on the sole ground that he should have proceeded by summons rather than arrest. Successful actions for false arrest have usually been based on the ground that there was no justification for the police to initiate a prosecution at all, rather than an objection to the method of initiating a prosecution. Once a defendant has been convicted it would be extremely difficult for him to persuade a court to find in his favour against a police officer simply on the basis of the procedure adopted to bring him before the court. The omission to arrest when there are grounds for doing so may amount to neglect of duty by a policeman, so the court would be reluctant to hold him accountable for any arrest which led to conviction even if a summons might have been equally effective.

Although this seems to be the present legal position, it is not satisfactory. This question is closely bound up with that of bail. If a defendant is granted bail soon after arrest, the deprivation of liberty which he suffers by being arrested is not severe. But the combined effects of being arrested rather than summonsed and of being unable to raise bail amount to a much more serious loss of liberty. It may be argued that many drunkenness arrests are a proper exercise of police discretion because it is necessary to take offenders into custody who are incapable of looking after themselves. But the present system by which a person properly arrested in this way is then detained for one or two days because he is unable to raise bail must cause grave concern. Possible solutions are suggested in the next chapter.

Further, although the exercise of the discretion in this way seems justifiable where the defendant is seriously drunk and disorderly, the same argument does not apply to all offences for which Aborigines have been arrested. For example, one man was arrested for the offence of 'Native receiving liquor'. According to police evidence, he was visibly affected by liquor but was not drunk enough to be charged with drunken driving. The defendant stated that he had drunk about four cups of wine. He had no prior convictions. In these circumstances it might well be thought that the arrest was unnecessary and that the defendant would have answered to a summons.

Some policemen have attempted to justify the use of the arrest procedure in such cases on the ground that Aborigines would not understand what a summons meant and would not attend court on the day fixed for hearing. There is no evidence that Aborigines who are proceeded against on summons or released on bail are any more unreliable about attending court on the due date than whites are. In one South Australian town the police were forced by circumstances to adopt an experimental procedure. They had arrested a number of Aborigines on charges of drunkenness, disorderly behaviour, and assault, but were unable to convene a court because all the local justices were away. Instead of releasing the Aborigines on bail, they simply let them go and later served summonses on them. All these cases were later heard by the court. Since these Aborigines were relatively tribalised and unsophisticated in white culture, this experience disposes of the myth that the summons procedure is not appropriate for use with Aborigines.

INTERROGATIONS AND CONFESSIONS

In cases of offences against good order, the evidence against a defendant usually consists of the observations of the arresting officer. In the majority of cases of other offences, the evidence includes a statement the defendant makes to the police admitting his guilt. An examination of 150 police 'briefs' involving Aboriginal defendants charged with these more major offences in South Australia showed that the police had obtained a confession in eighty-nine cases; in twelve cases there was no confession but other evidence was available; in the remaining forty-nine cases there is no information on the evidence available to the police. The confession was the sole evidence in twenty cases. The evidence in the police files was not often tested in court as most of the defendants pleaded guilty.

Similar information is not available for Western Australia. It seems probable that in the southern part of the State a similar pattern to that in South Australia would appear in relation to the nature of the evidence on which the police rely. In the northern part of the State, this is not necessarily so, for reasons which will appear later.

Since confessions do figure so prominently in evidence against defendants, it is important to know the legal limits on the powers of the police to interrogate suspects and how interrogations are actually carried out. If there is any substantial difference between practice and theory (the rules of law and administrative directions which are supposed to be observed) it will be worthwhile examining whether the rules should be changed. This might be either in the direction of a relaxation of the rules in order to give the police more powers or, alternatively, in the direction of further controls and checks so that the rights of suspects are more effectively preserved.

There are two distinct but closely interrelated issues which often arise in connection with confessions and the interrogations by which they are obtained. The first is the question of whether the police have observed the requirements of the common law or the statute concerned, as well as any obligations imposed by regulations governing police conduct. The second is the issue that often faces the court, namely, should a statement made by an accused person to the police be admitted in evidence? The answer to this question does not necessarily depend on whether the police have observed all the correct procedures.

In general, the following obligations are imposed on the police in the conduct of interrogations. First, they should caution a suspect as soon as they have made up their minds to charge him with an offence. If he is in custody they should caution him immediately before asking any questions. Secondly, they should not obtain or attempt to obtain a confession by the use of threats or promises or of violence. Thirdly, if a suspect indicates that he wishes to make a statement, the police are entitled to ask him questions for the purpose of elucidating anything in his statement that is unclear, but are not entitled to cross-examine him on his statement.

The High Court in *R.* v. *Lee*[12] took the opportunity to set out in detail the law relating to the admissibility of confessions in evidence. The court considered both the common law position and modifications made by the Evidence Act in Victoria. The main test which a court should apply to determine whether a confession should be admitted in evidence is whether it is 'voluntary' or not. 'The word "voluntary" does not mean "volunteered". It means "made in the exercise of a free choice to speak or be silent"' (p. 149). However, the High Court also recognised that the trial judge has an ultimate discretion as to whether he will admit a confession as evidence, that is, he can refuse to admit it even though it is 'voluntary' in the usual common law sense.

[12] (1950) 82 C.L.R. 133.

The following extract from the judgment (pp. 159-60) is particularly relevant to many Aborigines.

> The uneducated—perhaps semi-illiterate—man who has a 'record' and is suspected of some offence may be practically helpless in the hands of an over-zealous police officer. The latter may be honest and sincere, but his position of superiority is so great and so over-powering that a 'statement' may be 'taken' which is really very unreliable . . . Such persons stand often in grave need of that protection which only an extremely vigilant court can give them. They provide the real justification for . . . the Chief Commissioner's Standing Orders in Victoria, and they provide (if we are to assume that the requirement of voluntariness is not enough to ensure justice) a justification for the existence of an ultimate discretion as to the admission of confessional evidence. . . . Each case must, of course, depend upon its own circumstances considered in their entirety.

A recognition that Aborigines are very often helpless in the hands of the police underlies attempts that have been made to provide them with special protection in connection with police interviews. Because of State variations, each will be considered in turn.

VICTORIA

The case of *R.* v. *Lee* sets out the position relating to confessions of the ordinary defendant in Victoria. Apart from common law principles and the provisions of the Evidence Act, the procedures to be followed by the police are set out in some detail in the Standing Orders of the Chief Commissioner of Police. The relevant Standing Orders as at the date of that case (1951) are set out in the judgment of the High Court. As the Standing Orders are not made public, it is difficult to know the precise extent of subsequent amendments.

In 1965, following criticism by Mr Justice Sholl of police methods of interrogation and complaints by other persons against the police, the Solicitor-General, Mr B.L. Murray, conducted an inquiry and reported on police interrogations (Murray 1965—referred to hereafter as the Murray Report). He received complaints of the use of violence and threats by the police in order to obtain confessions and also allegations that confessions had been fabricated. He concluded that these abuses took place 'more often than on occasional or isolated instances' (p. 5). There is no information as to whether such abuses affect Aboriginal suspects more than whites. Mr Murray did express the view (p. 5) that threats of violence or actual violence occurred more often at inner suburban police stations than elsewhere and also that the victims were usually either young and arrogant men or men who are well known to the police and have long criminal records. Many Aborigines fall into the latter category and if they are arrested in Melbourne it is usually in the inner areas rather than in the outer suburbs. It would be expected that, to the extent that such abuses do occur, Aborigines would be amongst the victims. I have not obtained any well documented accounts of police violence to individual Aborigines in Victoria but this certainly does not establish that it does not occur. Aborigines are relatively powerless in the hands of the police and marks of violence are not readily visible on a dark skin. On the other hand, it has been said that Aborigines are so helpless and so submissive to the authority of the police that they confess readily and violence would be unnecessary. It is quite impossible at present to say how frequent or how serious any such abuses are in relation to Aboriginal suspects. Mr Murray recognised (p. 6) that there is no way in which the absolute truth of any such allegation could be determined. An independent witness is rarely present and it becomes a matter of the word of the suspect against that of the police. The suspect has a strong motive for lying but, if what he says is true, the police have an equally strong motive.

One of the recommendations of the Murray Report which has been partially implemented is that tape recorders should be used at Russell Street Police Headquarters and some other police stations to record statements made by defendants. Mr Murray saw this as a protection for the police against false allegations as well as a protection for suspects. He clearly took it for granted that suspects would be informed that the interview was being tape recorded. The Victorian Supreme Court, however, has now held that a tape recording of an interview is admissible in evidence even though the suspect has not been informed and has not been cautioned again before the tape recorder is switched on.[13] Since tape recorders have so far only been used at Russell Street Headquarters the effect of this new procedure has been marginal.

Special provision was made for Aborigines in the Police Standing Orders. In 1962 Standing Order 254 was amended to read:

> When a person whose appearance clearly indicates aboriginal ancestry is charged with a serious offence, or (being a child or a young person) is to appear before a Children's Court for the hearing of a Protection

[13] *R.* v. *Nilson* [1968] V.R. 238.

> Application, the Superintendent of Aborigines Welfare should be informed so that he will be in a position to arrange, if he considers it necessary or desirable, for an officer of the Aborigines Welfare Board to attend the Court when the case is being heard.[14]

It will be observed that this provision did not clearly state the time at which the Superintendent should be informed. It is clear that it required notification before the court hearing.

In 1965 and 1966 the Aborigines Welfare Board made representations about the amendment of this Standing Order. The Board felt concern about some cases in which the Standing Order had been completely ignored by the police. It was also desired to resolve ambiguities in the Order and to strengthen the position of a welfare officer who desired to assist an Aboriginal charged with a criminal offence. The Board also wanted it made clear that the notification by the police that they had charged an Aboriginal should be made at a point in time earlier than just prior to the final hearing of the case.

The case which primarily sparked the concern of the Board was one in which an Aboriginal, aged nineteen, was convicted of assault occasioning actual bodily harm and rape. He was sentenced to imprisonment for twelve years, with the direction that he serve a minimum of ten years before being eligible for parole (the sentence is discussed further in Chapter 6). In the present context it may be noted that the defendant was interrogated by the police without anyone else present. The police had made abortive attempts to notify the local welfare officer through third parties. When the welfare officer discovered what had happened and queried the procedure, the police replied that the wording of the Standing Orders was 'should be informed', not 'must inform'. Their argument against the mandatory effect of the Order would have been stronger if it had read merely 'may be informed'.

The formal caution was not given as soon as it should have been in the interrogation. The defendant's confession was incorporated in the depositions through the evidence of the policeman who interviewed him. If he had had expert advice available to him at the time of his interrogation, the defendant might have refused to make a statement. Alternatively, he might well have included in his statement other facts favourable to him; for example, on the degree of his intoxication at the time of the offence.

There was independent evidence of the commission of the offence and

[14] Information on the history of the amendment of Police Standing Orders was largely supplied by Professor C.M. Tatz.

it seems quite likely that the defendant could still have been convicted on this evidence even if he had refused to confess and had pleaded 'not guilty'. But the original sentence might well have been reduced if the mitigating circumstances had appeared in his confession.

It is quite clear that the police concerned were in breach of the Standing Order. Subsequently, an instruction was issued to all police in which the method of notification used in this case was described as 'wholly unsatisfactory'. Police were instructed to ensure compliance with the Standing Orders 'requiring the Superintendent of Aborigines Welfare to be informed'.

But within a short period a member of the Aborigines Welfare Board had become aware of four more cases of non-compliance by police with this Standing Order; two were protection applications concerning children.

Police Standing Orders were then amended (in May 1966) to require police officers to notify the Aborigines Welfare Board or approved persons, by telegram, of the arrest of any Aboriginal for all offences other than drunkenness.[15] This amendment still does not specifically provide that the notification should take place before the police interview an Aboriginal suspect. This had been requested by the Aborigines Welfare Board so that a welfare officer could advise a suspect of his rights on arrest. The Chief Commissioner of Police considered such an amendment would be impracticable, but agreed that there could be no objection to an accused person having access to a welfare officer or similar person from the time of his arrest and subsequently.

The Report of the Ministry of Aboriginal Affairs for the year ended 30 June 1968, stated that police had been notifying the Department when Aborigines were arrested, but foreshadowed a statutory amendment on the matter.[16] Section 37 of the Aboriginal Affairs Act, 1967 (Vic.) already imposed an obligation on a court to notify the Director of Aboriginal Affairs of any case concerning an Aboriginal. In introducing an amendment of this section in September 1968 the Minister made the following explanation:

> It has been pointed out to me that in many instances the court is not aware that an Aborigine is involved in a case until he appears before it, and that adjournment of the case in these circumstances may cause

[15] *Report of the Aborigines Welfare Board for the year ended 30th June, 1967* (1967), p. 21. Melbourne: Government Printer.

[16] *Report of the Ministry of Aboriginal Affairs for the year ended 30th June, 1968* (1968), p. 14. Melbourne: Government Printer.

> considerable inconvenience to the accused and to witnesses . . . Accordingly, it is now proposed to amend this section to place a statutory obligation on the police to notify the Ministry when an Aborigine is to be charged.[17]

It is interesting that the Minister did not refer to the fact that the police were already under a similar duty under their own Standing Orders. Thus belated and silent recognition had been accorded to the fact that internal police regulations are not the most satisfactory means of imposing duties on the police, when the main purpose is to protect members of the community.

The amended section provided that the police officer 'shall forthwith after the charge is laid . . . notify the Director of Aboriginal Affairs by telegram'.[18] The section does not apply to charges of being drunk or being drunk and disorderly in a public place.

This is certainly a great improvement, but still does not provide complete protection for an Aboriginal suspect. To illustrate: an Aboriginal defendant was tried in Tasmania on three charges of breaking and entering. The only evidence against him consisted of confessions he was alleged to have made to police in Victoria and Tasmania. He was unrepresented at trial but endeavoured to set up a defence that the confessions were fabricated and that he had an alibi for the third offence. He was nevertheless convicted. On appeal, the court was sufficiently impressed with the defendant's allegations against the police to say that this matter should have gone to the jury. The date of the defendant's arrest in Victoria was June 1966 so it is apparent that disputes about confessions have not ceased since the Murray Report. It is possible that if its recommendations had been more fully implemented, for example, by providing tape recorders at more police stations, difficulty might have been avoided in this case. Although it preceded the amendment of the Aboriginal Affairs Act, that amendment would not have made any difference. Section 37 still only imposes an obligation on the police *after* the charge is laid, so the police have retained the right to conduct interrogations free of outside interference. The original Aborigines Welfare Board proposals were directed to providing Aborigines with advice on arrest as well as with representation at trial, but only the latter is advanced by the present

[17] *Victoria Parliamentary Debates* (Hansard), Forty-fourth Parliament, Second Session, 1968, p. 142.

[18] Aboriginal Affairs (Amendment) Act, 1968 (Vic.). Section 8 substituted a new section 37 in the principal Act.

provisions for notification by the police. Further consideration of possible remedies in Victoria will be postponed until after the situations in South Australia and Western Australia have been examined.

SOUTH AUSTRALIA

At least two South Australian cases involving Aboriginal defendants reveal highly questionable methods of conducting police interrogations. These methods were objectionable even under the general law, leaving aside for the moment the question of whether Aborigines should be given extra protection.

A young Aboriginal was charged with breaking and entering. At the preliminary hearing the police gave evidence that the defendant had been interviewed in a police mess room. While being questioned he was very nervous and while standing near some lockers he fell backwards in a limp condition and slid down the front of the lockers onto the floor. It appeared that he had fainted and he was taken to hospital where he stayed about 30-40 minutes. According to one policeman, the doctor who examined him said that he had suffered an extreme shock.

Defence counsel cross-examined the police witnesses as to whether the defendant had been assaulted in the course of questioning, but the police denied it. The police claimed that there was no better place than the mess room to question him at the time and that he had not been standing for the duration of the interview but had just stood up about ten or fifteen minutes before he fainted. One police officer stated: 'I did not make arrangements for anyone from (the) Aborigines Board to be present during questioning. I have heard roughly that someone should be present.'

Before defence counsel began cross-examining the last police witness, the magistrate held that no reasonable jury properly directed could convict the defendant and dismissed the information. It is not possible to interpret this as a definite finding that the police had used violence in the course of the interrogation, although considerable uneasiness must be experienced by anyone reading the depositions. It seems reasonable to assume that the magistrate's decision was based on the non-voluntary nature of the confession coupled with the vagueness of the statements made by the defendant when he was taken to the scene of the offence, and his repudiation of the confession four days later. Reading the depositions as a whole there is substantial doubt, not just a reasonable doubt, about his guilt even on the police evidence alone. This defendant, who was not even committed for trial, spent at least ten days in custody. Bail was refused by the court when the police objected to it. The main reason for the objection, according to police documents, was that his release would seriously impede police inquiries, in relation both to other offences which he was supposed to have committed and also the location of his alleged accomplices.

The second case concerns an Aboriginal who was charged by the police with 'assault with intent to rape'.[19] The cross-examination of the detective at the preliminary hearing was very revealing as to his method of interrogation. The following exchange between defence counsel and the detective is instructive:

> Q. (by defence counsel) At p. 13 of your notes it appears you suggested to the defendant that 'you were going to bowl (the complainant) over, that is have intercourse with her or have some indecent connection with her'. That is the first mention of rape or illegal intercourse.
>
> A. (by detective) Yes I suggested that. . . . I was not primarily going to accept this version of going in to steal. I've had experience with aborigines! I've learnt that they are somewhat devious . . .

When further cross-examined on his method of interrogation the detective stated: 'It is probably a habit to suggest an answer that is logical.'

Such an interrogation is hardly calculated to produce a confession which is 'voluntary' in any sense or even one which has much likelihood of being true. It also fits ill with the rule that a defendant should not be cross-examined on his statement but should only be asked questions to clear up any ambiguity. On the contrary, it amounts to putting words into his mouth. It is particularly reprehensible when it is realised that this defendant left school at the age of twelve years while in Grade 3.

The local justices nevertheless committed him for trial for the offence charged. By the time the case reached the Supreme Court, the charge had been reduced to 'common assault' to which the defendant pleaded guilty. Chamberlain J. said that he did not think there was any evidence to support the more serious charge.

One of the major criticisms made by Inglis (1961) in his examination of the Stuart case (the *cause célèbre* in South Australian Aboriginal affairs) concerned the absence of a welfare officer during the initial police interrogation of Stuart. Inglis comments (p. 317) that no one appears to have considered the possibility of the welfare officer being present

[19] Supreme Court, Adelaide, File No. 40, May 1965.

during the interrogation though he waited outside the room where it was being conducted. After having observed the hostility of police officers to what they regarded as interference by departmental officers in other cases, I can understand that a welfare officer would not thrust himself forward in such a situation in the absence of specific authority to do so and in a town which does not have a particularly good reputation for race relations.[20]

In 1965 negotiations started between the Department of Aboriginal Affairs and the Police Planning and Research Division with a view to amending the Police General Order Book in connection with the interrogation of Aborigines.[21] One amendment suggested by the Department of Aboriginal Affairs was in the following terms:

> 1. A senior officer of the Department of Aboriginal Affairs must be advised when an Aboriginal . . . is about to be questioned prior to being charged with an indictable offence of a serious nature.
> 2. That senior officer will then advise as to whether or not a Department of Aboriginal Affairs officer must be present at such questioning. If he decides that a Department of Aboriginal Affairs officer must be present he will make the necessary arrangements.

But the relevant police regulation was changed to read:

> *Serious Offences* . . . An Officer of the Department of Aboriginal Affairs should be notified in the case of any allegation of a serious offence against an Aboriginal as soon as possible so that any assistance which may be necessary may be given to the Aboriginal.

The regulation does not unambiguously confer a right on a welfare officer to attend an interrogation. Nevertheless, the police have, since the Stuart case, in some cases notified a welfare officer so that he can be present during the interrogation of an Aboriginal for a serious offence.

Two cases illustrate the new approach of the police to the presence of

[20] The problem of lack of attendance of the welfare officer at interrogations continues in this area. In a recent case Bright J. commented: 'It seems to me that when the police in the present case invited the community welfare officer at Ceduna to participate in the subsequent interview by the police with the accused it was unfortunate that the community welfare officer found himself unable to accept the invitation. I do not reflect on him personally for I do not know what other duties necessitated his attention, but here was an Aboriginal charged or about to be charged with murder and I should have thought that in such a case assisting that Aboriginal would have a high priority.' (*R.* v. *Gibson*, Supreme Court of South Australia, November 1973).

[21] D.A.A. File No. 594 of 1965.

a welfare officer at interrogations. The first concerns an Aboriginal who was originally charged with murder. He spoke English but was illiterate. A detective interviewed him twice in the absence of a welfare officer. On the second occasion he informed the defendant that he had tried unsuccessfully to contact the local welfare officer. He asked whether the defendant wanted a welfare officer present. The defendant replied: 'I am not a mission native. I don't need any welfare.' The next day a welfare officer was present when the detective read to the defendant a report of the two previous interviews. The defendant said that his statement was true. The welfare officer then interviewed him alone and he confirmed that he had made the statement attributed to him.

A senior officer of the Department of Aboriginal Affairs was satisfied with the procedure adopted in this case. But it did not provide as much protection as if a welfare officer had been present at the first interrogation. It may be queried why the attempt to contact the welfare officer was not made until the second interview. Once the welfare officer was present it might have been preferable to have asked the defendant the questions again and waited for his answers rather than to read over the record of previous interviews. The only advance in this case as compared with the Stuart case was that the police did attempt to contact a welfare officer to attend an interrogation and did permit him to see the defendant alone after the third interview.

An Aboriginal woman was interviewed in hospital four days after she had killed her husband (a case already referred to in this chapter). She was questioned by a detective in the presence of another detective, a policewoman who took shorthand notes, and a welfare officer from the Department of Aboriginal Affairs. The Department had taken the initiative in contacting the police and requesting information on the time of the interview. At the outset of the interrogation, the detective informed the welfare officer that she was not permitted to interrupt, raise any objections to questions or interfere in any way. He refused to delay the interview to allow a solicitor to be contacted. The interview itself was conducted with sympathy and understanding. At its conclusion the detective asked the welfare officer to apply for legal assistance for the defendant, who had just been charged with murder.

It is quite clear that the police were prepared to allow the defendant to obtain legal assistance only after she had made an incriminating statement. They permitted the welfare officer to remain at the interview knowing that she was not in a position to give legal advice. In such circumstances the only protection afforded by the presence of the welfare officer is against violence or threats. A welfare officer who had been given some training in the legal rights of suspects could also observe whether correct procedures were observed, for example, in relation to the caution. The welfare officer could also take notes of the interview in order to check the accuracy of the police record. In this case there is no reason to doubt the accuracy of the record and it seems that the defendant made the statement quite voluntarily. But the police would be more entitled to claim that they had been completely fair to her if they had not been obstructive when the request for delay to enable a solicitor to attend was made.

WESTERN AUSTRALIA

Western Australian law on the interrogation of Aborigines was quite different from that in Victoria and South Australia. The difference is due to section 31(1) of the Native Welfare Act, 1963 (W.A.): 'No admission of guilt or confession before trial shall be sought or obtained from any native charged or suspected of any offence punishable by death or imprisonment in the first instance, and if any such admission or confession is obtained it shall not be admissible or received in evidence.' Section 31(2) provided that the section should not apply to Natives living or domiciled in the south-west corner of the State. The section originally applied to the whole State.[22]

This section has been the subject of judicial consideration on appeal on at least three occasions. In *Thomson* v. *Brockman*[23] a police constable obtained from a Native a confession in a case where he was suspected of the offence of carnal knowledge, which was punishable by imprisonment in the first instance. The confession included a statement that he was responsible for a girl's pregnancy. She later sought to use the confession in proceedings for an affiliation order. It was held by the appeal court that the confession had been rightly rejected in this case, even though the proceedings in dispute did not involve an offence punishable by imprisonment in the first instance. The fact that the confession had originally been obtained in connection with an offence covered by the section was sufficient to prohibit its use in evidence in any proceedings.

[22] It was introduced in 1936. Whenever section 31 is mentioned in this chapter, the reference is to the Native Welfare Act, 1963 (W.A.).

[23] (1939) 42 W.A.L.R. 36.

In *Bolton* v. *Neilsen*[24] the proper construction of section 60 of the Native Administration Act, 1905-47 (W.A.) and the extent of the duty placed on a Protector of Natives by that section were in issue. Section 60(1) was in substantially the same terms as the later section 31(1), quoted above. Section 60(2) and (3) imposed other requirements. Section 60(2) provided that a court should not accept any plea of guilty by a Native unless the provisos in section 60(3) were satisfied. The proviso in the latter sub-section, which was in issue in this case, was 'that the protector approves of such plea of guilty being pleaded'.

Three Aborigines appealed against convictions on charges of stealing. They had all pleaded guilty, the protector had approved of the pleas and the trial court sentenced each defendant to six months imprisonment. Dwyer C. J. held, on appeal, that a protector before approving a plea of guilty 'should satisfy himself of the actual guilt of the accused, and that there is admissible and credible evidence to support it, and unless he does that his statutory duty is not done' (at p. 51). The main evidence against the defendants consisted of confessions or admissions obtained from them in contravention of section 60(1). Since this evidence was not legally admissible against them, the protector should not have approved the plea of guilty. Section 60 had not been complied with in substance, so the court on appeal quashed the pleas, the findings and the sentences.

The decision in *Louis* v. *R.*[25] again turned on the proper construction to be given to section 60(1) of the Native Administration Act. The appellant was an Aboriginal who was convicted of unlawful and indecent assault by a jury at the Court of Sessions, Broome. The court admitted statements made by the accused while in custody in evidence against him. An officer of the Department of Native Affairs, who appeared for the defence, objected to the admission of this evidence but the court received it, overruling his objections.

On appeal, it was argued for the respondent that nothing can be an admission of guilt or a confession unless it is substantially a recount of all elements which constitute the crime, or a definite statement by the accused that he is guilty, using those words. The Court of Criminal Appeal preferred the argument for the appellant. In the words of Dwyer C. J.:

[24] (1951) 53 W.A.L.R. 48.
[25] (1952) 53 W.A.L.R. 81.

> In my view admission or confession covers not only a statement made in the verbiage of the section; not only a case where all the elements which constitute the crime are admitted; but also cases where in effect the admission of the accused is sufficient to fill out the case against him by supplying proof of such necessary matters as have not already been proved or is so materially incriminating as to furnish an important link in the chain of evidence against him . . . (at p. 83).

The second ground on which the statements were admitted by the trial court was that they were not 'sought or obtained'. The appeal court was not impressed with this finding by the trial court and held that it was obvious that the statements had been obtained contrary to the section. Dwyer C. J. may be quoted on this aspect also:

> In my view statements made to officers of the Police Force must on nearly every occasion be suspect. It is obvious that they are interested in prosecutions, and it is generally, though not always the case that they make opportunities for statements to be given; necessarily therefore statements given to them will nearly always be obtained by design contrary to the prohibition mentioned in section 60 (at p. 84).

It appears that the police felt hampered by the requirements of section 60 and attempted to evade its restrictions. A perusal of the original Evidence Book of the Broome Court of Session raises a strong suspicion that the evidence given to the trial court was altered either at the time of the original hearing or when notes of the hearing were sent down to the appeal court, apparently in order to make it less obvious that the statement had been 'obtained' contrary to the section. For example, the words of the police officer's evidence have been changed from 'obtained a statement from him' to read 'he made a statement quite voluntarily' (fieldwork notes). It is impossible now to say who made the alteration or when it was made, but it strongly suggests that either the police or the trial court or both were trying to evade what they knew was the real intention behind the section.

Some policemen I interviewed claimed that the section unduly hampered their work and they clearly resented the special protection given to Aborigines. Without, at this stage, wishing to indicate a final opinion on the merits of their complaints, it is interesting to read the explanation of the original section 60 put forward by Dwyer C. J. (at pp. 82-3): 'the Legislature had in view the giving in full measure to Natives all the advantages which could be claimed by the ordinary citizens of the community whether the Native claimed these privileges to which ordinary citizens are entitled, or did not'. He did not see the section as providing special privileges for Aborigines but rather as putting them on an equal footing with more educated or more powerful members of the community who would be aware of and be able to assert the privilege against self-incrimination and the right to plead not guilty. This overlooks the fact that poor whites may also not be aware of these privileges and rights or be in a position to assert them. Nevertheless, the statement of principle is an important one.

More recent cases show that the police continued to infringe section 31(1) in certain areas; whether deliberately or in ignorance of the requirements of the law is not clear. In one outback town in 1966 the magistrate dismissed charges against two Aborigines because the only evidence was statements made by them which had been obtained by the police contrary to the section. They had been held in police custody for some time before the hearing. If the police claim that they did not know the requirements of the section, then one can only say that they should have known.

In another 1966 case an Aboriginal was charged with common assault on a woman. At the court hearing a welfare officer pleaded guilty on behalf of the defendant. The prosecuting sergeant explained that the police had charged the defendant with the lesser offence of common assault, although it had been alleged that he had sexually assaulted the woman. The police could not prove anything more than common assault because the Native Welfare Act prevented them using the defendant's admissions in court. The welfare officer then spoke on behalf of the defendant and pointed out that since he had only been charged with the lesser offence that was all the justices could take into account in fixing sentence. The defendant was sentenced to three months' imprisonment.

The police officer had acted illegally in obtaining admissions from the defendant, even though he did not introduce these in evidence in court. Section 31(1) states quite clearly that: 'No admission of guilt or confession before trial shall be sought or obtained from any native charged or suspected of any offence punishable by . . . imprisonment in the first instance. . . .'

Although the point seems never to have been considered it is interesting to speculate on whether a police officer who obtained a confession in these circumstances could be charged with an offence against the Act. The prohibition against this conduct seems to be expressed at least as strongly as that against bringing intoxicating liquor into a reserve in Regulation 24(1) of the Native Welfare Act Regulations, 1964 (W.A.). Under this provision, Aborigines have been convicted and sentenced in accordance with the general 'Penalties' provision of the Regulations. A reasonable case could be made out for similar action to be taken against a police officer who offended against section 31(1) but no such prosecution has ever been launched.

Having considered the actual operation of section 31, it is time to turn to a consideration of its merits. Should it have been retained in Western Australia?[26] Would it be desirable to adopt a similar provision in those States which do not have it at present?

Arguments against section 31 were put forward by some police officers who claimed that it unnecessarily hampered them in their work. Yet one police sergeant stated that section 31 was not a great handicap to the police because usually the Department of Native Welfare co-operated with the police (apparently by persuading Aborigines to plead guilty, so that the police did not have to lead any evidence).

One magistrate expressed the view that it should be repealed because it produced too many anomalies. For example, it was often difficult for a police officer who attended the scene of a traffic accident to know whether any individual Aboriginal should be regarded as a suspect for a traffic offence or as a witness. Should he refrain from questioning every Aboriginal found at the scene? The magistrate mentioned other anomalies arising from the geographical limitation on the operation of the section and from its restriction to offences 'punishable by death or imprisonment in the first instance'. How did a policeman know whether he was investigating that type of case? And what exactly was meant by the phrase? In the case mentioned earlier the defendant was actually sentenced to three months' imprisonment for common assault. Yet that offence was regarded as not within the prohibition of the section, presumably because the court could have chosen to impose a fine.

This magistrate also believed that the section actually operated against the interests of Aborigines. If the police did not take a statement from an Aboriginal suspect or defendant, he lost the chance of putting his side of the story; of raising a possible defence. He thought a more satisfactory protection for every defendant would be to have an independent person present at police interrogations.

On the other hand, some welfare officers and another magistrate main-

[26] Section 49 of the Aboriginal Affairs Planning Authority Act, 1972 (W.A.) adopts a different method of offering protection to Aborigines in relation to confessional evidence.

tained that section 31 was still needed for the protection of 'bush natives', who do not speak or understand English well, and who may be unfairly prejudiced by the admission of a confession in evidence when they have not really understood the questions they have been asked.

In my view, section 31 as it stood was unsatisfactory. The blanket prohibition against obtaining or using in evidence any confession by an Aboriginal in cases involving the offences defined went too far. It meant that, no matter how scrupulously fair the police might be in obtaining a statement, it could not be used against an Aboriginal defendant unless it was wholly volunteered and did not result from any activity on the part of the police. One can understand police frustration at seeing Aboriginal defendants freed of charges in circumstances where white defendants would quite properly be convicted. On the other hand, the rights of Aborigines in interrogations do require protection and frequently they do require more protection than most whites in order to ensure that theoretical 'rights' have some real effect. Some middle ground between a total ban on confessions and an 'open go' for police interrogations seems to be required. The reasons for this and possible solutions are discussed next.

SUGGESTIONS FOR REFORM

The problem of protecting the rights of Aborigines in police interrogations is only one facet of the protection of the rights of all suspects. The problem has not been solved for the general community so it is not surprising that it is difficult to find a satisfactory solution for the specific problem of the minority group.

Although elaborate rules have been drawn up to protect the rights of suspects, the Murray Report shows how difficult it is to ensure that these rights really exist in practice and equally how difficult it is to know to what extent the rules are actually observed or disregarded. The problem arises because the general police attitude is that interrogations are an essential part of their investigation of crime and the less interference there is with their performance of this function the better. They would prefer not to have any third party present at interrogations and when the presence of an independent witness cannot be avoided the conditions on which he or she is permitted to attend are as restrictive as possible.[27]

[27] See, for example, press reports of statement by Inspector Crowley (*Age* 8/7/65 and 5/11/65) and the case discussed in this chapter of the Aboriginal woman who killed her husband.

The police no doubt have some justifiable grounds for these attitudes. The presence of a third party may inhibit a suspect from speaking freely, even though in the absence of that third party he would make a confession which is quite properly obtained within existing rules of law. On the other hand, unless an independent person is present it is quite impossible to find out how often the police use improper methods to obtain a confession. Allegations can be made by defendants and denied by the police and it is not possible to decide with absolute certainty where the truth lies. Any suspect in the hands of the police is to some extent in a situation of powerlessness and the temptation to use improper methods to obtain a confession is always inherent in the situation, although this is not to say that the police often succumb to the temptation. The competing claims of the police to pursue their task without interference and of the suspect to have his rights effectively and adequately protected must somehow be balanced and a solution found that provides for both.

It may be, as an eminent medico-legal expert claims, that if all suspects were actually able to enforce the legal rights which at present they theoretically possess, there would be very few convictions indeed.[28] If that were found to be so, after all suspects were put in this position, then the police would have good grounds for asking for a reduction in the legal rights assured to suspects. The present situation is that strong-willed and influential people are able to insist on strict enforcement of all their legal rights, including the right to have a solicitor's advice before saying anything, while the weak and uneducated are in a relatively unfavourable position, being unable to compel recognition of rights supposedly guaranteed to them by law.

Of all these weak and uneducated people, Aborigines are in the least favourable position. Unless they have the assistance of a strong welfare officer who is really interested in protecting their rights, or of a solicitor who acts as he would for any other client, they usually have no effective resistance to offer to any police officer who is not prepared to accord them their rights as suspects. Aborigines need special protection because of their high susceptibility to police action; their low standard of education which obviously leads to ignorance of legal rights; their lack of money to employ a private lawyer; and in some cases language difficulties. Many of these disabilities are shared with other persons of low socio-economic status and it is submitted that any special provision designed to enable

[28] Quoted Sargant 1959: 207; see also Glasbeek and Prentice 1968: 475.

Aborigines actually to enforce their rights should also be extended to these other persons. Many migrants, for example, could make a showing of need as a basis for special protection in interrogations in the same way that Aborigines can. None of the methods so far adopted in Victoria, South Australia or Western Australia has effectively provided protection for Aborigines.

In the United States considerable attention has been focused on the problem of police interrogations in recent years. In *Escobedo* v. *Illinois*[29] the Supreme Court held that a suspect must be permitted to see his lawyer before being interrogated if he asks for him. In *Gideon* v. *Wainwright*[30] the court had held that every accused person was entitled to a lawyer at trial. The *Escobedo* majority said that if the argument put forward by the State, that this right to counsel applied only at trial, were to succeed, the trial would be 'no more than an appeal from the interrogation'.[31] The actual decision in *Escobedo* was rather narrow and depended on the particular facts of that case. The defendant's lawyer had actually been present at the police station but had been unable to see his client. The defendant's requests to see him had been refused by the police.

The decision gave rise to considerable controversy as to how far it would extend. In *Miranda* v. *Arizona*[32] the Supreme Court resolved the controversy and again demonstrated its concern for the rights of suspects. The court held that: 'the prosecution may not use statements stemming from custodial interrogation of the defendant unless it demonstrates the use of procedural safeguards effective to secure the privilege against self-incrimination' (at p. 444). The procedural safeguards required were spelled out as follows: 'Prior to any questioning, the person must be warned that he has a right to remain silent, that any statement he does make may be used as evidence against him, and that he has a right to the presence of an attorney, either retained or appointed' (at p. 444). The warning to be given is thus analogous to the caution required by Australian law, with the addition of information about the right to a lawyer. The judgment is extremely interesting for its examination of the reasons underlying the privilege against self-incrimination and for its recognition that rights on paper do not mean much unless they can be effectively enforced.

[29] (1964) 378 U.S. 478.
[30] (1963) 372 U.S. 335.
[31] (1964) 378 U.S. 478, 487.
[32] (1966) 384 U.S. 436.

It may be argued that these American decisions do not have much relevance in Australia since the privilege against self-incrimination is specifically set out in the Fifth Amendment to the U.S. Constitution and the Australian Constitution does not contain any comparable provision. The privilege originally came from the English common law, however, and it is supposed to apply in Australia, except to the extent that legislation has abolished it in relation to specific offences. The Australian citizen has a right to refuse to answer any questions put to him by the police which might incriminate him. Although the police have a right, and indeed a duty, to ask people questions in an endeavour to solve crimes, this right only extends to the point where it can be exercised without infringing the privilege against self-incrimination. The police are entitled to ask questions as long as the suspect is willing to answer in the exercise of his free choice to speak or remain silent, but no longer. It is worth emphasising this point because many policemen seem to feel that because they have an acknowledged right to ask questions it is an unlimited right, or alternatively, that it should be an unlimited right.

Leaving aside for the moment the question of whether the privilege against self-incrimination is too restrictive on police activities and accepting that the law as applied to the general community does embody this privilege, I turn to a consideration of arguments in favour of special procedures being provided for Aborigines.

Australian law embodies the notion that all citizens are entitled to equal protection of the law and to be treated equally in the administration of justice. This principle is not included in the federal Constitution as it is in the United States but it is inherent in specific provisions of other laws. The police are required to take an oath to serve 'without favour or affection, malice, or illwill',[33] in other words, to treat all citizens equally under law.

It has also been recognised that the Aborigines constitute a group of people who require special attention in order to guarantee the effective exercise of rights which they theoretically possess. The United States Supreme Court recognised that unless care is taken: 'Rights declared in words might be lost in reality.'[34] It has already been recognised by the legislatures of Victoria, South Australia and Western Australia that

[33] Police Act, 1892 (W.A.) section 10.

[34] *Weems* v. *U.S.* (1910) 217 U.S. 349, 373; cited in *Miranda* v. *Arizona* (1966) 384 U.S. 436, 443.

Aborigines require special protection in the course of the interrogation process. This protection is required because of special factors which apply to them as a group, including language difficulties, educational standards, ignorance of legal rights, and economic status. The special procedures required to be followed in the case of Aborigines are designed to make them equal with other citizens when they face a police interrogation; not to give them an advantage over other citizens as many policemen believe.

When people are unequal in social status and economic resources they do not really have the same opportunity to enforce their rights. Unless special procedures are provided for Aborigines, the privilege against self-incrimination will remain a dead letter as far as they are concerned, whereas people who are more strong-willed or who can afford to insist on a lawyer's presence can effectively enforce their 'right to silence'. So the law may need to be expressed in different terms for different groups in order to provide equal protection for all.

This fact has been recognised in general terms in Australia, in the passages from *R.* v. *Lee* and *Louis* v. *R.* already quoted. A similar argument applies to other disadvantaged groups, such as foreign migrants. On the other hand, although the Aboriginal group as a whole possesses these disabilities and is therefore in need of special protection, there will always be some Aborigines who are not in this category. For this reason it is suggested that any special law which is framed should not be expressed in absolute terms as applying to the whole racial group, but should rather be based on a showing of special need. It might be expressed to apply to all illiterate people, to all people with no secondary education, and to all people whose native language is not English. Alternatively, it could be expressed to apply to all Aborigines but with a proviso that if the police can show that the particular defendant did not suffer from any of the disabilities mentioned then they would not be bound to follow the special procedures.

The main argument against the requirement of special procedures for Aborigines is that special laws create resentment amongst people who regard them as placing Aborigines in a privileged position, instead of recognising that they aim only at equalising the position. Another argument is that special laws encourage attitudes of dependency and irresponsibility in those who are intended to benefit by them. Even if true, this disadvantage is outweighed by the considerations already put forward in support of special laws.

If the argument in favour of special laws for Aborigines is accepted, specific suggestions can be made for putting it into effect. One way to make the privilege against self-incrimination effective is to provide for lawyers to be present at interrogations. The Yale Law School study ('Interrogations' 1967: 1615) on the impact of *Miranda* found that warnings alone did not make suspects' rights fully effective and recommended that counsel should be assured to each suspect before the police interrogate.

The Report of the International Commission of Jurists on 'The Right of Arrested Persons to Communicate with those whom it is necessary for them to consult in order to ensure their Defence or to protect their Essential Interests' considered, amongst other topics, the question of the notification of the fact of arrest to the legal adviser and access to the legal adviser.[35] The Commission's view (p. 94) was that

> the Rule of Law requires that the following minimum principles be observed in connection with the right of the arrested person to communicate with his legal adviser:
> 1. The arrested person should have a legal right to communicate orally with his legal adviser.
> 2. It should be the duty of the police to inform the arrested person without any delay of his right in this regard.
> 3. The arrested person should be entitled to exercise this right as soon as is practicable after the arrest . . .
> 7. The arrested person should be entitled to have a legal adviser or a friend present to protect his interests at any identification parade at the instance of the police relating to him.

The Commission left open the question of whether a legal adviser should be permitted to be present during police investigations (p. 93). Further, the principles formulated do not make any special provision for the person who is not able to engage his own legal adviser. But they are only designed to set minimum standards. The amendment of Police Standing Orders in Victoria referred to earlier followed a submission in which this I.C.J. Report was referred to and the view expressed that, in the Aboriginal context, these principles should be read to include a reference to the right to communicate with a legal adviser or welfare officer or both.[36]

Mr Justice Sholl's suggestions for the improvements of police methods of interrogation included the presence of an outsider, such as a licensed

[35] *Journal of the International Commission of Jurists* **5** (1964).

[36] Correspondence from Dr C.M. Tatz to Mr Rylah, 15/10/65.

shorthand writer or justice.[37] The Murray Report (p. 16) also recommended that a solicitor who desires to be present at a police interrogation should ordinarily be permitted to do so but it should be made clear to him that if it appears he is deliberately trying to impede the interrogation he will be requested to leave. This recommendation has apparently not yet been adopted. These suggestions were not specifically directed to the position of Aboriginal suspects but if they are desirable for the general community they are equally so for the Aboriginal population.

It is suggested that the following proposals should be adopted in the form of legislation, or at least in the form of administrative regulations binding the police and Aboriginal welfare staff. It should be provided that before the police interrogate an Aboriginal in connection with any offence, they should contact a welfare officer to enable him to arrange for a lawyer or another independent person or the welfare officer himself to be present. With the growth of Aboriginal Legal Services this would be an appropriate function for their field officers to perform. The police should not proceed with the interrogation until one of these persons is present or until the welfare or field officer has indicated his decision that it is not necessary for anyone to be present. The obligations laid on the welfare or field officer should be to arrange, if possible, for a lawyer to be present at the interrogation or, failing that, to attend himself or arrange for another independent witness to be present. Because of the difficulty of obtaining lawyers in remote areas, some discretion would have to be allowed to the welfare or field officer. Possibly a scale of offences should be drawn up with different requirements imposed on the police and welfare or field officers in respect to different classes. It is necessary to provide that the police should take the initiative in notifying the welfare or field officer (or an independent person where no such officer is stationed) because the Aborigines who most need protection are the very ones who would not think of asking for it or would not persist in asserting their rights if the request were refused. The obligation therefore needs to be laid on the police. Protection for the police should be provided so that, if the welfare or field officer has not appeared within a reasonable time after notification, they should be entitled to proceed with the interrogation. It will be necessary to provide also for notification of a welfare or field officer in other cases where no interrogation is contemplated, for the purpose of arranging bail or appearing in court.

[37] *R.* v. *Governor of Metropolitan Gaol; ex parte Molinari* [1962] V.R. 156, 169.

Another desirable reform would be to provide further education for police, Aborigines, welfare and field officers relating to their respective rights, functions and duties. A limited start has been made on such projects in Victoria and South Australia.

So far, reforms have been discussed on the assumption that the existing privilege against self-incrimination will be retained in the law. Since this is a very contentious issue, it is desrable to discuss briefly the issue of whether the law on interrogations and confessions for the general community should be changed. Police complaints that too many suspects are becoming aware of their rights are not worthy of serious attention, because they imply the unacceptable proposition that the police do not mind a few people exerting their full rights, as long as the great majority of people are not in a position to do so. But if the police complain that the law is too generous to all suspects and that the full enforcement of their rights would seriously hamper law enforcement, then the argument deserves to be examined.

Those who argue that the existing privilege against self-incrimination should be retained are seeking to preserve some or all of the following values. Some regard the privilege against self-incrimination as a positive value in itself. The court in *Miranda* v. *Arizona* rested its position largely on the English history of dislike of the Star Chamber process, and the decision to adopt an adversary system of justice instead of an inquisitorial one. Proponents of this view regard the suspect as primarily a citizen, who has rights and dignity to be protected. They do not see the contest as one in which the police and respectable society are ranged against the criminal but rather as one between the citizen (who at the moment is a suspect) and the government, of which the police are agents.

Another value sought to be preserved is truth. The law could be expressed so as to embody this as the only value to be sought, for example, to provide that a confession would be excluded from evidence only if there were a substantial risk that it was untrue. But the strongest supporters of the privilege against self-incrimination do not regard this as a sufficient test. They agree that one of the reasons for excluding confessions which are not voluntary is that there is a risk that they will be untrue, but they see value in prohibiting the police from obtaining or using involuntary confessions, whether they are true or not. Police may claim that confessions are always true, even if they have used some violence or coercion to obtain them. There are enough substantiated cases of miscarriages of justice based on false confessions to make one very sceptical of this claim.[38]

Another value underlying the position of supporters of the present law, is that the community should be able to respect the police and the police should not use violence, threats or lies to obtain confessions and should act strictly according to law. Almost everyone would accept that the police should not use violence or threats to obtain confessions; the disputed question is how far the law should go beyond this in restricting the activities of the police. For example, should the police be permitted to use clever psychological techniques which involve some degree of coercion?

Police activities in obtaining confessions may be regarded as falling on a continuum, with those that should clearly be prohibited (such as violence) at one end and those that are clearly permissible (the passive reception of a freely volunteered statement) at the other. The real question is what is to be done about the 'twilight zone' falling between these extremes. For example, should the police be permitted to interrogate a suspect held incommunicado at a police station for a limited period? Existing legal norms impose considerable restrictions on the powers of the police and most of the 'twilight zone' theoretically falls in the prohibited category at present. It may be that it is only because the rules are more honoured in the breach than in the observance that the police are so often able to obtain confessions, but information is lacking at present. The police claim that the rules unduly hamper law enforcement may be interpreted as a claim that the activities in the 'twilight zone' should henceforth be regarded as falling within the permissible category. The statement that the police should obey the law does not answer the question whether the law should be changed.

Underlying the police view also are several value judgments and factual assumptions. First is a belief in the great importance of society's interest in the detection and conviction of criminals. The police do tend to see the contest as one between the police and respectable society on one side and the criminal on the other. Many police also do not really accept the adversary system and the presumption of innocence but regard a suspect as already a criminal. Truth is the only or the main value which is sought. If a confession is true, it does not matter how it was obtained.

[38] Sargant (1959: 180-6) discusses the trials of Evans and Christie and shows how false confessions may be obtained even by police of acknowledged integrity.

One factual assumption underlying this position is that confessions must necessarily play an important part in obtaining convictions. Empirical studies carried out in the United States have found that confessions are less necessary than is commonly supposed. Usually the police have other evidence available that would be sufficient for a conviction ('Interrogations' 1967: 1588). Proponents of the view that existing rules should be retained point to the positive value of compelling the police to seek out objective evidence and not to take the lazy way out of obtaining admissions from the suspect's own mouth (*Miranda* v. *Arizona* (1966) 384 U.S. 436 at 447, 460).

It may be that in Australia at present most convictions are obtained on the basis of confessions. It is possible that as suspects become more aware of their rights and are able to enforce them more effectively, the number of confessions obtained will decrease. It does not necessarily follow that the number of convictions will then decrease or that more guilty persons will escape punishment. The police view that suspects are given too many rights should not be accepted and acted on in the absence of empirical evidence supporting it. It would be worthwhile carrying out a research project in Australia designed to provide facts on which informed decisions on matters of policy could be based, perhaps on the lines of the Yale Law School study ('Interrogations' 1967).

It must be obvious that my sentiment is in favour of retaining the privilege against self-incrimination. To counterbalance this expression of opinion, it should be mentioned that the opposite view is held not only by the police but has attracted increasing support from other quarters. Glanville Williams (1963: 37-74) sets out criticisms which have been made of the right not to be questioned. But he discusses the right in the context of trial procedure, not of police interrogation; the relevant considerations may well be different.

The British Section of the International Commission of Jurists recommended that the privilege of the defendant to keep silent before trial should be abolished but with the important safeguard that a confession should only be admissible in evidence if made at an interrogation controlled by a magistrate.[39]

Possibly such a change will eventually be introduced by legislation in Australia. In the meantime the law pays lip-service to the privilege against self-incrimination. While the law remains unchanged, action

[39] 'Interrogation of Suspects', *A.L.J.* **41** (1968).

should be directed towards helping the least privileged members of Australian society to enforce effectively rights which the most privileged members are already able to enforce without outside assistance.

ILLEGAL ACTIONS BY THE POLICE

HARASSMENT

Harassment by means of arrests for trivial offences has already been mentioned. Such action by the police may be considered legal, although not always the best exercise of their discretion. In addition, there are some cases of harassment of Aborigines, where there is no legal justification for the police action.

The most blatant example of this was a 1966 Western Australian case. Police constables arrested an Aboriginal for drunkenness, apparently because they regarded him as having been 'cheeky' to them when they tried to force their way into his house the night before. After his arrest, the sergeant asked if he wanted a solicitor or doctor. He asked for both. A blood sample was taken and scientific analysis showed no alcohol in the sample. A solicitor appeared for the defendant at the hearing and the charge was dismissed. The magistrate believed the evidence of the three arresting policemen that they had observed signs of drunkenness, but he gave the defendant the benefit of the doubt because of the result of the blood test. In spite of the magistrate's remarks, the evidence of the defendant about the malicious nature of the arrest and the violence used by one policeman on the way to the police station has the ring of truth about it. If the police sergeant in this case had not acted correctly in asking the defendant if he wanted a doctor and solicitor and in permitting the doctor to attend him in the cell, the defendant would have had little hope of avoiding conviction (cf. Bowden 1965: 354-5).

In a similar case in the same town, an Aboriginal was convicted in spite of what the local welfare officer regarded as strong defence evidence offered by reputable witnesses. The welfare officer and the local solicitor regarded this case as a miscarriage of justice. The papers were sent to the Crown Law Department for opinion. That Department's opinion was that there had been no miscarriage of justice and no further action was taken. The Crown Law opinion points out that a magistrate is entitled to assess the worth of each witness and to weigh them in the scales accordingly. This is of course perfectly true but one would have thought that where two independent witnesses were prepared to appear for the defence and state that they had not observed any signs of drunkenness, the magistrate should have had a reasonable doubt sufficient for an acquittal. The independent witnesses were not able categorically to state that the defendant was not drunk, but it is always difficult to prove a negative. The onus of proof is not on the defendant and although the magistrate said that he preferred the evidence of the police, he gave no reason for rejecting the evidence of the independent witnesses.

The Crown Law opinion also states that the only reason put forward in support of the allegation that the police swore falsely is that one of them was well known for his dislike of Aborigines. The opinion states: 'The allegation must be disregarded; not only is it not substantiated, but the matter of prejudice on the part of [the police officer] is strictly irrelevant. All that is important is to know whether or not he swore falsely.' This statement again is strictly correct but it is not very satisfying. A prejudiced person will not necessarily act in a discriminatory fashion towards Aborigines, but he is quite likely to do so and is surely more likely to do so than a person who is not prejudiced. It is very unfortunate that the possibility of an independent inquiry into all the circumstances surrounding this case was not considered. While there may not have been a miscarriage of justice in any technical sense, it is surely not only technicalities which should concern those charged with the administration of justice.

A South Australian police sergeant admitted that he had arrested an Aboriginal, who was a nuisance to him, on framed charges as a technique of persuading him that he would be better off in another town. Other instances of the same technique are apparently quite often practised, for example, warning Aborigines that they will be charged with 'insufficient means', or that they will have their children taken away from them, if they do not do something which the police wish them to do, such as leaving a particular area where they are camping.

One Aboriginal man came from his home mission to another mission to be near his wife while she had a baby. The police stopped him in the street of the nearby town and warned him to get a job. In relating this, he did not appear to see anything out of the ordinary in his experience. The police would not dream of treating most visitors to the town in this way. They could easily have regarded this young man as being on holiday if it had not been common practice to warn Aborigines that they must get jobs.

Another technique of which Aborigines complain is that the police deliberately provoke retaliation so that an Aboriginal can be charged with an offence. They may repeatedly ask for his name and when he finally loses patience and refuses to say it again they charge him with the offence of refusing to give his name to a police officer. No specific substantiated cases of this nature were found and it is difficult to say how often it actually occurs.

VIOLENCE

The question of police violence has been referred to in connection with interrogations. It may also occur in the course of an arrest or after arrest quite apart from the interrogation situation. Allegations of violence have been made by white defendants as well as Aborigines. Some of these allegations are found to be false on investigation;[40] others have been found to be true. As in the interrogation situation, it is often a matter of one man's word against another's and it is impossible to determine exactly where the truth lies. It is therefore not possible to state precisely how frequently the police do use violence or whether it is more frequent against Aborigines than against other defendants. Aborigines themselves are convinced that it is.

One clear case of police brutality occurred in South Australia in 1962. An elderly Aboriginal was severely beaten by a police sergeant in an attempt to make him confess falsely that he was drunk. Owing to the intervention of local people, including the welfare officer, the matter was investigated and the sergeant dismissed from the police force. It is significant that, although the Aboriginal was sufficiently badly injured to be off work for six days, he did not want to take any action against the policeman and it was only because other people became aware of the incident that action followed.

A special committee appointed by the Aboriginal Advancement Council of Western Australia (a voluntary organisation) investigated the fatal shooting of an Aboriginal by a policeman at Laverton Native Reserve in 1969. The Coroner's finding was that the policeman fired a shot between the victim's legs at close range and that he acted in defence of another policeman and did not intend to kill or injure the deceased. No further official action has been taken.

> The Committee feel that many questions are left unanswered by the evidence submitted at the inquest. Several people closely concerned were not called on to give evidence. There are reports of police intimida-

[40] At least one example of false allegations by Aborigines in each of the three States, Victoria, South Australia and Western Australia, seems to have been reliably established (fieldwork notes).

tion. Since then a shot gun has been used against an Aboriginal at Kalgoorlie and a policeman has fired a revolver in connection with a trivial offence concerning an Aboriginal at Narrogin.[41]

Severe brutality is probably rare and confined to a few individuals in each police force. It is likely that some other policemen do use lesser degrees of physical force, perhaps not causing any injury, in order to persuade defendants to confess or to co-operate in other ways.

UNWARRANTED ENTRY INTO PRIVATE HOMES

In general, the police cannot enter on private premises without the consent of the owner or occupier, unless they have a search warrant or are entering in order to carry out a lawful arrest (Campbell and Whitmore 1966: 48-9). Complaints have been made by Aborigines that the police have tried to force their way into their homes, particularly on reserves. One false charge of drunkenness mentioned earlier apparently arose because the police were annoyed that an Aboriginal had successfully prevented them from entering his house on a previous occasion.

In a Victorian case, three policemen entered a house occupied by Aborigines at 1.00 a.m. They had no warrant. Later they returned with three policewomen and removed four children, aged from two to eight years, from the house. The children were in bed with their mother. The children later appeared at the children's court on a care and protection application. The court ordered that they should be placed on probation for one year and be returned to their parents forthwith. Quite apart from the fact that the police probably should have obtained a warrant before entering the house,[42] it is difficult to see what urgency could possibly have justified disturbing young children in this way at this hour of night, particularly as the court subsequently found that the home conditions were suitable for the children to be returned there immediately.

ACTIONS AGAINST THE POLICE

Several cases have now been described in which the police exceeded their authority or otherwise acted illegally. The law provides actions which may be taken against individual policemen in such circumstances. Only one case was found in any of the fieldwork States in which court action was

[41] *Aboriginal Welfare News* **11** (1970), pp. 3-4. The policeman who fired the fatal shot in the Laverton incident later left the police force. In 1973 he was sentenced to six years' imprisonment (minimum twenty-three months) on six stealing offences (*West Australian* 22/8/73).

[42] Children's Welfare Act, 1958 (Vic.) section 17.

actually taken against a policeman,[43] although other cases appear to have provided good grounds for legal action.

Government departments concerned with Aboriginal affairs should consider legal action in such cases in the future, instead of relying on interdepartmental pressure on the Police Department. This should also be a fruitful field of action for the recently established Aboriginal Legal Services.

In the past, the practice has been to leave such matters to be dealt with by internal police discipline. The result has been that in many cases, instead of an offending policeman being dismissed, he has merely been transferred to another area. This is unsatisfactory, not only because it means he is able to continue abusing his authority as a member of the police force, but also because the secrecy surrounding the disciplinary process makes it impossible for the public to know whether the complaint was found proved and whether the transfer was actually a punishment or a reward for work well done.

The experience of a former Northern Territory solicitor shows that a sustained policy of taking legal actions against policemen on behalf of Aborigines can produce an improvement in police behaviour.

THE FUTURE RELATIONSHIP BETWEEN ABORIGINES AND THE POLICE

The police are under a duty to act 'without favour or affection, malice, or illwill'. In Western Australia the Police Regulations related this general requirement specifically to Aborigines. 'The police generally are required to render all the aid in their power to ameliorate the condition of the aborigines', and, 'In the general treatment of aborigines members of the Force must exercise the utmost patience and humanity, combined with firmness and decision. Any violent or improper treatment of an aborigine on the part of any constable will be visited with dismissal from the service or heavy punishment.'[44] This chapter has shown how seriously the police take this duty.

[43] Policeman charged with assault on Aboriginal; charge dismissed; policeman transferred to another district.

[44] *Regulations and Instructions for the Government and Guidance of the Police Force of Western Australia* (*Government Gazette* (W.A.) 4/12/44, p. 54, Regulation 1). These regulations were in force during the fieldwork period. They have since been revoked (in 1968). Current regulations do not mention Aborigines specifically.

Hope for the future improvement of relations between police and Aborigines rests on the fact that some senior police officers have recognised the need for change and have taken steps to end some discriminatory practices. Some welfare officers have also become aware of the problem and are prepared to interpose their authority between that of the police and the relatively powerless Aboriginal. It is vitally necessary that police who do act illegally or officiously against Aborigines are proceeded against, preferably in open court, so that all members of the police forces realise that their duty to treat people equally is not merely a meaningless statement of principle.

Other fruitful approaches would be to provide educational programs for the police on the special problems faced by Aborigines in Australian society and to devise programs in which police and Aborigines meet in a relationship other than that of prosecutor and defendant. Militant young Aborigines in Sydney feel that they and police officers benefited from an 'encounter group' session arranged by the New South Wales Aboriginal Legal Service and suggest further ventures on these lines.

It is disappointing to have to record that the Minister for Police in Western Australia in late 1971 said that police 'training is directed to preparing him to serve the interests of all members of the community, not to special consideration of ethnic groups'. He refused a request for special training for police posted to country areas where they would be dealing with Aborigines.[45]

The outlook in Victoria and South Australia is more promising. The participation of police Search and Rescue Squad members in the adventure camp at Lake Tyers reserve should lead to better understanding on both sides.[46] The South Australian initiative in appointing a liaison officer with special responsibilities for Aboriginal-police relations is also worth emulating in other States (Calvesbert 1974). This scheme needs to be expanded but at least it is a step in the right direction.

[45] *A New Era* **2** (1972), p. 16.

[46] *Police Life* 15/2/69, p. 1.

3 BAIL

One of the ways in which the legal system attempts to translate the principle of the presumption of innocence into practice is by granting bail to persons arrested as suspects. If a defendant is presumed innocent until proved guilty, it follows that he should not be deprived of his liberty until he has been convicted in a properly constituted court. By being released on bail as soon as possible after arrest, the accused retains his freedom while awaiting trial, subject only to safeguards necessary to ensure that he does then appear in court. This is the basic theory of the bail system. How does it operate in practice?

OPERATION OF THE BAIL SYSTEM IN PRACTICE

THE GRANTING OR REFUSAL OF BAIL

By the police. In each of the three States studied, police have a discretion or, in some cases, a duty, to grant bail after an arrest for most types of offence.[1] The Western Australian Police Act provides that, in the case of persons arrested without warrant, the policeman in charge of a lock-up 'may, if he shall deem it prudent, take bail by recognisance, with or without sureties'. Section 64 of the Justices Act, 1902 (W.A.) goes

[1] Police Act, 1892 (W.A.) section 48; Justices Act, 1902 (W.A.) section 64; Justices Act 1958 (Vic.) (Act No. 6282) section 39(2); cf. Summary Offences Act 1966 (Vic.) (Act No. 7405) section 51, and Vagrancy Act 1966 (Vic.) (Act No. 7393) section 14; Police Offences Act, 1953 (S.A.) sections 78 and 80. See also Campbell and Whitmore 1966: 43-4.

further and imposes a mandatory duty on the police officer in charge of a station. If it is not practicable to bring a person arrested without warrant before a justice within twenty-four hours, then the policeman 'may and *shall* inquire into the case, and, except where the offence appears to such . . . police officer, to be of a serious nature, *shall* discharge the defendant upon his entering into a recognisance, with or without sureties, for a reasonable amount, to appear before Justices' (my emphasis).

Appendix 2.6 shows the number of Aborigines and whites respectively released on bail by the police in 1965 in the Ten Towns Sample. Only 14.3 per cent of Aborigines were released on bail; 33.6 per cent of whites were granted bail by the police.

Many of the defendants who were held in custody and not granted bail were so held for longer than twenty-four hours. Appendix 2.7 sets out details of the periods for which defendants were held in custody before their first appearance in court. Many of the longer periods occurred over weekends, the defendant being arrested on Saturday and not being brought before a court until Monday. Such cases do not mean that the arresting officer has failed in his duty to bring the defendant before a justice as soon as possible, since courts do not sit on Sunday. In a few cases a delay of three days occurred before the first appearance in court, which does suggest a breach of this duty. Section 140 of the Criminal Code (W.A.) provides a maximum penalty of two years' imprisonment for any person who 'having arrested another upon a charge of an offence wilfully delays to take him before a justice to be dealt with according to law'. Without further evidence it is not possible to state whether any of these cases really do represent wilful delay on the part of the police concerned. It is possible that the reason for delay was the unavailability of a justice at the relevant time. Many of these remote towns have few justices. In some of the cases the apparent delay may be due to incorrect record keeping.

Could any of these defendants have brought an action against the police for false imprisonment based on a breach of duty under section 64 of the Justices Act, 1902 (W.A.)? The officer in charge of a police station is under a duty to inquire into the case and to discharge the defendant on bail in all cases, except those of a serious nature. There is no judicial authority on the meaning of 'serious nature', but most of the cases concerned are clearly not of this class, since most are cases of drunkenness or disorderliness.

The duty under this section arises only if it is not possible to bring the defendant before a justice within twenty-four hours. In the sample there are 223 cases (205 Aborigines and eighteen whites) in which the defendant was detained for more than one day before being brought to court (Appendix 2.7). Unfortunately there is no clear evidence whether the police officer in each of these cases addressed his mind to the question of bail and 'inquire[d] into the case' as required. It is possible that decisions to detain were taken after insufficient inquiry. It is also not known whether the defendants who were detained actually asked for bail. But ignorance of rights and failure to assert them should not affect a defendant's situation since section 64 is not expressed to apply only after application by the defendant.

The main reasons why Aborigines were not released on bail in these cases appear to be their poverty and, in some cases, discrimination against them by the police. The former reason may supply a justification for the police, since section 64 refers to a 'reasonable amount'. Where the latter reason operates, it provides ground for legitimate complaint by the Aborigines affected.

The low economic status of Aborigines in general is clear. In practice, release on bail is largely dependent on the ability to provide a financial guarantee that the defendant will appear in court. The principle has been stated that a man has a *prima facie* right to be at liberty before conviction,[2] but bail procedure rests on the assumption that a financial sanction is necessary to ensure attendance at the hearing. The recognisance of bail fixes the amount to be forfeited if the defendant fails to appear.

Information is available in police records on the amount of cash in the defendants' possession at the time of arrest. In the case of Aborigines who have little or no cash when arrested, and who are kept in custody, the reason for non-release is probably poverty rather than discrimination by the police (Appendix 2.8).

On the other hand, in some towns the local police have a definite policy against allowing bail to Aborigines. In one Western Australian town (not in the Ten Towns Sample) no Aborigines had been released on bail in 1966 up to October, the latest date for which records were available. Fifteen Aborigines had been arrested during the year and charged with a total of twenty offences. The police did not expressly state that it was not their policy to grant Aborigines bail. They explained that they always required cash or a surety before releasing a defendant on bail. This may

[2] *R.* v. *Light* [1954] V.L.R. 152, 157 *per* Sholl J.

be a valid explanation of some of these cases in which the defendant was detained in custody. But a full-blood Aboriginal woman charged with two minor offences (drunkenness and obscene language) was held in custody for two days yet was later able to pay fines and costs of $13.80 (including $1.80 for meals while in custody). Another Aboriginal was arrested and charged with unlawful possession. He was not granted bail by the police or the justices who remanded him until the magistrate's visit. He was held in custody for seventeen days, then the charge was dismissed by the magistrate. The court charge sheet bears an endorsement by the latter: 'Accused Full-blood Aborigine—says he did not apply for bail', suggesting that the magistrate was concerned that the question of bail had not been properly considered by the police or by the justices.

One South Australian policeman stated that in the period he had been in charge of a police station (almost two years), only two Aborigines had been released on bail. It had never been the practice at this station to grant bail and he did not propose to encourage it. In this town a large percentage of defendants were Aboriginal. There is no legislation in South Australia corresponding to section 64 of the Justices Act (W.A.). Section 78 of the Police Offences Act, 1953 (S.A.) is in similar terms to section 48 of the Police Act (W.A.) and allows the policeman to decide whether it is 'prudent' to grant bail. Thus in all cases in South Australia and in cases in Western Australia which are not covered by the 'twenty-four hour rule' of section 64 of the Justices Act, the police have a discretion rather than a duty.

Discretion does not mean caprice: it must be exercised according to law. A blanket policy of not releasing Aborigines on bail is clearly contrary to law, since the police are required to examine each case on its merits. Far from regarding the accused person's race as the one determining factor, the police should consider only whether the individual defendant will later appear if released on bail.

Most police in Western Australia do not operate such a blanket policy, as shown by the fact that they have admitted a few Aborigines to bail. But the circumstances in some individual cases raise doubts about the performance of their duty. A fifty-nine year old Aboriginal woman was arrested for drunkenness and detained in custody for over twenty-four hours although she had over $9 in her possession. She was then fined only $4. Whatever interpretation is given to the words 'reasonable amount' in section 64 of the Justices Act it is clear that this defendant had enough cash to provide bail in a reasonable amount.

By the courts. If the case is not finally determined the first time the defendant appears, the court has to decide whether he should be released on bail or detained in custody. Legislation in each State empowers justices and magistrates to grant bail to defendants in specified circumstances (Campbell and Whitmore 1966: 44-6). In some cases an obligation is imposed on the court to grant bail; in others the matter is left to its discretion.[3] Even when the court is under a duty either to admit the defendant to bail or to certify for his admission to bail,[4] this does not mean that every defendant will regain his freedom before trial. The defendant must still enter into a recognisance and the justice is entitled to decide whether he must provide sureties and to fix the amount in which he and the sureties (if any) are to be bound (sections 146 and 147 of the Justices Act, 1921 (S.A.)).

In Victoria the grant of bail is in every case discretionary. The general principle on which the discretion should be exercised is that 'in a non-capital case the presumption would be in favour of the granting of bail'. The onus is on the Crown 'to show that a man's *prima facie* right to be at liberty until he is convicted should not be given effect'.[5] The same principle should govern the court whenever it exercises its discretion, both in deciding whether to grant or refuse bail and in fixing the amount of bail. The same principle should apply in all States, since none of the legislation lays down guidelines for the courts to follow in exercising their discretion.

Most of the cases studied were finally disposed of the first time the defendant appeared in court, so that the court did not have to make any decision about bail. The number of Aboriginal and white defendants in the Western Australian Ten Towns Sample who were allowed or refused bail by the courts is set out in Appendix 2.9, which shows that bail was set for 56·5 per cent of Aboriginal defendants; the remaining 43·5 per cent were remanded in custody. 64·8 per cent of white defendants were allowed bail; 35·2 per cent were refused it. Unfortunately the records available did not permit a distinction to be made between those cases in which the refusal of bail followed a request by the defendant and those cases in which the matter simply went by default.

Not all those defendants allowed bail by the courts were actually

[3] Compare, for example, section 143 (discretionary) and section 144 (obligatory) of Justices Act, 1921 (S.A.).

[4] Section 144 of the Justices Act, 1921 (S.A.).

[5] *R.* v. *Light* [1954] V.L.R. 152, 155 and 157 per Sholl J.

released from custody. Although the court decided that the defendant could properly be released on bail, in some cases he did not enter into a recognisance. Appendix 2.10 shows the number of cases in which the defendant did not enter into a bail bond even though the court had set bail. Thirteen per cent of Aboriginal defendants were in this category, compared with only 2·6 per cent of whites.

The main reason for the difference between Aborigines and whites in this table would be the inability of the Aboriginal defendants to find the necessary money or property or to find a person with enough assets willing to act as a surety.

One would expect that any defendant admitted to bail would want to be at liberty if he could possibly raise it. In this study there is little direct confirmation of this. It is possibly unwarranted, however, to conclude that in every case the reason for remaining in custody after being allowed bail is lack of money. In a bail study carried out in New York,[6] several defendants interviewed gave non-financial reasons for remaining in custody (pp. 709-10). One reason given by some New York defendants, 'Afraid that time served is lost when prisoner goes out on bail', would probably be applicable here, even though in Australia there is no legislative provision for credit to be allowed for time spent on remand before trial. Some magistrates and judges do date any sentence of imprisonment back to the date of arrest, but this is by no means universal.

The New York researchers found that poverty was the reason given by over half the prisoners interviewed for their failure to go out on bail and suggested that some of the non-financial reasons 'might well be rationalizations, formulated after they had concluded that they could not afford bail' (p. 711). Comparable extensive interviews probably would reveal that a similar pattern in which financial reasons predominated also existed here.

THE AMOUNT OF BAIL

The second major question which the police or the courts have to decide is the amount at which bail should be set. Here too they have a discretion but the amount should not be excessive and should be fixed having regard to the main purpose of bail. That is, the amount should be sufficiently large to ensure that the defendant will appear at court, forfeiting his bail money if he does not.

[6] 'A Study of the Administration of Bail in New York City', *U. Pa. L. Rev.* **106** (1958), p. 693 (cited hereafter as New York Bail Study).

The Bill of Rights[7] provides that excessive bail ought not to be required: the amount should therefore not be so excessive that it constitutes a virtual refusal of bail (Nash 1965: 46). A magistrate or justice who sets excessive bail is guilty of a common law offence, or, in Western Australia, of an offence against the Criminal Code (Campbell and Whitmore 1966: 45).

Amounts set by the police. It appears that the police usually fix the amount of bail by reference to the offence. This approach has some justification in that the more serious the offence the greater the temptation to abscond from bail. In *Light's* case Sholl J. (at p. 155) recognised that the nature of the crime charged and the severity of the punishment that may be imposed were both relevant to the probability or otherwise of the accused appearing at trial and could be taken into account by the court in deciding whether to grant or refuse bail. The same considerations are relevant to the question of the amount of bail, whether the question falls to be decided by a court or by the police.

These are not the only relevant considerations, however, and an examination of the actual practice of the police suggests that many defendants are needlessly detained. In some cases this is due to the police setting unnecessarily high bail. In others, the police have exercised their discretion properly under existing law, which suggests that the law needs to be changed to mitigate its harshness.

Appendix 2.11 sets out the amounts of bail required by the police in those cases in the Ten Towns Sample in which Aboriginal and white defendants were released on bail. The information on the amount of bail has been further broken down into offence categories, to show the influence of this factor (Appendix 2.12).

The amounts which have been required by the police for bail are relatively high. In these Western Australian towns sixty-three defendants released on bail on drunkenness charges were required to furnish over $9 bail. These amounts may be compared with the practice in the Melbourne suburb of Fitzroy, where the usual amount required for bail on drunkenness charges is $1 or $2 (interview with clerk of courts). Statistics are not available but a higher proportion of defendants would be released on bail when the cash required is as low as this. The court does not issue a warrant for the arrest of a defendant who fails to appear in this type of case. Sentences imposed when the defendant does appear are in general

[7] [1688] 1 William & Mary, Sess. II. c.2. See Imperial Acts Application Act 1922 (Vic.), section 6 and Second Schedule.

less severe than in the Western Australian country towns. It is quite common in Fitzroy for a defendant who has been detained in custody to be convicted and discharged without any further penalty being imposed. This is rare in rural Western Australia.

In many minor cases in Western Australia the police are really fixing bail at the level of the fine which they expect to be imposed if the defendant is convicted. The police do not expect defendants to drunkenness charges who are released on bail to appear later in court. In such cases the court estreats bail but does not issue a warrant for the defendant's arrest; he is never compelled to stand his trial.

This practice is completely contrary to the theory underlying bail. There is not necessarily anything sinister about it, however, and it makes good sense from the defendant's point of view, particularly in outback areas. Defendants charged with drunkenness in one outback town were released on bail on these terms and returned to their home sixty miles away. They would have found it a considerable burden to have had to stay in the town for the weekend and miss work on the Monday in order to attend court for this minor offence.

On the other hand, the practice is certainly open to objection in principle and does offer opportunities for abuse. First, it does not fulfil the need of the community for suspected offenders to be brought to trial. No conviction is recorded against the offender; this may give a wealthy man an advantage over a poor one. If the accused is able time after time to find bail money and thus avoid a recorded conviction, his criminal record will appear less serious than that of a poorer man who has only been arrested for the same number of offences but who has never been released on bail. One magistrate criticised the police practice of making bail in effect a fine, using the illustration of a person of high social status who had been able to avoid numerous convictions for drunkenness in this way.

Secondly, as implied above, a man may be regarded as tacitly admitting guilt for an offence if he fails to answer to his bail in such cases. This may be an unwarranted assumption, and this danger is more likely to occur with Aborigines who do not clearly understand the legal process. If they are told by the police that they can leave on payment of a certain amount and need not appear in court, they are unlikely to attend even if they have a valid defence. One Aboriginal, relatively well educated, related an incident in which he had been arrested on a charge of drunkenness. He protested his innocence. He was unaware that a passenger had left bottles in his taxi and it was on this evidence that the police based the charge. He was released from the police station on payment of a sum which he regarded as a fine but which must have been bail. He sought the help of a welfare officer and the money was returned to him. This man, although not fully aware of the legal position, was able to protect his rights. Other Aborigines, less educated or without the status which steady employment gives, would be less favourably placed in a similar situation.

In the case of drunkenness and other minor offences, it would be desirable to provide a recognised procedure to permit defendants to have their cases disposed of quickly. A modification of the current practice, more in accord with legal principle, would be to grant the police power to impose 'on-the-spot' fines for specified minor offences, including drunkenness. The maximum fines which they could levy should be less than the maximum which a court can impose. The police should also have to inform the accused that if he wishes to contest the charge he is entitled to be released on bail and attend court for the hearing. The police should also be under a duty to provide reasonable facilities for him to contact relatives or friends who may be able to bring the necessary cash.

An alternative procedure would be the issue of a 'summons on the spot', which would avoid the need for the defendant to find money in advance of the hearing.[8] Such a procedure would allow the defendant time to pay any fine imposed and should eliminate discrimination between poor and wealthy defendants in relation to pre-trial detention. For this reason it is preferable to the first reform suggested, which still depends on money being furnished before the court hearing.

Similar procedures, which enable defendants to avoid being detained

[8] Assistant Commissioner W.D. Crowley of the Victoria Police suggested to the Statute Law Revision Committee that police be accorded a more practical method of issuing 'summonses on the spot' with a view to reducing the current number of arrests. He said: 'A much better system would appear to be that where a constable has, in fact, detained the offender but has decided that a summons would meet the case, the legislation be amended so that he could serve on the offender at the time an information, counter-signed by an inspector or a justice of the peace, compelling the offender to appear at a certain court on a certain date. This would obviate the time and expenditure involved with the subsequent service of the summons and, to a large extent, remove the possibility of the defendant absconding.

Over a period, this would reduce substantially the number of prisoners in police watch-houses on remand and would save the community considerable expense in the need for additional watch-houses, transport of prisoners, meals for prisoners, police time, paper-work, &c., and of course, would certainly be more humane.' I am grateful to Assistant Commissioner Crowley for giving me permission to quote his statement. His suggestion has not yet been implemented. But see Crimes (Powers of Arrest) Act 1972.

at all, are already provided for many traffic offences. The reasons why different procedures operate in these two fields, traffic and street offences (of which 'drunk and disorderly' is the most common example) are largely historical. There is no reason in principle why the modern procedures devised for the former class should not now be applied to the latter. The only difference is that arrest rather than summons may be justified as the police method of initiation of proceedings where a defendant is drunk and there is an immediate need to remove him from the street for his own protection. But this need for arrest in the immediate situation should not justify continued detention until hearing, just because the defendant is unable to furnish cash or find a surety satisfactory to the police.

Under existing law the police are not acting illegally in detaining persons who have no cash or assets to provide as security for their appearance in court (provided the initial arrest was lawful). The reference in section 64 of the Justices Act (W.A.) to a 'reasonable amount' rests on the assumption that money is at the core of the bail system. If the police, on inquiry, find that the defendant has no assets, they are entitled to detain him in custody. Regulation 137(i) of the Police Regulations in Western Australia[9] instructs the police that: 'They should not accept personal recognisances unless they have good reason to believe that the prisoner has sufficient property which will be forthcoming to levy on if the condition of the recognisance is not complied with.'

Even if the police have acted perfectly properly in all the cases in which defendants have been held in custody, the large number of such cases and the fact that a high percentage of all arrested persons is detained in custody by the police (Appendix 2.6) suggest that it is time for a thorough reappraisal of the whole bail system, including its underlying assumptions.

Overseas experience shows that the issue of pre-trial detention or release need not be determined solely on financial considerations. 'In Sweden, there is total and blunt rejection of the bail process as favouring the rich over the poor' (Botein and Sturz 1964: 206). The criteria on which the decision to detain or release is based are not concerned with the defendant's means. Even in the United States, where bail practice formerly was severely discriminatory against the indigent, recent experiments based on non-financial criteria are claimed to be very successful. The Vera Founda-

[9] *Regulations and Instructions for the Government and Guidance of the Police Force of Western Australia* (*Government Gazette* (W.A.) 4/12/44, pp. 54-123). (Revoked in 1968, but in force during fieldwork period.)

tion conducted experiments with release on own recognisance, and found that most defendants turned up for trial (Ryan 1967: 545-6). The basis for the recommendation for release was the defendant's ties with the community rather than his financial status. The specific criteria adopted were employment record, family, references, length of local residence, current charge, previous record and special factors. After an interview to assess these factors a recommendation for release was either made or withheld by the interviewer. The Vera project recommended 40 per cent of the 10,000 prisoners they interviewed. The only security required of these prisoners before release was a promise to appear for trial. The Vera program success rate (in terms of those who subsequently appeared for trial) is not quite as outstanding as it appears at first glance, since certain categories of offences and offenders were excluded from the pilot project. But it does demonstrate that a financial sanction is not the only effective device to ensure attendance at court for trial. The Vera Foundation also conducted the Manhattan Summons Project. In this experiment some suspects were recommended for procedure by way of summons instead of arrest. Thus, these defendants also avoided both pre-trial detention and the necessity to provide a financial security for their appearance at trial.

It may be objected that the topic of police bail is unimportant because most of the defendants detained by the police are held in custody no longer than a weekend. But the fact that a high proportion of arrested defendants are not released on bail by the police should concern the community. Even a weekend represents a substantial deprivation of liberty when it occurs in advance of conviction. The total time spent in custody before hearing by defendants in the course of a year is substantial. Apart from the interference with defendants' rights which this represents, it also means considerable custodial costs to the community. The only people who have an interest in preserving the present situation are certain unscrupulous police officers who make a profit out of the meals supplied to prisoners. The Comptroller General of Prisons in Western Australia gave the meal racket as one of the main reasons for his policy of closing police gaols and transferring as many prisoners as possible to prisons under the control of the Prisons Department. This Prisons Department action will alleviate the situation as far as sentenced prisoners are concerned but will have no effect on defendants held in custody before hearing, who will still be held in police cells.

It is clear that a majority of the defendants detained by the police do not constitute a serious menace to the community. Most have been arrested on comparatively minor charges. If they can find the cash required for bail the police readily release them and in many cases do not even ask for a warrant to be issued if they later fail to appear. The estreatment of bail is considered sufficient satisfaction of the defendant's debt to society.

Propositions about the defendant's right to bail which have been laid down in more serious cases surely apply *a fortiori* to these minor cases. It could be argued against this that the court in cases like *Light* was concerned with situations where the defendant will spend a longer period in detention if he is not bailed. But the legislature has explicitly shown its concern with people detained longer than twenty-four hours[10] and I would argue that any pre-trial detention for a period longer than four hours cannot be justified unless there are very compelling reasons in its favour. It seems ridiculous that the outright refusal of bail in some cases, combined with the setting of amounts which the defendant is unable to raise in others, results in large numbers of defendants being detained before hearing for offences like 'Native receive liquor' and 'drunkenness'. If any reasonable change in current practice can avoid this result, it should be adopted. Further suggestions for reform will be made later.

Amounts set by the courts. Appendix 2.13 sets out the amounts fixed by the court in those cases in which the court granted bail. On its face, this suggests that there is no discrimination against Aborigines in the amounts that are set. It is legitimate in fixing bail for the court to take into consideration the offence charged. In fact, the amount of bail fixed seems largely to depend on the offence and the penalty that may be imposed on a conviction. Appendix 2.14 has therefore been produced to show the way in which the amount of bail set varies with the offence. Appendix 7 is a more detailed version of similar information, for one town only, and correlated with the race of the defendant. The only offences in this table on which a direct comparison is possible are 'driving under the influence', assault and dangerous driving. On the first of these, the bail set was $60 for all Aboriginal and white defendants. On the assault charges, the Aboriginal defendant was allowed bail at $20 and the white defendant at $200. On the charges of 'driving in a dangerous manner' the Aboriginal defendant was granted bail of $20 and the white defendant bail of $100. Thus there appears to be no discrimination against Aborigines; if anything the discrimination is the other way. The court may have taken the defendants' means into account in setting bail. Alternatively, the explanation for

[10] Justices Act, 1902 (W.A.) section 64.

the difference in the assault cases may be that the Aboriginal offence was much less serious than the other one. In the dangerous driving cases the explanation for the difference may be that the Aboriginal defendant was charged at the same time with two other offences and the total amount of bail which he had to find was more than that fixed for the white defendant who faced only the one charge. The magistrate may well have taken this into account in fixing bail for this particular offence.

Although there is no obvious discrimination in the amounts of bail set, it has already been seen that the number of Aborigines who were actually admitted to bail after it was set by the court is proportionately lower than the number of whites who were actually released from custody (Appendix 2.10). This suggests that, even when bail is set at equal or lower amounts for Aboriginal defendants than for whites they are less able to find the cash required or to find a surety to act. Even if the courts have taken the defendant's means into account in setting bail it appears that they have not gone far enough in decreasing the amount to a point where the Aboriginal defendant is able to furnish it.

The ability to furnish bail also depends partly on the form in which bail is required, that is, whether the defendant is required to deposit cash or to provide a surety or neither. It will obviously be easiest for a defendant to satisfy bail requirements if the court has approved of his being released on his own recognisance. The courts generally have complete discretion as to which form of bail is required and the practice varies between different courts. One magistrate stated that he never required cash or a surety. Therefore any defendant granted bail by this magistrate would be released from custody.

Appendix 2.15 sets out the form of bail specified by the courts in all cases in which bail was granted in the Ten Towns Sample. The categories are graded in order of the difficulty the defendant might be expected to face in satisfying the requirements. On this scale, 'no surety—no cash' is considered the least difficult and 'two sureties—cash' the most difficult. Again there is no obvious discrimination against Aborigines in terms of the requirements imposed.

The reason for the defendant's failure to enter into a bail bond would in most cases be financial. In the remaining cases the probable explanation is that the defendant was unable to find someone to act as a surety. Appendix 2.16 analyses the cases in which the defendant did not enter a bail bond to show the amounts of bail which he was required to furnish. It does not confirm the view that the higher the amount of bail the fewer defendants are able to furnish it. But the total number of defendants who did not enter bail is perhaps too small to allow any conclusion to be drawn either way.

The New York Bail Study found that a decreasing percentage of defendants were able to furnish bail as the amount increased. The researchers point out (p. 707) that 'although bail is not by law excessive simply because it is more than the defendant is able to furnish, but only if it is more than necessary to compel appearance, it would seem that in most cases an amount greater than the defendant is able to furnish would also be greater than that necessary to deter him and, hence, excessive'. The defendant for whom bail has been set in an amount which he is quite unable to provide is hardly comforted by the thought that he has not been refused bail outright. In both cases he is equally behind bars before trial.

In those cases where the defendant was unable to furnish bail even after a lapse of time, it is probable that this was because the amount was set too high rather than that he was unable to provide any cash at all. If the amount had been set lower he might have been able to find it and have been released from custody. There may be a few cases where the charge is so grave and the defendant's access to assets so restricted that the court would not be justified in reducing the amount of bail to an amount he is able to furnish. Such cases must be rare and in general I agree with the authors of the New York Bail Study that the court should take the defendant's means into account and set an amount which the individual defendant is able to find. Any amount which he is unable to furnish himself or with the assistance of friends and relations will usually be excessive.

The process of setting bail is really an exercise in prediction (New York Bail Study 1958: 706). The main purpose of the court should be to predict the amount of bail necessary to ensure the appearance of the individual defendant at the hearing. Some defendants are unable to find the amount set; they remain in custody so that their reliability is never tested. It is interesting to examine the reliability of those defendants who did make bail and see whether the courts accurately assessed the amounts necessary to persuade them to attend court. This can be done by looking at the number of defendants who appeared for trial after having been released on bail and comparing the number whose bail was estreated for non-appearance.

Appendix 2.17 shows the comparative record of Aborigines and whites in this respect. It includes the estreatment of both police and court bail. It is clear that Aborigines are quite as reliable as whites in fulfilling the conditions of the bail bond and appearing in court. For both groups the number of cases in which bail was estreated is relatively high. This suggests considerable unreliability on the part of defendants and failure by both the police and the courts to make accurate predictions. This first impression is misleading. The great majority of cases in which bail was estreated are those in which the police did not really expect the defendants to appear. These are represented by the category 'Bail estreated—no record of subsequent action' in the table. The cases in which a warrant was issued as well as the bail being estreated represent the only really genuine cases of failure to appear. In this category there are only three Aboriginal cases (in one of which the warrant was later withdrawn) and eight white cases. In all but four cases in which a warrant was issued to compel the appearance of the defendant, he did later appear. In those four cases the record is not clear as to whether he ever appeared for trial. On the basis of these figures it would be fair to say that the non-appearance of defendants for trial is not a great problem and that the police expenditure of time and money required in order to find those few defendants who have taken flight is not very large.

This finding suggests that the police and courts have been overcautious in making decisions on the questions of the grant or refusal of bail and the amounts at which bail is set. Those who were detained in custody would probably turn out to be equally reliable if given the chance to prove it. This can only be ascertained by the bold step of releasing more defendants either on their own recognisance or on lower bail amounts than are presently set. Such an experiment would be well worthwhile.

EFFECTS ON DEFENDANT OF NOT BEING RELEASED ON BAIL

PERIOD SPENT IN CUSTODY

The immediate and obvious effect on the defendant of not being released on bail is that he spends a longer period in custody before his case is finally determined than the more fortunate defendant who is out on bail. Appendix 2.18 provides a comparison between the periods spent in custody before final hearing for 'bail' and 'gaol' defendants, that is those granted bail by the court and those remanded in custody. The table is confined to those cases in the Ten Towns Sample that were not finalised on the defendant's first appearance in court. Thirteen 'gaol' defendants were detained for periods of twenty-five days or more, including six held for more than sixty-four days. None of the 'bail' defendants was held for longer than thirty-two days (Appendix 2.18).[11]

Many more Aborigines than whites spend the period before the hearing in custody, owing to the combined effects of the fact that they are more often proceeded against by arrest than by summons and the discriminatory operation of the bail system upon Aborigines. Information about the periods spent in custody by Aboriginal and white defendants respectively is set out in Appendix 2.19. This table includes cases finalised at the first hearing (in which only the question of police bail is relevant) as well as those in which the court was required to make a decision about bail.

It is apparent from this table that the greatest discrimination against Aborigines regarding detention occurs at the earliest stage of initiation of proceedings (in the relatively small number of summons cases), and in the large number of defendants held for short periods of pre-hearing detention (up to two days). Once periods of detention longer than two days are considered the discrepancy becomes less marked. In the Ten Towns Sample there are forty-eight recorded cases of Aborigines being detained for longer than two days and fifty-nine cases of whites so detained. But in the most extreme category (those detained for over two months) there are only two whites while there are four Aborigines.

Of the four Aborigines, two charged with breaking and entering were detained in custody for twelve weeks before trial. But it appears that they were in custody serving a sentence on another charge, so this period cannot really be regarded as 'pre-trial detention'. The third Aboriginal in the Sample, a full-blood tribal Aboriginal, was in custody for over sixteen weeks before trial. He was charged with manslaughter, to which he eventually pleaded guilty and was sentenced to twelve months' imprisonment. The sentence was dated back to the date of arrest. The fourth Aboriginal was also charged with manslaughter. He was arrested on 18 November 1965; at the preliminary hearing on 20 December 1965 he was committed for trial in March at the southern Court of Session. He was then taken to Fremantle Prison on remand and there is no record of his release until the Crown entered a *nolle prosequi* in April 1966. He was thus detained for four months on a charge that was eventually withdrawn.

The total number of cases in the Ten Towns Sample in the longest category (over sixty-four days) is probably not enough to allow any valid

[11] This table treats defendants who were granted bail but did not enter a bail bond as 'bail' cases. There are nine such cases which would more appropriately be treated as 'gaol' cases. The original code used did not allow this distinction to be made.

conclusions about discrimination against Aborigines to be drawn. Yet it is undoubtedly true that many Aborigines have spent very long periods in custody awaiting trial over the years. An idea of the excessive periods of some pre-trial detention can be obtained from individual illustrations drawn from outside the Ten Towns Sample.

The following are three Western Australian examples. A full-blood Aboriginal, charged with breaking and entering, was arrested on 23 December 1965 and tried on 1 March 1966, having been in custody in the meantime. He was not legally represented and pleaded guilty to the charge. It is not clear from the records whether he pleaded guilty at the preliminary hearing or only at trial. If he pleaded guilty at the committal proceedings the court could not release him on bail.[12] Another Aboriginal charged with manslaughter was in custody for over three months before the trial at which he was acquitted. An Aboriginal woman charged with wilful murder spent six months in custody before trial. She pleaded guilty to the lesser charge of manslaughter and was sentenced to five years' imprisonment with a non-parole period of eighteen months.

Long periods of pre-trial detention are not confined to Western Australia. In South Australia two tribal Aboriginal women originally charged with murder were remanded in custody for almost three months. Finally they were convicted of assault and each sentenced to imprisonment for one month. A Victorian Aboriginal was arrested on a murder charge in December 1966 and was held in the remand yard at Pentridge for almost ten months. At trial he was convicted instead of 'conspiracy to burgle' and sentenced to imprisonment for two and a half years. It is probable that the judge took the period on remand into account in fixing the sentence.

It might be suggested that one reason for long periods of pre-trial detention is geographical. Higher courts sit infrequently in outback areas. If a defendant is detained before trial, the period he spends in custody in an outback area is likely to be longer than it would be in the metropolitan area. In Western Australia the Supreme Court criminal sittings are held in Perth monthly, whereas on circuit the court sits only four times a year, at Geraldton, Kalgoorlie, Bunbury and Albany. Courts of Session sit regularly only at the same places and on the same dates as the circuit courts but may also sit in certain other towns as required.[13]

On the defence side the arguments in favour of holding the trial

[12] Justices Act, 1902 (W.A.) section 114.

[13] *Law Almanac for 1966* (1966), pp. 13, 16. Perth: Government Printer.

locally are that the defendant will have the advantage of familiar surroundings and will find it easier and less expensive to obtain the witnesses he requires. He may consider this outweighed by the disadvantage of the long delay before trial in country areas. In a State as vast as Western Australia a so-called 'local' trial may in fact take place hundreds of miles from the defendant's home. He may live at Carnarvon, for example, and be tried at Geraldton, 300 miles away. In such cases, the main reason for holding the trial in Geraldton rather than Perth is the Crown's desire to save the expense of transporting prosecution witnesses the additional distance, even at the cost of keeping the defendant in custody for a longer period. In my opinion, those responsible for the administration of court calendars should recognise more realistically the problems created by a State having a large area with the population concentrated in one corner. If they are not prepared to send superior courts on circuit more often, then they should arrange for the case to be heard in the city to avoid excessive delay.

This latter course would have some disadvantages for the defendant; a better course would be to enable magistrates to constitute Courts of Session more often in remote areas.[14] Alternatively, the practice of release of defendants on their own recognisance (or on conditions such as reporting to the police), without requiring cash or a surety, should be encouraged in any case where a lengthy period is likely to elapse before trial. New South Wales courts, at least, have recognised that the length of the period likely before trial is a relevant factor in setting bail.[15] This geographical factor does not affect only Aborigines, but they are more often adversely affected because of the concentration of the Aboriginal population in remote areas.

The geographical factor may also be used to explain the disturbing cases in which juveniles were remanded in custody. A full-blood Aboriginal boy, aged fourteen, was detained for five days before he was tried on three traffic offences, including dangerous driving. He was then committed to a Child Welfare Institution. The reason for the delay in bringing on the hearing was that it was desired to bring the defendant before the magistrate rather than the local justices. The magistrate had to travel from another town in the Kimberleys to the place of trial. It may be claimed by

[14] The establishment of District Criminal Courts may relieve the situation. District Court of Western Australia Act, 1969 (W.A.).

[15] *R.* v. *Pascoe* 78 W.N. (N.S.W.) 59; (1960) N.S.W.R. 481.

the police that it was necessary to keep the boy in custody in these circumstances, but it is difficult to believe that he would not have appeared for trial if he had been released to the custody of his parents. The same boy had previously been detained in custody for a day on a charge of 'Native receive liquor'.[16] The police evidence was that he was arrested because he had his feet on four bottles of beer, attempting to hide them. This is a clear case of unnecessary arrest and pre-trial detention. A summons would surely have been appropriate here, if indeed any police action at all was necessary.

CONDITIONS IN REMAND PRISONS

My study of the conditions in which prisoners are held on remand in the three States studied confirms the 'ironic finding' of the New York Bail Study that 'accused, whom law presumes to be innocent and who are not to be punished, are confined pending trial under conditions which are more oppressive and restrictive than those applied to convicted and sentenced felons' (Foote 1958: 689). In country areas it is perhaps not true to say that the conditions are *more* oppressive. Defendants on remand are held in the local police cells or local gaol, depending on the length of time on remand. Generally speaking, no distinction is made between them and sentenced prisoners in the same prison. In large city prisons, like Pentridge in Melbourne, remand prisoners are held in a separate divison (Johnston and Fox 1965: 212). As inmates of a maximum security prison, remand prisoners are subjected to the same security arrangements as the rest of the prison. They are thus subject to more stringent security precautions than many sentenced prisoners held in other Victorian prisons. The physical conditions of the remand division are no better than most other divisions in Pentridge. Certain special concessions are allowed to remand prisoners; they are not obliged to work, but may do so if work is available. This is a mixed blessing. Deterioration in morale may occur when defendants are not working and have little to occupy their time. Remand prisoners are not entitled to canteen facilities unless they are working. They are entitled to write and receive mail and have visitors more often than convicted prisoners (Johnston and Fox 1965: 173-4).

An anomaly arises in the case of a prisoner who is both a sentenced and a remand prisoner, that is, one who has been sentenced on one charge, but is awaiting trial on another charge. In order that the time he spends in

[16] Licensing Act, 1911 (W.A.) section 150(2). Case from fieldwork notes.

prison will count as part of the sentence already imposed, he will prefer to stay in the appropriate division as a convicted prisoner. But if he does so he loses the benefit of the regulations relating to remand prisoners. This may seriously hamper him in the preparation of his defence. This would be a relatively simple matter to resolve by appropriate regulations or reasonable exercise of administrative discretion by prison authorities.

Even for prisoners in the remand yard, the conditions for preparation of a defence are far from ideal. Confinement in itself reduces morale and enthusiasm for one's own cause. It is difficult to obtain witnesses. Provision is made for the prisoner's lawyer to see him in private at specified times on weekdays but the task of representation must be more difficult for the lawyer of a 'gaol' defendant than of one who is free on bail.

This *a priori* reasoning about the adverse effects on the defendant of being detained before trial has been tested by American researchers and an attempt has been made in this study to ascertain whether the 'gaol' defendant is really at a disadvantage at the hearing as compared with the 'bail' defendant.

OUTCOME OF PROCEEDINGS

The New York Bail Study attempted to discover whether pre-trial detention had a demonstrably adverse effect on the outcome of the case. It was found (pp. 726-7) that the 'gaol' defendants entered a higher percentage of guilty pleas; their cases resulted in a higher percentage of convictions; and they were sentenced to penal institutions in a much higher percentage of cases, whereas the 'bail' defendants were much more often given a bond.

The authors point out that the relationship is not necessarily one of cause and effect. Detention is not necessarily *the* factor that produces the result of a plea of guilty, or conviction, or a prison sentence, as the case may be. Other unknown factors may be operating to produce the variation between 'gaol' and 'bail' defendants. A study of English bail practice found a high rate of convictions of persons who were refused bail or were unable to provide it. This was interpreted as being due to 'the shrewdness with which bail determinations are made' (Botein and Sturz 1964: 219). But another American study, which specifically considered the influence of other factors, more strongly supported the conclusion that 'a causal relationship exists between detention and unfavorable disposition' (Rankin 1964: 655).

For the Western Australian Sample, information on the rate of guilty pleas for 'gaol' and 'bail' cases is set out in Appendix 2.20. The percentage of 'gaol' defendants who plead guilty (94·8) is much higher than the percentage of 'bail' defendants who so plead (71·4).

Detention in custody probably induces many defendants to plead guilty at their first appearance in court. Remands are almost invariable on pleas of not guilty. The prosecution is rarely ready to proceed immediately if the defendant pleads not guilty, even in summary prosecutions. The period of remand granted by the court is usually eight days. Eight days is often a longer period than the sentence of imprisonment the defendant could expect if convicted. The expectation that if he pleads not guilty he will be remanded in custody and that if he is remanded it will be for a period of eight days probably persuades many a defendant to plead guilty initially.

It should not be necessary to remand for eight days in every case. If the police have sufficient grounds to justify an arrest, they should not need that period to prepare evidence or arrange the attendance of witnesses, at least in most summary cases. The main reason for fixing the period of remand appears to be administrative convenience, and possibly in some cases the improper motive of inducing the defendant to change his plea. Eight days is the *maximum* period fixed by section 79 of the Justices Act, 1902 (W.A.) for remands where a defendant is charged with an indictable offence. Section 86,[17] which empowers the justices to commit a defendant during an adjournment of a hearing of a simple offence, does not specify any time limit for the adjournment. It certainly should not be for longer than eight days. It may be arguable that in the case of a simple offence even the period of eight days is too long to be consistent with the principles of the Bill of Rights.[18] For an Aboriginal defendant in an outback town, without access to a lawyer, it is hardly a practical proposition to apply for a writ of *habeas corpus*. Even if he knew, or suspected, that a remedy was available to him for unlawful detention in such circumstances, the time that would elapse before any effective action could be taken rules out any existing legal remedy.

A better approach to the problem of unnecessarily lengthy remands would be to instruct magistrates and justices that where defendants are charged with simple offences they should not remand them in custody for longer than twenty-four hours unless it is at the defendant's request, or for very good reasons put forward by the police. It should be pointed out that section 86 of the Justices Act, 1902 (W.A.) offers the court a wide choice

[17] Cf. Justices Act 1958 (Vic.) sections 56, 59(2), and 39.

[18] [1688] 1 William & Mary, Sess. II. c.2.

on the adjournment of a simple offence. The justices 'may suffer the defendant to go at large, or may commit him, or may order his discharge upon his entering into a recognisance . . . '. By section 87 the committal may be to a gaol or to other safe custody. Justices should be encouraged to make use of the less severe powers granted to them by these sections, instead of using the harshest power, that of committing the defendant to gaol for the maximum period of eight days. To reinforce such instructions the legislation should be amended to make clear to the courts that the preferred alternatives are those that involve the least interference with defendants' liberty before the hearing.

The New York Bail Study also found (p. 727) that at trial the 'gaol' defendants were convicted in a higher percentage of cases than the 'bail' defendants were. There are not enough fully fledged trials in the Ten Towns Sample to make such a comparison meaningful, so a table has been prepared instead showing the final disposition of all cases in the Sample for which the information is available and the relationship of the granting of bail to the ultimate result (Appendix 2.21). An overwhelming majority of defendants who were not granted bail after arrest were convicted. But in the category of those granted bail, almost as many defendants had bail estreated and no further action taken against them as were convicted. In cases where bail is estreated in this way, no conviction is recorded. In addition, it is striking that of the few cases which were dismissed or in which the defendant was acquitted, a disproportionate number had been granted bail or had been proceeded against by summons. These favourable results for 'bail' defendants may be due to some other factor, such as legal representation, rather than to the release on bail in itself, but the findings do suggest that the bailed defendant is better able to prepare his defence than one who is detained until the hearing.

As has been shown, Aborigines have been released on bail less often than whites. They have also been convicted in a higher percentage of cases and have received the benefit of fewer acquittals (Appendix 2.22). In the Ten Towns Sample, Aborigines were convicted in 90 per cent of cases and were acquitted or had the charges against them dismissed in only 0·3 per cent of cases. By contrast, whites were convicted in 89 per cent of cases and received the benefit of dismissals or acquittals in 1·6 per cent of cases. The difference may not appear great but it is evidence of a continuing trend throughout the State. Apart from the ten towns in the Sample, statistics are available for the whole State and also for other years, and these consistently demonstrate a higher rate of Aboriginal convictions.[19] It is unlikely that this is due to a higher rate of Aboriginal guilt. It is far more likely to be due to other factors which influence the outcome of the case. Amongst these is the fact that Aborigines are more often detained in custody before the hearing than whites are. The extent to which this particular factor influences the unfavourable disposition of Aboriginal cases cannot be assessed at this stage.

The other prejudicial effect of pre-trial detention which the New York Bail Study found, and in which there was the most clearcut difference between 'bail' and 'gaol' defendants, was that of the type of sentence given (p. 727). It was found that 'gaol' defendants were sentenced to penal institutions in a much higher percentage of cases and put on a suspended sentence in a much lower percentage of cases.

A similar finding was made in connection with the Western Australian Sample (Appendix 2.23). The really striking difference lies in the differential imposition of fines and sentences of imprisonment in the two categories. Those defendants not granted bail were more often sentenced to immediate imprisonment and less often given the opportunity to pay a fine. Defendants granted bail were more often given the chance to pay a fine and avoid going to gaol.

In some courts the magistrate or justices adopt the practice of asking the police how much cash the defendant had in his possession when arrested. If he had little or no cash and has not been released on bail, they then assume that he will be unable to pay a fine and so impose a sentence of imprisonment or fix a fine but give the defendant no time to pay. Sometimes in the case of Aboriginal defendants, an additional punitive element seems to move the court, which is not present in white cases. This is the belief that an Aboriginal defendant should not 'bludge' on his relatives. In white cases the court does not inquire where the money will come from and does not perceive any duty to prevent relations and friends from assisting the defendant. But in some Aboriginal cases the court has not been willing to give relations and friends the opportunity to exhibit generosity and the communal spirit that is a common feature of Aboriginal life.

The differences between the type of sentences imposed on Aboriginal and white defendants are set out in Appendix 2.24. This demonstrates that Aborigines are sentenced to imprisonment in a disproportionate number of

[19] See, for example, the figures for the year ended 31 December 1961 reproduced in Appendix 8.

cases, whereas whites are more fortunate in being ordered to pay fines in a higher percentage of cases.

The whole topic of sentencing will be considered in more detail in Chapter 6. The explanation for the more frequent imposition of the more severe type of sentence (imprisonment) on Aborigines is not that they commit serious offences more often than whites do. It must be sought elsewhere. One possibility is that the fact that Aborigines are detained in custody more often before trial in itself operates to put them at a disadvantage in the sentencing process. For example, pre-trial detention makes it more difficult to arrange to have the services of an advocate who can make a plea in mitigation of sentence. Then the fact that the defendant has not been released on bail suggests to the court that he will be unable to pay a fine. The period in detention may demoralise the defendant so that he makes an unfavourable impression on the court.

The factor of release or non-release on bail does play some part in producing the imposition of a particular type of sentence. But other factors are also involved and possibly a better way of expressing the relationship is to say that a common factor, poverty, influences the probability of the detention of the defendant both before and after the hearing.

The New York Bail Study (p. 727) also provided information on the number of defendants sentenced to 'time already served' which appears to correspond to the practice of some Australian courts of dating a sentence of imprisonment back to the time of arrest if the defendant has been in custody in the meantime. In Western Australia there is no legislative requirement that the court should take any period of pre-trial detention into account. It depends on the discretion of the individual magistrate or justice. In one town (not included in the Ten Towns Sample) it was the invariable practice of the magistrate to date sentences for drunkenness offences back to the time of arrest. The sentences fixed were usually imprisonment for one or two days and this period had already been served before the hearing by most Aboriginal defendants. They were therefore released from custody immediately after the hearing. This was a sensible way to redress the balance operating against poor defendants who had been unable to raise bail, but few other courts have adopted the practice.

Sometimes when an indictable offence is involved the court also takes a period on remand into account in fixing a sentence of imprisonment. If the offence is serious, the defendant may still have a substantial period to serve after taking pre-trial detention into account. As the practice of counting the pre-trial period as part of the sentence is by no means universal, the defendant may not be aware that he has been granted credit for the period spent on remand. He may feel resentful about the time spent in prison awaiting trial. The Victorian Aboriginal who spent nine months on remand in Pentridge thought this period should be taken into account in fixing the date for his release on parole. It was not clear to him whether the judge had taken the remand period into account in fixing the term of imprisonment.

That case illustrates the problems of leaving a matter like this to the discretion of the court. It is preferable to have a definite rule embodied in legislation, as in some American States. Then a consistent policy of recognition of periods spent in custody before trial would be enforced in the courts. Defendants would learn that all were treated equally in this respect.

SUGGESTIONS FOR REFORM

The bail system as it operates at present cries out urgently for reform. The chief objection to unnecessary pre-trial detention is that imprisonment is the most serious punishment which can be imposed after conviction. (The execution of the death penalty is so infrequent that it can be ignored in this discussion.) Pre-trial detention is equivalent to imprisonment—defendants are held in similar conditions as when imprisoned *after* conviction—yet this is not supposed to be punishment and at this stage they have not been found guilty of any offence.

On the other hand, arguments may be put forward to justify pre-trial detention. First and most persuasive is that having identified an offender against whom there is a strong *prima facie* case, the community has an interest in his appearance at trial. There is a risk that the defendant, if not detained, will fail to appear. There are actually two possibilities here. The first is that the defendant may never again be found. The second is that he may fail to appear when he should, but may later be arrested on warrant and stand trial. The first is the more important and is the only situation in which the community interest in the punishment of criminals is really in jeopardy. The second involves only a question of administrative convenience, and possibly of cost. The police are put to the extra trouble and expense of tracing the defendant and executing a warrant. But the overall expense to the community of a more liberal bail system may be no more than the cost of the present system. At present hundreds of defendants are kept in custody before the hearing. The custodial costs must be considerable. If most of these defendants were released from custody the saving of expense would probably not be offset by the increased costs of pursuing defendants who abscond from bail.

An American study referred to the problems raised by the fact that a defendant was able to move to another State and out of the jurisdiction of the State where the offence was committed.[20] A similar problem arises in Australia, but if the crime is sufficiently grave, extradition is possible. Moreover, as the American study points out (p. 973), 'modern methods of identification, such as the nationwide exchange of fingerprint and photographic information by the police, probably make the lure of other jurisdictions less attractive than in pioneer days'.

In the usual case, then, the police should be able eventually to find the defendant for trial. This optimistic note is perhaps contradicted by Milte's (1968: 231) finding that 17 per cent of defendants (indictable offences but not summary offences) failed to appear for trial. It is not clear whether these represent defendants who were never tried or whether they are those who failed to appear when first required. If the latter, some would have been later apprehended and tried.

In the case of indictable offences, it is perhaps fair to argue that the interest of the community in the punishment of crime is so great that interference with the liberty of the suspect before trial is justifiable to overcome the risk that he will never be tried. The argument does not apply with the same force to summary offences and cannot justify the pre-trial detention of large numbers of defendants charged with nothing more serious than drunkenness.

The second major argument in favour of pre-trial detention is that it is necessary for the protection of the community from the commission of further offences in the interim period between arrest and trial. This argument has received its fullest recognition in England where Atkinson J. said in *R.* v. *Phillips*: 'The Court wishes magistrates who release on bail young housebreakers such as this applicant to know that in 19 cases out of 20 it is a very wrong step to take.'[21] This view has been rejected in American law.

The Australian position is midway between these two extremes. If the defendant has a previous history of committing offences while on bail, Sholl J. said in *R.* v. *Light* that the Crown could put this forward as a

[20] 'Bail: An Ancient Practice Reexamined', *Yale L.J.* **70** (1961), pp. 966, 967.

[21] *R.* v. *Phillips* (1947) 45 L.G.R. (Eng.) 410, cited in 'Release of Offenders on Bail', *A.L.J.* **21** (1947).

reason for opposition to bail and the court should take it into account in exercising its discretion (at p. 158). But the defendant's general history of prior convictions was irrelevant in his view.

On principle, the American view is preferable to the English view or even Sholl J.'s more liberal approach. If the principle of the presumption of innocence is accepted, it is no more justifiable to detain a suspect for the protection of the public before trial than it is to impose preventive detention *after* the completion of his sentence. If he is a recidivist, it is quite likely that after release he will commit further offences but that is rarely held to justify locking him up after the completion of his sentence. In my view any sentence of imprisonment should bear some relation to an offence which it is proved he has committed. The only possible justifications for Sholl J.'s view (that a previous abuse of bail is relevant to the question of bail now), are that the previous abuse of bail shows a contempt for the court and the legal process which in itself is sufficient to justify the refusal of bail, and possibly that the temptation to which an indigent defendant who wishes to obtain funds for his defence will be exposed is so great that the probability that he will commit further offences if released on bail is very high.

Sholl J. recognised only two grounds as legitimate in opposition to bail (pp. 157-8). These were the necessity to ensure the attendance of the defendant at trial and the protection of the community against further offences committed by a man who could be shown to have abused bail on a previous occasion. Other factors which he said could be taken into account could be considered only insofar as they were relevant to these two major grounds.

In my view, the aim of any reforms should be to reconcile the conflicting interests of the defendant in retaining his freedom before trial and of the community in ensuring that accused persons appear for trial, while at the same time as far as possible reducing the inequality between the poor and the rich in this area of legal procedure. A system which relies mainly on a financial sanction will obviously discriminate against the poor. Reliance on a financial sanction as the main method of enforcing the attendance of the defendant should be abolished and alternative methods of reaching the same result devised.

Turning now from principles to practical proposals, the first need seems to be for education of the police and courts towards greater respect for the freedom of individuals, including suspects. It would be an improvement even to enforce the existing law in the spirit in which it was intended. For example, section 36(4) of the Justices Act 1958 (Vic.) empowers the court to commit or admit to bail any person arrested on warrant. This appears to give the court a wide discretion but it should be read subject to the opening words of section 36: 'The following rules shall be observed *for the purpose of enforcing the appearance of any person . . .* ' (my emphasis). If the courts really directed their attention mainly to the question of whether the defendant before them was likely to appear for trial, a great many more defendants would be released on bail than at present. Education of the police and courts to accept the view that *prima facie* a man is entitled to his liberty before trial is not helped by the attitudes of some higher officials as exemplified in the instructions issued by an Attorney-General of Victoria (cited in Milte 1968, pp. 234-5). Newspaper reports of rebukes to courts over bail usually seem to be for too readily releasing defendants on inadequate bail.[22] The rebukes in these cases may be justified, but the Crown Law authorities have not shown comparable concern in the reverse situation, where defendants have been detained before trial for long periods.

There is, for example, no evidence of official concern over cases in which the court refused bail improperly on the ground that the police wanted to investigate further. In one South Australian case, the police reason for wanting a remand was that further inquiries were to be made, when the Aboriginal defendant would be charged with further offences of a similar nature. In another South Australian case, the police successfully objected to bail on the ground that the defendant's release would seriously impede police inquiries.[23] Later a magistrate dismissed the information and discharged the defendant, holding that no reasonable jury properly directed could convict him. He had spent at least ten days in custody.

If the proposed educational program were successful it would lead to greater use of summons procedure by the police and greater willingness to release on bail. The police and the courts should be encouraged to make more use of 'release on own recognisance' or with conditions such as reporting to the police, rather than relying exclusively on financial sanctions as at present. In addition, legislation would be required to enable new procedures to be used, such as 'on the spot' summons.

[22] See for example, report in Melbourne *Herald* 8/7/65 under headline, 'Man gone: JPs must explain bail'.

[23] Fieldwork notes. The police reason for wanting a remand in custody is shown on the police Remand Form. It is not known whether this is the reason they gave in court. Other aspects of this case are discussed in Chapter 2.

In cases where it is still considered necessary to proceed by way of arrest and to require cash to be furnished for bail, better facilities should be provided for contacting relatives and friends who may furnish bail. In more than 500 cases in the Ten Towns Sample the defendant was not released on bail and yet later paid the fine imposed by the court (Appendix 2.25). Many of these defendants could have provided bail if encouraged to do so and given adequate opportunities to contact persons to help them raise it.

Even under a more liberal bail system some defendants will no doubt still be detained in custody before trial. In order to mitigate the hardship imposed on these defendants, legislation should be enacted providing that credit for any period of pre-trial detention should always be given by the court when fixing sentence.

Conditions in remand prisons should also be upgraded, preferably by building new facilities separate from ordinary prisons. Meanwhile, conditions in existing remand yards could be improved by relaxing still further the regulations about visits and writing letters and taking steps to facilitate the inmates' preparation of their defence.

Finally, some form of automatic review of periods spent in custody before trial should be instituted. It would be desirable to fix, by legislation, maximum periods for which defendants could be detained before trial for various types of offence, and then to appoint an officer to oversee the actual operation of the bail system and take steps to release any defendant where the permissible limit has been exceeded. Existing remedies, such as *habeas corpus*, which require the defendant to exercise the initiative, are clearly not sufficient to protect uneducated, indigent persons from unwarranted or excessive pre-trial detention. Section 608 of the Criminal Code (W.A.)[24] which sets a limit on the period for which a defendant can be detained before being brought to trial, is expressed in such a way that the maximum period for which a defendant may be held in outback areas where superior courts sit infrequently may be very long indeed. It is preferable to express the maximum period in terms of actual time instead of in relation to sittings of the court, perhaps with a proviso that the period may be extended where delay occurs at the defendant's request.

Aborigines have been shown to be particularly in need of protection against unnecessary pre-trial detention. The suggested reforms would, of

[24] For the position in other states see Campbell and Whitmore 1966: 45.

course, cover Aboriginal defendants as well as whites. But in addition, it may be possible to appoint an officer of a government department (such as the Crown Law Department) to examine police and court records continuously to see that the proposed new procedures are functioning satisfactorily in relation to Aborigines. Ideally the person appointed would be a lawyer. Such an officer should also have the function of overseeing sentences imposed after conviction. The justification for this special treatment rests on the large number of Aborigines who are at present detained before trial. But it is hoped that the improvements in the administration of criminal justice which would result from the introduction of a reviewing officer would also benefit other defendants.

4 REPRESENTATION

One of the rights the law recognises today is that of a defendant to a criminal charge to be represented by counsel on the hearing of the charge. Like the right to silence, already discussed, this is of greater or lesser efficacy depending on the status, financial resources and education of the defendant concerned. Representation by a lawyer of his choice is theoretically available to every defendant to a criminal charge. In practice, the actual exercise of this right is heavily dependent on the financial resources of the defendant or his friends. In recognition of the fact that the right to legal assistance remains an abstraction unless one is in a position to pay for the services of a lawyer, each Australian State has set up a legal aid scheme.[1]

Since most Aborigines live in poverty and are relatively uneducated, it would be expected that they would not be able readily to employ lawyers in the ordinary solicitor-client relationship. The defendant with no one to represent him will generally be in the least favourable position in criminal proceedings. A welfare officer or some other third party, especially if he has some training in law, will usually represent the defendant better than he can himself. A lawyer supplied by a legal aid scheme will provide even better representation. But from the point of view of the defendant, the best lawyer will be one chosen and paid for by himself.

[1] Cranston and Adams (1972); Letter to Editor from A.R. Watson, *A.L.J.* **47** (1973), p. 54.

THE ROLE OF LAWYERS

VICTORIA

Precise figures of the number of Aborigines who arrange legal representation on their own initiative and at their own expense are not available. On the basis of general knowledge of their lack of education and finance it seems that the instances of such private legal representation must be rare.

In Victoria legislation authorises two bodies to provide legal assistance to poor persons: the Public Solicitor and the Legal Aid Committee.[2] Individuals and voluntary associations concerned with the welfare of Aborigines and the Aborigines Welfare Board (now the Ministry for Aboriginal Affairs) have found, however, that the mere existence of these official dispensers of legal aid is not enough to ensure that all Aboriginal defendants are adequately represented. Lack of money is not the only disability. In order to make effective use of facilities like legal aid, a defendant needs to know of the existence of such facilities, to realise that legal representation will be an advantage to him and to have the confidence to approach the relevant agency. Voluntary organisations have played an important role in directing Aborigines to the Public Solicitor or the Legal Aid Committee or in directly arranging private legal representation.

Two voluntary associations, the Aborigines Advancement League and the Council for Aboriginal Rights, have been particularly interested in legal representation for Aborigines. As an illustration of their work, Appendix 9 sets out details of cases from 1964 to 1969 in which an Aboriginal defendant was represented by the honorary solicitor of the Aborigines Advancement League. In many of these cases an officer of the League also attended court as a character witness. The table demonstrates the value to a defendant of being legally represented. In most cases where an Aboriginal defendant was represented by the honorary solicitor at the original hearing an acquittal resulted or a lenient sentence was imposed. In most cases where the solicitor acted on appeal, the appeal was successful. Out of eight appeals in which this solicitor acted, one resulted in the conviction being quashed and one resulted in a new trial being ordered; five defendants had their sentences varied and in each case the sentence substituted was less severe than the original sentence; only one defendant had his appeal dismissed.

[2] The text sets out the situation which existed prior to the Legal Aid Act 1969 (Vic.). It deals with legal aid available to poor persons generally, not that available to particular groups, such as ex-servicemen or trade unionists.

It is significant that of these sixteen defendants, eight were represented by this solicitor only at the appeal stage; seven having been totally unrepresented at the original hearing. If these defendants had had representation at an earlier stage, they might not have been convicted or might have received lesser sentences initially. A good deal of hardship, including time spent in prison on remand, might have been avoided. Better legal representation at an earlier stage might in individual cases actually save the community money (including costs of prison administration and the legal costs of appeals as compared with the costs of original hearings), as well as being fairer to the individual defendant. The Tasmanian Court of Criminal Appeal recognised the problems faced by an unrepresented defendant in these words: 'The lack of representation led, as often happens, to difficulties in the conduct of the trial itself; it also brought about successive delays in the prosecution of the appeal.' (Appendix 9—see 1967-8 case).

The absence of legal representation on the original hearing of so many of these cases represents a failure of communication between the authorities supplying legal aid and the Aboriginal defendants. After the passing of the Aboriginal Affairs Act 1967 some of these cases also indicated a breach of section 37 of that Act. Section 37(1) provided:

> Where an aborigine is a party to any criminal proceedings the court or the justices hearing such proceedings shall inform the Director of Aboriginal Affairs thereof and if it considers that it is in the interests of the aborigine may adjourn the hearing to enable the Director or his deputy to appear on behalf of the aborigine.

The Act came into operation on 1 January 1968 and section 37 remained in that form until amended later that year.[3] Thus the court in each of the 1968 cases listed in Appendix 9 was under a mandatory obligation to inform the Director of Aboriginal Affairs that an Aboriginal was appearing before it. In at least two of these cases there is definite evidence that this was not done. In one case the honorary solicitor had already been informed of the case before the inquest and appeared for the Aboriginal before the coroner so there was no need for the court to advise the Director. In another case, it appears that the defendant may have asked the local welfare officer to help in obtaining a solicitor and been refused. The evidence on this point is unclear. In any event, it appears that the magistrate made no effort to notify the Director of the case; the defendant

[3] Aboriginal Affairs (Amendment) Act 1968 (Vic.). (Date of commencement 13/12/68.)

was unrepresented and subjected to rather a severe sentence, later varied on appeal.

The information in the column headed 'Arrangements for Representation' in Appendix 9 is an indication of the haphazard way in which these cases came to the attention of someone who was in a position to take effective action on the defendant's behalf. In many cases the defendant himself did not ask directly for legal representation but the matter became known to someone who believed that legal representation was necessary and arranged it. How many more cases must there be in which legal representation is equally necessary but no such action is taken?

Section 37 was enacted in an effort to overcome this communication problem, to ensure that in every case the Director, who is one of the persons primarily charged with promoting the social and economic advancement of Aborigines in Victoria, becomes aware of the fact that an Aboriginal is involved in criminal proceedings. This object could clearly not be achieved if the section were more honoured in the breach than in the observance.

Apart from the problem of the non-observance of the mandatory requirement of the section, section 37 in its original form did not always assist an Aboriginal defendant because of the discretion reposed in the court and in the Director. The latter part of section 37(1) provided that the court 'if it considers that it is in the interests of the aborigine *may* adjourn the hearing to enable the Director or his deputy to appear on behalf of the aborigine' (my emphasis). The court could comply with the section by notifying the Director and then, even if he intended to attend court, it could continue with the hearing in his absence, since it was within its discretion to adjourn the hearing or not. Section 37 was then amended (in 1968) to transfer the obligation to notify the Director from the court to the police. The court retains the discretion to adjourn the hearing.

The Director has a discretionary power to decide whether or not to appear on behalf of the Aboriginal. Section 37(3) now provides: 'the Director or some other person authorized in writing by the Minister *may* appear on behalf of the aborigine and *may* make any application to the court which the Director or the person appointed may deem necessary in the interest of the aborigine'.[4] The purpose of section 37 'is to ensure that

[4] Emphasis added. Section 37(3) substituted by Aboriginal Affairs (Amendment) Act 1968 (Vic.). Section 37(2) of Aboriginal Affairs Act 1967 (Vic.) was in almost identical terms.

no Aborigine goes before a court without legal aid if he is in need of it'.[5] It was intended that the Director would appear to make an application for adjournment in order to arrange legal aid, rather than that he would himself represent the Aboriginal.

In 1968 newspaper reports of statements attributed to the Director raised grave doubts as to the manner in which he was exercising the discretion reposed in him by section 37.[6] The Director was quoted as saying that a new policy had been adopted: where an Aboriginal defendant had a number of prior convictions related to allied or similar offences, or where he had committed a variety of offences, legal aid might not be provided. The policy came to the notice of the newspaper because it was referred to by a welfare officer in a case before a Court of Petty Sessions. The magistrate very properly asked the welfare officer whether he wanted an adjournment so that the defendant could be legally represented. The welfare officer refused on the grounds of the new policy.

This policy was open to criticism on two grounds. First, the decision about the grant of legal aid is not entrusted by law to the Director. The Public Solicitor and the Legal Aid Committee are the bodies entrusted with the function of providing legal aid to accused persons, including Aborigines. The final decision about whether an Aboriginal defendant should have legal aid or not should be left to those bodies. Secondly, the announcement of this policy may have been prejudicial to Aboriginal defendants. It may have led a court to draw an inference that an unrepresented Aboriginal must have prior convictions. Trained magistrates or judges may be able to shut out of their minds such an inference but there is the danger that lay justices will be influenced.

It was not long before the Minister for Aboriginal Affairs gave the following answers to questions in the Legislative Assembly.[7]

1. Whether he is aware of the policy, expressed by the Director of Aboriginal Affairs, with respect to legal representation of Aboriginal persons?
   A. Yes.

[5] Mr Meagher (Minister of Housing), introducing the legislation. *Victoria. Parliamentary Debates* (Hansard) Forty-fourth Parliament, First Session, 1967-8, p. 541.

[6] Melbourne *Herald* 5/9/68, p. 13.

[7] *Victoria. Parliamentary Debates* (Hansard) Forty-fourth Parliament, Second Session, 1968, p. 98. Each answer is set out immediately following the relevant question for clarity.

2. Whether he accepts that Aboriginal persons with a number of convictions should be refused legal aid by his Ministry?
   A. No. Each case will be dealt with on its merits.
3. What was the decision of the Ministry of Aboriginal Affairs if, and when, it was consulted?
   A. The answer to this question appears in part 2.
4. Whether he will ascertain and inform the House whether Aboriginal persons have, prior to the establishment of his Ministry, been convicted without having had the benefit of legal aid?
   A. As free citizens subject to the same laws as others, Aboriginal persons may in the past have been convicted without having had legal aid. Since the Ministry came into being on 1st January, 1968, the number of Aboriginal persons assisted with legal aid has increased substantially.

Although this appeared to be a repudiation of the policy on Aborigines with previous convictions, the words 'on its merits' still left room for the exercise of discretion by welfare officials. It did not mean that all Aborigines wanting legal aid would automatically be referred to the appropriate agencies. The Minister later spelt this out when he said in the same session (pp. 1137-8): 'the object of the Ministry is to help Aborigines who are in need of assistance but not to help those who tend to make a racket of legal aid. If an Aborigine persists in refusing to learn from the assistance that my Ministry gives him, for his own good it will reserve the right to withdraw that assistance'. Under this punitive philosophy an Aboriginal could be in a worse position than a white defendant, because his access to the sources of legal aid could be effectively blocked by the department set up to promote the welfare of Aborigines.

Officials of the Ministry of Aboriginal Affairs and its predecessor, the Aborigines Welfare Board, have been responsible for arranging legal aid for Aborigines in a number of cases. Without their assistance, these Aborigines probably would not have obtained representation, mainly owing to difficulties of communication with the appropriate authorities.

In some cases, however, the official has decided that no legal aid should be arranged for an Aboriginal. The police notified the Aborigines Welfare Board that one Aboriginal would be appearing in court on a vagrancy charge but the Board official who was informed did not arrange any representation because he 'thought he deserved it'.

At a later date, the Aborigines Welfare Board established a practice of approaching the Public Solicitor, the Legal Aid Committee or a private lawyer whenever it knew of an Aboriginal defendant. The Legal Aid Committee agreed that it would take all Aboriginal cases. Thus the Ministry policy of deciding each case 'on its merits' instead of forwarding on all Aboriginal requests for legal aid, was a retrograde step.[8]

It is suggested that it should not be the function of any member of the Ministry of Aboriginal Affairs to make a final decision about the grant or refusal of legal aid to an Aboriginal defendant. No staff members are legally trained and the only person who can make a rational decision, based on proper legal criteria and excluding irrelevant factors, is a lawyer. The useful function which the Ministry can perform is to act as a liaison between Aboriginal defendants and either the Public Solicitor or the Legal Aid Committee. If legal representation is not available from either of those bodies and there are special reasons why the Aborigines should be represented, it should be open to the Director to arrange private legal representation. The first approach should be made to the Public Solicitor or the Legal Aid Committee, and this should always be done, regardless of the views of any official on the desirability of the grant of legal aid to the particular Aboriginal. This view has now been accepted by the Ministry.[9]

It is very important for the morale of the Aborigines that they should feel that everything possible has been done to provide adequate legal representation. It is not enough that they should be advised in the abstract about rights to legal aid; every effort should be made to help them actually obtain it.

Another function the Ministry could perform is that of providing welfare officers to represent Aborigines in areas where solicitors are not readily available. In Victoria, no instances have been found of this function being performed. Since South Australia and Western Australia use welfare officers in this way quite often, further consideration of the advantages and disadvantages of this practice will be deferred until later in this chapter.

The provisions of the Aboriginal Affairs Act 1967 are intended to facilitate Aboriginal applications to the Public Solicitor and the Legal Aid Committee. As these bodies were the chief sources of legal representation

[8] Personal communication from Professor C.M. Tatz. See also *Victoria. Parliamentary Debates* (Hansard) Forty-fourth Parliament, First Session, 1967-8, pp. 1143, 1550.

[9] The Victorian Aboriginal Legal Service, established in 1972, now provides a source of legal assistance to which the Ministry refers many Aboriginal clients. The Service has recommended to the Victorian government that section 37 of the Aboriginal Affairs Act should be amended so that the Legal Service and not the Ministry is notified of Aborigines charged with offences.

of Aborigines during the fieldwork period, their functions will now be examined.

The Public Solicitor. Before the Legal Aid Act 1961 came into operation on 11 December 1963, the Public Solicitor was the only official source of legal aid for poor persons in Victoria. Since that date a dual system has been operating. This in itself produces some problems of duplication of services and confusion of clients, but it has also filled some of the gaps in the service provided by the Public Solicitor. These deficiencies are largely caused by the terms of the legislation which authorises the appointment of the Public Solicitor. Section 7 of the Poor Persons Legal Assistance Act 1958 provides for the appointment of the Public Solicitor and section 8 sets out the circumstances in which he is to act. In criminal cases, the Public Solicitor is to act where a solicitor is assigned by the Attorney-General to an appellant under Part VI of the Crimes Act 1958 and where the Attorney-General assigns a solicitor for the defence of an accused person under Part I of the Poor Persons Legal Assistance Act 1958. Part VI of the Crimes Act 1958 provides generally for appeals by persons who have been convicted on indictment and section 575 provides specifically for the assignment of a solicitor by the Attorney-General on such appeals in certain circumstances. Part I of the Poor Persons Legal Assistance Act 1958 provides in section 3 as follows:

> (1) Any person committed for trial for an indictable offence . . . may at any time within fourteen days after committal and before the jury is sworn apply in writing . . . to a Judge of the Supreme Court or to a chairman of a court of general sessions or to a stipendiary magistrate for legal aid for his defence . . .
>
> (3) The Judge or chairman or stipendiary magistrate . . . if he is of opinion . . . that such person is without adequate means to provide legal aid for himself shall certify accordingly to the Attorney-General who may thereupon if he thinks fit cause arrangements to be made for the defence of the accused person and the payment of the expenses of all material witnesses.

There are thus severe limitations on the scope of the duty imposed on the Public Solicitor to act for poor defendants. First, the Attorney-General has considerable discretion both under section 575 of the Crimes Act 1958 and under section 3(3) of the Poor Persons Legal Assistance Act 1958. In the case of an appeal he need not grant legal aid unless in his opinion 'it appears desirable in the interest of justice' and the defendant 'has not sufficient means to enable him to obtain that aid' (section 575 of the Crimes Act 1958). In the case of a trial he may assign the Public Solicitor to the defence 'if he thinks fit' but no criteria are laid down for the exercise of this discretion.

Other restrictions follow from the terms of these authorising sections. The appeals referred to in section 575 of the Crimes Act 1958 are only those from decisions of the County Court or the Supreme Court. The section does not extend to appeals from Magistrates Courts to the County Court.[10] Section 3 of the Poor Persons Legal Assistance Act 1958 provides for applications for legal aid to be made only in cases of indictable offences, only *after* committal for trial and the application must be made within fourteen days after committal. In negative terms, this Act does not provide for legal aid in Magistrates Courts where most criminal prosecutions are finally decided or in the Children's Court. It does not provide for representation at an inquest or at committal proceedings. It is doubtful whether it applies to defendants who have pleaded guilty at committal proceedings and have been committed for sentence only. The time limit within which the application must be made is very short.

The Attorney-General has taken the view that the Public Solicitor is not entitled to act in any cases other than those specifically referred to in the sections quoted. In the light of the decision and certain dicta of Sholl J. in *Borradale* v. *Davenport* this view may be unduly restrictive. In that case Sholl J. held that the Supreme Court had an inherited common law jurisdiction to admit the applicant as a pauper party, where the applicant was the respondent to an order *nisi* to review the decision of a Court of Petty Sessions. He reviewed the legislation on legal aid and found that it was not applicable to this type of proceeding. Nevertheless he ordered that the Public Solicitor should be assigned as the solicitor for the applicant. This decision could be applied to the case where the applicant for legal aid was the party who had obtained an order to review, but whether it would have still wider scope is uncertain. Some of Sholl J.'s words (at p. 474) suggest wider possibilities: 'It may be that any court, or at all events any superior court of record, in this country, has an inherent power to admit persons as pauper parties to prevent the possibility of injustice, save in cases where so to act would contravene some statutory provisions as to costs or fees.' He found it unnecessary to decide the point in this case. The question may be considered somewhat academic now that a Legal Aid Committee exists to fill the gaps in the Public Solicitor's service.

[10] *Borradale* v. *Davenport* [1958] V.R. 470, 472 per Sholl J., referring to section 601 of the Crimes Act 1928, the forerunner of the present section 575.

One recent case, however, demonstrates that the capacity of the Legal Aid Committee to act in cases where the Public Solicitor is not authorised or declines to act is dependent on efficient communication. Injustice may result if communication breaks down between the defendant, prison authorities, the Public Solicitor, the Attorney-General and the Legal Aid Committee. Two appellants, Aboriginal brothers aged seventeen and nineteen, made applications for legal aid from Pentridge Prison where they were serving sentences of twelve months' imprisonment each on charges of having insufficient lawful means of support (see Appendix 9—defendants in 1967 case). The Attorney-General refused the application on the ground that there was no legislative authority for the Public Solicitor to act on such an appeal. It is unfortunate that the Attorney-General did not take adequate steps to ensure that the defendants understood that his decision did not close all doors and that they were still entitled to apply to the Legal Aid Committee.

On the contrary, the appellants were possibly not even aware that their application had been refused and were certainly not advised or encouraged to apply to the Legal Aid Committee. It was only by chance that I (as a member of the Aborigines Advancement League) learnt that the Public Solicitor was not acting when I telephoned to ask about the progress of the case. This was not long before the appeal was listed for hearing and hurried arrangements were made through the Legal Aid Committee for the honorary solicitor for the Aborigines Advancement League to act. Otherwise the appellants would have been unrepresented, which would have made it more difficult for justice to have been done. With legal representation, the sentences of imprisonment were set aside and an order made for the entry of good behaviour bonds instead. This case illustrates vividly the plight of appellants trying to conduct their affairs from gaol, where normal communication with lawyers and other advisers is impossible, and particularly the helpless position of uneducated people who are not aware of their legal rights and are unable to arrange adequate representation without the intervention of some interested person.

The restrictions imposed by section 3 of the Poor Persons Legal Assistance Act 1958 create other difficulties for poor persons and the Public Solicitor. The Public Solicitor sometimes finds it a disadvantage not to have acted for the defendant on committal. Almost all lawyers and magistrates who were interviewed agreed that it is at committal proceedings that the defendant's lawyer finds out the real strength of the case against his client: he sees the witnesses, and has an opportunity to cross-examine them. In some instances, the Legal Aid Committee has arranged representation at committal proceedings and the case has subsequently been transferred to the Public Solicitor. This is unsatisfactory, since it involves duplication of effort on the part of lawyers and, in some cases, the lawyer who acts at the trial would have acted differently at the committal proceedings.

The time limit of fourteen days after committal[11] would also impose hardship if it were rigidly enforced, but the Attorney-General sometimes exercises a discretion in favour of the applicant even if he is out of time. Aboriginal applicants have been given special consideration in this respect. The Legal Aid Committee has suggested that the period should be extended to six weeks for all defendants and that the Public Solicitor should as well be accorded a discretion to entertain some applications which are out of time.[12]

Other restrictions on the Public Solicitor's jurisdiction have also been mitigated by his practice of acting in some cases where there appears to be no specific legislative authority. The Public Solicitor will sometimes appear to make a plea in mitigation of sentence on behalf of a defendant who has pleaded guilty on committal. He has appeared at inquests.

In those cases where he is authorised to act, the Public Solicitor appears to provide an adequate and sympathetic service. No statistics are available of the number of Aboriginal clients who have been assisted but it is estimated that the office has about six Aboriginal cases each year. This could be an indication that few Aborigines are charged with indictable offences, or it could mean that those so charged do not apply for legal aid.

The Public Solicitor stated in an interview[13] that an Aboriginal application for legal aid is never refused, whether the applicant appeared to have a good defence or not and whatever the number of his prior convictions. The Public Solicitor's statement must, however, be read subject to the qualifications imposed by the criteria of eligibility. An Aboriginal application may be refused if it relates to a case of a type in which the Public Solicitor is not empowered to act. Further, he considers that appeals are different from trials. A defendant who wishes to appeal has already had his day in court and has a decision against him. Careful consideration

[11] For the meaning of 'committed for trial' and this time limit see *R.* v. *Peirce* [1961] V.R. 496.

[12] 'Report of Legal Aid Committee', *L.I.J.* **42** (1968), p. 28.

[13] In March 1968; the text refers to practice at that date.

should therefore be given before public money is spent on representing him. The Public Solicitor can act on appeals from the County Court but he needs an opinion from a barrister recommending the appeal before he does so.

The asterisked case in Appendix 9 illustrates the disability of a poor defendant as compared with other defendants. The solicitor who instructed at the trial, a member of the Public Solicitor's staff, did not consider the possibility of an appeal against sentence. In view of his verbally expressed lack of interest in an appeal no formal application for legal aid for an appeal was made to the Public Solicitor and the matter was dealt with instead by the honorary solicitor to the Aborigines Advancement League with the co-operation of the Legal Aid Committee. The appellate proceedings were ultimately successful: the minimum period of the sentence was reduced from ten to six years.

Another disadvantage in the Public Solicitor's service is that his staff is overworked. There are only four solicitors on his criminal staff to handle about 350-400 trials per year. On the other hand, the Public Solicitor's clients do have the benefit of representation by specialist solicitors. The client's wishes about a barrister are taken into account if he expresses any preference. The Public Solicitor has no power to assign cases to outside solicitors, even when his staff is overworked.

The Victorian Public Solicitor has money available to spend on obtaining evidence and searching for witnesses. This was one of the weaknesses of the South Australian legal aid scheme brought to light by the Stuart case (Inglis 1961: 317-18).

No action is taken to publicise the service offered by the Public Solicitor. It is considered a breach of ethics for a solicitor to advertise his services, but the considerations which make this a valid rule for the private practitioner do not apply to the Public Solicitor. Information is available in gaols about the Public Solicitor and the application forms under the Regulations to the Poor Persons Legal Assistance Act[14] are also provided there. Uneducated people in general and Aborigines in particular are often ignorant of the existence of such facilities or diffident about making use of them. An educational campaign, including encouragement to use the Public Solicitor's service, would therefore be desirable. Such a campaign might well be carried out by the Ministry of Aboriginal Affairs. Com-

[14] Regulations under the Poor Persons Legal Assistance Act 1928 (*Government Gazette* (Vic.) 11/11/31, p. 3188).

munity education about law and legal services is now the responsibility of the Aboriginal Legal Service.

In some cases where the client is not eligible for the Public Solicitor's assistance, he is informed that he can apply to the Legal Aid Committee. There is no formal liaison with the Legal Aid Committee, however, and, as we have seen, the client is not always made aware that an alternative source of legal aid may be available.

The Legal Aid Committee. The Legal Aid Act 1961 set up a scheme suggested by the Law Institute and Victorian Bar Council. It was intended to overcome the inadequacies of the assistance provided by the Public Solicitor's office. The purpose was clearly set out in the preamble to the Act:

> Whereas the members of the Legal Profession of Victoria believe that no person should be without legal assistance by reason of his being unable to pay therefor:
> And whereas . . . the Victorian Bar Council and . . . the Law Institute . . . have voluntarily offered to provide legal assistance for poor persons and to appoint a committee to establish and administer a scheme for that purpose . . .

The Committee began to consider applications for assistance in April 1964. Practitioners were advised in a letter of 1 April 1964 from the President of the Law Institute to Institute members that the Committee did not intend initially, save in exceptional circumstances, to grant assistance in criminal matters. A certain number of criminal applications have been granted, chiefly as a means of filling the gaps in the Public Solicitor's coverage. As a matter of policy, the Legal Aid Committee does not assist applicants who are eligible for the Public Solicitor's assistance, but usually suggests that they go to the Public Solicitor.

The following table[15] shows the number of criminal applications dealt with in four years of the scheme's operation:

Period	Total	Dealt with by Secretary	Referred to Committee	Approved
1/7/64-30/6/65	133	51	87	55
1/7/65-30/6/66	278	92	186	135
1/7/66-30/6/67	293	84	209	155
1/7/67-30/6/68	550	196	354	240

[15] The table was compiled from information in reports of the Legal Aid Committee as follows: *L.I.J.* **39**, pp. 229, 383; **40**, p. 441; **42**, p. 25; **43**, p. 63.

The Legal Aid Act is framed so widely that the Committee can provide legal aid in any court and before administrative tribunals. Everything depends on the decision of the Committee and they do not refuse an application simply because of the court involved. In the criminal field summary matters are covered as well as indictable offences. Thus the Committee is able to supplement the service offered by the Public Solicitor. The Committee has approved legal aid for some defendants in the early stages of criminal matters, and it has acted on inquests, appeals from Magistrates Courts to the County Court and in the Children's Court. It has also accepted cases not assisted by the Public Solicitor because the application was made out of time. It considers that the rigidity of this rule is unfair to many applicants, particularly to those who do not know their rights.

The Committee has a wide discretion in the operation of the scheme. No specific criteria for eligibility are laid down. The Committee does not use a rigid means test but considers the sufficiency of each applicant's means in relation to the type of legal proceeding for which he requests aid.[16] In civil cases, some legal merit must be established before the Committee will approve the application. The Committee probably would not refuse aid in a criminal case on the grounds of merit: every accused is entitled to be represented on his day in court. Where a defendant has pleaded guilty, the Committee may approve legal aid to help with his plea regarding sentence.

Legal Aid is available at any stage of the proceedings. In criminal cases it is available from the time the defendant has been charged with the offence. If necessary, the defendant or the Legal Aid Committee could negotiate an adjournment to enable his application for legal aid to be considered. When interviewed, the secretary of the Committee did not think it was necessary to adopt the Scottish system of granting legal aid to a defendant in custody on his first appearance in court without any investigation of his means (cf. Dandie 1966: 255). He did not consider there was any need for a 'duty roster' of solicitors, as established in Scotland. He thought that relying on the magistrate to grant an adjournment was satisfactory. This may be so where the Legal Aid Committee has become aware of the case before the hearing and arranges for the adjournment. In some cases where Aborigines have been arrested, however, the

[16] The information about the Committee's practice comes from interviews with Mr Heffernan, the secretary of the Legal Aid Committee.

matter has never reached the Legal Aid Committee. Although the defendants wanted legal representation, they have not been able to communicate with the Legal Aid Committee and have not known they could ask for an adjournment for this purpose. If the idea of a 'duty roster' is thought to impose too great a burden on the legal profession in Victoria, it would be desirable to achieve the same end by requiring the police to notify the Legal Aid Committee of all defendants who have requested legal aid and taking steps to ensure that the police actually carry out this duty.

In general, the assisted person is simply assigned a solicitor and barrister. If the applicant has previously consulted a solicitor, that solicitor is offered the case. Solicitors do refer people to the Legal Aid Committee and some Aborigines were represented by the honorary solicitor of the Aborigines Advancement League under this arrangement (Appendix 9).

The Legal Aid scheme has been publicised to a limited degree through the press and radio. There is not the same ethical objection to publicity about this scheme as there is to advertising by individual practitioners. The secretary stated that the Legal Aid scheme will 'lean over backwards to help Aborigines'.[17] He recognises a duty to represent them. The scheme is not intended to cover people residing in other States who are charged with an offence in Victoria. In the case of Aborigines, the Committee is prepared to act for some out-of-State defendants. In one case in Echuca, Aboriginal children residing in New South Wales were charged with an offence; Legal Aid representation was arranged. The special position of Aborigines along the River Murray is recognised. Many Aboriginal homes are on the bank of the river in New South Wales opposite a Victorian town.

In a number of cases (including some in Appendix 9) the assistance of the Legal Aid scheme has been very valuable to Aboriginal defendants. But there is still a vast untapped reservoir of potential Aboriginal clients. In November 1965 the Secretary stated that about ten Aboriginal clients had been assisted since the scheme began. These had come of their own accord or been referred by the Aborigines Welfare Board, clerks of courts or the Public Solicitor. The great majority of Aboriginal defendants still do not have legal representation in Magistrates Courts or on appeals from Magistrates Courts to the County Court.

The crux of the matter is publicity and communication. A number of

[17] Interview with Mr Heffernan. See also 'Report of the Legal Aid Committee': 'Special consideration has been given by the Committee to applications received from the Aboriginal Welfare Board' (*L.I.J.* **42**, p. 29).

Aboriginal prisoners in Pentridge have expressed the wish for legal aid but have not obtained it. I became aware of this during monthly discussion groups at the prison. It appears that in most cases the lack of legal aid was not due to a refusal to act by the Legal Aid Committee but occurred because the request for assistance had never reached the Legal Aid Committee.

One can sympathise with the early reluctance of the Committee to publicise its service widely, since it believed this would bring a flood of applications which it would be unable to handle. Without increased staff and funds, too great an increase in the number of applications would produce difficulties of administration and might lead to the breakdown of a scheme which depends on the voluntary co-operation of members of the legal profession. So far very few lawyers have refused to participate in the scheme. The main disadvantage to a practitioner of taking an assisted case is that he recovers less costs than from a private client. In the year ended 30 June 1967 the dividend to the profession was approximately 52 cents in each dollar of professional costs.[18] On the other hand, he is assured of getting some costs whereas some of his private clients' accounts will turn out to be bad debts. Further, the legal aid case provides work for the profession which otherwise may not come to it at all. This is perhaps particularly important to members of the junior Bar.

The idealistic expression of intention by the legal profession in the preamble to the Legal Aid Act 1961 that 'no person should be without legal assistance by reason of his being unable to pay therefor', can only be achieved if poor persons both know about and are able to contact the Legal Aid Committee in time for effective action to be taken.

To improve the Legal Aid scheme in relation to Aboriginal defendants, it is suggested that a voluntary panel of barristers and solicitors should be set up, consisting of lawyers with a special interest in Aborigines, who are prepared to assist them. This panel could function on an informal basis. When an Aboriginal is to be defended a member of the panel should be approached first by the Legal Aid Committee to see whether he was able to appear. His right to refuse the assignment would be preserved. A number of lawyers have expressed interest in staffing such a panel.

The reasons for favouring a legal aid arrangement with private solicitors for Aboriginal defendants, rather than making the Public Solicitor solely responsible for their defence, are as follows. First, Aborigines tend

[18] *L.I.J.* **42**, p. 31. The Legal Aid Act 1969 (Vic.) guarantees a higher dividend.

to distrust authority in any form, largely because of past and recent history (for a documented study in Victoria see Lippmann 1973). One Aboriginal prisoner mentioned as his reason for preferring the Legal Aid Committee the fact that the Public Solicitor was 'government'. In fact, the Public Solicitor has considerable independence but the objective situation is not reflected in his image in Aboriginal eyes. For the same reason the role of voluntary associations such as the Aborigines Advancement League is important. Their members are often trusted more than government welfare officers. They can often perform a useful function in arranging legal aid. The value of voluntary organisations has been recognised in the Aboriginal Affairs Act 1967.

The second reason is that lawyers who have indicated their interest in Aborigines are likely to be the best advocates for them. Some solicitors have said that they find Aborigines difficult clients; they are unreliable about keeping appointments and it is difficult to elicit the facts of the case from them, possibly because of their general distrust of white people. Lawyers with a special interest in Aborigines and understanding of their problems are likely to prove their most effective representatives.

Such a scheme would, in effect, give Aborigines a choice of solicitors and put them on more of an equal footing with defendants able to afford private representation, while at the same time providing the selected solicitor with the assurance that he will recover some costs. The right to choose a lawyer has been regarded as an important element of overseas legal aid schemes and it is surely just as important in criminal as in civil cases (see papers on 'Costs and legal aid' in Woodman 1966: 217-60).

SOUTH AUSTRALIA

In South Australia a dual system of legal aid also operates, but on rather different lines from the Victorian one.

The Poor Persons Legal Assistance Act, 1925 empowered the Governor to appoint a Public Solicitor and provided (in section 8) that certain provisions should come into operation upon the appointment of a Public Solicitor. These provisions are similar to those in section 8 of the Victorian Poor Persons Legal Assistance Act 1958. They were operative for only eight years. There has been no Public Solicitor in South Australia since 1933.

In that year the Law Society made an agreement with the government that the profession would take over all the work of the Public Solicitor's office and extend the legal aid offered so 'that no person would be without proper legal assistance if he were deserving of such assistance and would be unable to obtain it without the help of the Society's members'.

The scheme was given some legislative recognition by the Poor Persons Legal Assistance Act, 1936 entitled 'An Act to make further and better provision respecting legal assistance for poor persons'.[19] Section 3 enabled the Attorney-General to give directions for the remission of court fees and any other fees payable to the State in cases under the scheme. The Act did not directly embody the Law Society scheme within a legislative framework or provide any rules for its operation.

Most legal aid work in South Australia is carried out under the Law Society scheme.[20] In 1964/65 1664 cases were assigned to solicitors, including 460 criminal cases. The coverage of this scheme in the criminal field compares very favourably with the combined coverage of the Public Solicitor and the Legal Aid scheme in Victoria, which dealt with approximately 455 criminal cases in that year and approximately 555 criminal cases in 1966/67. The contribution made by the South Australian legal profession is particularly praiseworthy when it is realised that the population of the State, the number of lawyers and the amount of costs which they recover under the scheme are all much smaller than in Victoria.

Before 1960 the State government provided only the administration expenses of the scheme. Nothing was provided for disbursements or professional costs. If he did not obtain out-of-pocket expenses from the applicant, the solicitor had to bear them himself. The assignment in each case was made on terms specifying the amount of costs, if any, which the applicant was required to pay and that was the maximum the solicitor could look forward to receiving in criminal cases.

From 1960 the government made available an additional sum of $9000 a year. This was used to pay out-of-pocket expenses in full and the balance was available as a dividend to be paid to participating practitioners. The Law Society's Instructions to Applicants still stated: 'The applicant must provide the actual out-of-pocket expenses, including witnesses' expenses and the costs of service of process . . . ', but if the applicant could not, or did not, pay these expenses, he still obtained legal aid.

[19] No. 2322 of 1936 (S.A.). The text sets out the situation during the fieldwork period. The Poor Persons Legal Assistance Act, 1936 has since been repealed by the Legal Practitioners Act Amendment Act, 1969 (S.A.). For a recent case setting out the current position and providing a useful review of the history of legal aid in South Australia, see *R.* v. *Van Beelen* (1972) 3 S.A.S.R. 330.

[20] Most of the information on the Law Society scheme comes from an interview with Mr Maitland, secretary, Law Society in March 1966. See also Maitland 1966.

The Poor Persons Legal Assistance Act, 1936 did not repeal or amend the earlier Act (No. 1689 of 1925). Section 3 of the 1925 Act therefore still provided an alternative avenue of legal aid for defendants in a limited class of case. Section 3(1)—which has since been amended—provided that: 'Any person committed for trial for an indictable offence against the laws of South Australia may at any time before the jury is impanelled for the trial of such offence apply to a judge for the appointment of counsel for his defence.' Section 3(2) provided that the judge might assign counsel or a solicitor or both if:

> (a) the offence for which the person is committed for trial is punishable with death, or is such that in the opinion of the judge the person committed for trial should be defended by counsel; and (b) the judge is satisfied that the person committed for trial is without adequate means to retain counsel or summon witnesses.

Thus, assigned counsel under this provision was available *after* committal to any poor person charged with murder or with other grave crimes. Since this type of legal aid was available only at the post-committal stage of proceedings and in a limited class of case, it might be wondered why applications were still made under this section. The explanation lies in the concluding words of section 3: 'the judge . . . may order such sum as [he] . . . deems sufficient to be paid by the Sheriff for the purpose of the defence to such persons as the judge directs, and the Sheriff shall pay every such sum accordingly in like manner as he now pays the expenses of witnesses for the prosecution.' It appears that counsel and solicitors recovered more costs under this provision than they did under the Law Society's scheme. More money could also be made available under this section for the purposes of the investigation of the defence case, including searching for witnesses. The significance of this will become apparent when the Stuart case is examined.

An examination of other features of the Law Society's scheme reveals other points of similarity and difference when compared with the Victorian scheme. The Law Society will provide legal aid in any type of case, except minor traffic offences and 'drunk and disorderly' charges. The policy of the Victorian Committee is not to lay down in advance any restrictions on the type of case which will be assisted. In practice, the extent of the coverage of either scheme depends to a large extent on the type of case in which defendants actually apply for legal aid. Although the schemes may theoretically cover all jurisdictions it is clear that a large number of defendants tried summarily never consider applying for legal aid.

In South Australia the stage of the proceedings for which the assignment is made depends on the type of case. If a defendant desires to plead guilty to a charge of breaking and entering or larceny, a solicitor is assigned only for the Supreme Court and not for the preliminary hearing. The solicitor then appears to make a plea in mitigation of sentence. For sexual offences, the Law Society usually assigns a solicitor for the preliminary hearing, because it is considered that a solicitor can play an important role at that stage in dealing with the evidence introduced by the prosecutor. In any case where the defendant wishes to plead not guilty the Society will assign from the outset or assign 'for advice'.

The Society always assigned 'for advice' before granting legal aid for an appeal. In its 'Information for guidance of solicitors', it stated: 'Appeals from decisions of inferior Courts must not be instituted without the approval of the Committee. The Council alone can give permission to appeal from the decision of a Supreme Court Judge.' This presumably applied to both civil and criminal appeals proposed to be instituted under the Law Society scheme.[21]

As in Victoria, the Law Society has absolute discretion as to whether it accepts or rejects an application. In reaching its decision, it is mainly concerned with the question of means, but the means test applied is flexible. The Committee is not so interested in the *prima facie* case aspect, that is, in whether the applicant's case has sufficient legal merit to justify the granting of aid.

Again, there is no duty roster of solicitors. Theoretically, legal aid could be made available on arrest but it does not usually happen that a solicitor is assigned so early in the proceedings. Sometimes solicitors are called on in a private capacity at the arrest stage of a case which later becomes a Legal Aid case.

The fact that legal representation is rarely available at the arrest stage of criminal proceedings and that there is inevitable delay before legal aid applications can be approved and solicitors assigned, is one of the weaknesses of this scheme, as of the Victorian scheme. A member of a voluntary organisation mentioned this as the main objection to the scheme as far as Aboriginal defendants were concerned. He said that in many cases there was no point in an Aboriginal applying for legal aid, because he was rarely able to raise bail and it only meant he spent longer in prison on

[21] It should be noted that an alternative source of legal assistance is available in certain criminal appeals under section 360 of the Criminal Law Consolidation Act, 1935 (S.A.). See also section 363.

remand while waiting for his application to be approved. This attitude is perhaps unduly defeatist but it is probably shared by many Aborigines. If reforms in bail practice are carried out, as suggested in Chapter 3, this objection to the legal aid scheme would lose much of its force and one would expect that more Aborigines would apply. The Law Society might even be able to help to bring about these reforms by assigning solicitors to make bail applications on behalf of Aboriginal clients.

The legally aided client is usually given no choice of counsel and the scheme mainly works on a roster basis. The Committee does take the specialisation of solicitors into account in assigning cases.

There has been no active publicity campaign about the South Australian scheme. The Social Welfare Department, the Department of Aboriginal Affairs, and almoners at hospitals are aware of its existence. Police stations at main country centres and gaols have application forms but no notices are displayed. The Committee tends not to publicise the scheme because it already receives as many applications as it can handle, particularly with its limited financial resources.

The shortage of solicitors in country areas of South Australia is even more acute than in Victoria (see front endpaper map for country areas of South Australia—Victoria is better supplied with country solicitors, though this is not apparent from the map, which shows only fieldwork areas). Preliminary hearings in serious criminal cases are sometimes heard in a country town where there is no solicitor. In such cases the Legal Aid scheme can send a solicitor from Adelaide or the nearest country town if a special grant is obtained from the government. This has sometimes been done, particularly in murder cases.

As there is no Public Solicitor in South Australia the problems of duplication of services and delimitation of jurisdiction between two legal aid services do not arise.

The South Australian Committee also has a policy of special treatment for Aborigines. Legal aid is usually granted to Aborigines, even if they have long lists of prior convictions (which they are asked to supply, along with other information). It would be a very rare case in which an Aboriginal who applied would not be assisted. Most Aboriginal applications come from gaol or from the Department of Aboriginal Affairs. Sometimes they are sent by the police. Precise figures of the number of Aboriginal applicants are not available.

Rupert Max Stuart, a part-Aboriginal, was represented by a lawyer assigned by the Law Society at the preliminary hearing in January 1959 when he was committed for trial on a charge of murder (Inglis 1961: 16). At the preliminary hearing, the trial and the applications to the Full Court and High Court of Australia this solicitor appeared without fee. Funds raised by public appeal provided the expenses for his journey to London to apply to the Privy Council for leave to appeal. Finally, in the course of proceedings before the Royal Commission the government offered to pay the expenses of counsel for Stuart. The fees of Mr Starke Q.C. and two juniors were paid by the government (Inglis 1961: 60, 64, 139, 202, 205).

Professor Julius Stone, in a broadcast news commentary (quoted Inglis 1961: 146), pointed out 'the inadequacy of legal aid to persons accused of grave crimes, if such aid is limited to free services of lawyers. For this overlooks other costs, such as that of searching out and sifting evidence on behalf of the accused'. The Royal Commission in this case was set up largely as the result of the production of fresh evidence obtained by the independent investigation of a priest, whose expenses were paid by a newspaper. The investigation involved a journey from Adelaide to Queensland, a distance of over a thousand miles. Under a scheme in which the solicitor receives no fee for his professional services and nothing towards out-of-pocket expenses, he cannot be expected to undertake such an investigation as well as conducting the case in court.

It appears not to have occurred to the solicitor and the members of the Law Society involved in the case that an alternative source of legal aid might have been available under the Poor Persons Legal Assistance Act, 1925, which would have provided more funds for the conduct of the defence. Stuart's counsel could have asked for a special government grant for travelling expenses to search for witnesses. No information is available as to the practice of the judges in ordering payments 'for the purpose of the defence' under section 3(2) of the Poor Persons Legal Assistance Act, 1925 prior to the Stuart case. The fact that the government stepped in so late in the proceedings with its offer of payment for Stuart's counsel suggests that Stuart's advisers in the early stages may have been correct in thinking that it was not a practicable proposition to ask for a special government grant. Since the Stuart case a number of these applications have been made and granted.

Inglis's conclusion (1961: 317-18) is that Stuart was not harmed by an inadequate system of legal aid for poor people, since there is no evidence that his solicitor ever wanted to search for the witnesses, who were later found by the priest and who gave evidence to the Royal Commission.

Further, even after hearing the fresh evidence, the Royal Commissioners found the verdict against Stuart wholly justified and said they would have no hesitation in coming to the conclusion to which the jury came at the trial (Inglis 1961: 272-3). It could be argued, then, that even if the original solicitor had had unlimited funds available and had called all possible witnesses at the original trial, this would not have made any difference to the verdict. It is difficult to accept this argument. It seems that the fresh evidence was entitled to more weight than the Royal Commissioners gave it (Inglis 1961: 278); the Commissioners' support of the jury's verdict really only represents their opinion about what the original jury would have found if it had had all the evidence before it. The case illustrates the desirability of all relevant evidence being available at the original trial, rather than having to be introduced at later stages in the proceedings, either on appeal or before a Royal Commission. The Commissioners themselves recognised this when they said (Inglis 1961: 293):

> We feel obliged to point out that the need for this enquiry could hardly have arisen if the evidence which we have taken had been made available to the court of trial . . . (T)he plain fact is that the prosecution was content to rest its case upon the confession, without seeking for the testimony by which it has now been fortified.

I agree with Inglis that Stuart would probably have been no better off even if he had been a private client able to afford his own solicitor. Private legal representation is not always perfect. The search which eventually produced new evidence probably would not have been undertaken by a solicitor for a private client either. The case demonstrates the enormous disparity in investigatory facilities available to the police and to the defence, whether the defendant is a private or a legal aid client (cf. Blom-Cooper 1963: 50). Although the Royal Commissioners said that in this sort of case the obligation was on the Crown to provide witnesses which the defence wanted, Mr Starke Q.C. pointed out that a solicitor whose case involved a direct attack on the police would be unlikely to ask them for help in his search for evidence (Inglis 1961: 317-18).

The 1967-8 case in Appendix 9 shows the difficulties that may arise when the defendant is forced to rely on the police to obtain witnesses for him. The Aboriginal defendant, who was unrepresented at his trial in Tasmania, applied to the judge for leave to subpoena certain witnesses in Melbourne. The judge suggested that the Crown might arrange for statements to be obtained from the witnesses and if it appeared that they could give material evidence the Crown might provide the funds. The

Crown agreed to do this. At the adjourned application the Crown produced signed statements from the Melbourne witnesses who had been interviewed by policemen already connected with the case. The judge considered that they did not support the defendant's alibi for the crucial period and dismissed the prisoner's application. These witnesses were therefore not available to him at his trial. One of the grounds of appeal was that the judge was wrong in dismissing the application to subpoena witnesses. The Court of Criminal Appeal held that the appeal succeeded on other grounds and said: 'it is unnecessary to say more as to this ground than that, on the material before him, his Honour was entitled to refuse the application'.

As a member of the Aborigines Advancement League, I interviewed two of the witnesses concerned before the appeal and considered that their evidence would assist the defendant in relation to his alibi. By this time he had obtained legal representation and these witnesses and other new witnesses were called on his behalf at the retrial. Although he was again convicted, it would have been preferable that these witnesses should have been called at the original trial so that the court had more relevant evidence available to it and so that the defendant could feel that he had had a fair trial. Although the police are supposed to be interested in investigating an offence to find out the truth, it is clear that once they have charged a suspect they are unlikely to question potential witnesses for the defence with such persistence and in such detail as the defendant would like. There may be policemen who are capable of such impartiality but they must be rare. I am not pretending that I was completely impartial either. I did not put words into the witnesses' mouths but I asked questions designed to find out whether the defendant really did have an alibi. The point is that Australian criminal trials are adversary proceedings and both sides, prosecution and defence, operate within an adversary framework. It seems to be forgotten by many of the critics of rules designed for the protection of suspects and defendants (for example, the privilege against self-incrimination) that any accused person is at a substantial disadvantage with respect to the funds and facilities available for investigation and obtaining the attendance of witnesses, in comparison with the police. The fact that the trial is conducted as a contest and that police and prosecution regard it as such, often provides a justification for rules which may otherwise be thought to be too tender to defendants.

Since the Stuart case, there have been improvements in the South Australian legal aid situation. As already mentioned, since 1960 the government has provided an additional grant for the Legal Aid scheme so that practitioners can recover out-of-pocket expenses and a proportion of their professional costs instead of having to take on some cases completely free as previously.

The Department of Aboriginal Affairs has become more aware of its obligations to Aborigines charged with criminal offences and has taken a more active role in arranging legal aid, particularly in the most serious cases. The attempt by the welfare officer in one case to obtain legal representation for the defendant at the police interrogation has been discussed in Chapter 2. After the interrogation, the Department arranged for the Law Society to appoint a solicitor to act for the defendant. She was represented at the preliminary hearing and subsequently by a Port Augusta solicitor. The preliminary hearing took place at Marree, over two hundred miles from the solicitor's office. The charge here was originally murder, and in other cases of serious offences the Department has similarly arranged legal aid.[22]

Departmental welfare officers also sometimes represent Aborigines in court and this is discussed in more detail later in this chapter. The number of cases in which Aborigines are not represented at all, by either a lawyer or a welfare officer, is still considerable, although precise figures cannot be given.

Voluntary organisations have also played some part in arranging legal aid for Aborigines in South Australia. Dr Duguid, as president of the Aborigines' Advancement League, played a major part in the Stuart case (Inglis 1961: 51-2), but, apart from that case, the League has preferred other fields of action.

The secretary of the Aborigines' Friends' Association (A.F.A.) stated in an interview in March 1966 that there was a great need for legal advice for Aborigines. The Association had made representations to the authorities in the following terms (from its Annual Report for 1964, p. 8):

> In order that respect and confidence in justice and law be fostered among the aborigines the Association has strongly urged that provision should be made for legal advice and representation to be readily available in all cases of aborigines appearing before the Courts. Where this is not practical, that suitable representation be made on their behalf by

22 For example, in one case counsel was assigned after initial police interrogations but before the preliminary hearing. In another case the defendant was originally charged with murder. The Department of Aboriginal Affairs sent an application for legal aid to the Law Society. A solicitor was assigned after initial police investigations but before the date set for the preliminary hearing (D.A.A. File No. 112 of 1965).

persons other than officers of the Aborigines Affairs Department or other Government officials.

The secretary of the A.F.A. has helped Aborigines apply for legal aid but he said that in many cases it was not practicable to apply to the Law Society. The delay involved in making an application usually meant that the Aboriginal was remanded in custody for a longer period, since he was rarely able to raise bail. It was particularly difficult in country areas because of the problem of contacting the Law Society and the shortage of country solicitors.

The secretary has appeared in court on behalf of Aborigines. He regretted the legislative change regarding representation for Aborigines made in 1962. Previously section 46 of the Aborigines Act, 1934-1939 (S.A.) provided: 'At the hearing of any proceedings in respect of an offence against this Act the court may permit any person to address the court and examine and cross-examine witnesses on behalf of any aborigine.' This was repealed by the Aboriginal Affairs Act, 1962 (S.A.) and the relevant section (34) then read: 'At the hearing of any proceedings in respect of an offence against this Act the court shall permit the Director or any officer of the department to address the court and examine and cross-examine witnesses in the interests of any Aboriginal.' The secretary of the A.F.A. regarded this as reducing his standing to appear in court on behalf of Aboriginal defendants.

This view may not be correct, for the following reasons. First, the Aboriginal Affairs Act referred only to 'an offence against this Act'. Aborigines were often charged with offences against the Aboriginal Affairs Act and Regulations but many of their appearances in court were on charges under the general criminal law. The question of representation on such charges has not been the subject of legislation and is governed by the common law. Secondly, even in relation to offences against the Aboriginal Affairs Act, it is possible to argue that the court may still permit any person to appear for an Aboriginal. It will be observed that section 46 of the earlier Aborigines Act, 1934-1939 gave the court a discretion to allow any person to appear on behalf of an Aboriginal. The 1962 legislation imposed a mandatory duty on the court to allow the Director or any officer of the Department of Aboriginal Affairs to appear. It is submitted that this does not affect the power of the court under the common law to regulate its own procedure and to exercise a discretion in favour of allowing any person to appear on behalf of any defendant, including an Aboriginal.

In *O'Toole* v. *Scott*[23] the Privy Council considered the effect of section 70(2) of the Justices Act, 1902 (N.S.W.) which provided: 'The prosecutor or complainant may himself, or by his counsel or attorney, conduct his case . . . ' The appellant had been convicted by a Court of Petty Sessions, at a hearing when the case for the prosecution, with the permission of the magistrate, had been conducted by a police officer who was not the informant. The appellant argued that that police officer could not be given a right of audience because section 70(2) provided a list of the only persons who might conduct a prosecution. The Privy Council rejected this argument and held that magistrates had had from the earliest times a discretion to permit persons to act as advocates for other persons. In the Board's view section 70(2) of the Justices Act, 1902 (N.S.W.) did not deprive magistrates of their discretionary power to allow any person to conduct the case for the informant. It should be regarded as proper for a magistrate to exercise the discretion in order to secure or promote convenience and expedition and efficiency in the administration of justice (at p. 1170).

Although this case relates to the conduct of the prosecution, the same principles should apply to the conduct of the defence. In cases involving Aboriginal defendants who are often ill educated, inarticulate or shy, it would certainly make for an improvement in the quality of the administration of justice in inferior courts, if magistrates and justices adopted the practice of permitting members of voluntary organisations or other responsible citizens to appear on their behalf. This would be particularly valuable in areas where there are no lawyers.

It might even be better to impose a mandatory duty, by legislation, on the court to permit any person to appear on behalf of an Aboriginal in any type of case. At present, it remains a matter for the discretion of individual magistrates or justices; it would be desirable to establish uniformity of practice and set out explicitly the principle that Aboriginal defendants are entitled to be represented by laymen. Alternatively, the suggested provision could apply to any defendant in remote areas where no lawyers practise.[24]

[23] [1965] 2 W.L.R. 1160.

[24] Since this was written, the English Court of Appeal has held in *McKenzie* v. *McKenzie* [1970] 3 W.L.R. 472 that every party has the right to have a friend present in court beside him to assist by prompting, taking notes and quietly giving advice. While the case does not go to the extent of permitting the friend to provide full legal representation, it does confer a right on a party rather than leaving this

The A.F.A.'s main reason for suggesting representatives other than departmental officers appears to be that Aborigines do not trust government officials. The secretary informed me that in Adelaide the magistrates had adopted a practice of refusing to try an Aboriginal without a member of the Department of Aboriginal Affairs being present. But he thought it would be more useful if members of voluntary organisations appeared on behalf of Aborigines.

I believe that the Association is overpessimistic about the legal aid service. Surely it would be better to encourage Aborigines to apply for it and then complain about any deficiencies actually experienced, rather than to decide in advance that it is useless to apply? A similar attitude was expressed by a social worker in Victoria who thought in one case that it was too late to apply for legal aid and that the Committee would be likely to regard the matter as too trivial to justify legal representation. Yet when the Victorian Legal Aid Committee has been approached by the Aborigines Advancement League on behalf of other defendants, it has been most co-operative and the Aborigines have received good representation.

WESTERN AUSTRALIA

The Law Society of Western Australia was appointed by the Governor to carry out the objects of the Poor Persons Legal Assistance Act, 1928-1931.[25] The legal aid this Act provides is very limited. In the criminal field it is confined to indictable offences and the application has to be made within fourteen days after the committal for trial. There is also a fixed means test, which means that a successful applicant has to be virtually destitute. Since 1960 applications have been referred to a Committee of the Law Society for decision and assignment of solicitors to approved applicants.

The Legal Contribution Trust Act, 1967 makes provision for a more

matter to the discretion of the trial court. English lawyers concerned about the adequacy of legal representation have hailed the case as a landmark decision and forecast a big role for 'McKenzie men' in the future. But I maintain the argument that full representation by lay advocates should be permitted, at least in courts where professional legal assistance is not readily available. I am grateful to David Turnbull, a student in my Legal Aid seminar, for an interesting essay on the topic.

25 Poor Persons Legal Assistance Act, 1928 (W.A.) (No. 43 of 1928) as amended by Poor Persons Legal Assistance Act Amendment Act, 1931 (W.A.) (No. 28 of 1931).

extensive legal aid scheme and for larger funds to be made available to the Law Society to finance it. The Poor Persons Legal Assistance Act, 1928-1931 is not repealed or amended by this Act, and it is specifically provided that the powers conferred and duties imposed on the Law Society by the 1967 Act are in addition to those under the earlier Act.[26]

Even before the Legal Contribution Trust Act, 1967 was passed, the Society had granted legal aid in some cases not specifically provided for in the earlier Act. It was really operating a voluntary scheme in addition to the statutory one. For example, it did not enforce a rigid means test and it reserved a discretion to decide each individual application on its merits.

By 1967 the Law Society had adopted a policy of assigning a solicitor for committal proceedings in some cases, if requested. At an earlier date, the Law Society had advised the Department of Native Welfare that it was 'most unusual to assign counsel to represent the accused at committal proceedings, especially on a charge of murder where committal is almost a certainty'.[27] Some departmental welfare officers were unaware of the change of policy and took no steps to lodge applications on behalf of Aboriginal defendants until after committal proceedings.

When interviewed early in 1967, the secretary of the Law Society advised me that the Committee would not assign a solicitor for committal proceedings in a breaking and entering case.[28] It would wait to examine the depositions to ascertain the merits of the case. If the defendant pleaded guilty at committal proceedings, the Committee would carefully consider the case to decide whether he should be assigned a solicitor to make a plea in mitigation of sentence. The Committee can consider only applications that are forwarded to it; it seems likely that most defendants would believe that once they had pleaded guilty there was no point in applying for legal aid.

At the pre-committal stage, if a defendant wanted advice on arrest and on answering police questions, the advice would usually be provided by the secretary himself, rather than by assigning another solicitor. Some Aborigines have asked for advice at this stage, but it is not common.

Legal aid is available in the Children's Court, at inquests (provided that

[26] Legal Contribution Trust Act, 1967 (W.A.) (No. 74 of 1967) section 55.

[27] Memo. from Native Welfare Officer dated 7/5/62.

[28] Interview with Mr Wood, Law Society of Western Australia, 7/2/67. Most of the other information about the operation of the scheme was derived from this interview. It took place before the enactment of the Legal Contribution Trust Act, 1967 (W.A.).

there is a possibility of committal) and on appeals, though the merits of these are scrutinised more carefully than are the merits in proceedings at first instance.

Legal aid is not available for minor criminal matters. Since the enactment of the Legal Contribution Trust Act, 1967 it would be open to the Committee to approve aid in such cases. When interviewed, the secretary stated that he did not foresee that the legal aid scheme would ever be extended to cover minor criminal matters. He hoped that the scheme would be extended to a wider class of people, but not that its coverage would be extended for those poor persons already covered. The policy of the Committee regarding minor criminal cases remains the same, though some members of the Committee indicated recently (early 1974) that they would like the scheme to extend to representation in these cases, if sufficient resources were available.

According to the secretary, in deciding whether or not to grant legal aid there are no distinctions made between Aborigines and other defendants. The Committee uses the same criteria. He said that perhaps there was a slight tendency to help Aborigines more, because if the Native Welfare Department was sponsoring them, the Society knew the solicitor would be paid. But this would not prevent the Committee rejecting an application, in appropriate circumstances. If an Aboriginal with a long list of prior convictions wanted to plead not guilty, the Committee would still scrutinise the merits of his defence in the particular case and decide whether to grant legal aid or not. If he seemed to have grounds for pleading not guilty his prior convictions would not debar him from receiving aid. The same would apply to a white defendant with prior convictions.

The reference to the Native Welfare Department's sponsorship of legal aid applications requires explanation. A brief history of the special arrangements made between the Native Welfare Department and the Law Society regarding legal aid for Aborigines follows.[29]

In 1945 the Native Welfare Department clearly recognised that one of its duties was to provide representation for Aborigines appearing in court. It accepted that in the case of any 'Native' (as defined in the Native Welfare Act) who was unable to pay for counsel, it was the duty and responsibility of the Department to do so.[30] The recognition of this duty

[29] Mainly drawn from Native Welfare Department file 497/52.

[30] Memo. to Minister for Native Welfare from Commissioner of Native Welfare 14/1/57, confirming the policy adopted earlier.

extended only to indictable offences, however, and in other cases representation by welfare officers was usually considered adequate.

The District Officers' Conference in 1953 adopted the principle that a local solicitor could be engaged at departmental expense for either an opinion or a court appearance at the discretion of the District Office. Also in 1953 five Aboriginal criminal cases were accepted under the Poor Persons Legal Assistance Act, 1928-1931 (W.A.). Apart from these five cases the Department briefed counsel and paid ordinary counsel fees in all cases in which it intervened until 1957.

In 1957 part-Aborigines were brought within the Poor Persons Legal Assistance Act. The Native Welfare Department continued to accept responsibility for the provision of legal representation to full-bloods. It is interesting to note that the Poor Persons Legal Assistance Act did not discriminate between Aborigines and other poor persons and the exclusion of all Aborigines from the normal legal aid scheme prior to 1957 was due to ministerial policy and not the terms of the legislation. The Law Society wrote:[31]

> The Council feels that it is not competent to express an opinion so far as the question is a matter of departmental policy as its function is merely to administer the Act and that everyone irrespective of colour who satisfies the requirements of the Act should, subject to the discretionary power conferred on the Society, be granted assistance.

It did not matter to the Aboriginal defendant whether the counsel who represented him was briefed direct by the Native Welfare Department or was assigned under the Poor Persons Legal Assistance Act. From the point of view of the Department the latter procedure saved payments from its 'Relief to Natives' Fund.

In 1960 the Native Welfare Department offered, in the case of all applications forwarded by the Department acting as agent for particular Aborigines, to guarantee the costs and fees assessed and certified by the Law Society. The Department also suggested that the benefits of the Act should be extended to include full-blood Aborigines. The Society accepted these proposals.

The offer was made on the understanding that, amongst other things:

1. The assessment of costs was made according to the circumstances of the applicant.

[31] Letter from the Law Society to the Under Secretary for Law 17/4/57.

2. Accounts were not submitted to the Department until difficulty in recovery of costs had been experienced.

The Department understood that these conditions had also been accepted by the Law Society, but it subsequently became clear that the Society was not in fact assessing the costs on the basis of the Aboriginal applicant's ability to pay and was submitting accounts direct to the Department without attempting to obtain payment from the Aboriginal concerned. The Department then agreed to continue referring applications on this basis. The result was that the Department undertook to pay the assigned solicitor the costs certified by the Law Society, which usually amounted to about 60 per cent of normal fees plus full disbursements. Thus solicitors taking Native Welfare cases were paid more than they would receive if they acted for a white who was as poor as most Aboriginal defendants.[32] In such cases the Law Society would usually certify no costs and the assisted person would be liable to pay only the disbursements.

The Law Society also stated that its policy was that the Department, except in exceptional circumstances, should ask the Society to assign practitioners to assist Aborigines only when the circumstances were serious—for example, when an Aboriginal was charged with a serious criminal offence, such as murder.

Appendix 10 sets out all criminal cases which were referred to the Law Society for legal aid by the Department of Native Welfare from April 1957 to 1966. This table covers all Aboriginal defendants who approached the Law Society in this period. Even if the original approach was made by the Aboriginal himself the Law Society advised the Department and asked whether it was sponsoring the application, so such cases appear in this list. In most cases, the initiative for seeking legal aid came from the Department rather than from the Aboriginal concerned.

From 1956/57 to 1964/65 annual expenditure by the Native Welfare Department on legal aid and legal costs (including costs in civil cases) was: 1956/57 $734.65; 1957/58 $982.49; 1958/59 not available; 1959/60 $440.56; 1960/61 $766.60; 1961/62 $2247.98; 1962/63 $1250.60;

[32] 'In the great majority of cases where the assisted person is assigned at the request of your Department, it is obvious from the application that the assisted native could not pay costs.' Letter from Law Society to Native Welfare Department 16/7/65.

1963/64 not available; 1964/65 $2922.[33] In reading these figures and the table in Appendix 10 it should be remembered that only part-Aborigines were referred for legal aid between 1957 and 1960, so no full-bloods appear in Appendix 10 for those years, although costs incurred on behalf of full-bloods in briefing private counsel would be included in figures given in the previous sentence.

It will be observed that almost all the cases which have been referred to the Law Society have been for serious indictable offences. There have been occasions when the Department has asked the Society to assign a practitioner because of exceptional circumstances, but generally speaking, legal aid has been granted only for the most serious offences. The Law Society has not defined precisely what it means by 'exceptional circumstances'. It regarded a case in which an Aboriginal boy of considerable promise was charged in the Children's Court with carnal knowledge as falling into this category and therefore granted legal aid. Thus it is apparent that the arrangement between the Law Society and the Native Welfare Department did not even cover all indictable offences as a general rule.

If a comparison is made of the number of Aboriginal defendants who appeared before courts each year, and the number referred to the Law Society, it will be seen how few were reached by the legal aid scheme. In 1965 Aborigines were charged with 7491 offences, resulting in 7357 convictions. These charges included twenty-eight heard in higher courts, so that there must have been more than twenty-eight indictable offences charged, since some were decided summarily in lower courts (figures from Commonwealth Statistician). In that year only thirteen defendants were referred to the Law Society by the Native Welfare Department (Appendix 10). Private legal representation was arranged for at least three of the other defendants, but at least eight Aboriginal defendants who appeared in superior courts had no legal representation at all. Information on these superior court cases is set out in tabular form in Appendix 11. From this it appears that most of the defendants who were not legally represented pleaded guilty, in most cases to charges of breaking and entering. Although counsel may be considered less necessary in cases where the defendant pleads guilty than in cases where he wants to raise a

[33] *Report of the Special Committee on Native Matters 1958* and *Annual Reports*, Commissioner of Native Welfare, for years ending 30th June 1957, 1958, 1960, 1961, 1962, 1963 and 1965.

defence, it is still fair to say that a lawyer appearing on a plea in mitigation of sentence can make a difference to the sentence.

The former Chief Crown Prosecutor agreed that the absence of legal representation on pleas of guilty was a big gap in the legal aid scheme. He did not agree that this meant Aborigines received harsher sentences than whites in this type of case. All judges refused to sentence an Aboriginal until they had a report from the Native Welfare Department. He thought the departmental reports were usually good, because they say what they can in the defendant's favour but also present the other side of the picture.

Nevertheless, a Native Welfare Department report, however accurate, is hardly a substitute for a professional advocate making a plea in mitigation. Here, as at every other stage in criminal proceedings, defence counsel operates within an adversary system and in the normal case he is free to decide which character witnesses and what other evidence he will adduce on behalf of the defendant and which witnesses he will *not* call. Some inroads into this system have been made by the judge's power to call for a pre-sentence or psychiatric report. In the case of an Aboriginal, a Native Welfare Department report provides an additional source of information which may be adverse to him and which would not necessarily be supplied by a lawyer acting as a partisan for his client. This is not to say that the welfare officer who prepares the report is acting improperly in presenting all information available to him, but simply to point out that his function and the way he approaches the defendant are different from those of an advocate. This necessarily puts the Aboriginal defendant in a different position from that of a white defendant who is legally represented on a plea of guilty. Even if the Native Welfare Department report does not contain any material adverse to the defendant, it will not necessarily contain all the material favourable to him which a lawyer would think of including. A professional lawyer is more likely than a legally untrained welfare officer to adopt the same categories of reference as the judge.

Unfortunately no comparative information is available on the sentences imposed on whites in similar cases to these—that is, where they have pleaded guilty to breaking and entering charges. Nevertheless, it is clear that quite substantial sentences have been imposed on most of these Aboriginal defendants and it is suggested that legal representation should have been made available to them. In a resolution unanimously adopted in 1964 the House of Delegates of the American Bar Association stated

(Silverstein 1965: 2): 'Counsel should be provided at least in all cases where any serious penalty may be imposed and since, in fact, the advice and assistance of counsel would be desirable in all cases, the objective should be to extend rather than to limit the right to counsel.' This is an appropriate aim in Australia too.

The former Chief Crown Prosecutor suggested that a procedure could be instituted by which young counsel could take 'dock briefs'. They usually learn how to conduct trials by sitting at the back of the court. They could easily appear for defendants who have pleaded guilty and make a plea in mitigation, if they are going to be in court anyway. This seems an eminently sensible suggestion. Possibly it would need judicial or legislative encouragement to establish it firmly. Or perhaps the Law Society would be prepared to modify its attitude to representation on pleas of guilty if the government would provide a fund to enable nominal fees to be paid in such cases. These cases would undoubtedly provide good experience for young practitioners, and the system could possibly also be extended to cover applications for bail and other procedural matters.

The 'dock brief' procedure in England (Jackson 1964: 141) required payment of £2.4.6d. by the defendant and was available for the conduct of a complete defence. As far as Aborigines are concerned, it would be unsatisfactory to copy the English model exactly. Many Aborigines would not be able to produce even the equivalent of £2.4.6d. This method suffers from the defect that it gives very little time for the preparation of the defence. For these reasons, what is suggested here is a modified form of the 'dock brief' procedure. It should be available free to any poor defendant who wants help with a plea in mitigation or with an application for bail or other simple procedural application. He should be entitled to select any solicitor or barrister present in court to assist him in such circumstances. The funds required to make this coverage complete in superior courts would not be very large, if nominal fees only were allowed to counsel. Another objection which could possibly be made to this suggestion is that counsel would not be able to give satisfactory service to the paying client on whose behalf he is attending court if required to spend too much time and effort on 'dock briefs' before his private client's case is reached. There may be some merit in this objection. Possibly the scheme could be started on an experimental basis. If successful, it could then be extended to inferior courts also.

The Law Society's legal aid scheme provided representation for Aborigines in only a minute proportion of all Aboriginal cases. This would not matter, if Aborigines were adequately represented by lawyers whose services were secured privately or by welfare officers in the remainder of cases.

Appendix 2.26 shows the number of Aborigines in the Ten Towns Sample who had the assistance of the different classes of representatives (lawyers arranged privately, lawyers assigned by legal aid, or welfare officers), and the number who were not represented at all. It also provides a comparison with white defendants in these respects. From this it is clear that Aborigines less often obtain legal representation. Only 2 per cent of Aborigines in the Sample were represented by lawyers, compared with over 5 per cent of white defendants.

THE ROLE OF WELFARE OFFICERS

The Commissioner of Native Welfare in Western Australia claimed that Aborigines are in a better position than whites of the same socio-economic status as far as representation is concerned because they have welfare officers to represent them in court. To the extent that welfare officers do appear in court on behalf of Aborigines and do succeed in representing their interests in the same way that a lawyer might do, this is a fair claim.

Welfare officers do represent Aborigines in a number of cases every year, or are at least present in court when Aboriginal defendants are tried. The frequency of welfare officers' attendance at court is shown in Appendix 2.26. This table demonstrates that there are many cases in which Aborigines do not have any representation at all, even by welfare officers.

Some welfare officers do manage to defend their 'client's' interests ably and can be compared favourably with some solicitors. In general, though, such officers cannot be expected to be efficient advocates for Aboriginal defendants for the following reasons. First, they are not legally trained and therefore do not know the appropriate arguments which may be raised in many cases.

Second, and more fundamentally, welfare officers have varying views of their functions in court: some do not necessarily accept the duty of an advocate to his client. There may be some merit in such a welfare officer's contention that his function is analogous to a social worker rather than a lawyer. Thus, it might be proper for him to counsel his client to plead guilty, for example, in circumstances where a lawyer's duty would be to advise against such a plea. He might take the view that the experience of confession would be cathartic and could provide the basis for constructive change in his client's behaviour. However, many welfare officers are untrained and appear to have little psychological understanding of the Aboriginal people with whom they work. It appeared to me that their advice to plead guilty often rested on attitudes of disapproval and moralistic reactions to alleged offences rather than on any well considered view of what would be most helpful for the Aboriginal defendant.

In these circumstances, and particularly in view of the lack of lawyers in remote areas, I prefer the alternative view of the welfare officer's duty, that adopted by the Native Welfare Department in Western Australia. The Department issued instructions that the principle laid down in *Bolton* v. *Neilsen*[34] should still apply to departmental representation of Aborigines in court, even though the position of Protector no longer exists.[35] In the course of his judgment in that case Dwyer C.J. said (at p. 51):

> The protector may be said to be somewhat in the position of an advocate in ordinary practice in the courts. It is not for him to constitute himself the judge whether a native is guilty or not; it is for him to act on behalf of the accused person to the best advantage, so long as he does not manufacture or aid in the fabrication of evidence or wilfully mislead or deceive.

The decision specifically related to the approval of a plea of guilty but the remark applies equally to the duty of a welfare officer conducting a defence for an Aboriginal who has pleaded not guilty. Nevertheless, some welfare officers do not regard themselves as advocates and instead act as character witnesses. This may be quite valuable in itself, but it does not give the Aboriginal defendant the same protection as if he were represented by someone who could put forward every legal defence available.

Even if the welfare officer does accept the view that he should act as an advocate, he may face difficulty in giving effect to that intention. As he has not been socialised into the legal profession he cannot be expected to have the same understanding of professional ethics as a fully qualified lawyer. And in some situations even the trained advocate may have difficulty knowing where his professional duty lies.

The problem is particularly acute in relation to advice as to plea. What

[34] (1951) 53 W.A.L.R. 48.

[35] Native Welfare Department Instruction Manual. A later publication of the Department does not refer specifically to that decision but preserves the same principle (*Legal Representation for Aborigines: Notes for Guidance of Field Officers* (1969), p. 16. Perth: Department of Native Welfare).

should a lawyer or welfare officer do if he believes his client to be guilty? In one Western Australian case (discussed briefly in Chapter 2) the welfare officer had grounds for believing the Aboriginal defendant to be guilty, in the sense that he had committed the offence, since he had made a confession to the police. This, however, was not admissible in evidence, because of the provisions of section 31 of the Native Welfare Act. It appeared that the police had no admissible evidence to offer.

The duty of a lawyer (and by analogy, the welfare officer) in such a case is not entirely clear. Where counsel believes his client to be guilty but the client persists in pleading not guilty, the lawyer is faced with the competing demands of a duty to his client and to the court.[36] It is now settled that if a defendant makes a confession of guilt to counsel before trial, his barrister is entitled to withdraw from the case. Otherwise he would be seriously handicapped in presenting the defence. But if the confession is made in the course of proceedings, counsel should usually continue to act for his client. He must then take care not to mislead the court by allowing his client to give perjured evidence or by suggesting that some other innocent person may be guilty of the crime.[37]

Though it may be difficult for the layman to comprehend how a lawyer can ethically defend a man he knows to be guilty, the lawyer understands that a plea of not guilty is not an assertion of innocence but an invitation to the prosecution to establish guilt by admissible evidence, if it can. Sawer suggests (p. 32) this should be made clear by abandoning the phrases 'guilty/not guilty' and allowing counsel to say that the charge is contested or not contested.

The leading Australian case, appropriately enough, involved an Aboriginal defendant. In *Tuckiar* v. *R.*[38] the conviction for murder of a 'completely uncivilized aboriginal native' was quashed by the High Court because of the way in which the trial judge had directed the jury. During the trial, counsel for the accused had heard a confession from his client and had then said in open court that he was in the worst predicament of his legal career. After the Aboriginal had been convicted, his counsel

[36] The question is canvassed in depth in Sawer 1971. I wish to thank Professor Sawer for bringing the issue to my attention and making available his paper before its publication.

[37] Barry (1941: 203) discussing a ruling of the English Bar Council in 1915. This ruling is still in effect (Boulton 1971: 71-3).

[38] (1934) 52 C.L.R. 335. See also 'Responsibility of Defending Counsel', *A.L.J.* **9** (1935).

again made a statement in open court. This time he said that his client had admitted to him that the more serious evidence against him was true. The appeal court regarded counsel's action in making these public statements as improper.

> He had a plain duty, both to his client and the Court, to press such rational considerations as the evidence fairly gave rise to in favour of complete acquittal or conviction of manslaughter only . . . Whether he be in fact guilty or not, a prisoner is, in point of law, entitled to acquittal from any charge which the evidence fails to establish that he committed, and it is not incumbent on his counsel by abandoning his defence to deprive him of the benefit of such rational arguments as fairly arise on the proofs submitted.[39]

It is of some interest that this statement of defence counsel's duty has been adopted by the Victorian Public Solicitor as a useful test in considering applications for legal assistance. Legal aid will be recommended if there is any evidence which will support rational arguments by counsel on the accused's behalf at trial or if it appears that the prosecution will be unable to establish, by admissible evidence, its case against the defendant (Willis 1973: 253-4).

Thus, in the Western Australian case if the Aboriginal accused had definitely wanted to plead not guilty, it would have been proper for the welfare officer to appear for him in the role of advocate and require the prosecution to offer any admissible evidence available. As the police apparently had no evidence other than the inadmissible confession, the defendant would then have been acquitted.

But this still does not determine the welfare officer's duty if the Aboriginal defendant is undecided as to his plea. Is it open to the welfare officer to put pressure on the Aboriginal to plead guilty in these circumstances, where he believes he is morally guilty? Counsel's duty here is governed by *R.* v. *Turner*.[40] The court stressed that the defendant must retain a free choice to decide on his plea but that it is proper for counsel to advise him to plead guilty. However, the implication is that counsel should so advise taking into account legal considerations, including his assessment of the likelihood of a more lenient sentence on a plea of guilty. It seems to me that he should consider the legal effect of any evidence

[39] *Tuckiar* v. *R.* (1934) 52 C.L.R. 335, 346 *per* Gavan Duffy C.J., Dixon, Evatt and McTiernan JJ.

[40] [1970] 2 All E.R. 281.

which will be led. He should disregard any evidence which he considers will be inadmissible. So he should not advise a guilty plea on the strength of a confession which will not be admitted in evidence because of a rule of law forbidding its introduction. It should be noted that it is not only Aborigines who may make inadmissible confessions. Even in jurisdictions where nothing like section 31 of the Native Welfare Act is in force, Aboriginal defendants and others may confess to the police yet the court will not admit the confession if it is held not to be voluntary.

Section 31 expressed a legislative policy that Aborigines required special protection, probably because they were believed to be susceptible to suggestion and to be likely to make false confessions. A welfare officer should be particularly careful, therefore, not to believe that an apparent confession of guilt is necessarily true and not to exercise undue influence on his client in relation to his plea. It appeared to me in the Western Australian case referred to above that the welfare officer acted in a paternalistic way and influenced the Aboriginal to plead guilty. Despite the view of the court in *R.* v. *Turner* (at p. 285) that counsel must be free to give advice, even in strong terms, it is suggested that the position may be otherwise where the defendant is an Aboriginal. In order to preserve to the accused a real freedom of choice whether to plead guilty or not guilty it will be necessary for counsel to moderate the expression of his view and not express it too strongly.

In some cases it is really impossible for a welfare officer to act as an advocate. Where the welfare officer is launching the prosecution against an Aboriginal, it is impossible for him also to appear as defence counsel! Similarly, where two Aborigines are the antagonists in a particular litigious battle it is impossible for one welfare officer to represent them both adequately, and most do not even attempt to represent more than one side. This is sharply revealed in 'neglected children' actions. The welfare officer may be regarded as acting on behalf of the Aboriginal children against the parents. Alternatively, he may be regarded as taking action adverse to the Aboriginal family. Whichever way the situation is viewed, the interests of the Aboriginal parents are not adequately protected unless they have independent representation.

At an earlier period police officers, amongst others, were appointed as honorary Protectors of Aborigines. One of their duties as Protectors was to appear in court on behalf of Aboriginal defendants. The Moseley Royal Commission in Western Australia in 1935 recommended that police should not be appointed to this position (p. 21):

> . . . chiefly . . . because, when called upon to take police action against a native, a constable cannot satisfactorily at the same time act as his Protector. It must necessarily occur that the constable will be confronted with two conflicting sets of instructions, one from his superior police officer and the other from the Divisional Protector. I cannot see how such a system can be successful.

The Bateman Survey of Native Affairs (1948: 22-3) also drew attention to objectionable features of the practice. Finally, the Native Welfare Act, 1963 abolished the Protectorship system and provided instead for 'representatives'. Theoretically, a police officer could still be appointed as a 'representative', but in practice none has been and there is a policy against such appointments.[41]

The main objection to the Police Protector system was that it is impossible for one person to combine satisfactorily and fairly the two functions of prosecution and defence. Unfortunately, the same situation still arises in relation to welfare officers in some cases. The frequency of such cases is not great. Obviously a welfare officer is not in the position of informant or prosecutor against an Aboriginal as often as a police officer is. Nevertheless, the objection in principle is the same and can only be met by ensuring that the Aboriginal has independent representation. No matter how much the departmental officer may have the welfare of the Aboriginal population at heart, he inevitably faces a conflict of interest if he is charging an Aboriginal with, for example, wilful damage to departmental property. As a government officer, the chief consideration in his mind is likely to be the protection of government property. A minority of welfare officers also appeared to have little genuine interest in the welfare of Aborigines and to see their chief function as helping the police with a difficult section of the population and preventing Aborigines from being a nuisance to the rest of the community.[42]

The same problem arises in South Australia and a case from that State illustrates the need for independent legal representation whenever the Department is in effect the adversary of the Aboriginal defendant. Four Aboriginal boys were charged in the Juvenile Court at Port Augusta with

41 No. 79 of 1963 (W.A.) section 12. The Act came into force on 1 July 1964. In Queensland police ceased to act as Protectors in 1965. Now clerks of courts are Protectors (personal communication from Professor C.M. Tatz).

42 In one case a welfare officer giving evidence said that although the Aboriginal defendant had caused a small amount of damage to government property, the Department regarded it seriously. Another welfare officer stated in an interview that he had asked one Aboriginal to beat up another one.

storebreaking, escaping from legal custody, and wilful damage. The charges were based on incidents on an Aboriginal reserve and the property allegedly stolen was government property. The boys were tribal Aborigines with very limited understanding of English. An interpreter was provided for them in court but they were not legally represented. They pleaded guilty through the interpreter to all the charges. I was present in the court and heard the prosecutor present considerable detail in amplification of the charges. The magistrate questioned the defendants about their motives. They claimed they stole because they were cold and hungry. A senior officer of the Department of Aboriginal Affairs was then asked by the magistrate to assist the court. He was not sworn as a witness but gave information about conditions on the reserve, claiming that if the boys were hungry it was their own doing, because they could have taken work that was offered to them. He also gave the impression that these four boys were the only ones involved in lawbreaking. The representative of the Department of Social Welfare said only that he had no objection to a committal of these boys, and that no written reports were available to assist the magistrate.

In sentencing the boys the magistrate said that if the only reason they had done these things was because they were really hungry, because they could not obtain work, he would have let them go. He also referred to the statement made by the departmental officer that they were the only boys who made trouble and who stole from the store. Each was committed to Magill Reformatory until the age of eighteen years. This sentence was perhaps appropriate in the light of the information available to the magistrate from the court hearing. If the defendants had had legal representation a very different picture might have emerged. I saw the reserve in question. It seems to me that the picture given by the departmental officer who spoke in court was misleading, both about the work available and about the number of boys involved in the offences. He did not give sworn evidence and much of what he said was hearsay, yet the magistrate relied on it to a considerable extent in deciding on the sentences to be imposed. If the defendants had had independent counsel, with a proper opportunity to investigate the case, opposing evidence could have been called to support the defendants' statements, at least in mitigation of sentence.

The case illustrates the point that government servants cannot always be relied upon to put the interests of the people whose welfare they are supposed to be promoting before those of the government itself. This being so, it seems desirable, in order that justice should be done and should be seen to be done, that in all cases where the government department is the complainant or has any interest in the prosecution of an Aboriginal, independent legal representation of the defendant should be arranged. It is not enough to arrange an interpreter, however competent, and then stack the cards against the defendants by having a prosecutor and representatives of government departments speak against them, while they are not in a position to call any witnesses on their own behalf. It may be said that if the defendants had wished they could have arranged their own legal representation and their own witnesses, but this ignores the realities of the situation. These boys, because of their inadequate knowledge of English and of legal procedure, would not have known anything about legal representation. The Department set up to promote their welfare is a suitable agent to arrange legal representation for Aborigines, even if it means that the prosecution by the Department has less chance of success or that the sentence imposed after a successful prosecution is less punitive than some of its members would like it to be.

The suggestion for independent legal representation in such cases applies to all States. In remote areas, particularly in Western Australia, it may be difficult to arrange legal representation in every such case, particularly if the offence appears minor and the sentence is not likely to be heavy. Even then, it would be desirable if the defendant had some representation, for example, another welfare officer not involved in the prosecution, or a private citizen, such as a local minister or teacher or Aboriginal friend of the court who could speak on his behalf, so that he does not feel he is alone against all the might of the law and the government.

5

THE CONDUCT OF THE COURT HEARING

CONSTITUTION OF THE TRIBUNAL

JUDICIAL OFFICERS

Most criminal cases are finally disposed of in courts of summary jurisdiction, constituted by justices of the peace or stipendiary magistrates. Appendix 2.27 sets out the constitution of the tribunals which finally determined the cases in the Ten Towns Sample.

A sizeable proportion of the cases involving Aborigines were heard by justices rather than by magistrates. Western Australia has no legislation, as South Australia does in section 43 of the Justices Act, 1921, providing that justices may exercise their jurisdiction only if there is no magistrate available. But the Western Australian Crown Law Department has advised me that justices usually exercise jurisdiction only in those circumstances. The large number of cases heard by justices indicates how seldom a magistrate is available in remote areas. The magistrate stationed in Broome is responsible for the vast area of the Kimberleys and cannot often visit other towns on his circuit.

Although no similar statistics have been compiled for South Australia it is clear that justices conduct most of the courts in outback areas. All South Australian magistrates live in Adelaide and go on circuit to country areas as required. Thus the legislative policy preferring magistrates, and the similar administrative policy in Western Australia, is defeated in outback areas by geography and the scarcity of magistrates.

Magistrates are no doubt preferred because they have some training in the law and judicial work is their full-time occupation. In Western Australia under section 7 of the Stipendiary Magistrates Act, 1957 two classes of persons are qualified for appointment as magistrates. First, there are barristers and solicitors entitled to practise in an Australian State or in the High Court of Justice in England. The others are persons who have passed the prescribed examination in law under section 25 of the Public Service Act, 1904 (W.A.). Amongst present holders of this office are representatives of both these groups.

I was advised in 1966 by the Attorney-General's office in Adelaide that in South Australia it has been the practice for many years to appoint as magistrates only persons who are practitioners of the Supreme Court.

Justices of the peace receive no formal training in law. They imbibe their knowledge of the law from the experience of sitting on the bench, from discussion with clerks of courts and the police and from training programs initiated by their own voluntary associations. This education in law to date has been grossly inadequate.

Justices are not paid for their services; they do not even receive out-of-pocket expenses. This has the advantage that, as justices, they do not have any financial interest in the outcome of a case.[1] The cost of the administration of justice is lower than it would be if only a professional judiciary were employed. The registrar of the Royal Association of Justices, South Australia, was quoted as saying that, 'unfortunately, the public tends to take justices for granted when, in fact, they are saving taxpayers' money'. He added that South Australia is the only State making a profit, in revenue, from justices and that this happy situation was related to the free services of the justice of the peace.[2]

The disadvantage is that, since time in court is unpaid time, there are pressures on justices to speed through cases so that they can return to making money. Often the local justices most willing to spend time sitting on the Bench are retired men. But old age is not necessarily a valuable judicial attribute.

The ignorance of the law of some justices is displayed in too many cases where defendants are wrongly convicted or illegally sentenced. For example, one Aboriginal in Western Australia was convicted in 1966 of the offence of 'being a Native who loitered about licensed premises'. He

[1] Compare the practice in some counties in Ontario, Canada where magistrates formerly received part of the fines imposed. I am indebted to Professor H. Glasbeek for this information.

[2] *The Australian* 28/6/69, p. 14.

was charged under section 50 (2) of the Native Welfare Act, a provision which had been repealed two years previously.[3] Two justices fined him $6 with costs of $2. In South Australia the Crown appealed on behalf of an Aboriginal defendant against the action of two justices. They had wrongly proceeded in his absence to disqualify him from holding a driving licence.

In these cases justices were clearly ignorant of the effect of relevant legislation. It is equally difficult for some of them to appreciate the more subtle aspects of law, particularly evidentiary rules. In many cases the notes of evidence made by justices strongly suggest that the evidence led was insufficient to warrant conviction. In these cases the justices ignored the law that in criminal cases the benefit of any reasonable doubt should be given to the defendant. This criticism is subject to the reservation that notes of evidence may not accurately reflect the evidence that was actually presented to the court. The justices also had the benefit of seeing the witnesses, whereas I am basing my estimate of evidence merely on the written record. But some of the cases are too glaring to be explained away in such fashion.

An extreme example is the Western Australian case in which an Aboriginal defendant was convicted of fighting on the reserve. He pleaded not guilty. The only prosecution evidence was that of the arresting policeman which is quoted verbatim from the court records.

> At 11.30 p.m. on 29/7/65 complaint received at Police Station that brawl taking place at Native Reserve. Complainant stated that [named] boys were fighting with their father and they were all drunk.
> At 9.10 a.m. on 30th I interviewed defendant who was still showing effects of liquor and when questioned re fight he stated he had been there but was not fighting and was supposed to be the peacemaker. He denied he had struck anybody and stated he had only tried to stop the fight. Fight concerned was between defendant's elder brother and their elderly father. Elder brother mentioned was struck over head with some hard object and received laceration approximately 2″ long. Defendant was informed that complainant had advised that both boys were in a fight with their father and he was arrested forthwith.

The defence evidence consisted of the statement by the defendant: 'I was not in the fight'. There was no evidence of his involvement except hearsay evidence of the statement of an unnamed complainant; evidence

[3] The Native Welfare Act, 1963 (W.A.) (No. 79 of 1963) was proclaimed on 1 July 1964.

that should have been excluded by the court. It is impossible to believe that any court that knew of the hearsay rule and honestly applied the presumption of innocence could have convicted.

Some justices convey the impression that they will believe any police evidence. It is natural in small country towns that justices and police should be friendly. It would be almost impossible in some communities for justices to maintain the aloofness from local affairs that might be expected of a superior court judge. Friendliness between police and justices is not improper in itself but it is clear that in some towns it oversteps proper bounds. I was taken by the policeman of a South Australian town to visit the local justice to inform him that he was required to sit in court the next morning. Before the court hearing began the policeman told me the justice had decided to impose a prison sentence on the defendant. In the event, the policeman, in addressing the court on penalty, stated that he did not have the defendant's record of previous convictions and he must be treated as a first offender who could only be fined.

The conversation about penalty should not have been held before the hearing whether or not the policeman was trying to influence the justice. It seems that justices do pay considerable attention to police views on the appropriate penalty. A police inspector instructed police in his district to address justices on the question of penalty to the effect that they should impose fines on Aborigines, rather than gaol terms without the option of a fine. It is clear that he thought this change of policy by the police would have a substantial effect on the sentencing policy of justices.

This fault is not confined to justices. Some magistrates are known colloquially as 'police' magistrates because of their tendency to believe police evidence. For this reason, a country solicitor advised a white client charged with stealing a small amount that it would be worth the extra costs to go before a jury. He expected that the local magistrate would convict and impose a light fine, even though the prosecution evidence was insufficient to justify a conviction. His client was very anxious to avoid a conviction because of the effect on his employment. The jury speedily acquitted him.

A conviction can have particularly serious consequences for many Aborigines. A man will not be employed on a permanent basis by the railways if he has a conviction for stealing and this is an important source of employment for Aborigines. But their inability to find legal costs means that they often consent to having charges heard summarily, even though theoretically they have the choice of insisting on a jury. Thus they run the risk of being convicted in the lower court in circumstances where a jury may have acquitted.

The extent to which justices rely on the police for information on the relevant law is also illustrated by cases in which excessive sentences were imposed under repealed legislation. Two Aborigines were sentenced by two justices to six months' imprisonment for being drunk on a reserve, although an amendment had made the maximum penalty twenty-one days.[4] One justice explained that the court had imposed an incorrect sentence because the police had charged the Aborigines under an outdated regulation.

In other cases the sentences, while valid in the sense that they fall within the maximum limits permitted by legislation, appear unduly harsh. The whole topic of judicial discretion in sentencing is discussed more extensively in Chapter 6.

Justices in the Ten Towns Sample more often imposed prison sentences than magistrates did and correspondingly less often imposed fines (Appendix 2.28). This is largely explained by the different types of offence heard by justices and magistrates (Appendix 2.29). Magistrates hear most traffic cases and proportionately fewer drunkenness cases. A distinctly different sentencing pattern emerges for these two major categories of offence (see Chapter 6).

The reason for the practice of magistrates hearing most traffic cases is unknown. It is not based on a legislative requirement since the Traffic Act, 1919 (W.A.) provides that two lay justices may hear charges arising under the Act.[5]

On the whole justices appear to be willing to impose harsher sentences than magistrates are. Possibly this is because in small country towns the justice is intimately linked with the local community and feels a need to vindicate the interests of the 'respectable' section of the community. It is a plausible hypothesis that this explains differences in sentencing between the metropolitan area and country towns in South Australia (see Chapter 6). Probably it also reflects differences in attitudes between legally trained magistrates, who comprise the Adelaide courts, and country justices.

4 Melbourne *Herald* 28/6/66. Also fieldwork notes.

5 Some sections of the Traffic Act specify that the court shall be composed of a stipendiary magistrate, but otherwise justices may constitute the court. Justices Act, 1902 (W.A.) section 20.

Occupations frequently represented amongst justices are businessmen, including storekeepers, and farmers. One clerk of courts sensibly suggested that more use might be made of government servants and bank officials, who would be more likely to be unbiased than local residents of long standing. It appears that such people are not appointed precisely because the authorities consider that they do not stay in one area long enough to be useful.

Interviews with justices were informal. Knowledge about their attitudes to Aborigines was therefore largely impressionistic. Some information about attitudes was derived from other sources, including observation of court hearings. An afternoon spent in a northern court in Western Australia provided convincing evidence that some justices have no idea of the judicial manner in which a hearing should be conducted. All defendants were Aborigines. Two justices constituted the court but one completely dominated the proceedings. When asking the first defendant, who pleaded not guilty, whether he wanted to ask any questions he said: 'We haven't got much time so you'd better make it quick.' Another defendant persisted in asking questions of the prosecution witnesses in spite of the intimidating manner of the justice.

Unfortunately it appeared that the chairman's sole knowledge of procedure was that the defendant must first ask questions, not make a statement. He kept interrupting the defendant to remind him that he must ask questions.

His assessment of the evidence was extremely prejudicial to one defendant who was convicted of being 'disorderly by creating a disturbance'. The defendant claimed that he had ended up under the table after being pushed. The justice commented: 'It's obvious then that you weren't trying to avoid a fight. Anyone who ends up under the table must be seriously involved in the disturbance.' The possibility that the defendant was an innocent victim who should not be convicted of 'creating' a disturbance was not even considered. The police evidence may have been sufficient to justify the conviction, but the manner in which that conviction was reached had all the hallmarks of an inquisition.

In a later interview with the second justice who constituted this court he defended the treatment of one defendant on the grounds that from past experience the court knew that he would ramble on for hours about irrelevant matters if unchecked. It is true that prescribed procedure justifies the court in advising defendants that they must first cross-examine and only later introduce their own evidence. But this does not excuse the impatience and discourtesy exhibited by the chairman of the court.

The interview also suggests the possibility that the second justice's attitude to this defendant was not racist but was motivated by impatience with a habitual offender. He expressed tolerant views of Aborigines and pointed out that 'those who appear in court are only a hard core; the majority are quite decent people'.

Some justices clearly exhibit racist attitudes. In May 1967 the press reported that justices in Pingelly, Western Australia, advocated flogging Aboriginal offenders because gaol was no deterrent.[6] One justice claimed to have been misquoted; he meant that he would like to have the power to order a juvenile offender to be caned, not whipped.

In the Northern Territory *certiorari* was obtained against a justice who purported to hear a charge against two Aboriginal defendants.[7] One justice constituting the court was manager of the station on which the white complainant and the Aborigines were employed. Jurisdiction was challenged on this ground but Bridge J. held that this justice was not disqualified, though it may have been injudicious for him to sit.

The successful challenge was based on a statement made by the other justice between the two summary trials that 'Natives must be kept under the thumb'. Bridge J. held that a reasonable observer was justified in concluding that there had been an improper interference with the course of justice due to a real likelihood of bias on the part of the justice of the peace.

If justices allow racial prejudice to sway their judgment they are clearly not fulfilling the spirit of their oath of office. Under the Justices Act, 1902 (W.A.), third schedule the justice promises that he will 'do equal justice to the poor and the rich and discharge the duties of my office . . . without fear, favour, or affection'. Commenting on similar words in the judge's oath, Lord Denning (1967: 359) said that they meant 'without fear of the powerful, or favour of the wealthy, without affection to one side'.

In the early period of settlement of Western Australia the British government recognised the danger that justices might be prejudiced against Aborigines. An Act of 1840 was refused assent because the

[6] Melbourne *Herald* 17/5/67 and *Age* 8/5/67, p. 10. See also letters to the editor, *Herald* 9/5/67.

[7] *R.* v. *Justices of Rankin River* (1962) 3 F.L.R. 215. Also interview with Bridge J.

Colonial Office objected to provisions conferring summary jurisdiction on justices over Aboriginal offenders, jurisdiction which could not be exercised over white offenders (Hasluck 1970: 136).

Hasluck (1970: 139-42) traces the later history of similar legislation. In 1849 summary jurisdiction over Aborigines was conferred on justices.[8] The legislation included directions about the composition of the bench; to provide a safeguard for Aboriginal defendants. The court was to be constituted of two or more justices not interested in the subject matter of the complaint, one of such justices being a guardian or sub-guardian of Aborigines or the resident magistrate of the district. Reports on convictions were to be made to the Colonial Secretary.

Later legislation removed the safeguards in the composition of the Bench. By 1893 the position was that white offenders could also be tried summarily but they could elect to go before a jury (unlike Aborigines). Aborigines in outback areas were left to the tender mercies of justices of the peace who, as representatives of the settlers, regarded the Aborigines as their natural enemies in their efforts to establish pastoral properties.

During the fieldwork period section 30(1) of the Native Welfare Act, 1963 (W.A.) provided that: 'All offences against this Act may be prosecuted in a summary way before any magistrate or, in his absence, any two justices of the peace'. This provision applied to charges against both white and Aboriginal defendants.

Although it appeared to provide the minimal protection to the defendant of requiring two justices rather than a single justice, it was subject to the provisions of sections 29 and 32 of the Justices Act, 1902 (W.A.). The proviso to section 29 empowered a single justice to hear a complaint if all parties consented. Section 32 granted jurisdiction to a single justice 'whenever no other justice usually residing in the district can be found at the time within a distance of ten miles'.

It should be observed that section 30(1) of the Native Welfare Act, 1963 referred only to offences 'against this Act'. It is understood that the Police Circular Orders made in 1960 under section 9 of the Police Act purported to offer greater protection to Aborigines. They stated that at least two justices were required to adjudicate at the hearing of any charge against a Native. It is impossible to be precise about the wording of the Circular Orders, which are treated as secret documents.[9]

[8] Act 12 Vic., No. 18 (W.A.).

[9] Information about their contents was obtained in an interview with a senior police officer. Although I made notes during the interview it is possible that these do not

It is interesting to look again at the statistical table (Appendix 2.27) showing the constitution of courts hearing charges in the Ten Towns Sample. The number of charges against Aborigines heard by a justice of the peace sitting alone is comparatively high.

Closer examination of the cases heard in one Western Australian town (not included in the Sample) in 1965 reveals that twelve charges against Aborigines were heard by a single justice. For some of these cases there is a certificate that only one justice was available within ten miles. Accordingly, jurisdiction was legitimately assumed in these cases. But for five cases, in which the charges were laid under the Native Welfare Act or the Regulations, there is no such certificate. Jurisdiction was improperly exercised in these cases. With legal advice, the Aboriginal defendants could have challenged the assumption of jurisdiction in these cases.

In at least one South Australian town many cases against Aborigines were heard by a single justice. The defendants had signed consent forms under the proviso to section 43 of the Justices Act, 1921 (S.A.). Numerous consent forms signed with a cross by illiterate Aborigines were a poignant reminder of their lack of education.

An Aboriginal is more likely to receive justice from a magistrate than from a justice. It would be simple to suggest that legislation should provide that all cases against Aborigines should be heard by magistrates. But this would not necessarily solve the problems. In remote areas, unless current bail practice is substantially modified, such a requirement could itself produce injustice. In practice all juvenile cases in the Kimberleys are reserved for the magistrate. In one case Aboriginal boys were kept in custody for a considerable period waiting for the magistrate's visit. The charges were then dismissed because there was no police evidence other than an inadmissible confession. It is probable that by having their case heard by a magistrate the defendants avoided conviction and a sentence of imprisonment. But it is unfortunate that they were incarcerated for any period at all.

In my view a desirable objective in the administration of justice in the lower courts is the abolition of lay justices. The injustices produced by people untrained in law or procedure, and without any feeling for judicial tradition, outweigh any supposed advantages. An affluent community should not be content with justice on the cheap.

---

accurately record the terms of the Circular Orders because there may be qualifications to the general statement quoted here.

It is unlikely that this reform will occur for a long time. The difficulties in the way of appointing trained magistrates to all areas are formidable. The following recommendations are made on the assumption that the honorary justice system will continue.

First, every effort should be made to improve the training of justices. Some commendable steps in this direction have been taken through the initiative of justices themselves. The Royal Victorian Association of Honorary Justices runs a training course at which lectures are given by law professors and others. Associations of justices in South Australia and Western Australia have arranged regional conferences at which local magistrates have appeared with other guest speakers.[10]

Second, thought should be given to the appointment of a wider range of people as justices. So far there are very few Aboriginal justices. Sir Douglas Nicholls is a notable exception in Victoria. One factor inhibiting further appointments is the general level of education amongst the Aboriginal community. In one South Australian town it was considered that a local Aboriginal would make a good justice, but for the fact that he was illiterate. It is not suggested that a lower educational standard should be accepted for Aboriginal justices, although men like this should be eligible as assessors if special Aboriginal courts are ever set up (see Chapter 9). But amongst the younger generation of Aborigines, who have had greater access to formal education, candidates should be considered. The other source of suitable justices, so far largely untapped, consists of government servants, bank employees and teachers.

Third, greater control should be exercised over cases heard by justices. Legislation should restrict their powers as much as possible, consistent with practical limitations imposed by the shortage of trained magistrates. Cases heard by justices should be subject to automatic review, either by the local magistrate or by a specially appointed officer of the Crown Law or similar department. The supervisory officer should consider the validity of the exercise of jurisdiction; whether convictions appear justified by the evidence recorded; whether sentences are invalid or appear unduly harsh.

The Crown Law Department in Western Australia audits court records and occasionally annotations appear querying aspects of procedure. This

[10] Information on justices' and magistrates' meetings was obtained from the following sources: in South Australia I attended a meeting; Mr McGuigan, S.M., supplied copies of papers delivered at one Western Australian meeting; a Victorian conference of magistrates was reported in *Police Life* 15/8/67, p. 8.

audit is usually too late to be effective from the defendant's point of view. Rarely is any action taken to set aside wrongful convictions or sentences. There is no compensation for defendants who have already served gaol terms invalidly imposed. Effective protection of defendants requires prompt examination of court records and power to intervene quickly when injustice is apparent. Perhaps an itinerant reviewing officer would be the best solution.

JURIES

Few Aboriginal defendants are tried by juries. In the Ten Towns Sample only one case was so decided (Appendix 2.27). The nine cases heard by a judge alone were cases in which the defendant pleaded guilty at the preliminary hearing and was committed for sentence.

Similarly in South Australia a senior officer of the Department of Aboriginal Affairs stated that he could not recall a case for some years where a jury had tried an Aboriginal defendant. Most cases in superior courts were settled by guilty pleas.[11]

Although trial by jury is infrequent in the Aboriginal context, the jury system will be briefly examined to see whether its operation has a discriminatory effect on Aborigines. It may be that Aboriginal defendants are well advised to enter guilty pleas to indictable offences and avoid facing a jury. But if it appears that juries are likely to give Aborigines a fair trial, then it may be better for these defendants to exercise the right to trial by jury, requiring the prosecution to prove its case. The same considerations apply where defendants have consented to summary trial in lieu of jury trial.

Hasluck shows (1970: 131-4) that in the nineteenth century in cases involving an Aboriginal defendant and an Aboriginal victim, such as tribal murder, juries displayed sympathy for the defendant. They either convicted with a recommendation for mercy or failed to agree on a verdict. But when whites were charged with serious offences against Aborigines convictions were very difficult to obtain (pp. 143-6).

More recently Mr Justice Kriewaldt (1960) thought that juries should not be used in the trial of Aborigines in the Northern Territory, because they brought in too many verdicts of acquittal. He believed that many white citizens held the view that the ordinary criminal law should not be

[11] But more recently an Aboriginal was tried by a jury at Port Augusta (*Trans-continental* 16/4/70 and *Advertiser* 8/4/70).

applied to Aborigines and that they gave effect to this view when acting as jurors. In *R.* v. *Willie* he emphasised to the jury that they must judge the case as if the accused were a white person. The jury brought in a verdict of guilty (pp. 16-17). Kriewaldt also mentioned that Aborigines (by which he meant full-bloods) did not sit on juries in the Northern Territory.[12]

The Crown Prosecutor, Mr Scarfe, stated in an interview on 10 May 1966 that Aborigines had never sat on juries in South Australia. Until December 1965 by section 11 of the Juries Act, 1927-1937 persons qualified for jury service were men under sixty-five who were electors for the Legislative Council. Eligibility for enrolment as an elector depended primarily on a property qualification (section 20 of the Constitution Act, 1934-1936). Few Aborigines had the requisite qualifications. In 1965 the Juries Act was amended so that all persons who are electors for the House of Assembly and are twenty-five or over are qualified for jury service.[13] The franchise for the Assembly is wider than for the Council (section 33 of the Constitution Act); thus more Aborigines should now be eligible for jury service.

Qualifications for jury service in Western Australia are wider and several part-Aborigines have been included in jury panels; some have actually served as jurors. Section 4 of the Juries Act, 1957 (W.A.) provides that any person between the age of twenty-one (now eighteen) and sixty-five years who is enrolled as an elector for the Legislative Assembly is qualified and liable to serve as a juror. Section 5 disqualifies anyone who 'cannot read and understand the English language'. Many older Aborigines would be excluded by this provision but, with the spread of formal education, most younger Aborigines will be eligible for jury service.

A part-Aboriginal woman in a town in the Kimberleys was charged with the murder of her husband. In a list of persons whose names were selected as a jury panel and who were not summoned six Aborigines appear. One was the accused herself; the others were not summoned as jurors either because they were her relatives or because they were illiterate. The composition of the jury that heard the case is not precisely known. It is likely to have been an all-white jury, as the then Chief

[12] Aborigines are now eligible for jury service in the Northern Territory. It is not known whether any have sat on juries (see Tatz 1964a: 255).

[13] Juries Act Amendment Act, 1965 (S.A.) (No. 28 of 1965). Section 10 amends section 11 of the principal Act.

Crown Prosecutor informed me that he would always 'stand aside' an Aboriginal from a jury if the defendant were an Aboriginal.

In notes made before trial the police anticipated that the main line of defence would be on the basis of sympathy and that this defence would be strengthened upon a trial before a local jury. In the result the jury brought in a verdict of guilty of manslaughter with a strong recommendation for mercy. The police notes suggest that racial lines are not rigidly drawn in this town: 'She is considered a Native by the Native Affairs Department but not so by the people of the town who have known her possibly all her life.'

Although the Chief Crown Prosecutor indicated that he would 'stand aside' an Aboriginal in any case involving an Aboriginal defendant, he would not necessarily follow this procedure in other cases. He recalled at least one Aboriginal sitting on a jury in Perth. In his view white juries exhibited prejudice against Aboriginal defendants in any case where the victim was white. But in cases involving only Aborigines juries were inclined to be more lenient.

It remained difficult to obtain a conviction from a jury when a white defendant was charged with a serious offence against an Aboriginal. Only one such case could be found and the defendant was acquitted of unlawful wounding although the magistrate who conducted the trial thought that this verdict was against the weight of the evidence. Of course the prosecution does not stand aside white jurors merely on the grounds of race in such cases.

Aborigines are eligible for jury service in Victoria on the same basis as whites are.[14]

In recent years Aboriginal defendants have begun to challenge jury selection; so far without success. In *R.* v. *Grant and Lovett*[15] the defendants attempted to 'challenge the array'. Counsel for Lovett, an Aboriginal, argued that the jury was not representative of the community and did not offer his client a trial by his peers since it had no Aboriginal on it; nor did it have anyone following the same occupation as his client, a

[14] Juries Act 1967 (Vic.) (Act No. 7651) section 4: 'enrolled as an elector for the Legislative Assembly'. See the Constitution Act Amendment Act 1958 (Vic.) (No. 6224) sections 102 and 103.

[15] [1972] V.R. 423. Similarly, a South Australian Aboriginal defendant recently attacked the selection of the jury empanelled to try him, but the judge held there was no evidence that the sheriff had deliberately excluded Aborigines. *R.* v. *Gibson*, Supreme Court of South Australia, November 1973, Bright J. Similar challenges have been made in some cases in New South Wales.

labourer. It was also contended that the panel was not 'chosen indifferently'.

The trial judge held, however, that the mere showing that there was no Aboriginal on the jury panel was not sufficient; nor did it matter that 'the jury is of a composition which is not to the liking of the accused'. There was no evidence that the sheriff had failed to follow the requirements of the Juries Act. In order for the challenge to succeed it would have had to be established that the sheriff had been guilty of some default of duty in summoning the panel for jury service. The judge did refer to early cases in which a sheriff had been influenced by bias or prejudice in relation to the political views or religion of the accused. This seems to leave the way open for a successful challenge in future, but the necessary evidence would be difficult to obtain. Presumably it would have to be shown that the sheriff deliberately excluded Aboriginal names. It should be noted that the challenge was to the whole panel of persons summoned for jury service (the array), not to the twelve persons who actually constituted the jury that tried the defendants.

Similarly in the United States an attack can only be made on the initial selection of the jury list, not on the exercise of the prosecutor's challenges to particular jurymen, even though the effect of the latter is to keep non-whites off the jury. Some successful attacks on racial discrimination in jury selection have been made under the American Constitution by both blacks and American Indians. In *State of South Dakota* v. *Adolph Plentyhorse*,[16] for example, evidence was led that Indians constituted 29·9 per cent of the total population of the county in which the Indian defendant was tried but that only about 8 per cent were represented on the county jury list for a three-year period. The Supreme Court of South Dakota accepted this as sufficient evidence of Indian exclusion from juries and held that the defendant's motion to quash the jury panel should have been granted and a new panel ordered. But this is not to say that a defendant is entitled to have a jury selected to accord proportionate representation to different racial groups. All that the doctrine of equal protection requires (p. 656) is that members of his race have not been intentionally excluded from the jury because of race or colour.

Thus the law is directed to ensuring that the jury is impartially selected, rather than that it ends up with a particular racial composition. In this United States law resembles Australian law, even though the American

[16] 184 N.W. 2d 654 (1971).

defendant can rely on an entrenched constitutional Bill of Rights. The different success rate in jury challenges seems to be due to the thoroughness of data collection by the American lawyers and the greater willingness of courts in that country to listen to statistical evidence, together with greater sensitivity to racial issues. If Australian lawyers attempted to collect similar evidence for presentation to courts they would face formidable obstacles. In the Victorian case, for example, the judge said that the court's practice was that a copy of the panel was never made available to, or permitted to be perused by, counsel for the accused. He referred to the express prohibition in section 21(2) of the Juries Act 1967 in support of this rule of practice.[17]

Nevertheless, this should not be a bar to proper empirical research *after* trials have been concluded. If such research produces evidence of a consistent pattern of exclusion of Aborigines from jury panels, defence counsel should continue to challenge the juries so that the issue is at least kept constantly before those who are responsible for administering justice.

COMPREHENSION OF THE PROCEEDINGS

Kriewaldt (1960: 23) asserted that: 'If the rule requiring substantial comprehension of the proceedings were applied in the Northern Territory, many aborigines could simply not be tried'. In his opinion the majority of Aborigines did not have sufficient education or background of civilisation to understand the proceedings of a trial.

Kriewaldt was concerned with full-blood Aborigines who spoke an Aboriginal language and whose command of English was limited. From my fieldwork it appeared that two groups of Aborigines might experience difficulty in understanding legal proceedings. First was a group corresponding to that considered by Kriewaldt. Second were the fringe-dwellers, who often have a limited English vocabulary, even though they no longer commonly use an Aboriginal language.

The first group will be considered in relation to the possibility of using interpreters in court. Then follows a more general discussion of the extent to which both groups comprehend the proceedings when they are tried.

ABORIGINAL LANGUAGES AND INTERPRETERS

In *R. v. Lee Kun*[18] Lord Reading said:

[17] *R.* v. *Grant and Lovett* [1972] V.R. 423, 424, per McInerney J.
[18] [1916] 1 K.B. 337, 342.

> If the accused is fit to plead it may yet be that no communication can be made in the ordinary way; it may be that he is deaf and can only be approached by writing or signs, or dumb, and can only make his views known by writing or signs, or a foreigner who cannot speak English and requires the assistance of an interpreter to understand the proceedings and make answer to them. In such cases the judge must see that proper means are taken to communicate to the accused the case made against him and to enable him to make his answer to it.

Thus the court should always require an interpreter if the defendant's English is inadequate and if he speaks an Aboriginal language. Tatz (1964a: 256) found that, in the Northern Territory, interpreters had not been used in the courts since 1950 at least. He agreed that a scheme to supply interpreters could not be universal because of the number of Aboriginal dialects and languages, but he argued that this fact should not debar the use of interpreters where bilingual persons are available.

Interpreters have been used in a number of Aboriginal cases in South Australia and Western Australia. From personal observation of one juvenile court case it appeared that the interpreter (a Commonwealth patrol officer) was fluent in the Aboriginal language and a competent interpreter. He did not appear to have any great difficulty in translating the defendants' statements for the court or vice versa. The criticisms I have made of this hearing (Chapter 4) were not based on the quality of the interpretation.

Other competent interpreters are available. Jim Lester, an Aboriginal, is an outstanding interpreter. Several missionaries are fluent in Pitjantjatjara, which is spoken by a large population. Some departmental officers are also learning this language. One missionary has interpreted in two major cases. The first involved six defendants charged with conspiracy to murder (see also Chapter 9). Most of the men could understand English. The missionary interpreted for one defendant when his solicitor interviewed him in prison. He also interpreted the charge and the judge's remarks when passing sentence. In the second case two Aboriginal women were charged with assault following the death of a child, who had been killed in accordance with tribal custom. The women had little contact with white society and considerable interpretation was required. As they were unrepresented the missionary also to some extent acted as defence counsel.

Unfortunately not all interpreters reach the same high standard. One Western Australian magistrate indicated that he had been dissatisfied with the ability of some Aboriginal interpreters, but others he had found quite satisfactory. These were local Aborigines who obtained a reputation as interpreters.

Police trackers are also sometimes used as interpreters in police investigations to obtain statements from defendants and witnesses and later in court. Irrespective of the linguistic ability of the trackers, it is undesirable in principle that they should be used as interpreters, because of the conflict of interest between their employment and the impartiality required of an interpreter. It would be equally undesirable for a missionary or a government officer to interpret in any case where there was a potential conflict of interest. This was not the situation in any of the cases described above.

Even if bilingual people were available to act as interpreters Kriewaldt believed (1960: 22) it would be impossible to translate many legal concepts into an Aboriginal language. 'It is . . . quite out of the question . . . to translate an indictment into an aboriginal language . . . Neither "pidgin" nor any aboriginal language suffices to convey the meaning of "malice aforethought" or of "unlawfully" or of "fraudulently without a claim of right" or of "lawful custody" '.

Wurm, a linguist, examines the question whether and how far Aboriginal languages can, through the services of interpreters, be used to express the juristic ideas and principles involved in the operation of a white man's court of law. In an illuminating article (1963a) he points out that language is intimately bound up with the culture of the people who use it.

> [I]t follows . . . that the central problem is in fact not whether the aboriginal languages are suited for the expression of, and reference to, such ideas and principles, but rather whether these ideas and principles themselves are meaningful and intelligible to aborigines whose understanding of the white man's culture is so limited that they are wholly, or almost wholly, ignorant of English . . . (p. 5).

He concludes that the rare individual who is fluent in both languages, thoroughly at home in both cultures and has a gift for pictorial expression, would be able to convey the white man's concept of law and also certain specific juristic concepts, such as 'unlawfully', 'murder' and 'fraudulently without a claim of right'. There are corresponding concepts in the Aboriginal culture, so it is a matter of finding the appropriate symbols (language) to convey the correspondence. In relation to these concepts the major problem is an emotional one rather than one of language and culture (p. 7). The Aboriginal may be brought to an intellectual understanding that the white law regards a killing in particular circumstances as 'murder' and that this concept of 'murder' corresponds to the idea of unlawful killing in his own culture. Nevertheless, he will find it difficult to accept this categorisation of the killing if it is one which is considered lawful within his culture (this problem is further explored in Chapter 9).

Wurm considers (1963a: 9) that, even if an Aboriginal could be brought to a full understanding of the legal concepts applicable to his case, he would still find court procedure incomprehensible. 'The notions of judge, jury, prosecutor, counsel for the defence, etc., and of their respective functions are totally alien to his conceptual system . . . Similarly, the significance of pleading guilty or not guilty is outside his world of experience.' Again, an exceptionally qualified interpreter could perhaps convey these concepts if he had considerable time available for the explanation. But a court does not usually have access to such an interpreter nor does it have the time for the long process of explanation which would be required to make the court hearing fully comprehensible to a traditionally oriented Aboriginal.

Thus, while not adopting Kriewaldt's extreme position, Wurm does agree that in many cases the Aboriginal defendant comprehends little of the proceeding by which he is tried. The pessimism of these views is mitigated somewhat by the fact that some very well qualified men have acted as interpreters for Aborigines, not only at trial but at earlier stages of the proceedings.

The missionary interpreter stated in an interview that he was disturbed by the difficulty of interpreting our legal concepts to Aborigines; for example, it was impossible to explain to them the meaning of the caution. 'In one breath you're telling them "you must tell the truth," in the next you're saying, "you needn't say anything, in case you incriminate yourself".' In his view the difficulty of interpreting arises both because the appropriate words do not exist in the Aboriginal language and also because Aboriginal culture is so entirely different from white culture. Since language arises from culture these are two facets of the one difficulty.

He instanced the plea as another legal concept difficult to interpret to Aborigines. As Kriewaldt wrote (1960: 39): 'It would also be impossible in most cases to explain to the accused the effect of his plea, namely, that a plea of guilty is a confession which obviates the necessity for trial, but that a plea of not guilty is not a denial of guilt so much as a demand that the prosecution prove the fact of guilt.'

From personal observation of court proceedings and perusal of case records, this statement appears to be justified. The inadequacy of the Aboriginal defendant's comprehension of the proceedings is often made apparent by his response when asked to plead to the charge. For example, in one Western Australian case, the charge of manslaughter was read to the defendant, a tribal Aboriginal, who answered, 'Yes, I was drunk'. The judge accepted this as a plea of guilty. In this case it appears that no injustice was involved in this procedure since the defendant was represented by counsel who advised him to plead guilty to the lesser charge of manslaughter substituted by the Crown for the original charge of wilful murder.

In a Northern Territory case the intervention of a welfare officer prevented the police relying on an alleged confession of the Aboriginal defendant to a charge of rape. The welfare officer interviewed the defendant in gaol before trial and played a 'word game' with him from which he was able to estimate his comprehension of English. The welfare officer, as an expert witness, told the court that he thought the Aboriginal would understand that he was going to be asked questions by the police, but he would not understand the implications of the standard caution. He would not realise that he need not even speak when asked questions. The welfare officer considered that the defendant was typical of many Aborigines in that he would say what he thought a white interrogator wanted him to say and that, though he seemed to understand English, he in fact could not proceed beyond common small talk.

The judge directed that no evidence could be given of the alleged admissions made by the defendant to the police. Since there was no other evidence to link the defendant with the offence, the jury acquitted him.

Acquittal was the correct legal result, though it is probable that the defendant was morally guilty of the offence. It would have been unjust to him to admit his confession in evidence when there was considerable doubt as to how much of the interrogation he had understood. The welfare officer suggests that establishment of his legal guilt would have been assisted if there had been effective co-operation between the Welfare Branch and the police. Instead of proceeding to interrogate an uncomprehending defendant, the police might have asked the Welfare Branch to arrange for the attendance of a competent interpreter.

It should be noted that there is no evidence that all white defendants fully comprehend all the legal concepts involved in their trials. It is unlikely that they do so; in fact, there would be less need for legal representation if they did. Even police, justices and magistrates sometimes display an imperfect understanding of the function of a plea of not guilty and the requirements of proof beyond a reasonable doubt. Kriewaldt appears to have been measuring the comprehension of Aboriginal defendants against an ideal standard, unattainable by any defendant. Nevertheless, the point about incomprehension remains a valid one, since it is clear that tribal Aborigines will understand even less of the proceedings than other defendants.

What can be done to improve this situation? Kriewaldt suggests (1960: 22) that if the defence had raised the point that an accused Aboriginal did not have sufficient education or intelligence or background of civilisation to understand the proceedings, in many cases he would have acceded to it. The trial could then not have proceeded. It is not clear whether he thought that in such cases a jury should be sworn to ascertain whether the defendant was 'fit to plead' with the consequence of indeterminate detention if found unfit, or alternatively that the judge should simply refuse to proceed with the trial. Either approach seems undesirable if we accept the initial assumption that Aborigines are properly amenable to our law.

A more constructive approach would be to organise a system of qualified interpreters and ensure that one is available for the trial of every indictable offence, and, as far as possible, for lesser offences also. They should be made available at the earliest possible stage of the proceedings, preferably beginning with the police interrogation.

In South Australia and Western Australia it appears that interpreters were used in all cases where tribal Aborigines were charged with the most serious offences. It is desirable that interpreters should not be used unless they reach some recognised standard of proficiency. The number of qualified interpreters could be increased by continuation and extension of language courses like those sponsored by the Department of Aboriginal Affairs in South Australia. Welfare officers should be encouraged to take these courses to improve their representation of Aborigines in court, as well as the performance of their other functions. Downing suggests that trained people should be attached to the courts as interpreters.[19]

On the other hand, emphasis should be placed on the education of

[19] Letter to the editor, Melbourne *Herald* 23/4/68, p. 12.

Aborigines, not only in the English language but also in legal concepts and the functions and procedures of the white legal system. This is not to imply that there is no place for education in the vernacular. Wurm suggests (1963b: 5) that Aborigines can be made literate in English through making them literate in an Aboriginal language first. Edwards also strongly argues (1969: 272-88) the case for commencing the education of Aborigines in their native language and leading on to instruction in English. The vernacular could be used for explanations of the white legal system to Aboriginal adults and children.

UNDERSTANDING OF COURT PROCEDURE

In the previous section it was suggested that the most formidable task facing an interpreter was that of explaining to an Aboriginal defendant the procedure by which he is tried. Detribalised Aborigines are also likely to have an inadequate understanding of court procedure. In this case the incomprehension arises not because the defendant must have concepts translated from English into his own language, but because his English vocabulary and general education are limited, whether or not he speaks an Aboriginal language. The factor common to both groups of Aborigines is limited education about the legal system. The only way of overcoming the problem is positive educational programs directed at enhancing understanding of how courts work, and how they are meant to work.

Kriewaldt's remarks on the difficulties of comprehension by Aboriginal accused of the proceedings of a trial were intended to be confined to trials in the Supreme Court. He thought (1960: 24) that: 'So far as aborigines charged in the police court with minor offences are concerned, there is no similar problem.' While I agree that the problem is more acute with tribal Aborigines whose culture is so entirely different from white culture, the problem of incomprehension exists to a lesser degree for 'fringe-dwellers' and, it must be added, for white defendants of limited education.

St John refers (1968: 84) to the confusion of court and prosecution roles in the minds of defendants, particularly those unrepresented, in Courts of Petty Sessions in New South Wales. 'In essence the scene is such that it appears that the Court is staffed by the police service and is being run by that service.' This impression must be even more strongly presented to defendants in remote areas of South Australia and Western Australia where courts are held in police stations, where police act as clerks of courts and where an atmosphere of mateship between police and justices pervades the scene. In some towns the court sits in the very room which at other times serves as the police station; in others, it sits in a separate room in the same building. It is unfortunate that even where new buildings have been erected recently, many have been designed with police station and courthouse under the one roof. No doubt this was done for reasons of economy. But the extra cost of separate buildings would be justified if thereby the proposition that the prosecution and judicial officers have different functions to perform is illustrated to defendants and reinforced in the minds of the police and justices themselves.

Another reason for incomprehension lies no doubt in the complexity of legal procedure. Reforms might well be considered in procedure and the rules of evidence in order to simplify court hearings. These would benefit all defendants and it is suggested that particular attention should be given to hearings concerning minor offences. Care would need to be taken that changes did not reduce the protection the law presently affords to defendants; but it is submitted that simplification of procedure would help defendants, particularly unrepresented defendants, to put their case more strongly and clearly to the tribunal. The existing rules about the order in which evidence is presented and the requirement that defendants must cross-examine prosecution witnesses before making a statement themselves undoubtedly confuse many defendants. I have observed numerous cases in lower courts where unrepresented defendants have been informed that they must question prosecution witnesses and not make a statement, with the result that inarticulate defendants have been reduced to silence. They have been unable to frame their remarks to prosecution witnesses in interrogative form and, having been warned several times that they must not make a statement, have given up the effort even at the point in the hearing when they are entitled to do so. The solution to this particular problem may lie in a change in procedure or in full explanations to defendants about their rights or in more frequent provision of legal representation. The danger in modifying procedure would be that defendants would then make the full statements they are now prevented from making and incriminate themselves in the process.

Kriewaldt (1960: 36-7) made several suggestions for procedural reform, the major one being the abolition of the coroner's inquest and the preliminary hearing in the Police Court in all cases in which an Aboriginal is suspected of a serious crime. The suggestion was aimed at avoiding confusing Aboriginal defendants and witnesses who, the judge thought, often believe that the committal proceedings are the trial and cannot understand why they have to go back to court again later.

I found no one to support this particular suggestion. A magistrate with previous experience as defence counsel thought that if it were adopted the advantage of not confusing Aborigines would be outweighed by the disadvantage to defence counsel of not having available the prosecution's evidence from the committal proceedings.

Another magistrate suggested that the special procedure used in the Children's Court should be adopted (with appropriate modifications) for the hearing of all charges against undefended Aborigines other than simple drunkenness and like offences. A brief summary of the Western Australian Children's Court procedure is set out in Appendix 12.

PLEAS

The pleas entered by Aborigines and whites respectively in the Ten Towns Sample are shown in Appendixes 2.30 and 2.31. While Aborigines show a slightly greater tendency to plead guilty, the difference between the two groups is not statistically significant.

This finding is unexpected in view of the conclusions of other writers that Aborigines inevitably plead guilty (Tatz 1963: 38-9). The implication is that in this they differ from whites and that this is yet another example of the discriminatory operation of the law when Aborigines are involved. The fact is that the percentage of guilty pleas in all cases, whether the defendant is Aboriginal or white, is very high. While it is true that Aborigines frequently plead guilty in circumstances where a not guilty plea may be justified, the same is probably also true of many white defendants. The conclusion is that the administration of justice is unsatisfactory in this respect in relation to defendants of both racial groups, rather than that it discriminates against Aborigines.

The great frequency of guilty pleas accords ill with the legal theory that a presumption of innocence applies in every case and that the prosecution is required to prove the guilt of every defendant beyond a reasonable doubt. A plea of guilty in most cases effectively prevents the court from testing the strength of the prosecution's case. Conviction does not automatically follow a plea of guilty. The court may occasionally intervene to advise an unrepresented defendant to change his plea if it appears from the brief statement of facts by the prosecution that the plea of guilty is ill advised. But the power of the court to intervene in this way is limited. Appendix 2.30 shows that only four defendants in the sample changed an initial plea of guilty to one of not guilty. There were far more changes in the reverse direction.

It is unlikely that the court will intervene with advice on the plea if the defendant is represented by a lawyer. A study from New South Wales (Tobin n.d.: 7) refers to 'Plead Guilty Lawyers' and claims: 'They seem to be an institution among Aborigines, the lawyer involved being referred to as "Guilty Smith" etc. . . . Lawyers admit advising this method as the simplest and best way out for all; minimal trouble with the police, saves time and money of all concerned—lawyer, magistrate and accused.'

If lawyers improperly advise their clients to plead guilty, legal representation is more of a hindrance than a help to the defendants concerned. I found no evidence of impropriety, in the sense of lawyers advising guilty pleas simply to save themselves work for which they could not expect to be paid. There may be some borderline cases, where a defendant has been advised to plead guilty to save himself legal costs, even though he had some chance of obtaining an acquittal if he persisted with a not guilty plea and continued to retain a lawyer. One magistrate, in commenting on a case in which a lawyer obtained an acquittal for an Aboriginal defendant on a charge of drunkenness, expressed the view that the defendant would probably have been better advised to plead guilty because it would have cost him less. In this he showed little appreciation of the value an innocent accused may place on justice and on his reputation. Nevertheless, it does illustrate that a lawyer, advising his client realistically, may recommend a guilty plea on economic grounds. A defendant, to whom the consequences flowing from the alternative pleas have been explained, may well decide that he prefers to save money, even at the cost of suffering the stigma of an undeserved criminal conviction. It is a weakness of the legal system that the defendant should be faced with this cruel dilemma. But it is not a weakness that should be blamed on practising lawyers, so long as they have honestly and realistically counselled their clients.

The fact that no Aboriginal defendants faced a jury for some years in South Australia does suggest that some Aborigines charged with serious crime may have been advised to plead guilty in cases where a not guilty plea would have been more appropriate. Most of these cases were examples of 'plea bargaining', that is, the Crown agreed to accept a plea of guilty to a lesser crime than that originally charged. In some cases this occurred through the intervention of the Department of Aboriginal

Affairs rather than on the advice of a lawyer. The practice of 'plea bargaining' is strongly entrenched in the United States, and it is interesting to see it featuring so prominently in the Aboriginal field.[20] The defendant trades an uncertain outcome (acquittal or conviction of the more serious crime) for the certainty of conviction of a crime carrying a lesser maximum penalty. When offered this choice by the Crown, many defendants and defence counsel may reasonably prefer certainty. On the other hand, a solicitor indicated that one experience of plea bargaining had taught him a lesson, so that he intended to advise not guilty pleas in future. He advised a guilty plea to a charge of manslaughter, in exchange for the Crown dropping a murder charge. He believed this was in the best interests of his client and was horrified when the judge imposed a long prison sentence.

As indicated in the previous chapter, I consider that legal representation is of value to most defendants. Part of its value lies in the informed advice which a lawyer is able to give on the plea. A northern magistrate suggested that advising on the plea would be a useful function for welfare officers to perform. In his jurisdiction there are no resident solicitors and visits of lawyers are rare. Welfare officers would require further education in law, particularly aimed at helping them to understand that it is proper to advise a plea of not guilty where it appears that the prosecution does not have sufficient evidence against the Aboriginal defendant, even though the welfare officer believes him to be guilty (discussed in Chapter 4).

A number of reasons have been suggested by Tatz (1963: 38-9) for the Aboriginal tendency to plead guilty. Two preliminary points need to be made. Tatz confined his discussion to guilty pleas on Queensland Aboriginal settlements. To the extent that my findings differ from his the discrepancy may possibly be explained by the different situations in which Aborigines find themselves. Queensland Aboriginal settlements are closed communities with their own police and courts. The pressures on Aborigines to plead guilty are stronger there than they are on Aborigines living in the general community who come before the ordinary courts.

The second qualification on the following discussion is that, since my statistics do not show that the tendency to plead guilty is significantly

20 There are no general studies of its incidence in Australia. It has come in for some attention in England. See, for example, Davis 1971.

greater for Aborigines than for whites, if the suggested explanations are valid for Aborigines, they must apply equally to many whites.

Tatz mentions the following possible reasons for Aboriginal guilty pleas. First, an explanation of pleading is not made to Aborigines and they are by and large unaware of a right to plead not guilty. In the Western Australian and South Australian context, this would apply particularly to tribal Aborigines. The difficulties of interpreting the plea in an Aboriginal language have already been discussed (earlier in this chapter). To hear a court accept as a plea of guilty the mumbled assent of a defendant to the question whether he was drunk yesterday is to observe incomprehension in action. I have observed this procedure adopted with relatively detribalised Aborigines but the same magistrate also used it with a white defendant charged with drunkenness.

Secondly, Tatz mentions (1963: 39) the claim that the police force is so efficient that only water-tight cases are brought to court. A similar claim on behalf of the police forces of South Australia and Western Australia put forward as an explanation of the high rate of Aboriginal convictions is rejected below (in Chapter 6).

Thirdly, 'Aborigines are so honest that they almost always admit culpability' (Tatz 1963: 39). There is no reason to suppose that Aborigines are more or less honest than other people, though there may be special factors which affect their willingness to tell the truth in legal proceedings. Legislative provisions prohibiting the acceptance of Aboriginal confessions and pleas of guilty rest on the assumption that Aborigines will admit guilt more readily than whites. But it is not clear whether the legislation was based on the view that it was unfair to allow Aborigines to incriminate themselves, even if the confession was true, or alternatively on the view that innocent Aborigines were likely to make false admissions of guilt and so needed special protection.

Fourthly, Tatz refers (1963: 39) to the desire not to run counter to settlement superintendents. In the wider context police and welfare officers could be added to superintendents. The New South Wales study claimed: 'Police may encourage people to plead guilty by threatening to level other charges as well. One lawyer we interviewed claimed to have overheard a police officer instructing an Aborigine to plead guilty outside the court. At first the officer denied this though when pressed claimed it was policy from higher up' (Tobin n.d.: 7). I found no evidence of direct pressure being applied in this way. In fact I heard one policeman explicitly advise an Aboriginal defendant that he had the right to plead not guilty. It is unlikely, however, that any policeman who wished to apply improper pressure to a defendant would have done it in my presence.

In general, it seems that the pressures operating on Aboriginal defendants are less direct. Some Aborigines interviewed gave as their reason for pleading guilty their inability to raise bail.[21] In practice, a plea of not guilty often means a remand in custody for eight days, which is frequently longer than the sentence imposed on conviction. In one case involving a white defendant a change of plea from not guilty to guilty was brought about by the police threat to reserve the case for the magistrate's visit which could have meant a considerable period in custody before the hearing.

The hypothesis that a fear of remand in custody is largely responsible for the frequency of guilty pleas is not entirely borne out by the statistics. If it were true one would expect that defendants remanded in custody would more frequently change their plea to guilty to avoid further confinement, as compared with those remanded on bail. But the statistics (Appendix 2.30) do not support this expectation. The hypothesis may be further refined to state that the difference between those defendants who plead guilty and those who plead not guilty depends on a difference in personality, in terms of susceptibility to all the direct and indirect pressures favouring guilty pleas. Thus, many defendants who initially plead guilty do so because of their greater fatalism—their view that it is no use pleading not guilty. Amongst the factors leading them to adopt this view is their dislike of spending time in custody before the hearing and their desire to 'get the case over and done with'.

On the other hand, some Aboriginal defendants have shown remarkable tenacity in maintaining a not guilty plea in the face of legal advice that a plea of guilty to a lesser charge would be wise. In one case defence counsel obtained an unofficial assurance from the Crown that if his client pleaded guilty to common assault the charge of robbery in company would be withdrawn. The difference in potential sentences for the two offences is considerable. The defendant refused to plead guilty to any charge and the jury found him guilty on the more serious charge.

The Native Welfare Department adopted a policy of providing legal representation in every case where an Aboriginal was charged with an

21 Fieldwork notes. Also interview with secretary of Aborigines' Friends' Association (South Australia).

indictable offence and pleaded not guilty. Even in a case where the depositions disclosed strong evidence against the defendant and the defence counsel was not very optimistic, the Department was prepared to contribute its share of legal aid costs. Since legal representation is not always provided on a plea of guilty to an indictable offence this policy provided a positive incentive to plead not guilty.

Fifthly, Tatz refers (1963: 39) to the view put forward by some officials that 'gaol means good meals and no work, and as work is compulsory for Aborigines on settlements, a gaol term is convenient'. The view that Aborigines regard gaol as a holiday will be more fully examined in Chapter 6. Here I merely state my conclusion that this is not a weighty factor in inducing pleas of guilty.

Finally, Tatz expresses (1963: 39) the 'non-official view . . . that Aborigines have come to learn that pleading not guilty is useless, for pleas seem irrelevant to decisions: for example, of the 177 accused in 1956 and 98 accused in 1962 at Woorabinda, all were found guilty'. This is indeed an important point, though I draw different conclusions from it. The rate of Aboriginal acquittals in proportion to total charges is lower than the comparable rate for whites (Appendix 2.22). Since there is not a significant difference in the rate of not guilty pleas, this means that Aborigines are more often unsuccessful on not guilty pleas. Thus I disagree with Tatz that the realisation that pleading not guilty is useless has led to the large number of guilty pleas. It is remarkable that, in spite of being convicted so often after pleading not guilty and attempting to raise a defence, some Aborigines have persisted in pleading not guilty.

It may be argued that, contrary to the implicit assumption of the discussion so far, it would be disastrous for the legal system if many more defendants pleaded not guilty. There is already considerable delay in bringing contested cases on for hearing and it is only the fact that many defendants plead guilty that prevents the system breaking down entirely.

The first answer to this contention is that, if defendants were represented and encouraged to plead not guilty, the result might be to discourage the police from laying many charges rather than to maintain the rate of prosecutions at the present level, with inevitable serious delays. Many Aboriginal offences are liquor offences in which it seems difficult to set up a successful defence and in similar cases whites frequently also plead guilty. Proposals for representation by legal aid or welfare officers have so far not contemplated providing assistance in such cases,

Yet in New York, when lawyers were provided for derelict defendants and the prosecution was required to prove the element of disorderliness in drunkenness charges, the proportion of acquittals rose dramatically (Murtagh 1966: 6). The police were later instructed not to make arrests unless they had clear evidence of disorderliness and arrests for drunkenness almost ceased. This does not mean the breakdown of law and order but shows that for years undefended prisoners had been wrongly convicted on their own admissions of guilt.

Secondly, even if the contention is accepted that an increase in not guilty pleas would impose an intolerable burden on the legal system, this is not an argument in favour of the status quo. The existing system is unjust in enabling a wealthy or powerful defendant to take advantage of all the legal benefits involved in the presumption of innocence, while other defendants plead guilty or unsuccessfully plead not guilty because they do not have access to the legal representation which would give them more chance of an acquittal. There is something farcical about a legal system which talks nobly about a presumption of innocence and a requirement of proof beyond reasonable doubt, yet depends for its viable functioning on the fact that most defendants do not take it at its word.

It seems to me preferable that an attempt should be made to translate ideals into practice by providing legal aid in as many cases as possible and encouraging not guilty pleas. Then, if the system shows any signs of breaking down, in the sense that there are not enough lawyers or courts to enable cases to be heard reasonably quickly, the whole system should be re-examined. The aim should be to provide equal justice for all, even if this means modifying procedures which at present give the most favoured defendants every advantage against the Crown.

ABORIGINAL EVIDENCE

So far court procedure has been examined largely from the viewpoint of the Aboriginal defendant. The value of Aboriginal evidence and the weight given to it by courts will now be examined with reference not only to the testimony given by Aboriginal defendants but also that adduced from Aboriginal complainants and witnesses.

Aboriginal witnesses have been placed in a special category by legislation, by judicial decisions and by the administrative practice of law-enforcement agencies. In South Australia, for example, the Evidence Act provided that any Aboriginal 'who is uncivilised and appears on examination not to believe either in a God or a future state of reward and punishment, and who further appears not to understand the obligations of an oath, may give evidence without an oath and without any formality'.[22] The reception of such evidence, however, did not guarantee that the court attached the same weight to it as to the sworn evidence of other witnesses (section 13). But the Aboriginal whose evidence was given under this provision and who made a wilfully false statement 'which if made upon oath would subject him to the penalties of perjury' was guilty of a misdemeanour (section 14). Until 1968 the penalties were even more severe than for perjury since they included whipping.[23]

The restrictions imposed by legislation on the reception of Aboriginal confessions in evidence have already been discussed (in Chapter 2). Kriewaldt J. judicially imposed another restriction on the reception of Aboriginal evidence when he refused to admit a dying declaration made by an Aboriginal. It is paradoxical that he did so on the basis that the law applies equally to Aborigines and whites:

> because I have to apply the same rules to aborigines and whites I did not admit that evidence on the basis that the reason for admitting the evidence in the case of a white person is that he has a belief that God will punish him if he tells a lie just as he is about to die. So far as the aborigines are concerned we know that they have not that type of belief in the hereafter and therefore applying the same rule to aborigines as I do to whites, I excluded any statement the deceased might have made shortly before his death.[24]

Brazil (1960: 196) found that historically judges treated 'dying declarations' as an exception to the hearsay rule on the basis of the religious sanction operative at the moment of death. However, they did not require proof of religious belief since they assumed that nearly all persons have the necessary belief. Such an assumption is, of course, not universally valid today.

But Brazil concluded that Kriewaldt was right in holding that the law still requires belief in a God who will punish for falsehood. Since the case involved a comparatively uncivilised Aboriginal, the judge was put on

[22] Evidence Act, 1929 (S.A.) section 9. The section has since been repealed and a new section substituted.

[23] Evidence Act (S.A.) section 14: ' . . . liable to be imprisoned for any term not exceeding two years, and further to be once, twice, or thrice publicly or privately whipped'. The provision about whipping was repealed in 1968. 'It had, prior to its repeal, fallen deservedly into disuse' (Mitchell 1969: 3).

[24] *R.* v. *Wadderwarri* (unreported, 20/3/58), cited in Brazil 1960.

inquiry as to the existence of the belief. He acted by taking judicial notice of the religious beliefs of Aborigines, which is carrying judicial notice rather far.

Although Kriewaldt J. may have correctly applied the modern law on the subject, the question arises whether the law is appropriate in modern conditions. Most atheists will obtain the benefit of the presumption that the necessary religious belief exists, whereas the court will inquire into the religious belief of every Aboriginal deceased or even apply the opposite presumption. In fact, the motives for truthfulness on the death bed may be equally strong in both cases. Further, there may be great difficulties in practice in applying the rule to Aborigines. It is assumed that Kriewaldt J. was thinking only of Aborigines living in the tribal state but there will be many borderline cases. Should the court inquire into religious belief in every case where it is put on notice by the colour of the deceased's skin?

It is submitted that it would be better to adopt a new basis for this exception to the hearsay rule, which would enable the dying declarations of all adults to be admissible. The requirement of religious belief would then become part of legal history. Raine J. of the Supreme Court of the Territory of Papua and New Guinea adopted this secular approach. He rejected the nineteenth century justification for the exception to the hearsay rule and thought that in this century no distinction should be made between Christians and others in relation to dying declarations.[25]

The attitude of the police to Aboriginal complainants and witnesses is probably not sufficiently consistent to be dignified by the name of an administrative practice. But a pattern can be discerned whereby the police adopt a double standard towards witnesses and potential witnesses of the Aboriginal race. If an Aboriginal complains of an offence committed by another Aboriginal the police show little hesitation in launching a prosecution and the Aboriginal evidence appears to be given due weight by the courts. But the police seem more reluctant to take action when the Aboriginal victim complains of an offence by a white person. The reasons for this reluctance may be the wish to maintain friendly relations with local whites (for example, where Aborigines accuse a local station owner of assault) and the belief that Aborigines are not good witnesses. This belief may be an expression of the personal views of the police about the value of Aboriginal evidence or it may be a realistic assessment of the reaction of juries asked to convict a white man on the testimony of an Aboriginal.

[25] *R.* v. *Peagui Ambimp* (20/7/72). Noted in 47 A.L.J. 92 (1973). For a discussion of earlier cases in the Territory of Papua and New Guinea, see O'Regan 1972a.

Certainly in the past it was difficult to launch a prosecution against a white man who had injured an Aboriginal. T.G.H. Strehlow was a patrol officer in the Northern Territory for many years and stated in an interview in Adelaide in 1965 that he was constantly frustrated in his efforts to bring whites to justice for offences against Aborigines. Other whites would not give evidence in such cases; Aboriginal witnesses were likely to be confused in court.

On the other hand, Kriewaldt stated (1960: 11): 'I was satisfied that in the Northern Territory a white person who commits a crime against an aborigine will be prosecuted exactly as if the victim had been white.' The position has certainly improved, although it does not seem to have quite reached the ideal in South Australia and Western Australia.

The breakthrough in South Australia came with a case in 1945 in which the police prosecuted a white station owner for an assault on Aboriginal employees and the local justice of the peace convicted and fined him (Duguid 1965: 79 and Oodnadatta court records). This was an improvement on the previous situation where the white man would not have been proceeded against at all. But he was merely fined, whereas the Aborigines, whom he had not only assaulted but also had brought before the court on trumped-up charges, were sentenced to gaol on the latter. Naturally they did not receive any compensation for this wrongful imprisonment.

Appendix 2.32 correlates the race of the defendant with the race of the victim of the crime in the Ten Towns Sample. The figures are incomplete, but a pattern is suggested in which Aborigines are frequently charged with offences against whites while the reverse does not occur. (Many of the offences in the Ten Towns Sample are 'crimes without victims' and are not included in this table.)

It may be argued that the small number of charges against whites for crimes against Aborigines is attributable to the infrequency of such offences in fact, rather than to any exercise of discretion on the part of the police. But there is some evidence that the police still refuse to act on a complaint by an Aboriginal unless he is supported by a white witness.[26] Distrust by the police of Aboriginal complainants and witnesses is also expressed in police 'briefs' which assess witnesses. In some cases, too, the

[26] For example, police refused to take action under the South Australian Prohibition of Discrimination Act solely on an Aboriginal complaint but agreed to act when a white welfare officer turned up to support the allegation of discriminatory treatment.

police failed to initiate action against whites on behalf of Aboriginal victims who did not lay complaints, possibly because they did not realise that an offence had been committed.[27]

The difficulty of obtaining a conviction from a jury, when the accused is a white man charged with an offence against an Aboriginal, has already been noted. Judge Bevan, referring to his experience in the Northern Territory, wrote:

> Speaking generally I do not hesitate to say that where a European is charged with an offence against a coloured man, no matter what the evidence may be, the matter is decided on the question of colour. The records show this. . . . The injustice is made more glaring by the fact that it is not that 'coloured' evidence is disbelieved *qua* 'coloured' evidence, but that it is disbelieved because it is offered against a European; the same 'coloured' evidence against a 'coloured man' will be accepted, and, rightly, acted upon . . . (quoted Elkin 1947: 197)

The last way in which Aboriginal witnesses are subjected to differential treatment in practice is that restrictions are imposed on their movements before the court hearing. Formerly it was police practice to 'arrest' Aboriginal witnesses and bring them in 'on the chain' with the prisoners (Western Australia 1905: 14; Elkin 1947: 198). I have been unable to find out precisely what the modern practice is, but it appears that in some cases tribal Aborigines have been removed many hundreds of miles from their home 'country' and warned severely against leaving the town or the local reserve before the court hearing.[28] Thus, in many ways Aboriginal witnesses are subjected to differential treatment. This treatment clearly rests on an assumption that Aborigines are different from other witnesses; that they are more unreliable and less honest than others. To what extent is this assumption justified?

Elkin (1947: 184) examined the question exhaustively and concluded that the evidence of Aborigines in court was unreliable. This was not due to any inherent untruthfulness of Aborigines but to a number of factors which, from the Aboriginal point of view, made the unreliability of their court evidence perfectly explicable and reasonable.

[27] In one case an unsophisticated Aboriginal defendant was charged with assault. The charge was later withdrawn. The provocation offered to him by his white employer was a relatively serious assault, yet no action was taken by the police against the white station owner.

[28] In one case a magistrate felt obliged to impose a gaol sentence on the defendants because both defendants and witnesses had spent a considerable period 'on remand' before trial.

Chief amongst these factors was the social context in which the Aboriginal is a member of a subject race, dependent on the white pastoralist for his subsistence, and seeing the court as another instrument of white domination. It is natural that when called on in the unfamiliar surroundings of a court to give evidence against his employer, he will hesitate to repeat the strongest allegations and may contradict statements he has previously made in more favourable surroundings. Elkin strongly contends that to treat these contradictions as proof that the Aboriginal is a liar and particularly that the first story he told is untrue is to fall into error.

Secondly, court procedure is itself a cause of unreliable Aboriginal evidence. The witness does not understand why he is asked to tell the same story over and over again and, not wishing to offend the authorities he changes his story, believing that this is required of him. This makes the cross-examiner's task of trapping the witness in inconsistencies very easy. But Elkin points out that the rejection of the evidence on the ground of such inconsistencies often leads to injustice. Tatz (1964a: 260) quotes a former Darwin magistrate as saying that Aborigines tell their stories honestly on examination-in-chief but they miss out on cross-examination, because they do not understand its functions. When the witness's limited education is compounded by ignorance of English, the dangers of incomprehension and of resulting false evidence are increased. The earlier discussion in this chapter on incomprehension by Aboriginal defendants of court procedures, applies equally to Aboriginal witnesses.

From personal observation of Aboriginal witnesses I would say that many are not sufficiently fluent in English to convey their meaning to the court or to understand all court procedure. Many are also shy and inarticulate but would probably respond to sympathetic, patient questioning. In some cases special factors may inhibit Aborigines from telling the full truth to the court. A young Aboriginal victim of a rape was reluctant to give any evidence about it when her mother was present in court but had less hesitation when her mother was absent. This was interpreted by other observers as being due to the fact that she was still largely traditionally oriented. In other cases, Aborigines may not reveal the truth because it would involve speaking of tribal secrets to persons who are not entitled to know about them. This will be a powerful inhibiting factor when it operates.

Elkin makes a number of suggestions for reform of court procedure, designed to enable truthful Aboriginal evidence to be elicited by the court. His proposals for special Native Courts and for courts to sit in Aboriginal localities will be considered in Chapter 9. His other major suggestion is for the abolition of juries in Aboriginal cases. It certainly appears that the jury system operates unjustly, particularly in 'mixed cases', that is, those where complainant and defendant are of different races. I agree that there is a strong case for the abolition of juries in cases where whites are charged with offences against Aborigines, unless racially mixed juries are stipulated.

6 THE OUTCOME OF CRIMINAL PROCEEDINGS

THE FINDING

A criminal prosecution initiated by the police may never come before a tribunal for determination. The police may decide to withdraw the prosecution and apply to the court for permission to withdraw. If the charge is for an indictable offence, the decision to withdraw is made by the Attorney-General and is notified to the court by the entry of a *nolle prosequi.*

The defendant against whom the prosecution elects to proceed may enter a plea of guilty, which usually results in his conviction and saves the prosecution the trouble of proving its case beyond reasonable doubt by admissible evidence. Occasionally the court refuses to accept a proferred plea of guilty and enters a plea of not guilty on the defendant's behalf. He is then in almost the same position as if he had decided himself to plead not guilty. He suffers the disadvantage, however, that he is unprepared with witnesses and other evidence to support any defence which may be open to him. This course is likely to be adopted by a magistrate only if a defendant is not legally represented.

When the defendant pleads not guilty the court proceeds to a full hearing of the charge against him. In summary proceedings the court finally either convicts the defendant or dismisses the case against him. On the trial of an indictable offence the jury must convict or acquit the defendant or find him not guilty on the ground of insanity.

Appendix 2.22 shows the final result of the cases in the Western

Australian Sample, subdivided according to the race of the defendant. It has already been observed in Chapter 3 that the conviction rate for Aborigines is higher than for white defendants, and conversely that whites obtain the benefits of acquittal or dismissal in a higher proportion of cases than Aborigines do. The difference is quite striking and has been confirmed by an examination of statistics for the whole of the State and for an earlier period (Appendix 8).

It has been suggested that this difference between Aborigines and other defendants is partly caused by the higher incidence of pre-trial detention in the former group and also by their more restricted access to legal representation (these points have been discussed in Chapters 3 and 4). Another reason for the higher conviction rate may be the nature of the offences with which Aborigines are charged. They are more frequently charged with drunkenness offences, to which it is difficult to raise a successful defence. Even if the defendant was in fact not guilty, it is usually his word against that of one or more police witnesses and some justices and magistrates appear to be predisposed to accept police evidence. It is rare for a defendant to be in the position of the Aboriginal who was able to obtain legal representation and a blood test which showed conclusively that he was not drunk (discussed in Chapter 2). Legislation relating to other offences with which Aborigines are frequently charged, such as vagrancy, shifts the burden of proof to the defendant and thus makes it extremely difficult for him to plead not guilty successfully.

The higher conviction rate of Aborigines is probably partly due to prejudice on the part of justices and magistrates. Some prejudice undoubtedly exists, but it is difficult to assess its precise influence on decisions. One magistrate who had intervened in a number of cases to prevent injustice to Aboriginal defendants nevertheless expressed a low opinion of them when interviewed. Evidently, his professional training as a magistrate was sufficient to enable him to submerge personal prejudice in the performance of his duties. On the other hand, one explanation offered for the imposition of an excessive sentence on two Aborigines—a sentence not authorised by the relevant legislation—was that one of the justices had been assaulted by Aborigines and chose to make an example of the next Aboriginal defendants who came before him. Whether or not this was the true explanation the sentence was certainly excessive and, as in many other cases involving long prison sentences for Aboriginal defendants, it is difficult to imagine any reason for the sentence other than the influence of racial prejudice against Aborigines.

There is no evidence of any tendency for juries to acquit Aborigines on the ground that they should not be subject to the general law. There is still a slight tendency for juries to refuse to convict whites charged with offences against Aborigines and to be ready to convict Aborigines in the converse situation (see discussion in Chapter 5).

It is common practice for the prosecution to lay multiple charges of drunken driving and dangerous driving arising out of the same incident. If the defendant pleads guilty to the former charge the other is withdrawn. This practice partially explains the higher number of withdrawals of charges against white defendants. Appendix 2.33 which relates the offence charged to the outcome of the proceedings, shows that the highest concentration of withdrawn charges occurs in traffic offences. This practice may not be discriminatory in intention, since it is applied to many drunken drivers. But it is discriminatory in effect, because whites are charged more often than Aborigines with traffic offences and thus obtain the benefit of the dropping of the multiple charge more often. It is rare for one charge in a multiple series to be withdrawn against an Aboriginal defendant, even though all arise out of the same or closely related incidents. For example, one Aboriginal was charged with five counts of supplying liquor to other Aborigines and received cumulative sentences of imprisonment totalling ten months. The charges all arose out of the one incident in which younger Aboriginal men asked him to obtain liquor for them. It was quite lawful for the police to lay multiple charges but one may query the wisdom of this exercise of their discretion. A police inspector in South Australia who shares this view about the injustice of laying multiple charges in similar circumstances, instructed police in his district not to lay charges for both 'drunk on Reserve' and 'possess liquor on Reserve'. Although technically these were two different charges, he thought this amounted to charging the defendant twice for one offence if both arose out of the same set of facts.

The police claim that Aborigines are not charged and convicted unless they are guilty. This claim does not explain the discrepancy between Aboriginal and white rates of conviction, however. The police surely would not prosecute whites unless they thought that they had a strong case against them too. Even if the prosecutors consider that all persons acquitted should have been convicted, the fact remains that some defendants obtain the dismissal of charges against them by due process of law, and this occurs more frequently for whites than for Aborigines.

It is probable that the main reason for this difference is Aboriginal ignorance of legal rights and lack of access to legal representation and consequent failure to raise defences legally available. Perusal of Police Court Evidence Books discloses a number of cases in which it appeared that a defence could have been raised with some hope of success if a lawyer had appeared, so that, far from the police claim being correct, it appears that at least some Aboriginal defendants were improperly convicted (examples are cited in Chapter 5).

THE SENTENCE

Upon conviction, the court generally has a discretion as to the type of sentence and the severity of the sentence it imposes on the defendant. Nearly all criminal legislation sets maximum limits only; within those limits the court has a choice of sentence.

THE TYPE OF SENTENCE IMPOSED

Appendix 2.24 sets out the kinds of sentence imposed on Aborigines and whites in the Ten Towns Sample. The initial determination of the type of sentence may be regarded as involving a decision as to the severity of the sentence which should be imposed. From the point of view of the defendant, release on a bond is the least severe, followed by the imposition of a fine, with imprisonment ranking as the most serious. The death penalty is so infrequent as to have been excluded from consideration—no Aboriginal has been hanged in Western Australia since 1904 (according to the Crown Law Department) or in South Australia since 1906 (Griffiths 1970).

Aborigines are subjected to imprisonment proportionately more often than whites are (Appendix 2.24). The general trend shown by the cases in this Sample is confirmed by statistics available for the whole State of Western Australia for 1960: of 40,276 white offenders 2052 or 5 per cent were imprisoned; of 3206 Aborigines 642 or 20 per cent.[1] It is also confirmed by Prisons Department statistics of the number of Aboriginal prisoners. In the year ending 30 June 1965 for example, the daily average of prisoners for all gaols was 876·93. This average included 214·78 Aborigines. Thus, Aborigines formed 24 per cent of the total prison population.[2] This is far above the percentage of Aborigines in the general

[1] *Annual Report. Commissioner of Police for Western Australia* (1960). Perth: Government Printer.

[2] *Annual Report of the Prisons Department from 1st July, 1964 to 30th June, 1965* (1966). Perth: Government Printer.

population (2·5 per cent). It is even more important that it is above the percentage which Aborigines represent in the 'population' of persons convicted of offences (11 per cent).

Having made the primary decision as to the type of sentence to be imposed, the court then has to decide the amount of sentence, that is, the length of imprisonment or the amount of the fine.

The periods of imprisonment imposed on Aboriginal and white offenders in the Sample are set out in Appendix 2.34. From this table there appears to be no discrimination against Aborigines in the length of imprisonment imposed. The majority of Aboriginal defendants who are imprisoned are sentenced to the shorter terms. The proportion who are sentenced to the longer terms (over nine weeks) is lower than it is for whites. Thus, if the initial determination that imprisonment was the proper form of sentence was characterised as non-discriminatory, the actual terms of imprisonment imposed could not be criticised. But the periods of imprisonment need to be considered in conjunction with the fact that many more Aboriginal defendants are imprisoned, while many convicted whites serve no time in prison at all. The general pattern of comparison of the length of prison sentences for Aborigines and whites in the Sample is confirmed by the information available on peremptory commitments to prison from Magistrates Courts for the whole State in 1960:[3]

	Under 1 mth	1 mth & under 6 mths	6 mths & under 1 year	1 year & under 2 years	2 years & under 5 years	Total
Whites	888	934	182	43	5	2052
Aborigines	389	215	35	2	1	642

Appendix 2.35, which sets out the amounts of fines, also shows no obvious discrimination. This statement is also subject to the qualification that this table takes no account of factors such as the type of offence charged and prior convictions. Another decision which the court may be called on to make is whether to grant the defendant time to pay a fine. If the defendant requests time to pay, the court may either refuse the request or grant it and fix the time within which the defendant must pay. If time to pay is not granted and the defendant has no cash in his possession, he is immediately committed to prison in default of payment. In such cases,

[3] *Annual Report. Commissioner of Police for Western Australia* (1960). Perth: Government Printer.

the sentence of a fine is virtually one of imprisonment, though such imprisonment is not included in the table above. There is the advantage, from the defendant's point of view, that if he can obtain the money to pay the fine before completion of his sentence, he can make partial payment and obtain his release.

Appendix 2.36 shows how the defendants of the two racial groups fared in relation to the granting by the court of time to pay. A higher percentage of whites were not granted time to pay, so *prima facie* the practice regarding the granting of time to pay is not discriminatory against Aborigines. However, there are two factors which may make this table an unreliable indicator of the true position. One is the fact that in most cases it was not possible to ascertain from the records whether the defendant had actually made an application for time to pay which was refused, or whether he had simply not asked for time to pay either because he did not know that he could request it or because he did not require it. The other is the large number of cases for which there is no record of whether time to pay was granted or not. It is probable that white defendants, because of their higher economic status as a group, required time to pay less often than Aborigines did. The consequences of time to pay not being granted are likely to be more severe for the Aboriginal group, and it is these consequences which are important, rather than the practice itself.

Appendix 2.37 has therefore been produced to show the number of defendants of each group who paid fines or who went to gaol in default of payment. It will be seen that a higher percentage of white defendants paid the fines owing and a comparatively small percentage served imprisonment in default. It therefore seems that even if all the white 'no record' cases in the previous table were cases in which time to pay was not granted, this has not had a serious effect on the majority of these defendants. The percentage of Aboriginal defendants who paid their fines is lower, although such defendants still comprise a majority of those fined. A higher percentage of Aboriginal defendants was imprisoned in default.

Alternative explanations of this finding are possible. One is that the practice of the courts is discriminatory in effect, because the means of Aboriginal defendants have not been sufficiently taken into account in fixing the amounts of fines and in deciding whether to grant time to pay. In this view, the administration of the law has been largely responsible for the fact that a higher proportion of Aboriginal defendants has been imprisoned in default of payment of a fine. The other view is that Aborigines are unreliable about paying fines and that no matter how much consideration were accorded to them in the way of granting time to pay, no more fines would be paid. Some would actually prefer to serve the default sentence.

The argument may be advanced that justice, in the sense at least of equal treatment for all, requires that the same fine should be imposed on all defendants for the same offence without regard to individual means. In her study of Victorian stipendiary magistrates, Julie Jones (1963: 24) found that one magistrate fixed individual fines according to means. She (and the magistrate) interpreted this as an expression of bias and emotional feelings. Another magistrate 'firmly insisted that the same treatment should be given to rich and poor alike'.

Nevertheless, the opposing viewpoint may be more plausibly advanced. It is obvious that a fine of a specified amount is a greater imposition on a poor man than on the richer man who experiences no difficulty in raising it. The strongest proof of this argument is to be found in the prisons where poor people predominate, largely because they have been unable to pay fines or because they have been sentenced to imprisonment without the option of a fine, the court taking the view that they would be unable to pay the fine considered appropriate for the offence. The law in Australia has given little guidance to justices and magistrates facing this dilemma. In Sweden it is recognised that a fine of a fixed amount does not represent equal justice for rich and poor. The system of day-fines is the most rational approach to the problem which can be devised and, as the result of the adoption of this system, Swedish defendants rarely serve sentences in default of payment of fines (Botein and Sturz 1964: 215). In the United States it has been held by the Supreme Court that it is unconstitutional to limit punishment to payment of a fine and then to imprison an indigent defendant who is unable to pay the fine.[4] Similarly in England the Court of Criminal Appeal has said that it is completely wrong to sentence a person to imprisonment not because the offence merits a prison sentence but because he is not able to pay a substantial fine.[5]

One Western Australian magistrate interviewed stated that he did not make allowance for the fact that Aborigines generally have low incomes and large families. He fixed the same fine as he would for a white charged with the same offence. But he did take individual circumstances into

[4] *Tate* v. *Short*, 91 S.Ct. 668 (1971); Barton 1971.

[5] *R.* v. *Reeves* (1972) 56 Cr. App. R. 366.

account in deciding about time to pay. If he knew a defendant was a good worker and had a large family to support he would grant longer time to pay. But if the Aboriginal defendant was not a local and the police opposed the granting of time to pay, he did not grant the application. The police view is that the force would have to chase the defendant with a warrant and in the end he probably would not be able to pay and would have to go to gaol anyway. This attitude implies a certain discrimination against Aborigines, a certain willingness to believe that they are unreliable about paying fines imposed.

Oddly enough, there may be some truth in the view that Aboriginal defendants prefer to serve the default sentence rather than pay a fine. In Western Australia there is a practice that a defendant can call in all warrants outstanding against him if he is serving a gaol sentence. All sentences can then be served concurrently, which is an advantage to the defendant. In other cases, a defendant with very little money may prefer to save it and spend the default period in gaol instead. The latter course may seem to him a lesser evil than paying the fine out of his limited resources.

Nevertheless, the fact that the majority of Aboriginal defendants do pay the fines imposed, in spite of obvious poverty of the Aboriginal community, suggests that most would prefer to pay a fine if they possibly can. Furthermore, most Aboriginal defendants pay their 'debt to society' in one way or the other—by paying the fine or by serving the default. In this respect they are no more unreliable than whites. The argument about the police having to find them to execute warrants is nothing but an argument based on administrative convenience, which should not be sufficient to outweigh the claims of poor defendants to justice.

It is suggested that in all cases where fines are imposed on Aboriginal defendants of small means, the experiment should be tried of granting a reasonably long period of time to pay, possibly by instalments. This would at least give them the chance to pay the fine and avoid going to gaol.

IS SENTENCING DISCRIMINATORY?

This initial brief review of sentencing practices suggests that there is discrimination against Aborigines in sentencing and that this discrimination chiefly occurs in the choice of imprisonment as a suitable sentence in a higher proportion of Aboriginal cases, instead of the imposition of a lighter penalty.

Does this finding of a difference in punishments between Aborigines and whites really represent discrimination against the former group, or are other factors responsible, independent of race? This question requires an examination of the criteria courts may legitimately take into account in imposing sentences.

The first and clearest factor which should affect the court is the offence with which the defendant is charged. Legislation usually fixes the maximum sentence that can be imposed for each offence. It also specifies the type of sentence that may be given. The offence may be one for which the only penalty provided is a fine and the defendant then will only be imprisoned if he makes default in payment of the fine fixed.

The hypothesis may be advanced that the difference between the sentences imposed on Aborigines and whites is mainly due to the offences with which the two groups are respectively charged. From Appendix 2.38 it is apparent, as would be expected, that there is a relationship between the offence charged and the type of sentence imposed. The proportion of traffic offenders who are imprisoned is relatively low, whereas the proportion of defendants convicted of drunkenness, disorderliness and offences against the Native Welfare Act who are sentenced to imprisonment in the first instance, is much higher. This difference can be partly explained by the fact that for several offences under the Traffic Act the only sentence available to the court is a fine (e.g. section 30). On the other hand, the penalty for public drunkenness, even for the first offence, may be a fine or imprisonment for seven days (Police Act, section 53). This imprisonment is not in default of payment of the fine, but may be imposed initially instead of the fine.

Since Aborigines are more often convicted of offences against good order, which are more often punished by imprisonment, and, conversely, are less often convicted of traffic offences, the hypothesis seems plausible that the reason for the apparent discrimination in sentencing is not really the race of the defendant but rather the type of offence with which he is charged. The hypothesis is plausible until the statistics are examined more closely. When the Western Australian Sample is broken down into subsamples for each offence and then the sentences imposed on Aborigines and whites are again compared, it is found that the discriminatory pattern of sentencing is repeated for most of these sub-samples. Appendix 2.39 shows that in the offence categories of drunkenness, traffic, disorderly conduct, assault, offences against the police, unlawful use of a motor vehicle, other major offences and other minor offences, a higher percentage of Aborigines than whites are sentenced to imprisonment and a lower percentage are fined. These offences thus follow the pattern established for the Sample as a whole. The only category for which the opposite pattern is found is that of Native Welfare offences, and the offence of stealing is neutral in that both races have been sentenced to imprisonment to almost the same extent.

The second factor which courts may properly take into account in sentencing is the defendant's record of prior convictions. In order to test the hypothesis that the prior record plays a major role in determining the type of sentence imposed, offenders have been divided into categories of first offenders and recidivists and the sentences imposed on these groups have been examined. Appendix 2.40 shows that, as would be expected, there is a tendency for first offenders to be fined more often than recidivists, while defendants with long records are proportionately more often imprisoned. It appears from Appendix 2.41 that Aborigines are somewhat less likely to be first offenders than whites are. The actual extent of the difference may be exaggerated by that table, because of the large number of offenders for whom no record of prior convictions is available. This lack of information is even greater for the white group than for the Aborigines.

It is likely that the factor of a prior record partly explains the difference observed between the sentences imposed on Aborigines and whites, rather than outright discrimination on the ground of race. The precise extent of the influence of this factor awaits further research.

Even if the prior record of the defendant were found to be a major determinant of sentence, several comments may be made which tend to lessen the significance of any finding of non-discrimination. First, even if there were not obvious discrimination in the sentencing process the fact that Aborigines more often do have prior records is at least partly accounted for by discrimination at other stages of the legal process, for example, in the initiation of criminal prosecutions (discussed in Chapter 2). The cumulative effect of past injustices is that the Aboriginal defendant now before the court has a long criminal record which the court can look at to justify a heavy sentence in the instant case. Secondly, the crude classification into first offenders and recidivists is not very meaningful, ignoring as it does both the number and type of the previous convictions which make an offender a 'recidivist'.

Although it may be valid to state as a general proposition that courts are entitled to take prior convictions into account in fixing sentence, this does not mean that they should apply any mechanistic rule and look only at the total number of prior convictions. Some assessment of the gravity of the prior record and of its relevance to the particular offence now charged is required.

Further, the prior record is only one factor which may be taken into account. It should not outweigh all others and particularly it should not override 'the intrinsic character of the particular offence committed' which the Report of the Departmental Committee on Persistent Offenders stated to be the primary consideration in determining the nature of the sentence to be imposed.[6]

More extensive data collection and more sophisticated statistical techniques of multivariate analysis might enable a more meaningful assessment of the weight of the different factors in sentencing practice and of the complexities of the process to be made. In the meantime, an examination in more detail of the situation in a few districts and of individual cases may convey more of the flavour of sentencing practice than is revealed in general statistics.

EXCESSIVE SENTENCES—SOME INDIVIDUAL CASES

There are several cases in which Aborigines received excessive sentences. In some, the sentences were actually illegal in that they exceeded the maximum permitted by the relevant legislation.

In a South Australian town in 1962 an Aboriginal woman was charged with 'Aboriginal drink liquor'. Although she had no prior convictions she was sentenced to forty-eight hours' imprisonment. As this was her first (and only) offence, it is difficult to understand why she was not fined or released without penalty. Although forty-eight hours is not a very long period of imprisonment, it is difficult to imagine any white woman being imprisoned at all for a first offence of similar triviality.

In a Victorian case (asterisked 1965 case in Appendix 9) an Aboriginal boy was initially sentenced to ten years' imprisonment for rape and two years' for assault occasioning actual bodily harm. During the year in which he was sentenced, no other person convicted of rape received a sentence as long as twelve years. The Aboriginal was a first offender. He successfully appealed against sentence. The appeal and the implications of sentencing in his case will be more fully discussed later in this chapter.

Although severe, this sentence was not 'illegal'. It did fall within the

[6] *Report of the Departmental Committee on Persistent Offenders* (1932). London: H.M.S.O., Cmd. 4090, paras. 19-20.

maximum established by legislation for the offence. On the other hand, two Aborigines were charged with being under the influence of intoxicating liquor on a reserve under the Native Welfare Act Regulations, 1964 (W.A.). They were each sentenced by justices to six months' imprisonment, although the Regulations had been amended two years before to make the maximum sentence for this offence twenty-one days. By chance, the magistrate for the district became aware of the illegal sentence and, following his intervention, the balance of the sentence was remitted so that each defendant was required to serve only fifteen days. The magistrate regarded this as unsatisfactory as the illegal sentence should have been treated as a nullity. In an interview he pointed out, however, that white defendants have also been invalidly sentenced by justices. Although in this particular case, prejudice on the part of the court seems to have been responsible for the excessive sentence, it was also at least partly due to the ignorance of the justices about the relevant law.

The magistrate suggested that the solution to this type of problem lay in greater control over justices, for example, by providing a system of automatic review of sentences imposed by justices. In my opinion, such a reform is extremely desirable and would not be difficult to implement. The review could be conducted by local magistrates or by an officer of the Crown Law Department—a similar system operates in South Africa (Simons 1949: 67-9).

This example of an illegal sentence is not unique. On the record of a case against an Aboriginal in South Australia in 1963 appears the annotation: 'Sentence invalid and not enforced'. But, of course, illegal sentences are not as common as those which may be objected to on the ground that, though they fall within the permitted maximum, they are too severe. The latter are more difficult to criticise because of the wide discretion vested in courts in relation to sentencing. Some guidance as to the proper exercise of the sentencing process and as to the type of sentence which may properly be regarded as excessive may be obtained from an examination of the views of appeal courts.

APPEALS AGAINST SENTENCE

An Aboriginal defendant appealed against the sentence of six weeks' imprisonment imposed on him in a South Australian country town for the offence of being drunk in a public place. In support of the ground of appeal that the 'penalty inflicted is under the circumstances manifestly excessive', his solicitors introduced an affidavit made by their articled clerk. The affidavit set out a table of the sentences imposed on defendants who pleaded guilty to 'drunkenness' in the Adelaide Magistrates Court on two days when the clerk attended. Fines ranging from $2 to $20 were imposed on forty-one defendants and gaol terms ranging from seven days to eleven days were imposed on the remaining eight defendants. Those sentenced to gaol admitted the following numbers of prior convictions: eighty-two including eight for drunkenness in the last year; 466 including nineteen in the last year; seventy-nine including sixteen in the last year; twenty-five; sixty-one; seventy-nine including six in the last year; seventeen including five in the last year; 109 including fourteen in the last year. Those fined included some first offenders and others who admitted to anything from one to 183 previous convictions.

In allowing the appeal Hogarth J. did not refer to this evidence of comparative sentences but based his decision on what could be considered a technicality. It appeared that the justices were told of the defendant's previous convictions, including two for drunkenness, but he actually admitted only one previous conviction for drunkenness. The judge stated that it was therefore their duty to regard the conviction in the present case as being a second offence under section 9 of the Police Offences Act, 1953 (S.A.), that is, an offence carrying a maximum penalty of $10 or imprisonment for fourteen days. The sentence of six weeks was therefore beyond the maximum which could be imposed.

The judge substituted a penalty of eleven days' imprisonment, the period for which the appellant had already been in custody. Although he did not express an opinion about what he would have considered an appropriate sentence if he had had the duty of imposing it initially, the Judge did state: ' . . . I do not wish to be understood . . . to suggest that if the appellant had not already been in custody for that period of time, some other less severe penalty might not have been appropriate'. It seems clear that he would have regarded even the shorter period of imprisonment as excessive for a second offence of drunkenness and would have reduced the period still further if the defendant had not already been imprisoned.

It is likely that even if the technical objection had not existed, that is, if the defendant had in fact admitted his two previous convictions for drunkenness, so that the period of six weeks' imprisonment had come within the maximum fixed by the legislation, that period would still have been regarded as excessive.

The Adelaide Sample included some Aborigines who were fined and who were not discriminated against in comparison with other defendants sentenced in the same court. The sentence imposed on the defendant in this case could, therefore, represent no more than the difference between city and country sentencing practices, without any implication of discrimination against Aborigines, or it could indicate that it is mainly in country areas that the discrimination occurs. Certainly, the judge's remarks about a less severe penalty possibly being appropriate are ironical when the other sentences imposed in this particular country town are examined. This defendant was very fortunate that he had sufficient initiative to prosecute an appeal to the Supreme Court and was able to obtain legal aid for the purpose. Other Aborigines in the same town were regularly sentenced to long terms of imprisonment for minor offences and served them, apparently without even considering the possibility of appeal.

An examination of the court records for this town for the nine months following the decision appealed against, reveals that in this period 102 Aborigines were charged with 'drunkenness'. The following sentences were imposed in these cases: fines of $4 (nine cases), $5 (forty-four), $6 (five), $7 (two), $9 (one), $10 (eighteen), $15 (six), $20 (three); imprisonment of fourteen days (two), six weeks (six), two months (one); no record (five).

For the same period there is information available about only six white defendants charged with drunkenness. (It is not clear whether or not more were charged during this period.) For the six for whom records of sentences are available the results were as follows. One was fined $4; two were fined $5; one was fined $10; one was sentenced to fourteen days' imprisonment; and one was sentenced to five weeks' imprisonment.

Thus, one third of the white defendants were imprisoned for drunkenness, a higher proportion than for the Aboriginal defendants. *All* the sentences of imprisonment imposed in this court were longer than any of the sentences imposed for drunkenness in the Adelaide court. In one case in the Adelaide court the fact that the defendant had spent two days in custody before the hearing was taken into account in imposing a fine of $10 on a defendant with 101 prior convictions, including fifteen in the last year. By contrast, the country court gave no consideration to the fact that most of the defendants charged with drunkenness had spent some time in custody before the hearing, including some cases where the period in custody exceeded twenty-four hours.

It could be argued that the severe sentences imposed on Aboriginal defendants for drunkenness in this particular town are a function of the court's general sentencing practice rather than of discrimination against Aborigines as such. But this statement must be read subject to the overriding qualification that local police practice in charging defendants is strongly discriminatory against Aborigines so that a disproportionate number of them are rendered liable to the sentencing process—this is the town in which an Aboriginal was charged with wearing an R.S.L. badge (see Chapter 2).

The Victorian Aboriginal sentenced to ten years' imprisonment for rape (asterisked 1965 case in Appendix 9) provides another example of a successful appeal against sentence. At his trial he pleaded guilty and was sentenced to ten years on the rape charge and two years cumulative on a charge of assault occasioning actual bodily harm. A non-parole period of ten years was fixed. The defendant appealed against the sentence. Although he was unrepresented on the appeal, the court varied the sentence by reducing the minimum term to eight years but otherwise confirmed the sentence.

Later a Petition for Mercy under section 584 of the Crimes Act 1958 (Vic.) was presented to the Attorney-General who referred it to the Full Court of the Supreme Court of Victoria for hearing and determination as if it were an appeal by the applicant. On the hearing of the petition a great deal of new material was placed before the Full Court.

This additional material related to the applicant's drunkenness at the time of the offences and to his family background, personal characteristics and his employment record. The most interesting extra evidence was an affidavit relating to other sentences imposed for the crime of rape. Seventeen other cases were cited, making a complete record, as far as could be ascertained, of all convictions for rape in the Court of General Sessions at Melbourne and in the Supreme Court of Victoria at Melbourne in 1965 and in 1966 up to the date of the affidavit. Three earlier cases were also cited. (Appendix 13 reproduces the table of sentences included in the affidavit.) Sentences in these cases ranged from probation at the bottom (or lenient) end of the scale to twelve years' imprisonment at the top (or severe) end of the scale. The Aboriginal defendant with a twelve year sentence was at the very top of the scale, together with one other defendant sentenced four years previously. The latter had five previous convictions; three for assault and two for rape. The Aboriginal defendant had no previous convictions whatever. The other defendant was four years older than the Aboriginal defendant and his victim was a sixteen year old girl; the victim of the Aboriginal was a twenty-two year old married woman.

Even if the Aboriginal defendant's sentence is treated as one of ten years' imprisonment, omitting consideration of the additional two years imposed for the assault on the husband of the rape victim, he still falls at the top end of the scale with only four other defendants receiving sentences of the same length or longer (see Appendix 13). The only one who received a longer sentence is the defendant previously described. The three men who were also sentenced to ten years' imprisonment had prior convictions as follows: one; eleven, including four for offences against the person (one of these was a sex offence); eight, including one for a sex offence. Previous convictions are clearly one factor justifying a longer sentence than would otherwise be required for the same offence.

Another factor of aggravation in rape cases is the age of the victim. One might expect courts to sentence more severely when the victim is a teen-ager than when she is an older woman. The victims in the cases in which the longest sentences were imposed were respectively aged fourteen, eighteen, ten, twenty-one, sixteen, twenty-two and sixteen. The twenty-two year old woman was the victim of the Aboriginal defendant and on this basis one would expect that he might have received a shorter sentence than the other defendants.

On the basis of the factors examined in this table the sentence imposed on the Aboriginal defendant appears clearly excessive. In determining whether a particular sentence is excessive and harsh in all the circumstances, the most rational approach is to examine and compare other sentences imposed for the same offence in the way that was done in this affidavit.

Australian courts have been slow to acknowledge the merits of the comparative approach and to set up formal mechanisms for comparisons to be made of the sentencing practices of different judges. The reaction of the court in this case to the evidence of comparative sentences is worth quoting in full (from the unreported judgment of the Full Court):

> In our view such evidence is not of any great value to the Court in dealing with any particular case. We say that because it is quite plain to us that each case must depend peculiarly on its own facts and circumstances and beyond indicating some general trend in sentencing for offences of a like nature, we think that evidence of that kind is not much value and may be misleading in a particular case. In the present case, for example, some of the sentences included in the table were for convictions for rape with mitigating circumstances. In other cases the sentences imposed as shown by the table would, we think, be plainly inadequate for the case with which we are dealing; and so it is we

think that, although we may and should have had regard to the evidence contained in the table, its real use to us is as an indication that the sentence was, as I have already said, in the present case, a sentence of a very severe nature.

The court had already reached the conclusion that the sentence was too severe by taking into account the age of the applicant, the disadvantages and difficulties arising from his racial and family background, the absence of any prior convictions, the new evidence relating to his drunkenness at the time of the offence and the other evidence of his previous good character. It used the evidence of comparative sentences only as an additional support of its view that the sentence was too harsh.

In the result the sentence was again varied so that the applicant was sentenced to eight years' imprisonment for rape and two for assault, making a total of ten; the minimum term fixed was six years.

It may be regarded as an advance in sentencing practice that the Full Court was prepared to look at the evidence of comparative sentences at all but it is submitted that its approach still does not go far enough to recognise the real value of such comparative evidence. First, the comment that such evidence may be actually misleading and the selection of convictions for rape with mitigating circumstances as an illustration seems unduly narrow. If the Full Court is right and these sentences were completely misleading and irrelevant, then there was no need to deny the value of comparative evidence on that score. It would have been enough to criticise the selection of examples in the particular case and suggest that when such evidence is prepared in future more care should be taken to confine the material to convictions for exactly the same offence.

But it is suggested that this group of sentences is not quite as misleading as the Full Court considered and that instead it could have furnished quite a useful guide to the court. Section 44 of the Crimes Act 1958 (Vic.)[7] enables the jury to bring in a verdict of rape 'with mitigating circumstances' and such a verdict reduces the maximum sentence that can be given. In this case, the defendant's simple plea of guilty prevented any such verdict being reached.

[7] Section 44(2) provides: 'If on the trial of any person charged with rape the jury are satisfied that the offence charged has been committed but that there were circumstances connected with the commission of the crime which appear to mitigate the offence the jury may return as their verdict that such person is guilty of the offence so charged with mitigating circumstances.' Section 44(3) provides: 'A person convicted of rape with mitigating circumstances shall be liable to imprisonment for a term of not more than ten years.'

The possibility of a verdict of 'rape with mitigating circumstances' produces an anomalous situation. In *R.* v. *Webb*[8] the defendant upon arraignment pleaded guilty to rape with mitigating circumstances. A jury was empanelled and after direction by the judge, no evidence being offered by the Crown, the jury found the defendant guilty of rape with mitigating circumstances. This is a practical way around the theoretical impossibility of a defendant pleading guilty to 'rape with mitigating circumstances'. But in a case decided a few months later, where the same procedure had been adopted, the court referred to the 'procedural difficulties' of this course. 'There is but one crime, that is rape. There is no separate offence of rape with mitigating circumstances'.[9]

The Aboriginal defendant did not obtain the benefit of a verdict of 'rape with mitigating circumstances' which would have had the legal effect of reducing the maximum sentence possible from twenty years to ten. The mitigating factors eventually put before the Full Court on his behalf were of a kind which the courts in later cases have considered to justify the lesser verdict. These include the effect of alcohol.

It seems therefore that even though the Aboriginal defendant's guilty plea precluded the lesser verdict and meant that the maximum sentence which the court could legally pass was one of twenty years, the Full Court might well have considered that the sentences imposed in cases where the jury had found the alternative verdict were not totally misleading in the present case.

The second comment on the Full Court's approach is more general. It is of course true that 'each case must depend peculiarly on its own facts and circumstances'. It is true because the relevant factors which may be taken into account in sentencing are so many and the possible combinations of these factors are so complex, that we have not yet worked out techniques for rationalising sentencing practice. But to jump from that proposition to the one that comparative evidence is not of any great value is a great leap indeed. In my opinion, instead of regarding sentencing as a task that can be performed only by intuition, the courts should be far more willing

[8] [1971] V.R. 147.

[9] *R.* v. *Robinson* (Full Court, unreported, October 1970). It is suggested that a defendant could take advantage of an amendment to the Evidence Act (section 149A substituted by Evidence (Amendment) Act 1965 (Vic.)). A defendant who pleads not guilty may make admissions and need only put in issue the facts he does not want to admit. This would possibly overcome the 'procedural difficulties' referred to by the court. A better solution would be legislative reform to establish separate offences for rapes of lesser and greater seriousness.

to attempt to turn it into a rational process by examining comparative sentences for the same offence and by analysing the relevant factors in greater detail.

The affidavit of comparative sentences in this case may be regarded as a first tentative essay in this field. It is clear that other factors apart from those tabulated are relevant to sentencing. Chief among these is the gravity of the particular offence. For example, to categorise the offence here as one of 'rape' is hardly sufficient. Although all rapes are serious offences and by definition involve the use of force or at least the lack of consent of the victim, an individual offence may be less or more serious depending on the degree of force used and other surrounding circumstances, such as the fact, as occurred here, that the husband of the victim had already been immobilised by an assault.

Other important relevant factors are the family background of the offender and whether he has previously been of good character. It is suggested that all these factors should be set out in tabular form whenever any offender is being sentenced together with similar information about recent cases of the same offence. It is not suggested that it will be possible or would be desirable to reduce sentencing to a mathematical formula and hand the job over to a computer. What is suggested is that judges should be able to make more informed decisions about sentences if they have available evidence about how other judges have treated other cases and if they undertake the task of making explicit the assumptions on which they are acting.[10] If the courts are not prepared yet to go so far, it would at least be desirable if a full-scale research project on sentencing could be carried out, involving the collection of the type of material suggested and its subsequent analysis.

Courts overseas have accepted the principle that uniformity of sentencing policy is desirable.[11] Justice, in the sense of equal treatment, obviously requires that like cases should be treated alike and the best way to find out whether cases are alike is to collect and tabulate as much information as possible about them. Even though an imperfect instrument, such an analysis is surely superior to a 'system' which relies on the chance of individual judges' memories of other offenders they have sentenced.

The argument in favour of comparative sentences impliedly rejects the

[10] Cross (1965) argues for reasoned sentences. He suggests there should be a rule that reasons should be given for all prison sentences of three years or more.

[11] See, for example, *R.* v. *Lavin* [1967] Crim. L.R. 481.

view that punishment or 'treatment' should be individualised, at least in the extreme form that this view is put by some criminologists. Without wishing to argue the point here in great detail, it *is* my view that the sentence should be based on the offence rather than on the offender. Certainly some allowance should be made for factors adduced in mitigation, including those related to the individual offender rather than to the offence, but such factors should not be the main consideration influencing the sentence imposed. The view should not be accepted that the length of imprisonment should depend only on the length of time needed to 'treat' the individual offender.

LENIENT SENTENCES—SOME INDIVIDUAL CASES

The evidence so far produced suggests a pattern of discrimination against Aborigines in the matter of sentencing. On the other hand, the impression of some people working in this field is that, although this may be generally true in inferior jurisdictions, the converse is the case in higher courts.

A solicitor who has appeared for many Aborigines considers that, on the whole, the Victorian courts in which he has appeared have been sympathetic to Aborigines and have treated them leniently. His comment was not restricted to the superior courts. In support of his view he cited a number of cases, including one in which an Aboriginal was convicted for the second time of drunken driving. The magistrate imposed a fine and stated that it was otherwise his invariable practice to send a defendant to gaol on a second conviction for this offence (first 1965 case in Appendix 9). Of course, the fact that in these cases the defendants were represented by this solicitor, who was able to make a plea in mitigation, is probably extremely significant in producing the lenient sentences.

Pleas in mitigation of sentence based on the defendant's 'Aboriginality' appear to have had some success in influencing the court to be lenient. Where tribal Aborigines are concerned, tribal custom is sometimes used as a ground for an argument in mitigation of sentence. The topic will be more fully discussed in Chapter 9.

In the case of part-Aborigines, the plea in mitigation sometimes includes reference to the adverse circumstances in which the defendant has been brought up, his low standard of education and consequent difficulty in finding employment. To the extent that the defendant's plea rests on the disadvantages he suffers as a member of the most depressed section of the community, it may be considered as arising from his race. But as long as the factors of poor educational and family background are given weight in

Plate 1. Governor Davey's proclamation to the Aborigines, 1816 (reproduced by permission from the Rex Nan Kivell Collection of the National Library of Australia)

Plate 2. Aboriginal prisoners in Derby Gaol, 1899 (from the Leader, *20 May 1899)*

the same way as they would be in the case of a white defendant, the use of such material in mitigation of sentence is quite legitimate.

However, in one South Australian case the defendant's racial origin was presented to the court and accepted by the judge as a factor in mitigation of sentence in quite a different way—a way which, in my opinion, was unwarranted and unfortunate. The defendant was originally charged with the murder of his de facto wife. Subsequently he pleaded guilty to manslaughter. A welfare officer of the Department of Aboriginal Affairs called as a character witness stated: 'The practice of these people in punishing their wives or "de facto" wives is to give them considerable beatings.' He stated that he did not know whether the defendant was a part-Aborigine or a full-blood. It is clear that the defendant was not living in traditional conditions but was a fringe-dweller. It is difficult to accept that the beating he administered was in any sense justified by 'tribal custom'.

Nevertheless, the judge in sentencing him stated:

> I am told that it is the custom amongst the people of your race for a man to administer physical chastisement to their women folk for misbehaving and this is the explanation for the attack you made . . . But, although I propose to make allowance for your racial customs I must make it quite clear to you and other people of your race that if you are to live with white people and live as it is the ambition of the authorities that you should live on equal terms then you must conform to the white laws and customs and those customs seriously condemn the use of violence against even a misbehaving wife or woman with whom a man may be living.

He imposed a sentence of twelve months' imprisonment on the defendant.

The statement that wife-beating is an Aboriginal custom was misleading in the circumstances. It is true that in traditional Aboriginal communities men could physically punish women for offences, including adultery and transgressions against the rules governing sacred matters. But modern scholarship has shown that women were by no means the 'slaves and chattels' of men as earlier observers asserted (White 1970: C.H. Berndt 1970). Wife-beating was permitted but it was kept under control. In traditional society husbands could beat wives but not so severely as to inflict any real injury on them. As Meggitt says: 'A man should always berate his wife for such shortcomings . . . and he may occasionally beat her. But, if he strikes her too often, or too heavily, or sheds her blood, her father should upbraid him' (Meggitt 1962: 92).

The prevalence of wife-beating in fringe-dwelling communities appears to owe little to traditional custom. If the practice *is* more frequent amongst these communities than amongst the general community, this is unlikely to result from any perpetuation of tribal traditions.[12] The 'custom' would probably occur as often in some sections of the white community. For this reason, I consider that to take this into account as a supposed racial characteristic is an expression of racial superiority and degrading to the Aboriginal community, even if the result is leniency to a particular defendant, which may possibly be justified on other grounds.

THE PAINS OF IMPRISONMENT

The incidence of imprisonment is the major difference found in this study of the administration of justice and its effect on the two groups of Aborigines and whites. It is obvious that imprisonment is a more severe sentence than a fine or a bond, but since this is the most important point of difference between the two groups, it may be worth examining in a little more detail why it is more severe and what its overall effects on the Aboriginal community are. There is in prison at any time a higher proportion of the Aboriginal community than of the general community, and this must have some adverse effects on the group.

OPERATION OF THE PRISON SYSTEM IN PRACTICE

In general, nowadays, Aboriginal and white prisoners are treated in the same way and there is no segregation of racial groups in the prisons. Official segregation of Aboriginal and other prisoners ended as recently as 1966 at Fremantle Prison, the largest in Western Australia.[13] At this same prison, illiterates are now required to spend six months in school before they go through classification procedures. Since so many Aborigines are illiterate, this program should have more effect on them than on other prisoners.

Another difference between Aboriginal prisoners and others in Western Australia arises from their geographical location. Because the Aboriginal population is concentrated in remote areas away from the metropolitan

[12] There is, in any event, no evidence that wife-beating is more frequent in these Aboriginal communities. The extent of the practice in the general community is largely hidden from public view ('The shame of battered wives: why violence at home is kept a secret', *Age* 30/8/73, p. 14).

[13] *Sunday Times* (W.A.), 8/1/67. Also interview with Mr C.W. Campbell, Comptroller General of Prisons, W.A.

district, a higher percentage of Aboriginal prisoners is held in police gaols, instead of in common gaols, which are wholly operated by the Prisons Department. In the year ending 30 June 1966, for example, 36 per cent of Aboriginal prisoners were held in police gaols compared with 16 per cent of white prisoners.[14] The balance (64 per cent of Aboriginal prisoners and 84 per cent of white prisoners) were held in common gaols.

The conditions in some of the police gaols are shocking. In one such gaol in the north of the State anyone who is considered a security risk is chained to a concrete slab in the floor. (The only case in which I have direct evidence of this occurring concerned a white alcoholic who should probably have been in a mental hospital rather than in a barbaric prison.)

But imprisonment in some of the police gaols is less onerous than in an ordinary prison. Although the physical conditions may be bad, largely resulting from the age of the buildings, the prisoners are often given a substantial measure of freedom. They are not locked behind high walls all day but work around the police station or in the town.

The situation where gaols are operated by the same persons (the police) who initiate and conduct prosecutions is wrong in principle. Particularly dangerous is the situation where the police are in a position to make financial gains by keeping the gaols full. In some country towns a full gaol means that the local police receive quite a large sum in reimbursement of meals supplied to prisoners. If the officer in charge is dishonest, he can convert reimbursement into profit by supplying poor meals. The temptation to be quick to arrest powerless persons, particularly Aborigines, may be great. Another advantage to the local police in keeping a full complement of prisoners is that they constitute a labour force for keeping the garden in order (cf. Myrdal 1962: 548-9).

In 1904 a Royal Commissioner, Dr Roth, found (Western Australia 1905: 14-15, 91-2) that large numbers of Aborigines were being arrested for cattle-killing in the northern areas of the State.

> The larger the number of prisoners and witnesses, the better, pecuniarily, for the police, who receive from one and sixpence halfpenny to two shillings and fivepence daily per head, or as it is called in the North-Western vernacular 'per knob' . . . Your Commissioner is satisfied that the amount of purchased food, given to natives while on the road in, usually constitutes but a fraction of the native food supplied, e.g., lizard, kangaroo . . . It is no secret that the police say, if the ration

[14] *Annual Report of the Prisons Department from 1st July, 1965 to 30th June, 1966* (1967), p. 9. Perth: Government Printer.

allowance was cut down or taken away they would not arrest so many natives.

It appears that the situation is not so very different after seventy years. Although expeditions after alleged cattle-killers no longer take place, the police are still exposed to similar temptations to make a dishonest profit at the expense of the Aborigines and the same combination of the functions of prosecutor and gaoler in the one person still exists.

The Prisons Department is taking steps to replace the police gaols with new regional gaols under its immediate control. In the meantime a system of prisoner collection has been instituted which at least reduces the period for which prisoners are held in the police gaols.[15]

But the Prisons Department has no control over police lockups at all. Prisoners can be held in them for seven days and such sentences are not included in the Prisons Department statistics. Prisoners awaiting a hearing and those imprisoned in default of payment of a fine are not included in these statistics either. The number of Aborigines who spent some period in custody would therefore be even higher than the figures quoted earlier in this chapter.

Aborigines are also overrepresented in the special juvenile institutions for offenders set up by the Child Welfare Department (Gorton 1969: 3). Aboriginal children as young as fourteen have even been sent to ordinary gaols.[16] By contrast, Aborigines are underrepresented in Karnet, the special institution for alcoholics run by the Prisons Department. Considering the number of Aborigines who are convicted of liquor offences, including habitual drunkenness, they should have access to special institutions for alcoholics. But in the year ended 30 June 1966, only one Aboriginal was in Karnet Inebriate Section and the following year there were only three Aborigines there, whereas there were 105 whites.[17]

THE EFFECT OF IMPRISONMENT ON ABORIGINES

From interviews it appears that two contrary beliefs are held as to the subjective effect of imprisonment on Aborigines and on the question

[15] *Annual Report of the Prisons Department from 1st July, 1966 to 30th June, 1967* (1968), p. 5. Perth: Government Printer. Also interview with Mr C.W. Campbell, Comptroller General of Prisons, W.A. But a regional prison is still needed in the northwest of the State.

[16] *Daily News* 14/8/67.

[17] *Annual Report of the Prisons Department from 1st July, 1965 to 30th June, 1966* (1967), p. 9; *Annual Report of the Prisons Department from 1st July, 1966 to 30th June, 1967* (1968), p. 10. Perth: Government Printer.

whether they experience it in a different way from other prisoners. One school of thought asserts that they like prison or at least do not mind being imprisoned. The description by Maslyn Williams (1964: 20) of the reaction of New Guinea tribespeople brought to Port Moresby to see the wonders of civilisation could perhaps be applied to tribal Aborigines. 'They visited the prison, a place where criminals are fattened and protected behind fences so that their victims cannot be revenged . . . ' But in general, courts have considered that imprisonment will bear more heavily on tribal Aborigines than on other persons because they are unused to confinement and the conditions are such a complete change from anything they have known. So courts have fixed relatively short terms of imprisonment.

The folklore that Aborigines do not mind prison is usually put forward in relation to fringe-dwelling part-Aborigines and is accompanied by the assertion that they feel no sense of shame or stigma surrounding their imprisonment. It has not been possible to ascertain in this study the extent to which this folklore is justified by the actual attitudes of Aboriginal prisoners. It is considered unlikely to be generally true and this view is supported by interviews with a small number of Aboriginal prisoners, all of whom wished to be out of gaol, by statistics of the number of Aborigines who paid fines rather than going to gaol and by personal observation in court of the reaction of an Aboriginal girl to being sentenced to imprisonment when she had apparently hoped to be fined (see also Robinson 1969: 16). To the extent that the folklore does represent the truth about Aborigines' reaction to imprisonment it is a sad commentary on the standard of living which the community offers them outside prison walls. If many feel no stigma attaches to a prison term, may this not be because the legal system has sent them to gaol on trivial charges and, by operating in such a way that a much higher proportion of their race has had experience of imprisonment, has reduced the threatening power of that punishment? Eldridge Cleaver's assertion (1969: 46) that Negro convicts see themselves as prisoners-of-war rather than criminals probably applies equally to most Aboriginal prisoners.

Assuming then that Aborigines do experience the hardships of prison life, in much the same way as other people do, it becomes relevant to ask what are those hardships. Gresham Sykes lists (1962: 131-7) the main pains of imprisonment as being: the deprivation of liberty, the deprivation of goods and services, the deprivation of heterosexual relationships, the deprivation of autonomy and the deprivation of security.

Although at first glance these appear to be deprivations affecting the prisoner during the period of his sentence, it will be seen on closer examination that at least some of them will also adversely affect his ability to readjust to life outside the prison. The loss of autonomy resulting from the imposition of prison regulations will make it more difficult for the prisoner to make his own decisions after release. The effect of imprisonment is not only that the individual is deprived of his freedom for the period of imprisonment but that it is all the more difficult for him to obtain and keep steady employment; it is a bar to obtaining certain types of employment for ever and it disrupts relationships with his family. It therefore has a cumulative negative effect. And this effect relates not only to the individual himself but also has adverse consequences for members of his family. 'Stigma' has both a subjective and an objective meaning. Even if Aborigines do not feel shame or guilt about going to prison, they still suffer the real effects of stigmatisation as a 'criminal'.

In his classic study of total institutions, *Asylums*, Goffman (1968) suggests some of the reasons why institutions like prisons fail to change ('reform' or 'rehabilitate') those committed to them. Chief amongst these is that the institution must function in such a way that the needs of the institution rather than those of the inmates are met (p. 86). The rate of success in changing people is likely to be less in prisons—to which admission is involuntary—than in institutions like religious communities—in which conversion has occurred before entry (p. 69).

This approach suggests that, if possible, it would be preferable to find some alternative method of disposition of offenders which does not involve institutionalisation. Norval Morris (1965: 274) looks forward to a considerable reduction in the incidence of imprisonment as a sentence, stating: 'It is a truism of sound sentencing practice that a prison sentence should be imposed only when no alternative punishment is reasonably appropriate.' To the same effect is the American Law Institute's Model Penal Code which specifically directs the court not to impose a sentence of imprisonment unless it is of the view that such a sentence is necessary for the protection of the public.[18]

SUGGESTIONS FOR REFORM

Accordingly, the main improvement suggested in the sentencing of Aborigines is that greater use should be made of fines, bonds or probation as an alternative to imprisonment. A fine could be selected as a sentence more

[18] American Law Institute, Model Penal Code, section 7.01.

often if the view were taken that justice requires the amount of the fine to be adjusted to the offender's capacity to pay and if the same approach were adopted in relation to the question of time to pay. A system like that of the Swedish day-fine plan (mentioned earlier in this chapter) should be adopted in Australia for the benefit of those of limited means. A defendant wholly without means need not be imprisoned merely because he is unable to pay a fine. Mary Daunton-Fear, in an article that also makes other sensible suggestions about fining as a punishment, considers that it would be appropriate in such cases to require some form of community service to be performed by the defendant (1972: 326).

The improvement of social welfare services and education for Aborigines would help to reduce the incidence of imprisonment by providing employment opportunities and raising the general economic level of the Aboriginal community.

The substitution of other types of sentence for imprisonment is, of course, urged primarily on humanitarian grounds—in order to reduce discrimination against Aborigines in the sentencing process and to alleviate the disruption of Aboriginal society caused by having such a large percentage of its population in prison. But it can also be justified on economic grounds. It is expensive to keep men in prison. In Victoria, for example, it costs about $3.40 a day to keep a prisoner in gaol and more than 60 per cent of this is the cost of guarding him.[19]

In those cases where some form of institutionalisation is still thought to be necessary, serious consideration should be given to the establishment of new types of institutions which may have more success than existing prisons in fitting Aborigines for a stable life in the free community. Imprisonment could have positive value if it were used as an opportunity to provide Aborigines with education and work skills which they lack at present. This is rarely done in Australian prisons, although a start has been made in teaching illiterates in Western Australia.

In New Guinea special institutions for Native offenders have had some success in turning out people with skills valued by employers. The Periodic Detention Work Centre in New Zealand is also a hopeful precedent.[20] The Aborigines' Friends' Association in South Australia has

[19] Mr Whatmore, Director-General of Social Welfare, as reported in the Melbourne *Herald* 28/12/68, p. 13.

[20] P.N.G.: interview with Dr Rollo (fieldwork notes); N.Z.: personal communication from Professor C.M. Tatz. A number of Maoris have participated in the scheme and Professor Tatz considers it would be suitable for Aboriginal offenders.

for some years 'urged the establishment of a suitable training centre to assist in the rehabilitation of Aborigines where they have offended against the law'.[21]

It may be unwise to set up completely separate, segregated institutions for Aboriginal offenders. Reading the case histories of Aborigines who were formerly sentenced to the special institutions run by the Native Welfare Department as penal institutions does not lead to the conclusion that these institutions were any more successful in reforming the inmates than modern prisons are and they appear to have been, if possible, even more authoritarian. The managers were vested with a considerable degree of arbitrary and capricious power (even modern Aboriginal institutions —which are non-penal—are often authoritarian—see Chapter 8). Since the general prison system is undergoing some reform (however gradual and crippled by lack of finance) it would be preferable to establish any special institutions or programs for Aborigines within the Prisons Department's control. Nevertheless, special attention should be paid to the Aboriginal offenders within the prison population, both because they form such a large proportion of that population and because they may fairly be considered to have special needs in relation to their adjustment to the community outside prison walls. If Aborigines continue to be imprisoned in large numbers it is imperative that some thought be given to ways of making their prison experience a more constructive one.

Finally, improvement in the coverage of legal aid schemes may assist Aborigines in obtaining lighter sentences. Legal representation improves a defendant's chances of receiving a sentence of a fine instead of imprisonment (Appendix 2.42). Seventy-nine per cent of defendants represented by a lawyer were fined, compared with 64 per cent of those who were not represented. On the other hand, only 20 per cent of those represented were imprisoned, contrasted with 35 per cent of those not represented. Representation is valuable not only to a defendant who pleads not guilty but also to one who admits his guilt and for whom the only issue is whether there are any factors the court should consider in mitigation of sentence. In most cases, a lawyer can make a more effective plea in mitigation than the defendant himself and the former knows which matters are relevant to bring to the attention of the court.

Yet this is a field which is largely ignored by legal aid schemes. Often when a defendant has pleaded guilty it is assumed that there is no need

[21] Annual Report 1964, p. 8.

for legal assistance. This is one area where lawyers could be very useful at no great cost in time to themselves. If the proposals for a modified form of 'dock brief' procedure were adopted (see Chapter 4), they might make quite a difference to sentences imposed on Aborigines.

7 SPECIAL LEGISLATION

So far the position of Aborigines subject to the administration of the general law has been considered. There is also special legislation specifically directed to them and some examples of legislation which, though general on its face, affects them to a greater degree than other members of the community.

Hasluck in *Black Australians: A Survey of Native Policy in Western Australia, 1829-1897* (1970: 122-61) shows how the original ideal of British colonial policy, that Aborigines and whites should be equal before the law, was progressively eroded, so that Aborigines were eventually reduced to a status far inferior to that of the ordinary citizen. This was brought about by special legislation and administrative action.

Hasluck attributes this to three main causes. First, the desire to protect persons who suffered from natural disabilities. Second, the recognition of the hard fact that, if special provision was not made to make Aborigines amenable to the criminal law, the settlers on the frontier would probably take retribution into their own hands. Both these aims may be considered to be protective of the Aborigines. But third, there was a certain degree of pandering to the desires of the pastoralists for easy criminal prosecutions of Aborigines who had offended them.

Hasluck expresses the opinion (pp. 160-1) that there was a progressive reduction in the status of Aborigines by special legislation up to the modern period.

> The dominant feature of the later legislation has been this steady reduction of the status of the native, and, though the intention has been

> protective, legislation has now gone so far that it may well be asked what purpose or plan there is or what possible outcome there can be from a system that confines the native within a legal status that has more in common with that of a born idiot than of any other class of British subject.

Since Hasluck wrote, in the 1940s, there has indeed been a swing of the pendulum, so that much of the discriminatory legislation has been repealed (Hasluck recognises this in the preface to the second edition). However, a great deal still remains in force. The press reported in 1970 that: 'The Commonwealth Government has compiled a 19-page dossier listing State laws which discriminate unfavourably against Aborigines . . . It lists . . . discriminatory sections and regulations in Queensland . . . South Australia . . . Western Australia and . . . Victoria.'[1] Though the federal government at that time expressed the hope that any remnants of discriminatory legislation against Aborigines would shortly be eliminated this has not occurred, even under the present Labor government.

At this point it should be noted that the word 'discriminate' is ambiguous. I have used it to mean 'differentiate against'. Some of the legislation listed in the Commonwealth dossier may be considered to differentiate in favour of Aborigines. It is open to question whether all differential legislation should be repealed; but some people interpret as 'discriminatory' any legislation which treats Aborigines as a special class (an issue discussed further later in this chapter).

DEFINITIONS OF ABORIGINES

Before embarking on a detailed examination of discriminatory legislation, it is necessary to determine who belongs to the class of persons to whom the legislation applies. So far I have used the term 'Aboriginal' in a broad sense which accords more with social facts than with the definitions used in legislation.

Each State defines Aborigines in its own peculiar way.[2] In Victoria 'Aboriginal' now means 'any person who is descended from an aboriginal native of Australia'.[3] This definition is the broadest in any of the three States studied.

[1] *Age* 10/3/70, p. 1.

[2] The definitions set out are those operative at the time of fieldwork (1965-7). For the position at the beginning of 1967 see Rowley 1970: Appendix A.

[3] Aboriginal Affairs Act 1967 (Vic.) section 2. Compare section 7 of the Aborigines Act 1958 which also included a wide definition, though expressed in different terms.

The South Australian Act set up two categories of Aborigines. Full-bloods were known as 'Aboriginals' and part-Aborigines were 'persons of Aboriginal blood'.[4] Until 1968 there was provision for a Register of Aborigines and for the removal of the names of individual full-bloods from the Register if they were 'capable of accepting the full responsibilities of citizenship'.[5] As the Aboriginal Affairs Board never carried out the legislative injunction to compile the Register, the repeal of the relevant section made no difference in practice.

The Native Welfare Act, 1963 (W.A.) contained a long definition of 'native' in section 4:

> (a) any person of the full blood descended from the original inhabitants of Australia; and
> (b) any person of less than full blood who is descended from the original inhabitants of Australia or from their full blood descendants, except a person so descended who is only one-fourth or less than one-fourth of the original full blood;
>
> but notwithstanding the provisions of this interpretation, any person of the full blood or of less than the full blood descended from the original inhabitants of Australia who—
>
> (i) has served in the Territory of New Guinea or beyond the limits of the Commonwealth as a member of the Naval, Military or Air Forces of the Commonwealth; or
> (ii) has served a period of not less than six months' full time duty as a member of the Naval, Military or Air Forces of the Commonwealth,
>
> and has received or is entitled to receive an honourable discharge, has all the rights, privileges and immunities and is subject to the duties and liabilities of a natural born subject of Her Majesty who is of the same age.

In other words, any Aboriginal of more than quarter caste was subject to the restrictive legislation unless he was an ex-serviceman who fulfilled the specified conditions. In addition, under section 10, the Minister had a discretion to extend 'the benefits and privileges' of the Act to persons of quarter caste or less.

Section 28 provided for a presumption of 'Aboriginality' in relation to offences under the Justices Act and the Criminal Code. If 'there is an

[4] Aboriginal Affairs Act, 1962 (S.A.) section 4.

[5] Aboriginal Affairs Act, 1962 (S.A.) section 17. This section was repealed in 1968 with consequential amendments of section 4.

averment that a person referred to in the complaint, indictment or information is a native, courts and persons acting judicially shall presume the averment proved in the absence of proof to the contrary.' This provision applied to Aboriginal defendants and to cases involving Aboriginal victims.

Apart from military service, a person who was an Aboriginal by inheritance was sometimes able to remove himself from the status of 'Native' by making an application under the Natives (Citizenship Rights) Act, 1944-1964 (W.A.). The number of certificates of citizenship in force as at 30 June 1966 was 2117. The names of 1524 children were also included. The estimated Aboriginal population of the State was then 21,890.[6]

The situation was comparable in the Northern Territory where all except fifteen of the 16,000 full-blood Aborigines listed in a census were declared wards under the Welfare Ordinance 1953 (N.T.) (Lady Street cited in Fitzpatrick 1958: 405; see also Tatz 1964b: 51-2). 'Ward' is the euphemism for Aboriginal coined by the Northern Territory administration.

The use of the expression 'citizenship rights' in the Western Australian Act suggests either confusion over the meaning of 'citizen', or alternatively, that it is not a technical term but rather an emotive word governments use when they wish to convey the impression that they are conferring substantial rights on a group.

The Commonwealth Nationality and Citizenship Act 1948 (section 10) provided: ' . . . a person born in Australia after the commencement of this Act shall be an Australian citizen by birth'. Thus Aborigines born in 1949 or since were given the status of Australian citizens. But even this enhanced status in the federal sphere was different from that of most native-born Australians. Limitations were placed on the emigration of Aborigines by section 64 of the Commonwealth Migration Act 1958 (see also section 59 for the definition of 'aboriginal').

One attribute of citizenship is the franchise. All Aborigines are now entitled to enrol as voters for the federal Parliament and, once enrolled, are subject to all the usual responsibilities of electors. But, unlike other Australian citizens, they are not compelled to enrol.[7]

[6] *Annual Report for Year Ended 30th June, 1966, Commissioner of Native Welfare* (1966), pp. 62, 67. Perth: Government Printer.

[7] Commonwealth Electoral Act 1962 (Cwlth) (No. 31 of 1962).

The franchise has also been extended to Aborigines in the various States. In Western Australia since 1962 any 'Native' may be registered as an elector, whether or not he holds a certificate of citizenship.[8] Thus the notion of 'citizenship' is ambiguous and not very useful in analysing the nature and extent of the Aborigines' rights and duties. Possibly the idea of legal 'status' will prove more helpful to an understanding of the Aborigines' position before the law. Graveson (1953: 2) examines status in the common law, which he defines as:

> a special condition of a continuous and institutional nature, differing from the legal position of the normal person, which is conferred by law and not purely by the act of the parties, whenever a person occupies a position of which the creation, continuance or relinquishment and the incidents are a matter of sufficient social or public concern.

The definition is merely introduced here, as background to an examination of the details of the legislation applying to Aborigines. It is hoped that this will demonstrate, by concrete examples, the way that imposition of inferior legal status on a group has depressed the social and economic status of its members.

HISTORICAL SURVEY

Even repealed legislation still exerts some influence on current attitudes. An exhaustive historical survey of Aboriginal legislation in the three States studied would almost require a book to itself. All that is intended here is to indicate the complex net of regulations that surrounded Aborigines in earlier days. Particularly important categories of legislation will be discussed in more detail later.

EARLY HISTORY OF DISCRIMINATORY LEGISLATION IN WESTERN AUSTRALIA

Legislation in 1843 (7 Vic., No. 3 (W.A.)) prohibited the supply of liquor to Aborigines. A similar provision remained in force in some areas of Western Australia until recently.

In 1875 an Act[9] provided that Aborigines sentenced to capital punish-

[8] Constitution Acts Amendment Act (No. 2), 1962 (W.A.) (No. 48 of 1962). See also Electoral Act, 1907 (W.A.) sections 45 and 184.

[9] The Capital Punishment Amendment Act, 1871 Amendment Act, 1875. 39 Vic., No. 1 (W.A.).

ment might be executed in public and outside prison walls; the execution of white convicts had, since 1871, to be carried out in private.

The Aborigines Protection Act 1886 enabled an employer to enter into a binding contract with an Aboriginal child of fourteen, and if the child acted in breach of contract he could be sentenced to imprisonment.[10] The minimum contracting age for whites was twenty-one. This Act also imposed severe restrictions on freedom of movement.

Hasluck (1970: 160) notes that 'the practice of ordering natives to leave towns when they offended by their brawling or their nudity had been adopted as early as 1840, but without any sanction'. The 1886 Act empowered any justice of the peace to order any Aboriginal found loitering in town or not decently clad 'from neck to knee' to leave town, with immediate arrest and liability to imprisonment for a month if he disobeyed.[11] Similar legislation was in force until 1954.[12]

An Act of 1892[13] allowed justices of the peace to sentence Aborigines to be whipped for interfering with settlers' cattle. Aborigines were expressly excluded from the provisions of The Regulation of Whipping Act, 1884,[14] which controlled the manner in which whippings could be given.

The Aborigines Act, 1905[15] provided that the Chief Protector was the legal guardian of all Aboriginal children. In pursuance of its provisions, he proceeded to remove many children from their families and bring them to institutions away from the contaminating influence of the Aboriginal camps (Paterson 1957: 35-6). Section 42 of the same Act provided that female Aborigines had to obtain the consent of the Chief Protector before they could legally marry anyone other than an Aboriginal.

Restrictive provisions of the 1905 Act were continued by the amending Act of 1936.[16] No Aboriginal could be removed from one place to

[10] Aborigines Protection Act, 1886 (W.A.) (50 Vic., No. 25) section 18. See Hasluck (1970: 156) on imprisonment. See also section 37 re apprentices.

[11] Aborigines Protection Act, 1886 (W.A.) (50 Vic., No. 25) section 43.

[12] It was repealed by Native Welfare Act, 1954 (W.A.) section 42.

[13] 55 Vic., No. 18 (W.A.).

[14] 48 Vic., No. 5 (W.A.).

[15] No. 14 of 1905 (W.A.) section 8.

[16] Aborigines Act Amendment Act, 1936 (W.A.) (No. 43 of 1936). Some sections were modified but the essential restrictions remained as stated in the text. The amended Act was reprinted as the Native Administration Act, 1905-1936 (W.A.).

another without the permission of a protector and the giving of sureties (section 9). Aborigines could be ordered into reserves or institutions and confined there (section 12). They could be ordered out of towns or from prohibited areas (sections 41 and 42). Control over marriage and guardianship over children was retained by the administration (sections 8 and 45).

Restrictions on marriage were even extended by the 1936 Act, which provided for notice to be given to the Commissioner of Native Affairs of *any* proposed marriage of an Aboriginal. One of the grounds on which the Commissioner was given power to object to the marriage was that it was 'inadvisable as being in contravention of tribal custom' (section 45). Even adult Aborigines had to go through the humiliating experience of obtaining administrative consent to marry. This legislation was repealed as recently as 1954.[17]

The Aboriginal legislation was 'not regarded as being merely permissive and the general tenor of the administration up to 1939 at least appeared to be to exercise to the full the absolute control given' (Hasluck 1970: 161). Even after that date the degree of control exercised over individuals could be considerable, as shown in records of the Department of Native Welfare. One case history is set out in more detail in Appendix 14 to illustrate the breadth of interference in an individual's life permitted by this legislation. Without further research it is not possible to state definitely how typical this case is. But an examination of some other departmental personal files suggests that it is not too untypical. The files seen were those in which legal aid applications had been made because the Aborigines concerned had been charged with serious offences. This suggests that the authoritarian control exercised over Aborigines under earlier legislation had not been particularly successful in its objects.

RECENT HISTORY: 1940-65

To illustrate discriminatory legislation operative during this period, legislation restricting freedom of association has been chosen for extended treatment. It is historical in the sense that all the legislation to be considered here has now been repealed. The illustrations are drawn from Western Australia and South Australia.

Sexual laws. Legislation in South Australia aimed at protecting Aboriginal women by making it an offence for anyone other than an Aboriginal to

[17] Native Welfare Act, 1954 (W.A.) (No. 64 of 1954).

Plate 3. Aboriginal prisoners at Wyndham about 1894 (reproduced by permission of the Battye Library, Perth)

Plate 4. Aborigines demonstrating outside Fannie Bay Gaol, Darwin (reproduced by permission from Cheryl Buchanan, We Have Bugger All—the Kulaluk story, *Melbourne, A.U.S., 1974)*

have carnal knowledge of a female Aboriginal.[18] The protection offered Aboriginal women was potentially greater than that provided for white women, since it is an offence to have intercourse with the latter only if they are under age or if they have not consented. The consenting adult Aboriginal woman was to be protected (even against her will) from exploitation by unscrupulous white men. It cannot be claimed that the legislation was strikingly successful in achieving its objectives. Statistics are not available for the frequency of this offence in South Australia but the number of convictions was probably never high.

Three cases heard in 1961, the last year in which this conduct was still an offence, illustrate the operation of the legislation in practice. The first case involved a New Australian defendant with no previous convictions. He was sentenced to a total of five months' imprisonment on three counts of carnal knowledge of a female Aboriginal. The same woman was the 'victim' of the defendant in the second case. This defendant, another New Australian, was charged with an offence in Adelaide about four months after the first case. The woman, aged nineteen stated (in the police brief): 'I used to have sexual intercourse with men for money but I don't do it any more.' She also said about the defendant: 'It was his idea to have intercourse . . . I never tried to stop (him) from doing this, because I love him.' The defendant was convicted and put on a bond of $50, with a condition that he was not to associate with the Aboriginal girl. Later he was brought before the court for breach of the bond, because he had again been arrested for carnal knowledge of the same girl. He was fined $10 for the original offence and the bond was estreated. It is difficult to explain the difference between the penalties imposed in these two cases, except on the basis that the country court in the first case took a harsher view of the offence than the metropolitan court in the second case.

The third defendant had no previous convictions either. He claimed that he wished to marry the girl involved, who was then aged twenty-two, and whom he had known for two years. The girl agreed that they were going to marry and gave the same reason for waiting (he was paying off his car). The defendant was convicted and fined $30.

The girl had applied to the Department of Aboriginal Affairs for an exemption, but had been told to wait until she had been working as a nurse attendant for a year. In her statement to the police she said: 'I have

[18] Aborigines Act, 1934-1939 (S.A.) section 34a (inserted 1939; repealed 1962). Similar legislation existed in Western Australia but was much wider. Discussion here is confined to the narrower South Australian legislation.

been here over a year now but I haven't heard anything more about an exemption.' If she had been an exempted Aboriginal the man could not have been convicted. The following remarks reveal her attitude to this offence: 'I think a lot of (him) and I am not going to give him up because of the Aboriginal Department. (He) said he wasn't going to break with me just because of the Aboriginal Department; he didn't care what colour I was.' In this case, at least, the 'victim' who was to be protected from exploitation was ungrateful for the protection offered, seeing it as an interference with her personal liberty. She also saw it as a form of apartheid, aimed at keeping the races apart. It is interesting also to note the hint that the legislation may have as its purpose the protection of white men from contamination by coloured women.[19]

Repeal of the legislation makes discussion of its value somewhat academic. Nevertheless, the issue of protective legislation in general remains a live one. Some informants expressed the view that this particular legislation should be reintroduced while others believed that its repeal was proper.

The legislation was based on the view that Aboriginal women were in a particularly vulnerable position in the field of sexual relations with white men. This may well be true, but it does not follow that legislation of this type or any other special legislation to protect Aboriginal women is desirable.

It is probably not desirable if it is largely unenforceable or unenforced. It is apparent that most of the men prosecuted had formed relatively long-term relationships with the Aboriginal women, thus allowing the police to catch up with them. If most people who have actually offended against the law escape any legal consequences it may be because the law is too difficult to enforce, suggesting that it deals with private behaviour inappropriate for regulation by the criminal law. Similar arguments have been used in campaigns for reform of homosexuality and abortion laws, and seem well founded.

This and other 'protective' legislation has not had the effect of actually protecting the supposed beneficiaries—the Aborigines. This may be because 'protective' legislation which uses criminal sanctions is an instrument ill adapted to this end. Alternatively it may be because law-enforcement agencies really had no desire to protect Aborigines. In relation to sexual

19 Cf. Max Harris, *The Australian* 26/4/69, p. 14: ' . . . sexual apartheid laws in Australia to protect Europeans from Aboriginal nymphomaniacs'.

laws the question remains an open one. The infrequency of prosecutions may indicate that the police genuinely found it too difficult to obtain evidence of breach of the law or alternatively that they were not genuinely interested in prosecuting this offence. With this may be contrasted the high level of enforcement of other 'protective' legislation, the liquor laws, which also seem to have failed to achieve their aims.

Tatz (1964a: 240) argues persuasively that: 'Sex in a civilised society ought to be the concern of the individual. It would seem that there is little place for legislation . . . which prevents all the women of a racial group from making decisions of such a personal nature.' The third case discussed above illustrates the resentment felt by one Aboriginal woman over such interference. An Aboriginal woman may be more vulnerable than a white woman to sexual exploitation. But this vulnerability does not justify measures taken for her protection which affect her freedom to such a degree. If she is specially vulnerable, this is largely due to her low social status and insecure financial position. An Aboriginal woman employee in the outback may be in a situation of special duress.

These disabilities would be better overcome by measures directed to this end, rather than general prohibitions on sexual intercourse. When Aboriginal women are better educated and able to obtain better paid employment, any element of duress in sexual relations will reduce itself to a degree comparable with that obtaining in the case of the average white woman. The general laws prohibiting rape and unlawful carnal knowledge of girls will then protect them equally with other women.

Other legislation could have been better framed to produce the desired result of protecting Aboriginal women. It would seem better to strengthen the ability of Aboriginal women to take paternity actions against white men and to obtain maintenance for illegitimate children rather than to try to protect them by the means which have so far been used.

Other laws restricting contact between the races. It was formerly an offence in Western Australia to enter 'upon any place where natives are camped or where any natives may be congregated or in the course of travelling in pursuance of any native custom'.[20]

The appellant in *Hodge* v. *Needle*[21] had been convicted of this offence. The High Court allowed the appeal and set aside the conviction. The Court held that the words 'in pursuance of any native custom' were

[20] Native Administration Act, 1905-1936 (W.A.) section 39 (repealed in 1954).
[21] (1947) 20 A.L.J. 499.

attached to and modified both the words 'congregated' and 'travelling'. As there was no evidence that the Aborigines were congregated at the place where they were in pursuance of any native custom, the appellant was not guilty of any offence in visiting them.

Dixon J. considered (p. 500) that:

> . . . the reader unless his mind were controlled by some considerations external to the precise text or unless his sensibilities to English forms of speech had been dulled, would more naturally understand . . . the provision as dealing only with the case of aborigines, in pursuance of native custom, travelling or congregating.

Yet the Supreme Court of Western Australia had held that the words 'in pursuance of native custom' modified only the word 'travelling'. His Honour continued that it was a gratuitous assumption that the legislature had any policy in view beyond the exclusion of strangers when Aborigines were carrying out any tribal or native custom. The effect of the High Court's decision was to enlarge the Aborigines' freedom of association beyond that which the lower courts were prepared to allow.

In fact (although it does not appear from the report) the Aborigines gathered together were strikers from the surrounding pastoral stations—members of McLeod's Mob.[22] This attempt to use Aboriginal legislation as a strike-breaking weapon is paralleled by more recent events in the Northern Territory. It was alleged that the permit system in the Northern Territory, which was controlled by the Director of Welfare, has been used as a method of strike control.[23]

Section 47(1) of the Native Administration Act, 1905-1954 (W.A.) was framed widely to prohibit sexual relations and restrict other contact between the races. It provided: 'Any person (except a native)—(a) who habitually lives with natives or with any native not his wife or her husband; or (b) who cohabits with or has sexual intercourse with any native who is not his wife or her husband—shall be guilty of an offence . . . '.

This section was repealed in 1963 but a similar, though narrower, section still appeared in the Police Act and is considered below.

22 There is an extensive literature on this group which survives in some form to the present day. See, for example, Wilson 1961. *McKenna* v. *Fletcher* (1947) 20 A.L.J. 498 was a successful prosecution under the Native Administration Act, 1905-1936 (W.A.) section 47, in connection with the same strike.

23 Cecil Holmes, 'The unpermitted', *The Australian* 12/2/70, p. 13.

THE FIELDWORK PERIOD

LEGISLATION IN FORCE

In Victoria the legislation affecting Aborigines that was operative during the first part of the fieldwork period (1965-7) was the Aborigines Act 1958.[24] The Aborigines Welfare Regulations 1958[25] imposed restrictions on Aborigines living on reserves and dealt with permits for entry onto reserves. Regulations 24-9 also imposed conditions on the employment of Aborigines. The Aborigines Act 1958 was repealed by the Aboriginal Affairs Act 1967. There is now little differentiation in Victorian law between Aborigines and whites.

The Aboriginal Affairs Act, 1962[26] was the main legislation affecting Aborigines in South Australia in the fieldwork period. As in Victoria, the most severe restrictions imposed on Aborigines by this Act and the Regulations[27] relate to institutions and will be considered in Chapter 8. The Act also contained provisions relating to compulsory medical examinations of Aborigines (section 25); access to employed Aborigines (section 26); curatorship of Aborigines' property (subject to consent of the Aboriginal owner) (section 29); an offence of obstructing officers of the Department of Aboriginal Affairs (section 31); and representation by officers of Aborigines in court (section 34). Section 30, dealing with alcohol, is considered further below.

Other legislation enacted during the fieldwork period may be considered to confer benefits on Aborigines rather than to discriminate against them. The relevant Acts are: Aboriginal and Historic Relics Preservation Act, 1965; Aboriginal Lands Trust Act, 1966; and Prohibition of Discrimination Act, 1966.[28]

In Western Australia the Native Welfare Act, 1963 was proclaimed to

[24] Aborigines Act 1958 (Vic.) (Act No. 6190) as amended by: Aborigines (Houses) Act 1959 (Vic.) (Act No. 6498); Aborigines (Amendment) Act 1965 (Vic.) (Act No. 7267).

[25] Published in *Government Gazette* (Vic.), No. 80, 27/8/58, p. 2978.

[26] Act No. 45 of 1962 (S.A.). It was amended by the Aboriginal Affairs Act Amendment Act, 1966-1967.

[27] Aboriginal Affairs Regulations, 1963 (S.A.) (*Government Gazette* (S.A.), 28/2/63, p. 510). Amendments (during fieldwork period): *Government Gazette* (S.A.), 1/4/65, p. 749; 22/4/65, p. 937; 7/10/65, p. 1297.

[28] Act No. 33 of 1965 (S.A.); Act No. 87 of 1966 (S.A.); Act No. 82 of 1966 (S.A.).

come into operation on 1 July 1964.[29] Provisions of the Act and the Native Welfare Act Regulations, 1964[30] relating to reserves are discussed in the next chapter. The Act also contains provisions relating to the removal of Aborigines from the State (section 17); access to Aborigines in employment (section 21, also Regulations 47-9, 51-2); the management of Aboriginal property (section 23); the establishment of the 'Natives' Trading Fund' (sections 24-5); the distribution of estates of intestate Aborigines (section 26, also Regulation 50); representation of Aborigines in court (sections 30(2) and 32); confessions (section 31); and the Minister's power to acquire land for sale to Aborigines (section 9, also Regulations 4-12).

Other legislation in Western Australia made some reference to Aborigines.[31] The Electoral Act and the Native (Citizenship Rights) Act have already been referred to and the Licensing Act will be discussed later. The Fauna Conservation Act provides that Aborigines may take fauna for food. The Land Act confers on Aborigines a right to enter unenclosed and unimproved parts of land subject to a pastoral lease. Section 65(2) of the Police Act in terms imposes restrictions on whites but affects Aborigines and its operation will be examined next.

OPERATION OF DISCRIMINATORY LEGISLATION

Police Act (W.A.). In Western Australia, under section 65(2) of the Act, it is still an offence for anyone other than a 'Native' to lodge with Aborigines. At least three charges were laid for this offence in one northern town in 1965. In the first case the eighteen year old defendant pleaded not guilty and was acquitted by the justice of the peace. There is no direct evidence of the reason for acquittal. The police evidence certainly seems insufficient for conviction, particularly as it included hearsay. Moreover the defendant claimed that the Aboriginal he was staying with was a Citizenship Rights holder.

29 Act No. 79 of 1963 (W.A.). Proclamation: *Government Gazette* (W.A.), 26/6/64, p. 2526.

30 *Government Gazette* (W.A.), 25/6/64. (Available as a reprint.)

31 Electoral Act, 1907 (W.A.); Natives (Citizenship Rights) Act, 1944-1964 (W.A.); Licensing Act, 1911 (W.A.); Fauna Conservation Act, 1950 (W.A.) section 23; Land Act, 1933 (W.A.) section 106(2); Police Act, 1892 (W.A.). In addition to the legislation listed in the text the Native Mission Stations Act, 1923 (W.A.) (No. 31 of 1923) and Regulation 118 of the Prisons Act Regulations affect Aborigines. The Aboriginal Offenders Act, 1883 (47 Vic., No. 8) is still listed in the index to Western Australian legislation as not wholly repealed but appears to be obsolete.

The defendant in the second case, an Aboriginal, was charged with 'Not being an Aboriginal native, lodging with Aboriginal natives'. It appears that the justice of the peace was able to convict him because he had Citizenship Rights and was therefore not himself a 'Native-in-Law'. In the result he was fined $40. He had no previous convictions. The anomalous situation of Aborigines could hardly be better illustrated than by this case. On one hand, an individual Aboriginal clearly wanted 'Citizenship Rights' which brought with them certain advantages. But on the other hand, he then became liable to conviction for living with his Aboriginal friends or relatives who happened not to have their 'Rights'. The third defendant, a white man, pleaded guilty and was also fined $40.

The accepted aim of Aboriginal policy from 1937 until late 1972 was 'assimilation'. Legislation prohibiting members of the two races from living together should therefore have been considered obsolete for thirty years. Such legislation harks back to the days when it was considered that the only way in which 'advanced' Aborigines could 'succeed' in the wider society was to cut off all ties with their backward relatives and friends. The repeal of section 65(2) of the Police Act is long overdue (it was not removed in the amendment of 1972). Unlike most archaic legislation, however, it continues to be enforced in this town. This exercise of police discretion unfortunately reflects the colonial flavour of race relations in East Kimberley.

The recent official abandonment of the policy of 'assimilation' should not be taken as a justification for reversion to such archaic thinking. The modern emphasis on self-determination would leave it to the Aborigines themselves to decide whom they wish to associate with. Legislation should not intrude.

Licensing Act and Native Welfare Act (W.A.). From Appendix 2.1 it can be seen that the total number of charges laid for Native Welfare offences in the Ten Towns Sample for 1965 was 553. Of this total, 500 charges were laid against Aborigines and fifty-three against whites. The category of 'Native Welfare Offences' here comprises all offences against the Native Welfare Act and Regulations and also offences against the sections of the Licensing Act which deal with 'Natives'.[32]

[32] Figures supplied by the Commonwealth Statistician for the whole State of Western Australia in 1965 show under 'Breach of Native Welfare Act': Aborigines 420 convictions, five dismissals; whites 119 convictions, three dismissals (the Aboriginal figures are also published in the *Western Australian Year Book 1967* (1967: 206). Perth: Commonwealth Bureau of Census and Statistics). At first sight it is difficult to reconcile these figures with those quoted for my Ten Towns

Native Welfare offences thus constitute 26 per cent of all charges laid against Aborigines in the Sample. On the other hand, fifty-three charges represent only 2·6 per cent of the total charges laid against whites.

No distinction is made in Appendix 2.1 between reserve offences and others. Appendix 2.43 shows that at least 266 of these charges against Aborigines and six charges against whites concerned behaviour on reserves; a further eleven against Aborigines were for offences on missions. In general, consideration of reserve offences will be deferred until the next chapter, although some of the following discussion is also applicable to them.

It has already been shown (Appendix 2.39) that 'Native Welfare' is the one offence category in which sentencing favours Aborigines, in that they receive proportionately more fines and fewer gaol terms than whites do. Although no discrimination in sentencing exists, this legislation clearly affects Aborigines more than whites, thus enabling many more charges to be laid against them. If the penal clauses of the Native Welfare Act and the discriminatory sections of the Licensing Act had not existed in 1965, one quarter of the charges against Aborigines in the Sample could not have been prosecuted. This is not to say that the repeal of this legislation would immediately reduce Aboriginal offences by one quarter. The police might find it possible to lay alternative charges instead of those under the Native Welfare Act.

A more detailed breakdown of the Native Welfare offences in the Sample shows the following:[33]

	Aborigines	*Whites*	*Total*
Offences under Licensing Act			
'Native receive liquor'	155	0	155
'Supply liquor to Native'	56	36	92
Offences under Native Welfare Act	0	7	7
Offences under Native Welfare Regulations	281	2	283
Totals	492	45	537

Sample. But it appears that the Statistician's figures actually cover only two offences: 'Natives receiving liquor' and 'supplying liquor to Natives', which were breaches of the Licensing Act, 1911 (W.A.).

[33] This table has been produced from a second set of punched cards which coded offences in detail. The total is 537 instead of 553 as produced from the first set of cards. The difference may be due to insufficient information to enable detailed coding, or may be due to coding errors.

Charges of 'Native receive liquor' (155) represent 31 per cent of the 492 Native Welfare charges against Aborigines. Many of the offences under the Regulations also involve liquor. In addition, Aborigines in the Sample (see Appendix 2.1) were charged with 630 offences of being drunk in public under the general law (Police Act, 1892 (W.A.) section 53).

Alcohol is thus of crucial importance in the involvement of Aborigines with the criminal law. Does this mean that the white stereotype of the Aboriginal who 'can't hold his liquor' is more than a myth? Does it mean that 'protective' laws which prohibit or restrict Aboriginal drinking are necessary or desirable?

Legislation restricting access to liquor. Jeremy Beckett (1964: 33) accepts the truth of the stereotype to the extent of recognising that the consumption of alcohol 'goes far towards giving aboriginal life its distinctive character . . . ' The Aboriginal life he is concerned with is that of some 700 part-Aborigines who live in or near two small towns in far western New South Wales. 'Alcoholism is sufficiently prevalent for it to be a sign of adult male status . . . ' (p. 43).

He suggests reasons for the extent of drinking in Aboriginal society despite legal sanctions against it, the disapproval of the local white society, and of most Aboriginal women. First, in a monotonous life in a poorly organised society, drinking and getting drunk provide one of the few amusements and one way in which an individual can acquire prestige. A drinking song quoted by Beckett (p. 41) expresses this concisely:

The people in town just run us down;
They say we live on wine and beer.
But if they'd stop and think, if we didn't drink
There'd be no fun around here.

Further, drinking 'is perhaps the only means whereby a minority which has been terrorized in the past, and which remains disunited and politically impotent, can defy the white majority' (p. 46).

As I have not observed any Aboriginal communities in depth and for a sustained period as Beckett has, I cannot quarrel with his description of Aboriginal drinking sprees nor with his explanations of the motives behind Aboriginal drunkenness, which are very persuasive. His implied conclusion that alcoholism is comparatively frequent in the Aboriginal community does not necessarily follow. The comparison he makes is with the surrounding rural community and he claims that: 'The aborigine, with his taste for spirits and cheap fortified wine (notorious among whites as the drink of alcoholics) and his frequent bursts of drunkenness, comes closer to the old-time bushmen than to their modern descendants' (p. 38).

There is no solid evidence that excessive drinking is more prevalent among Aborigines than in the general Australian population. Perhaps it appears to be more prevalent because Aboriginal drinking is more visible by reason of a frequent lack of privacy. If in fact excessive drinking is more prevalent than in the general population, then it may still be no more so than among white groups of comparable socioeconomic status, such as Skid Row men and bush labourers (Rankin 1971: 15).

This contention may appear untenable to those who claim to have seen many drunken Aborigines. Certainly drinking patterns differ in different communities. It has already been noted (in Chapter 2) that Aboriginal 'visibility' is one reason for their susceptibility to arrest. But when it is realised that some large Aboriginal communities (for example, Ernabella Mission and Amata Reserve) consist almost entirely of teetotallers, while the incidence of hidden alcoholism in the white community is much higher than is popularly supposed (Stoller 1969: 21), my contention may not seem so extreme. On present information, it is not possible to prove that the frequency of alcoholism is no greater in the Aboriginal community than in white society. But it is strongly urged that the high rate of Aboriginal convictions for liquor offences is not a true reflection of the incidence of heavy drinking amongst Aborigines and that it depends to a considerable extent on other factors.

Even if we assume for the moment that Aborigines are peculiarly susceptible to alcoholic intoxication, does it follow that 'protective' legislation is justified? Even if a case can be made out for some 'protection', should it take the form that has been traditional in Australia? Before attempting to answer these questions, it is necessary to examine the legislation that was in force and how it operated in practice.

Section 150(1) of the Licensing Act (W.A.)[34] provided: 'Any person who . . . sells, supplies or gives any liquor in any quantity whatsoever . . . to any native for himself or for any other person . . . commits an offence.' The penalty was $200 or imprisonment for six months or both.

Section 150(2) was in these terms: 'Any native who knowingly receives or is in possession of any liquor commits an offence.' The penalty for this offence was $10 or imprisonment for one month.

[34] Licensing Act, 1911 (W.A.). The section in this form was introduced by the Licensing Act Amendment Act (No. 4), 1963 (W.A.) (No. 87 of 1963).

Sub-section (6) laid down that in this section and section 151 the word 'native' had the same meaning as in the Native Welfare Act, 1963. Section 151 prohibited natives from loitering about public houses. A few prosecutions were laid under this section but the majority of charges in connection with Aboriginal drinking were brought under section 150. Provisions similar to section 150 formerly existed in sections 172 and 173 of the Licensing Act (S.A.).[35]

Returning to the statistics, it is interesting that there were 155 charges against Aborigines for receiving or being in possession of liquor and only ninety-two charges of supplying liquor to them. Theoretically, for every receiver there must be a supplier.

The discrepancy between the number of persons charged with the two offences of 'supplying' and 'receiving' seems to be mainly attributable to the exercise of police discretion in investigating and prosecuting offences. The same pattern has been observed by research workers in other areas (Beckett 1964: 39-40; Tatz 1964a: 228, 230).

The discrepancy is not solely due to police choice. There are real difficulties in the way of prosecuting suppliers. Aboriginal receivers may not divulge the information necessary for conviction of a supplier, since they want to protect sources of supply for the future. It is more difficult to prove a case against a supplier than against the Aboriginal in possession of liquor. Few defences are available to the latter charge. On the other hand, police claim that suppliers display considerable ingenuity in hiding liquor in the bush for later collection by Aborigines, so that it is difficult to trace the identity of the supplier.[36] Again a defendant may only have to face one charge for supplying several Aborigines at the one time. Although strictly speaking each one represents a separate offence it seems a reasonable exercise of police discretion that only one charge should be laid.

Nevertheless, it is difficult to avoid the conclusion that at least some police use the liquor legislation as a means of harassing Aborigines. Their enthusiasm for enforcing this law against Aborigines contrasts strongly with the lack of enforcement of other sections of the Licensing Act. In

[35] Sections 172 and 173 ceased to have any effect in 1965. Proclamation in *Government Gazette* (S.A.), 1/4/65, p. 735. Similar legislation in Victoria was repealed by the Aborigines Act 1957 (Vic.) (No. 6086).

[36] 'They seem to take orders from the nigs and then dump it out in scrub anything from 5-6 miles from town. Nice and hard to catch.' (extract from police document in fieldwork notes).

South Australia the policy of non-enforcement was condemned by the Royal Commissioner.[37]

In Western Australia the Department of Native Welfare tried unsuccessfully to persuade police to enforce section 118 of the Licensing Act on behalf of Aborigines. This section makes it an offence for a licensee to refuse to supply any person with liquor or refreshment. It is often flouted by certain publicans who refuse to serve Aborigines, even now that they are entitled to drink. Welfare officers were concerned that the refusal of the publican in one town to allow Aborigines to drink in the hotel, although he would sell them bottles, was forcing Aborigines to commit an offence if they wanted to drink. The general prohibition on Aboriginal drinking had been lifted in this area but it was still an offence to take liquor onto a reserve. General prohibitions on drinking in the street and in other specified places exist. If Aborigines could not drink in the hotel, there was nowhere else that they could legally drink. A newspaper report of a Licensing Court hearing about this hotel indicates that the applicant for transfer of the licence stated that Aborigines were permitted to drink only in a separate bar.[38] From interviews and personal observation the previous year the situation was that they were allowed to use this bar only on Sundays, when the brief 'drinking sessions' made it uneconomical for the licensee to force them to take liquor away.

Aborigines themselves succeeded where the Native Welfare Department had failed. Finally (in 1972) three Aboriginal men obtained a conviction against the licensee of a country hotel, who had refused them full service.[39]

Individual prosecutions reveal the element of harassment in the enforcement of the discriminatory legislation. In one case an off-duty policeman followed a white man and two Aborigines into the bush in order to observe them drinking. The white man was charged with supplying liquor and the others with receiving liquor. One Aboriginal was in custody for three days before the hearing at which he was convicted and fined $2. In another case an Aboriginal faced five charges of supplying liquor to other Aborigines. He was sentenced to two months' imprisonment, cumula-

[37] *Report of the Royal Commission into the Law relating to the Sale, Supply and Consumption of Intoxicating Liquors and Other Matters* (*including Matters dealt with by the Licensing Act, 1932-1966*) (1966), p. 7. Adelaide: Government Printer.

[38] Melbourne *Herald* 2/8/67.

[39] *Aboriginal Welfare News* **13** (1972), p. 5.

tive on each charge, a total of ten months. It was lawful for the police to lay separate charges and for the court to impose cumulative sentences, but the effect on the Aboriginal supplier was unduly harsh.

Thus harassment occurs not only at the police level but also at the hearing stage in the process of law enforcement. A case from an earlier period (1955) nicely illustrates the potential for injustice contained in this legislation. An unrepresented Aboriginal defendant was charged with supplying liquor to another Aboriginal, who was charged with receiving. The receiver claimed that he was not a 'Native' but a quadroon and the charge against him was adjourned *sine die.* Nevertheless, the alleged supplier was convicted and a fine imposed. Since there was doubt about whether the receiver was a 'Native' within the definition in the Native Welfare Act, there should have been sufficient reasonable doubt to compel a dismissal of the case against the supplier.

The matter was taken up through administrative channels and the Minister for Justice ultimately recommended that the balance of the sentence 'be forthwith remitted'. Unfortunately the wheels of justice grind slowly and it was found that the defendant had already completed the term of imprisonment in default of payment of the fine and been discharged. The action for remission of part of his sentence was too late to be effective. He may never even have known of the mercy extended to him.

The frequency of charges against Aboriginal suppliers as compared with the number against white suppliers also shows discrimination. Tatz (1964a: 228) found in the Northern Territory that: 'The persons convicted are seldom the ones at whom the law aims: the white racketeers who exploit prohibition by supplying Aborigines large quantities of adulterated liquor at exorbitant prices, and the white males who use liquor as an inducement for sexual purposes.' The Northern Territory legislation (cited in Tatz 1964a: 221) specifically required heavy penalties where the liquor was supplied 'with the intent to derive monetary profit or other gain therefrom or with the intent of procurement for sexual purposes.' There was no similar provision distinguishing between suppliers with different motives in the Western Australian legislation. But it seems fair to infer that the Western Australian legislature did not intend that Aborigines should be more liable to conviction under the supplying provision than whites were. Further, it is clear that the motives of many Aboriginal suppliers rested on friendship or the obligations of sharing with other members of their community rather than on a desire for profit. For this reason they resented legislation which made a friendly, generous act an offence. The case of *Namatjira* v. *Raabe* in the Northern Territory is the most famous example of the harshness of this legislation in such circumstances.[40]

The 'receiving' provision was more obviously discriminatory than the 'supplying' section, since on its face it could apply only to Aborigines. They resented the fact that under this legislation they could be convicted merely for being in possession of liquor, without any requirement of proof that they had been drinking, much less that they were drunk. As one Aboriginal woman leader said to me: 'They made a fortune out of us for our little bottles of wine.' An Aboriginal taxi driver, in expressing the opinion that drinking rights should be extended to all Aborigines, said that when he visited Darwin it was marvellous 'to be free to go into the pub'. He was then still prohibited from drinking in Western Australia but when he crossed the Northern Territory border his status changed.

The liquor laws were an important point of contact and conflict between Aborigines and law enforcement authorities. The discrimination inherent in the law itself and the possibilities it opened for discriminatory law enforcement created resentment in many members of the Aboriginal community. For this reason alone, it seems that repeal of the legislation was desirable, particularly as it is clear that it had little deterrent value. Aborigines who wanted to drink were able to obtain liquor despite the law.

Nevertheless, a number of people were in favour of the discriminatory legislation. Some Aborigines accepted the underlying philosophy of the prohibitions, at least to the extent of making complaints to the police about the supply of liquor to other Aborigines and requesting the police to try to stop the liquor traffic. A white woman resident of a South Australian country town, who had proved herself a champion of the Aborigines, strongly deplored the change in the liquor laws. She claimed that 'the granting of alcohol to natives has been a definite step down . . . It is a nightmare to the Police and the public safety and a colossal expense to the Government and themselves, suffering!'[41]

[40] (1959) 100 C.L.R. 664. There is an extensive literature on the life of Namatjira, the famous Aboriginal artist, and on this conviction for which a sentence of six months' imprisonment was initially imposed. As he was permitted to serve the sentence at a mission station instead of in prison, the legislation actually bore less harshly on him than on other Aboriginal suppliers. See Hughes 1965: 302.

[41] Department of Aboriginal Affairs (Port Augusta) File No. 23 of 1966.

But most persons interviewed accepted the necessity for change, possibly because in many areas it was already a *fait accompli*. Some said that the change was long overdue; that Aborigines should have had legal access to liquor long ago.

The arguments for and against the Aboriginal liquor laws are set out in detail by Tatz (1964a: 222-34). They will not be repeated at length here. The general arguments advanced above in this chapter to support the abolition of the Aboriginal sexual laws are also relevant to the liquor laws. In some respects, the argument here is even stronger. In spite of a high level of enforcement of the liquor laws, in the shape of frequent convictions for offences against the restrictive legislation, it has proved largely ineffective as a method of preventing Aboriginal access to liquor. An odd feature of the liquor laws is that the 'victim' is 'protected' from the adverse effects of liquor by charging him with a criminal offence. In this respect the sexual laws were more rational, since the only possible offender against their provisions was the person who exploited the 'victim' (the Aboriginal woman).

The notorious failure of general prohibition of alcohol in the United States might have provided a historical warning that laws denying liquor to Aborigines were likely to fail. In any event, the lesson has now been learned and the legislation has been changed.

In South Australia the change was gradual and was carried out by means of proclamations which specified areas of the State in which the restrictive legislation should no longer apply to Aborigines. The change has now proceeded to the point where the only discriminatory liquor laws remaining are those on reserves.[42] In Western Australia a similar process was followed and the restrictions on Aboriginal drinking were finally repealed in 1972.[43]

Pessimists who forecast dire effects from the change in liquor laws no doubt felt justified by the annual report of the officer-in-charge of the

[42] Licensing Act, 1967-1973 (S.A.) no longer contains sections penalising Aboriginal drinking or the supply of liquor to Aborigines. Section 30 of the Aboriginal Affairs Act, 1962 (S.A.) was repealed in 1968. Section 17 of the Licensing Act, 1967-1973 (S.A.) authorises 'wet canteens' on reserves. But the Community Welfare Regulations, 1972 (as amended on 15 November 1973) still embody some restrictions in Part XII (Regs. 55-9).

[43] Liquor Act Amendment Act, 1972 (W.A.) repealing section 130 of the principal Act (which had replaced section 150 of the Licensing Act).

Far Northern Police Division (S.A.) for 1965/66.[44] Inspector Lockwood was reported as saying that in 1964/65 a large proportion of the charges against Aborigines were for the offence of consuming liquor.

In the 1965/66 financial year, with full drinking rights, there was a great increase in the number of offences brought about mainly by the consumption of liquor. The total number of offences at Port Augusta by Aborigines was 620 against 431 for the previous year. At Oodnadatta the rise was from fifty-seven offences to 253. Both Leigh Creek and Marree showed almost a 100 per cent increase. In Leigh Creek offences were seventy-six as against forty for the previous year and at Marree forty-four, against twenty-four. Throughout the police division the number of charges brought against Aborigines rose from 556 in 1964/65 to 1002 in 1965/66.

The Minister of Aboriginal Affairs was reported in the same sources as saying that these figures did not contradict his own reports. The reports he had received had shown a large increase in drinking offences by Aborigines soon after the restrictions on drinking had been removed. However, more recent figures had shown that in some areas the number of offences caused by drinking had reduced considerably. These reports did not show any significant increase in drinking by Aborigines who previously had not drunk excessively, but those whose drinking habits had been excessive previously were now drinking openly.

Statistics produced by the Department of Aboriginal Affairs for Port Augusta support the Minister's contention.[45] The average monthly convictions for liquor offences before the lifting of restrictions was twenty-four. The monthly rate over the year 1965/66 was thirty-four. But the figures for May and June 1966 were back to the average of twenty-four. However, a period of two months is hardly enough to show a significant trend. More interesting is a comparison of the last six months of 1965 with the first six months of 1966. In this period there was a decline from an average of thirty-six liquor convictions per month to thirty-four convictions per month. The fall in Aboriginal convictions for all offences in the same period was from fifty-seven per month for the first six months to forty-nine per month in the latter half of the financial year.

The 100 per cent increases quoted by Inspector Lockwood for Leigh Creek and Marree are not very significant either. The base rate of con-

[44] Reported in *Advertiser* 21/7/66, p. 1 and *Transcontinental* (Port Augusta), 21/7/66, p. 1.

[45] Department of Aboriginal Affairs (Port Augusta) File No. 23 of 1966.

victions used in the comparison (forty for Leigh Creek and twenty-four for Marree) is so small that an increase of almost 100 per cent still does not amount to many convictions.

The situation at Oodnadatta, though, is more striking. An increase in convictions from fifty-seven to 253 in the following year is not necessarily a reflection of the degree of use of liquor in the Aboriginal community. Another factor such as a change in attitude by the police stationed in the town could be responsible for such a change in the 'crime rate'. This does not appear to be the explanation, however, since the same police sergeant was in charge in both the years in question. The change in the liquor laws does seem to have changed drinking habits here to a marked degree and Aborigines with no previous liquor convictions were appearing in court charged with being drunk. The reason can probably be found in the extremely depressed conditions in which the local Aborigines were living and the fact that they were even more visible than in most country towns. Most Aborigines were squatting on a small area of land immediately opposite the police station. Any drunkenness was very obvious to the police.

The overall increase in Aboriginal offences for this police division represents a rise of 80 per cent when compared with the previous year. White crime also increased in the same period; but by only 23 per cent.

Does this mean that the repeal of the liquor restrictions was a mistake? Of course, this does not follow at all. The fact that Aboriginal convictions have increased since the change in the law does not invalidate the argument against continuing the previous legislation.

The Port Augusta Branch of the Aborigines' Advancement League expressed a constructive approach to the question.

> The League is fully aware that since the ban was lifted, there have been excesses, but it is unfortunate that the actions of a minority are being used as a weapon to condemn Aborigines and their actions in general . . . The lifting of the ban on Aboriginal drinking is only one facet of the progressive moves evident throughout Australia, to raise the status of the Aboriginal. When put in its true perspective, the matter of drinking socially is coupled with the need for decent housing, education standards, and equal opportunity for employment.

The lifting of restrictions was recommended by the Chairman of the Aboriginal Affairs Board and the Commissioner for Police. 'They have, no doubt, taken into account that following the lifting of restrictions, there would be some excesses with a levelling out after the novelty had worn off.'[46]

Aborigines, whose status had been considerably reduced by legislation, show themselves no more than human by rushing to take advantage of rights and privileges which the rest of the community takes for granted, once legal barriers are removed.

ABORIGINAL STATUS: LEGAL AND SOCIAL

The preceding survey of special legislation has demonstrated the truth of Hasluck's claim (1970: 160-1) that the legal status of Aborigines had 'more in common with that of a born idiot than of any other class of British subject'.

In terms of Graveson's definition of 'status' (1953: 2), an Aboriginal was subject to 'a special condition of a continuous and institutional nature' which differed from the legal position of the ordinary adult member of the community and which was conferred by law and not purely by his own act. The special status was attached to an Aboriginal because he had been born into a particular racial group. It is true that he could apply to a court to grant him a certificate of exemption and divest himself of the status. Although Graveson refers to the institutional, permanent nature of status, he also recognises that many forms of status can be brought to an end. The divesting of status may follow an application by the individual concerned but the essential point is that it 'can only be brought to an end by some . . . act of the State through the medium of its courts' (p. 100).

The comparison of the status of an Aboriginal with that of a lunatic is apt, because both are forms of involuntary status and both result in the attachment to the individual of many disabilities accompanied by few special privileges. With these forms of status can be contrasted examples of voluntary status, such as that of husband or wife. In the latter situation, the individual desires the status and performs some act of his own volition on which the status can be based (p. 135). An act of the State is still required for the granting of the status, but the fact that individuals voluntarily take the first step towards acquiring the status suggests that in these cases the benefits to be obtained outweigh any disabilities.

Examination of the special Aboriginal legislation suggests that there is

46 *Sunday Mail* 6/11/65. Letter reprinted in abridged form in Aborigines' Advancement League *Newsletter* (S.A.), December 1965, p. 5.

some relationship between legal status and social and economic status. Reference has been made frequently to the low socioeconomic status of Aborigines. In this context economic status refers to control over assets which are valued by the wider community; social status means prestige in the eyes of the wider society.[47] It is clear that in this sense Aborigines have never had high social status and their low standing antedates the enactment of the most restrictive legislation. Nevertheless, it seems plausible to suggest that the discriminatory legislation did not merely preserve the low status of the Aboriginal group but actually further depressed it. This result flowed partly from the institutionalisation of notions of inferiority in the legislation which must have reinforced the Aborigines' feelings of exclusion from the general community. It was also produced by the real barriers which the legislation set up to normal participation in the social and economic life of the community. For example, an Aboriginal who was not permitted to drink alcohol at all, must have found it difficult to share to the full in the life of many Australian groups. Similarly, restrictions on freedom of movement hampered equal participation in economic life.

ABORIGINAL STATUS IN THE FUTURE

Is there a place for special legislation concerning Aborigines in the future? As part of its program on Aborigines the federal government intends to abolish all discriminatory legislation at both federal and State levels. This policy has been welcomed by Aboriginal organisations and it has been shown above that the repeal of discriminatory legislation has already proceeded a long way in some States. On the other hand, Aboriginal organisations are continuing to press for preferential legislation, that is, legislation which differentiates in favour of Aborigines, to replace the repealed discriminatory legislation.

The line between discriminatory and preferential legislation is not always easy to draw, depending as it does to a large extent on a value judgment as to whether the legislation in question benefits Aborigines. No doubt there are clear-cut cases on either side of the line, but it has been shown that legislation which was intended to protect Aborigines from exploitation, such as the cohabitation legislation, was disliked and regarded as discriminatory by the Aborigines themselves.

[47] This is a colloquial meaning of 'status', rather than a technical sociological usage. But many sociologists still prefer the colloquial meaning. See Zelditch 1968: 250-7.

In the recent moves to sweep away discriminatory legislation some laws that clearly conferred privileges on Aborigines were also abolished. For example, the South Australian provision which formerly permitted Aborigines to keep two unregistered dogs was repealed.[48] It is true that historically most of the special legislation imposed disabilities on Aborigines and operated to their prejudice. But the questions remain: should all legislation conferring a special status on Aborigines be repealed, whether or not it discriminates against them or confers special benefits on them? Should new legislation be enacted which attaches 'status' to Aborigines as a group, but with different incidents (privileges and disabilities) from their former status?

I encountered a strong sentiment amongst some laymen and administrators that if Aborigines wanted equal rights they must be prepared to accept equal responsibilities. This was interpreted to mean that no special legislation treating Aborigines as a separate group should exist. While it may be suspected that persons adopting this point of view frequently do so because they dislike Aborigines and do not want any benefits offered to them, the argument is worth examining to see if anything can be found in its favour.

It has been argued above that the grant of a special status to Aborigines in the past contributed to the maintenance of their low socioeconomic status. If this is accepted, it could be further argued that any separate treatment in the future will reinforce the image of the Aborigines in the eyes of the rest of the community as different and thus perpetuate their inferior social position.

To put the same matter slightly differently: Graveson claims (1953: 114, 125) that 'One of the chief objects of status is the classification of society.' Is there now any basis for classifying society into Aborigines and whites?

The answer seems to be that the content of the special legislation should be designed to influence the community's image of Aborigines. Legislation which recognises the value of their cultural heritage, such as legislation for the protection of sacred objects,[49] should help to project a more

48 Registration of Dogs Act Amendment Act, 1968 (S.A.) (No. 37 of 1968). Section 18 repeals section 36 of the principal Act.

49 Aboriginal and Historic Relics Preservation Act, 1965 (S.A.); Aboriginal Heritage Act, 1972 (W.A.); Archaeological and Aboriginal Relics Preservation Act 1972 (Vic.).

favourable image of the race. In other cases, the legislation may confer material benefits which will improve their economic position and self-confidence and this should eventually, if not immediately, raise their standing in the eyes of others. The South Australian Aboriginal Lands Trust Act[50] belongs in this class of legislation.

Furthermore, the notion that Aborigines are being assimilated into a homogeneous society in which no groups have special privileges is obviously unfounded. Not only is 'assimilation' no longer official policy, but Australian society is far from being homogeneous. People who argue for no special privileges or benefits for Aborigines conveniently overlook the substantial benefits conferred on other interest groups in the community, such as returned servicemen (with their repatriation benefits) and farmers (with their subsidies).

No doubt there are sound reasons why these groups are offered special benefits and usually the benefits offered are ones they have themselves requested. The justification for special benefits in the Aboriginal case is that historically the white community has treated them in a way which has largely produced their present disabilities. Positive discrimination is therefore justified to overcome the legacy of past treatment and remove present social and economic disabilities. It is further suggested that special legislation will be most successful in this aim if it is enacted after consultation with Aborigines, rather than by others who believe they know what their best interests demand, as always happened in the past.

The rigidity of 'status' (in Graveson's sense) also suggests that any future legislation conferring special status on Aborigines should be framed so as to make it voluntary rather than involuntary status. Aborigines should be able to choose whether they want to be subject to the special legislation or not.

Detailed suggestions for the type of legislation which is needed, together with the justifications for it, have been excellently set out in a policy document of the former Aborigines Welfare Board of Victoria.[51]

As an alternative to special legislation applying to Aborigines as a designated group, it might be possible to enact provisions of universal

[50] Aboriginal Lands Trust Act, 1966-1973 (S.A.). For comments on this and other preferential legislation, see Shearer n.d.

[51] 'Aboriginal Policies of the Aborigines Welfare Board' in *Report of the Aborigines Welfare Board for the Year Ended 30th June, 1967* (1967), p. 12. Melbourne: Government Printer.

application but so designed as to have a differential impact.[52] An example is the proposal to provide for needy families by paying a substantial allowance to all families, but making it taxable, so that those who have enough already will automatically pay it back. Other legislation could apply to all poor people, which would include most Aborigines but would also include poor whites, so that the criterion would be need rather than race. In this way some of the sting should be taken out of the 'white backlash'. While I believe that fear of the 'white backlash' is overrated, there is no sense in unnecessarily provoking antagonism to Aborigines. Justice does demand consideration of the rights of poor whites as well as of poor Aborigines.

But until such general provisions are enacted, special legislation favouring Aborigines should continue. They should not be thrown on the resources of general community services, which, at present, are not well equipped to cope with their special needs.

EXCURSUS

'STATUS OFFENCES'

A considerable legal literature has appeared on the topic of 'status offences'. Most writers claim that these are offences which depend on *being* a particular kind of person, rather than on *acting* in a certain way.

The discriminatory legislation which has been considered in this chapter is specifically directed at Aborigines but it does not make the status of Aboriginal in itself a crime. It provides that a person with the status of Aboriginal who behaves in a certain way is guilty of an offence, whereas anyone else who behaves in the same way is not liable to any criminal sanction.

This excursus concerns rather persons who are penalised merely because they possess a certain status. The offences most commonly discussed under this heading are those of drunkenness and vagrancy. It so happens that Aborigines are overrepresented in the ranks of those convicted of these two offences. The legislation on its face does not discriminate against Aborigines but is general in its terms. The reasons why Aborigines particularly feel the impact of this legislation should become apparent when each offence is examined separately.

52 I am indebted to Alan Jordan for this suggestion and for constructive criticism of the rest of this chapter.

DRUNKENNESS

Section 53 of the Police Act (W.A.) is accurately described in the side-note as inflicting a 'penalty on drunkards'. It provides: 'Every person who shall be found drunk in any street, public place, or in any passenger boat or vehicle, shall for the first offence be liable on conviction to a penalty not exceeding' $2 or to imprisonment not exceeding seven days. The maximum penalty for any subsequent offence is $10 or twenty-one days' imprisonment. In the Ten Towns Sample there were 630 charges against Aborigines for this offence and 341 charges against whites (Appendix 2.1). 630 charges represent 32·9 per cent of all charges against Aborigines in the Sample.

Drunkenness is the offence where the traditional expressions of the criminal law: 'proof beyond a reasonable doubt', 'innocent until proved guilty' and so on, seem most remote from reality. Many writers (for example Murtagh 1966: 2-3; Jordan 1966: 60) have described the morning 'drunks parade' in court; the very frequent guilty pleas, inarticulate unrepresented defendants, the speed with which justice is dispensed. My observations of courts dealing with drunkenness charges revealed no essential variation from this pattern.

Detailed statistics on the drunkenness offences in the Ten Towns Sample (Appendixes 2.5, 2.33, 2.44, 2.45) confirm the subjective impressions gathered from watching courts in action. These tables show that all drunkenness offenders are proceeded against by arrest, not by summons; that pleas of not guilty are infrequent; that there are few dismissals; that most defendants are unrepresented.

When a comparison is made between Aboriginal and white drunkenness offenders, it is seen that there is a significant difference between the grant of police bail to the two groups and the difference is favourable to whites (Appendix 2.46). It is thus not surprising to find that many more whites had their cases disposed of by estreatment of bail without a conviction being recorded. (Of the 181 drunkenness cases shown in Appendix 2.33 as having had bail estreated, 103 were whites, seventy-seven Aborigines and the race of one was not stated.)

Sentencing also shows a marked difference in favour of whites, with many more Aborigines receiving sentences of imprisonment (Appendix 2.39). The gaol terms imposed are, of course, relatively short, since the maximum penalty provided by the legislation is twenty-one days. But Aborigines gaoled for drunkenness represent a significant part of the prison population.

'For many years almost everyone in the criminal justice system and out of it has recognized that the criminal process is an irrational means of dealing with drunks.'[53] In the first place, it is inefficient and costly. The high rate of recidivism amongst drunkenness offenders shows that the short gaol terms have little deterrent value and effect little in the way of reformation or treatment. Appendix 2.47 shows the number of drunkenness offenders in the Sample who already had convictions for the same offence.

The ultimate in recidivism is found in the report of an Irishman who had 500 convictions for drunkenness, a record for Western Australia.[54] The Aboriginal with the record number of convictions in Western Australia has over 400; most are for drunkenness.

Jordan (1966: 3) shows that in Victoria for the year 1963/64 drunkenness offenders, who made up 19 per cent of all individual men committed to prison during the year, were responsible for 60 per cent of all admissions, each man serving an average of 5·4 sentences for this one offence.

In an intensive study of 'homeless men',[55] he found a pattern of frequent convictions for drunkenness, vagrancy, begging and similar offences. He concluded (p. 40): ' . . . we may be sure that the very great majority of homeless men are not and never have been serious criminals.' 'Only about one quarter have ever been convicted of offences serious enough to be punished by gaol sentences of six months or more, and even fewer men have repeatedly been convicted of such offences.' (p. 52).

It is not yet possible to state definitely what proportion of Aboriginal offenders fall into the pattern described by Jordan. After looking at numerous criminal histories, the impression gained is that many Aborigines are petty offenders of the type he pictures, but further analysis is necessary.

One Aboriginal case history, presented in Appendix 15, illustrates the way an individual may be repeatedly convicted of liquor offences. This man has been charged with thirty-nine offences of which only one (for

[53] *The Challenge of Crime in a Free Society*, 1967: 14.

[54] Melbourne *Herald* 20/8/68, p. 3.

[55] Defined as: 'Adult or adolescent males who are not currently living with any relatives (except occasionally in the case of brothers), who are chronically dependent on the community for material support, either continuously or intermittently, and who use inner-city night shelters, hand-outs and other Skid Row facilities, at least on occasion.' (Jordan 1966: 15).

creating a disturbance) is not for a liquor offence. Admittedly this is an extreme case. Most of the case histories derived from the same source (C.I.B. records, Western Australia) have at least one charge of petty theft or minor assault.

The expense to the community of keeping chronic drunkenness offenders in prison is high. The cost would not matter if worthwhile results were being achieved, since any alternative mode of dealing with these people, by medical or social welfare services, is likely to be just as expensive. But the proved failure of the penal system to produce changed behaviour amongst this group (as demonstrated by the high rate of recidivism) suggests that a radical rethinking of the problem is necessary.

A more fundamental objection to the present system is an ethical one, which questions the criminal punishment of any 'status offence'. Should a man be punished criminally for *being* a certain kind of person? This question has been presented to American courts in a constitutional context. In the leading case of *Powell* v. *Texas*[56] the defendant was convicted of 'being found in a state of intoxication in a public place.' On appeal, the United States Supreme Court affirmed the conviction but the five majority judges did not agree on an opinion.

The defendant argued that the conviction and penalty was invalid as a 'cruel and unusual punishment' under the Eighth Amendment as applied to the States by the Fourteenth Amendment of the Constitution. He claimed to be suffering from the disease of chronic alcoholism and therefore his appearance in public in a condition of intoxication was not of his own volition. He might well have had some hopes of success. Convictions of chronic alcoholics for violations of public drunkenness statutes had been invalidated on Eighth Amendment grounds by two federal Circuit Courts of Appeals in *Easter* and *Driver*.[57] The Supreme Court itself in *Robinson* v. *California*[58] had declared unconstitutional a State statute which made it a crime to 'be addicted to the use of narcotics'.

Four of the majority judges (Warren C.J., Marshall, Black and Harlan JJ.) rested their decision to a certain extent on the inadequacy of the record of proceedings in the lower court. In their view, the evidence failed to establish that chronic alcoholics were unable to abstain from

[56] (1968) 392 U.S. 514, 20 L. Ed. 2d 1254.

[57] *Easter* v. *District of Columbia* (1966) 361 F. 2d 50; *Driver* v. *Hinnant* (1966) 356 F. 2d 761.

[58] (1962) 370 U.S. 660.

drinking and that the defendant in particular was under an overwhelming compulsion to drink. There is at least a hint that they would recognise a constitutional defence if the record was right, that is, if an individual defendant brought forward stronger evidence of the nature of his disease of chronic alcoholism. After insisting on the conceptual distinction between 'loss of control' once an individual has started to drink and 'inability to abstain' from drinking in the first place they say: 'Presumably a person would have to display both characteristics in order to make out a constitutional defense, should one be recognized.'[59]

Later parts of the judgment, however, make it apparent that these judges would be unlikely to declare a conviction under this statute unconstitutional, no matter what the individual defendant's circumstances were. They distinguished *Robinson* v. *California* because in the present case the defendant was convicted, not for being a chronic alcoholic, but for being in public while drunk on a particular occasion.

> The State of Texas thus has not sought to punish a mere status, as California did in Robinson; . . . Rather, it has imposed upon appellant a criminal sanction for public behaviour which may create substantial health and safety hazards, both for appellant and for members of the general public, and which offends the moral and esthetic sensibilities of a large segment of the community. (p. 1267).

Thus they categorised the offence of being drunk in a public place as one which involved an act on the part of the defendant; not one which punished mere possession of a status or a state of *being*. By interpreting *Robinson* as a case concerning *actus reus* rather than *mens rea* they held that it was inapplicable here. 'The entire thrust of Robinson's interpretation of the Cruel and Unusual Punishment Clause is that criminal penalties may be inflicted only if the accused has committed some act . . . which society has an interest in preventing, or perhaps in historical common law terms, has committed some actus reus.' (p. 1268).

Furthermore, they would not accept a general constitutional doctrine of *mens rea*. Black and Harlan JJ., in a separate concurring opinion, express personal sympathy with the view that criminal sanctions should be imposed only if conduct is morally blameworthy, but this does not mean that the States should be held constitutionally required to embody that same view in their legislation (p. 1271).

[59] *Powell* v. *Texas* (1968) 20 L. Ed. 2d 1254, 1263.

White J. concurred with the majority in affirming the conviction, but his conclusion was based entirely on the specific facts in this case. His opinion was that some chronic alcoholics could prove 'that resisting drunkenness is impossible and that avoiding public places when intoxicated is also impossible.' (p. 1278). If both elements were established he would uphold a constitutional defence. In a more realistic view of chronic alcoholics than some of his colleagues he recognised that 'for all practical purposes the public streets may be home for these unfortunates, not because their disease compels them to be there, but because, drunk or sober, they have no place else to go and no place else to be when they are drinking.' (p. 1278). But Powell had a home and a wife, and if there were reasons why he had to drink in public or be drunk there, they were not offered in evidence.

The four dissentients (Brennan, Douglas, Fortas and Stewart JJ.) held that Powell's conviction constituted cruel and unusual punishment. They accepted the trial court's findings that the defendant was a chronic alcoholic who could not resist the constant, excessive consumption of alcohol and did not appear in public by his own volition but under a compulsion which was part of his disease. On these findings they held that any criminal penalty imposed on him violated the Eighth amendment (p. 1288).

Fortas J. agreed that the public intoxication statute covered more than a mere status and was thus unlike the statute involved in the *Robinson* decision (p. 1287). But he also refused to say that Powell had committed any criminal *act.* Instead he delineated an intermediate category—the *condition* of being intoxicated in public (p. 1282).

Since he also adopted a wider view of *Robinson* than the majority did, he was able to hold that it covered the instant case. In his view the rationale of *Robinson* was that 'criminal penalties may not be inflicted upon a person for being in a condition he is powerless to change'. (p. 1286). In traditional common law terms, this looks much more like viewing *Robinson* as a decision concerning *mens rea* or moral blameworthiness and as imposing limits on State legislative powers in terms of a general *mens rea* doctrine.

Before the decision in *Powell* v. *Texas* was handed down it was hoped that it would produce some finality on the question of the constitutional validity of public intoxication statutes. This hope was not realised because of the split majority, and the extent to which the decision rested on the inadequacy of the record in the particular case.

The constitutional issue is not directly relevant in Australia. The Bill of Rights with its prohibition on 'cruel and unusual punishment' is in force here,[60] but it has no more force than any other statute. It is not entrenched in the federal Constitution. Our legal tradition of non-enforcement of such rights is so strong that it is impossible to imagine that a court could be persuaded to invalidate a public drunkenness statute on the ground that it conflicted with the Bill of Rights of 1688. What I am concerned with here is rather the wider social policy issue: whether the result reached in *Powell* v. *Texas* is desirable or whether the dissent has more to commend it.

Murtagh, a New York judge, is strongly opposed to the indiscriminate arrest of drunken derelicts. He therefore agreed (1966: 9) with the result reached in the *Driver* and *Easter* cases. But he criticised the rationale of the decisions which depended on the defendant being a 'chronic alcoholic'. No doubt he would have criticised *Powell* v. *Texas* if it had been decided when he wrote, since even Fortas J., dissenting, was careful to restrict his decision to the case of a chronic alcoholic (p. 1282). Murtagh's view is that public intoxication statutes are fundamentally unconstitutional, that is, when they are applied to anyone whether a chronic alcoholic or not.

He rejects the approach (taken by Fortas J.) that an alcoholic is without free will and that it is therefore unconstitutional to hold him responsible for his conduct. He criticises (1967: 53) this concentration on the 'disease' of alcoholism, which ignores the more fundamental problem represented by the status of chronic human deterioration. It is the total pathology of the derelict 'that affronts society, and leads to arrest for public drunkenness. These are "status" offenses; the offense consists in being a derelict. The immediate condition of inebriety may be the occasion, but it is not the fundamental reason for an arrest.' (Murtagh 1966: 10-11).

Once again there is an ambiguity in the word 'status'. It is being used here in the sense of economic station. On its face the law does not penalise the possession of a 'status' in this sense. It makes it an offence for non-derelicts as much as derelicts to be drunk in public; on the other hand, teetotal derelicts can avoid prosecution under this law. It is unusual for lawyers to look behind the veil, as Murtagh has done, to see how the law actually operates in practice. To the extent that persons of higher social standing are not arrested, even though they may be drunk in public, and

[60] [1688] 1 William & Mary, Sess. II. c. 2. Senator Murphy, the former federal Attorney-General, introduced a Human Rights Bill into the Senate on 21 November 1973. It is uncertain whether this Bill will become law.

that sober derelicts may be arrested (as sometimes occurs), the law does in practice penalise low socioeconomic status. These reasons largely explain the overrepresentation of Aborigines amongst drunkenness offenders in the Western Australian Sample.

First, Aborigines are more likely to be on the streets when drunk, because they have fewer alternative places to go. Second, when the police see them they are more likely to arrest them, because they believe, rightly or wrongly, that there is no alternative. Other persons found drunk on the street are far more likely to be sent home without prosecution.

Murtagh's realism is attractive and so also is his expression of the rationale for his rejection of public intoxication statutes. He quotes John Stuart Mill: 'the only purpose for which power can be rightfully exercised over any member of a civilized community, against his will, is to prevent harm to others.' Therefore, the public intoxication statutes should be interpreted as having been intended to penalise public drunkenness only insofar as it interferes with peace and tranquility—that is, when it is accompanied by disorderly behaviour which has a tendency to cause a breach of the peace (Murtagh 1966: 12).

To summarise these three main approaches in terms of traditional common law doctrines of *mens rea* and *actus reus*: the first view, that of the majority in *Powell* v. *Texas*, is that there should be no criminal penalty without an *actus reus*. The majority hold that 'being found drunk in public' constitutes an act and since they also reject any constitutional requirement of *mens rea*, they uphold the validity of the conviction.

The second view, represented by the dissentients in *Powell* v. *Texas*, is that there should be no criminal penalty without *mens rea*. While accepting the majority view of the necessity for an *actus reus*, they impose another requirement, that only morally blameworthy people should be dealt with by the criminal law. Anyone who acts under a compulsion he is powerless to resist should not be liable to criminal punishment.

The third approach, that of Murtagh and Mill, requires not only an act but an act of a really socially harmful nature. This view says nothing about the presence or absence of *mens rea*. Public drunkenness should not be a criminal offence. Even if appearing drunk in public is an 'act' and even if the defendant was not a chronic alcoholic so that he could be said to have *mens rea*, his behaviour is not sufficiently serious to be subjected to criminal penalties.

In my view, the third approach is the most persuasive. It crystallises the objections to legislation which makes public drunkenness a criminal offence. It should perhaps be noted that not everyone agrees that public drunkenness causes no harm to others. The reference by the majority judges in *Powell* to offence to 'the moral and esthetic sensibilities of a large segment of the community' (p. 1267) suggests that they would not agree that public drunkenness (without disorderliness) is not socially harmful. But in my view offended sensibilities are a poor reason for locking up a drunken man.

For these reasons of social policy I believe that public drunkenness should be taken right out of the criminal justice system. The first moves in this direction have already been taken in the United States and England. The President's Commission on Law Enforcement and Administration of Justice recommended that drunkenness alone (as distinguished from disorderly conduct) should not continue to be treated as a crime. It proposed instead the development of public health facilities for detoxification and the enactment of civil legislation authorising the police to pick up any drunks who do not co-operate.[61]

In England, the offence of being drunk and disorderly remained under the Criminal Justice Act, 1967 but it was intended that imprisonment should not be imposed. As Lord Parker said in *Osgerby* v. *Rushton*:[62] 'The idea behind Parliament was that there should no longer be imprisonment for drunks but suitable accommodation should be provided for their treatment. Needless to say, that has not yet come into force because the suitable accommodation has not been found.'

I have discussed elsewhere (Eggleston 1972: 181) the dangers of substituting a medical model, which regards alcoholism as a 'disease', for the existing legal model which regards it as a crime. It is unjust to the alcoholic to compulsorily subject him to 'treatment' under civil legislation if the period of detention is thereby lengthened and treatment is still not provided. Thus, I support a change from criminal procedure to civil procedure only if the new civil legislation involves more than a mere semantic change and provides adequate safeguards for the protection of individual liberty. After all, Mill's dictum relates not only to the coercive power of the state expressed through the criminal law but to any power exercised over the individual against his will.

[61] *The Challenge of Crime in a Free Society*, 1967: 235.

[62] [1968] 3 W.L.R. 438, 441.

VAGRANCY

Vagrancy is another 'status offence' in the sense that punishment is imposed for being a particular kind of person rather than for any specified behaviour.

Section 65 of the Police Act, 1892 (W.A.) provides that anyone who commits one of a series of offences shall be deemed 'an idle and disorderly person' and shall on conviction be liable to a maximum of six months' imprisonment. The first offence specified (section 65(1)) is: 'Every person having no visible lawful means of support, who being thereto required by any Justice, . . . shall not give a good account of his means of support to the satisfaction of such Justice.'

Vagrancy legislation dates back to the fourteenth century in England (Stephen 1883: 267). Many writers consider it obsolete and inapplicable to modern social conditions (Campbell and Whitmore 1966: 20-1). Nevertheless, similar legislation has been re-enacted as recently as 1966 in Victoria and it is still enforced by the police, particularly against Aborigines.[63]

The total number of charges of vagrancy in the Western Australian Ten Towns Sample was fifty-seven: thirty-seven against Aborigines, nineteen against whites and one case in which there was no record of the race of the defendant.[64] Figures supplied by the Commonwealth Statistician for the whole of Western Australia for 1965[65] show a different pattern: of 173 Aborigines charged, 165 were convicted and eight dismissed; of 376 whites, 339 were convicted and thirty-seven dismissed.

The figures are not directly comparable because the Statistician's 'vagrancy' category covers other offences besides 'insufficient means'. It is not known whether the different pattern results from the different definitions used or whether the Ten Towns Sample is unrepresentative of the whole State in this respect. In any event, even if in absolute terms Abori-

63 Vagrancy Act 1966 (Vic.) (Act No. 7393) section 5. In late 1973, for example, an Aboriginal who served a month's sentence for vagrancy had the sentence quashed in the County Court at Sale. According to the press report, 'In reversing the JPs decision, Judge Vickery said it was "a bit rough" when a person who had left gaol only two weeks previously and had gone to see his sister-in-law had been arrested for vagrancy' (*Age* 15/11/73).

64 These figures come from the second set of punched cards with more detailed categories of offences.

65 Fieldwork notes. The Aboriginal figures are also published in the *Western Australian Year Book 1967* (1967: 206). Perth: Commonwealth Bureau of Census and Statistics.

gines do not outnumber whites in relation to vagrancy charges, the number charged is very high when considered in relation to population.

What is it, in practice, for which these defendants have been convicted? In his study of the enforcement of the Victorian vagrancy law, Jordan (1966) found that at present it seems to be used primarily against homeless men, but it is probably used quite often against persons who are more likely to commit serious crimes. 'In such cases, the purpose of the vagrancy charge may be to forestall criminal acts, or to permit detention of the person until the police are ready to lay charges for the offences which are the real occasion of arrest.' (p. 49). Examination of the records of individual Aboriginal cases suggests that in most of them the defendant is being penalised for his poverty and social inadequacy, rather than that the vagrancy charge is being used as a holding device pending the laying of a more serious charge.

Police often appear to lay these charges against those they regard as 'undeserving poor'; Aborigines who have little money and are not trying to find work. But in many cases even the evidence of lack of means and failure to seek employment is inadequate. It may be that in these cases the vagrancy charge was laid as a holding charge and when evidence of any more serious offence failed to eventuate the police decided to proceed with the vagrancy prosecution. Alternatively, these may simply be cases where the police are harassing individuals.

Selected individual cases will illustrate these points. An eighteen year old Aboriginal girl pleaded not guilty to a vagrancy charge. She was convicted and placed on a bond for twelve months with a condition that she remain at a mission. Police evidence was that she had been found in a room in the men's quarters at the meatworks. She had no money when arrested. The arresting policeman had not seen her in employment since she returned to town from the mission three weeks before. He had noticed her on several occasions at the men's quarters.

On this evidence the magistrate held that the prosecution had raised a reasonable presumption that the accused was without lawful or sufficient means of support. The defendant then made an unsworn statement in which she claimed that she had returned from the mission two weeks ago. She worked for three days as a domestic and was paid \$2. She then lived with her sister and helped her in return for her keep. 'I didn't try and get any more work. I went to the meatworks to see the boys. They didn't do anything to me at the meatworks.' Presumably this charge was laid because the defendant was suspected of being a prostitute, but any offence under section 59 of the Police Act (W.A.) would have been difficult to prove. This appears to be one quite common function of vagrancy prosecutions.

Another function is suggested by the following extract from a memorandum by a Native Welfare inspector (dated 1 March 1960): 'I'll attempt to find employment for him and, should he fail to accept it, I suggest a vagrancy prosecution might convince him he has obligations to his father and children.'

Idleness was the essence of the offence in the Victorian case of two Aboriginal brothers aged seventeen and nineteen years. The police report on both boys included the following information. They were arrested on 5 October 1967 on a charge of having insufficient means of support. They were remanded for four weeks for presentence report.

They live with their mother in an Aboriginal Welfare house. The police report (quoted Bartholomew 1967: viii) said:

> Both . . . have not worked since last Christmas and despite frequent warnings from the police and members of the Aboriginal Welfare Board they have refused to register with the employment bureau to enable them to get social service.
>
> There are seven aboriginals living in the house and the only income is the widow's pension and child endowment. They came under the notice of the police when one of the children, a 3 months old baby girl died of malnutrition. These two youths were eating the food which was supplied by the Aboriginal Welfare Board and the younger children would have to go without.
>
> (The younger brother) appears to be very dull. . . . He spends most of his time in . . . hotels . . . trying to get free ale. The last time he tried to get work was in January this year.
>
> (The older brother) arrived in (the town) in April from Melbourne. He was employed in a clothing factory in Melbourne. He was a good worker. He was at this stage staying in a boys' hostel but he left there because the other youths called him names. He has never tried to get work . . . since his arrival in April.
>
> At the Court both the youths pleaded 'Guilty' to the offence and informed the magistrate that they were living off their mother.

The psychiatrist reported of the younger brother:

> Intellectually he is extremely dull, but not to such a degree as to warrant certification to an appropriate institution. He is not suffering from any psychiatric disorder . . .
>
> Essentially his troubles stem from the aboriginal culture in that . . . he is prepared to live in a communal fashion even at a sub-standard level. He presents a sociological problem in that his dullness limits the

> scope of employment he can do. Imprisonment will not help him at all for it will only make him further dependent on others.

The report on the older brother read:

> Intellectually he is of average intelligence and he is not suffering from any psychiatric disorder . . . Like so many aboriginals he is quiet and pleasant but shy; consequently he was hurt by disparaging remarks (about his colour and aboriginal blood) made by other youths at work. On returning for the weekend to (his mother's) new home . . . he found the love and security he was lacking so elected to stay on. Having been brought up at Lake Tyers it is not surprising he soon readily fell into the aboriginal cultural attitudes: lackadaisical and dependent upon others.
>
> Imprisonment will not help this boy at all. I would suggest he be given a period of probation conditional on his returning to Melbourne where he held his job for about a year . . .

In spite of the psychiatrist's reports the court sentenced both boys to twelve months' imprisonment. It appears that the magistrate intended that the sentence would be served in a Youth Training Centre but, because of an anomaly in the relevant legislation, he was unable to express his intention in the sentence.[66] His recommendation to that effect was not followed by the Prisons Division and the boys commenced to serve their sentence in Pentridge. On appeal the sentence was varied to a bond.

The sentences imposed on vagrants are by no means light. In one Western Australian town in 1965 ten Aborigines were imprisoned for periods of one month (two), two months (one), three months (six) and the permissible maximum of six months (one). The average gaol sentence was 2·8 months. Six whites were gaoled for terms of seven days (one), two months (one), three months (two), four months (one) and six months (one), with an average of three months. The sentences here thus showed no discrimination against Aborigines, particularly as one Aboriginal was placed on a bond and another was fined (all whites were imprisoned).

So much for the operation of the vagrancy laws in practice at the police and lower court level. Fortunately there are some reported cases in higher courts which enable testing of this practice against the standard set by higher judicial authority.

In *Zanetti* v. *Hill*[67] Kitto J. said, with reference to the Western Austra-

[66] Justices Act 1958 (Vic.) (Act No. 6282). Section 102CA refers only to indictable offences.

[67] (1962) 108 C.L.R. 433.

lian legislation: 'Clearly the provision is not directed to the punishment of poverty . . . ' (p. 441). *Daniel* v. *Belton*,[68] a decision of the Supreme Court of the Northern Territory is even more relevant. The defendant, a noted Aboriginal leader, appealed against his conviction on a vagrancy charge and the sentence of fourteen days' imprisonment.

Blackburn J. allowed the appeal and quashed the conviction and sentence. He emphasised (p. 104) that

> in directing its mind to the question whether there is an absence, or an insufficiency, of means of support, the court must take the defendant's actual standard of existence and address itself to the means that he has for support at that standard. It is an error to assume that there is some one standard of living which is to be regarded as a norm for all persons in the community.

He accepted that the law applies equally to whites and to Aborigines but the application of this particular law in any particular case must be in accordance with this principle. 'Unless that principle is applied, it is obvious that many aboriginals in the Northern Territory are habitually committing the offence, for they are living in conditions which for white men would entail that they were without lawful visible means of support.' (p. 109). Applying the principle that it is the individual's actual standard of existence that must be considered, he concluded that Dexter Daniel, an Aboriginal living at a mission, could not be convicted of the offence.

Is this decision applicable to all Aborigines? Dexter Daniel is a full-blood Aboriginal who at the time of his arrest was living at the Roper River Mission and Blackburn J. had no doubt that he was perfectly capable of living off the land. Many Aborigines live in similar situations. Aborigines living on the fringes of country towns may not be able to live off the land in the same sense, but their actual standard of existence is such that the decision should apply equally to them.

Should the vagrancy legislation be repealed? There is the highest judicial authority for saying that it is inapplicable to modern social conditions.[69] Most commentators agree that it has so many faults, both in its formulation and in the way it is enforced, that it is undesirable (Bartholomew 1967; Jordan 1966; Campbell and Whitmore 1966: 20-1; Lacey 1953; Douglas 1960). One exception is Perkins (1958: 252-3), who believes that: 'In metropolitan centers . . . the vagrancy law is one of the

[68] (1968) 12 F.L.R. 101.

[69] *Zanetti* v. *Hill* (1962) 108 C.L.R. 433, 441.

most effective weapons in the arsenal of law enforcement, and if the officer's use of this weapon should be seriously impaired the security of the citizen would be grievously weakened.' But there is really no evidence that the vagrancy law does fulfil the crime preventive function claimed for it. The theory is that persons arrested for vagrancy would otherwise have committed more serious crimes. Bartholomew (1967) and Jordan (1966), in their studies of Victorian vagrancy offenders, both found that the men imprisoned for vagrancy rarely had a record of more serious crime. The same appears to be true of many Aborigines convicted of this offence.

Vagrancy law may perform a crime prevention function when it is used as a holding charge. But such a use of the law is illegitimate, since it is being used for a purpose not intended by the legislators and to overcome restrictions on arrest and interrogation powers imposed on the police by law.

The same objections apply to vagrancy as to other status offences. The defendant is being punished although he has performed no specific wrongful act. The basic objection has already been extensively discussed in connection with public drunkenness.

For clarity, it must be repeated that the word 'status' has a number of different meanings. Graveson (1953: 128) emphasises that if a person can voluntarily attain or relinquish a certain condition, for example, that of being a car-owner, that condition is not a 'status' in his sense of the term. Since persons can, theoretically at least, cease to be vagrants by reformation, vagrancy is not a 'status' in this sense. The qualification is inserted because, in practice, persons like Aborigines, who belong to the lowest socioeconomic class, find it very difficult to 'reform' (that is, to attain sufficient means by the standards of the rest of the community).

It does not follow that 'status offences' can be committed only by persons of low socioeconomic status. It so happens that convictions for the two offences considered here (drunkenness and vagrancy) are most often obtained against persons of the lowest social class. But with other 'status offences' there will not be the same coincidence. Burns (1968: 52) defines status offences as 'those statutory offences that do not require proof of any act or omission on the part of the accused as an ingredient of the offence' and his illustrations include vicarious liability and other offences which would more commonly be committed by persons of higher social status.

Other objections, mainly procedural and evidential, have been made specifically to the offence of vagrancy. Lacey (1953: 1209-17) presents a detailed analysis of the differences between status offences (typified by vagrancy) and other crimes. It is only necessary to add the further point that Australian vagrancy laws shift the burden of proof to the defendant once the prosecution raises a reasonable or probable presumption of the insufficiency of means of support. As Blackburn J. said in *Daniel* v. *Belton*:[70] 'It is unfortunate that the wording of the provision thus provides an exception to what might be regarded as the most important rule of law that lay justices of the peace should understand—that before they can convict the evidence should satisfy them beyond reasonable doubt.'

Another serious objection to the way the vagrancy legislation is formulated is that it is so vague, and its elements are so imperfectly understood, that it provides an opportunity for harassment of persons who are innocent of any offence.

My main objection to the vagrancy legislation is that in practice it does punish poverty. Blackburn J. (p. 107) found it difficult to accept that Dexter Daniel could have believed that a person who is unemployed is, by reason of that fact alone, guilty of an offence. He ultimately accepted this explanation of the defendant's guilty plea. 'The charge as read to the accused alleged that he was "deemed to be an idle and disorderly person," and it is not unreasonable that an unemployed man who is apparently charged with idleness should believe that he has no defence.' (p. 108).

It might be surmised that another reason for the defendant's belief might be his knowledge of how the law has been applied in practice in the lower courts and his knowledge of the facts on which other Aborigines have been convicted or threatened with prosecution. Bartholomew (1967: 14) found that over 80 per cent of his sample of Victorian vagrancy prisoners had been charged simply for wandering and/or not working.

Pronouncements made in the rarefied air of superior courts are ineffective so long as vagrants are unrepresented in lower courts and so long as the only mechanism of control over police and inferior judicial practice is the appellate procedure. It appears that Daniel appealed only because he is relatively sophisticated in the ways of the white community.[71] Most persons convicted of vagrancy do not have effective access to the appellate procedure, so injustice continues to be dispensed to the poor in the lower courts whatever 'the law' as interpreted by the higher courts may say.

[70] (1968) 12 F.L.R. 101, 104.

[71] Melbourne *Herald* 7/12/67, p. 1.

8 INSTITUTIONS FOR ABORIGINES

Many Aborigines in Victoria, South Australia and Western Australia live on areas of Crown Land set aside for the use of Aborigines, generally by proclamation of the Governor in Council under the relevant legislation.[1]

The front endpaper map shows missions and reserves visited on field-work. Missions are established by church mission societies on land reserved for the use of Aborigines and are staffed by those societies.[2] The South Australian reserves shown on the map are controlled by resident white staff, employed by the government. In addition, there are reserves in or near most of the Western Australian country towns on the map, but these do not have resident white staff.

The word 'reserve' is ambiguous. It may mean the land reserved for Aborigines or it may mean the institution established on that land. Termi-

[1] Since this book is concerned with criminal law, it is not intended to enter into the important question of land rights for Aborigines. But briefly, the legislation under which the reserves which existed at the fieldwork period were established is: Land Act, 1933 (W.A.) section 29; Native Welfare Act, 1963 (W.A.) section 18; Native Mission Stations Act, 1923 (W.A.); Aboriginal Affairs Act, 1962 (S.A.) section 18; Pastoral Act, 1936 (S.A.) section 140; Crown Lands Act, 1929 (S.A.) sections 5 and 9; see also Aboriginal Lands Trust Act, 1966 (S.A.); Land Act 1958 (Vic.) section 14. For example, on 18 May 1965, Lake Tyers was permanently reserved as a site for the use of the Aborigines by Order in Council (*Government Gazette* (Vic.), 26/5/65, p. 1664).

[2] Usually missions are established on reserves by agreement with the government and obtain a government subsidy. But Ernabella holds four pastoral leases in addition to reserve land (Hilliard 1968: map facing p. 91).

nology varies from one writer to another. The definitions adopted in the legislation of the various States also vary. Unless otherwise specified, my usage is as follows. 'Reserves' mean government-controlled institutions and 'missions' mean church-controlled institutions.[3] 'Supervised reserves' are those on which there is resident white staff; 'unsupervised reserves' have no resident staff.

'Institutions' is used to cover Aboriginal communities on both missions and reserves. 'Institutions' is used in Goffman's (1968: 15) sense of 'social establishments', the popular meaning of the term, rather than in any technical sociological sense.

This chapter is concerned with the control of behaviour of persons entering and residing on reserves and missions. Legislative definitions of 'reserve' and 'institution' are set out in the next section.

THE LEGAL FRAMEWORK

Aborigines in institutions are subject to the general law but, in addition, their behaviour may be the subject of special legislation and regulations applying to all Aboriginal institutions. Before examining the way these institutions operated in practice the legal provisions available to the authorities who controlled them will be discussed.

VICTORIA

In 1957 Mr Charles McLean S.M. reported on the operation of the Aborigines Act 1928 and the regulations and orders made under it (McLean 1957). He devoted one section to Lake Tyers, the only supervised reserve in Victoria. The practice of issuing licences to reside at Lake Tyers was discontinued in 1937. Mr McLean pointed out that the only power to make regulations for the control of residents of Lake Tyers was contained in section 6 Clause VII of the Act, and related only to half-castes residing there under licence. The position was therefore that none of the regulations regarding discipline and control 'have application to any of the present residents who, if not full blood, are half-castes not under licence' (p. 12).

Apart from this difficulty arising from the practice of not issuing licences, Mr McLean mentioned that some of the regulations on discipline were clearly *ultra vires* the limited powers conferred by the Act. This had

[3] Compare, for example, Dunstan 1966: 314-44. He uses 'reserves' to cover both. His paper is an excellent summary of the former status of South Australian reserves.

been pointed out by the Crown Solicitor in 1946, when he advised that certain prosecutions under the regulations should be withdrawn. The Crown Solicitor suggested the repeal or amendment of these regulations but nothing had been done about this suggestion. Mr McLean thought (p. 12) that this inaction was not without reason, 'since the invalid regulations, though unenforceable at law, probably retain some persuasive influence, and without them, control by management would be even more difficult than it is now.' Although this seems an extraordinary statement to come from a magistrate, it represents an attitude which is not unusual in the context of Aboriginal institutions. The staff often seem to feel such a compelling need to control Aboriginal residents that they will use extra-legal or illegal methods if the legal methods are considered insufficient. Mr McLean did go on to say (pp. 12-13) that, 'Since some rules to maintain discipline and control are essential, the only real remedy would lie in widening the regulation-making powers conferred by the Act.'

It is not known whether any Aborigines were subjected to punishment for breaches of discipline on Lake Tyers during the period when these *ultra vires* regulations remained unrepealed. It would have been possible for prosecutions to have been instituted even though the Crown Solicitor had advised that, in his opinion, the regulations were *ultra vires*. It would then have been left to the Aboriginal to raise the issue of *ultra vires* in his defence and also the fact that he was not a half-caste 'under licence'. However, since the government was aware of the view of the Crown Solicitor, who had specifically recommended that certain prosecutions should be withdrawn, it is probable that no action was taken thereafter to enforce these regulations in the courts. On the other hand, the manager of Lake Tyers may have imposed punishments on residents, purporting to act under these regulations, or he may have used them as a means of moral compulsion, or as a basis for threatening action he had no intention of carrying out. It is indicative of the low priority of Aboriginal welfare in this period that no legislative action was taken to remedy this obviously unsatisfactory situation in the eleven years between the Crown Solicitor's advice and the McLean Report.

However, after Mr McLean reported, the Aborigines Act 1957[4] was enacted. The definition of Aboriginal was widened (section 7 of the

[4] Act No. 6086 (Vic.). The Act was consolidated the following year and became the Aborigines Act 1958 (Vic.) (Act No. 6190).

Aborigines Act 1958) to include any person of Aboriginal descent. The Governor in Council was empowered under section 11(1)(d) of the 1958 Act to make regulations for the control of Aboriginal reserves. The Aborigines Welfare Regulations 1958 contained detailed provisions concerning permits to reside on reserves and applications for permission to visit reserves. A number of reserve offences were also created.[5] A wide range of behaviour was penalised, including gambling and being indecently clothed. These regulations were in force during most of the fieldwork period.

Section 42(d) of the Aboriginal Affairs Act 1967 continues the power to make regulations. No regulations were made under this provision during the fieldwork period, so the entry of Aborigines onto reserves in Victoria was legally uncontrolled once this Act came into force.

SOUTH AUSTRALIA

The Aboriginal Affairs Act, 1962 defined 'Aboriginal institution' to include 'any mission station, . . . reserve, or other institution for the benefit, care, or promotion of the welfare of the Aboriginal inhabitants of the State'.[6] 'Reserve' means 'a reserve for Aborigines declared under this Act'.[7] Thus in South Australia all 'reserves' proclaimed under the Aboriginal Affairs Act, 1962 were also 'institutions'.

The Act distinguished between full-bloods, who were called 'Aboriginals', and part-Aborigines, who were known as 'persons of Aboriginal blood' (section 4). The two groups were given different rights to enter and remain in Aboriginal institutions, the former group being in a preferred situation. 'In order to promote the welfare or to facilitate the training of Aborigines, the Minister may refuse the entry of any Aboriginal or group of Aborigines into an institution.' (section 20(1)). It was an offence for an Aboriginal to enter an institution after a refusal of his entry by the Minister (section 20(3)).

Thus a full-blood was entitled to enter or remain in an Aboriginal institution unless the Minister specifically refused him entry. On the other

[5] Aborigines Welfare Regulations 1958 (Vic.) (*Government Gazette* (Vic.) No. 80, 27/8/58, p. 2978), Regs. 11-14, 18-20, 21.

[6] Act No. 45 of 1962 (S.A.) section 3. The text in this and the following paragraphs deals with legislation in force during the fieldwork period (1965-7). There have been a number of amendments since that date.

[7] Aboriginal Affairs Act, 1962 (S.A.). The power to proclaim reserves is conferred by section 18.

hand, a part-Aboriginal had to obtain written permission from the Aboriginal Affairs Board to avoid the commission of the offence of being unlawfully in the institution. This was laid down by section 23 which stated:

> Any person who enters or remains or is within the boundaries of an Aboriginal institution, without the written permission of the board, unless he is—
>
> (a) an Aboriginal or the wife or child of an Aboriginal residing with him thereon;
>
> . . . shall be guilty of an offence against this Act.

This section clearly applied to all persons other than full-bloods. It did, however, exempt certain other categories of people, including police, and there was a proviso enabling the superintendent of the institution to admit other persons under certain circumstances.

It will be seen that these sections gave the Minister, the Board and individual superintendents considerable power to decide who might reside on missions and reserves and even who might visit them. It will be shown later how these powers were exercised in practice.

Section 40 empowered the Governor to make regulations for many purposes including: 'VII. For the maintenance of discipline and good order in Aboriginal institutions'; and 'VIII. Authorizing entry to an Aboriginal institution by specified persons or classes of persons for specified objects . . . '

These powers were exercised in the Aboriginal Affairs Regulations, 1963.[8] Regulations 4-6 provided for the issue, cancellation and forfeiture, respectively, of permits to reside in an Aboriginal institution. The police were empowered to remove anyone who failed to leave an institution immediately his permit became void for any reason (Regulation 7). Regulation 9 was headed 'Removal from an Institution' but actually it did not provide any method of removal. It authorised the Minister in certain circumstances to deliver a notice forbidding a person to be within an institution and provided that the person was guilty of an offence if he was present within the institution thereafter.

The superintendent was to 'be responsible for the enforcement of discipline and good order' (Regulation 8). His specific duties and powers enabled him to exercise considerable control over the lives of the Aboriginal residents.

[8] *Government Gazette* (S.A.), 28/2/63, p. 510.

Offences on institutions were specified in Regulation 10.[9] For example, it was an offence to fail to obey the orders of the superintendent; to be guilty of any immoral conduct within the institution; to fail to keep any house clean and in good order to the satisfaction of the superintendent; to play 'cards or any other game for money or for any other thing'. The penalty for a first offence was a fine of a maximum of $20, and for a second or later offence the maximum penalty was a fine of $50 or imprisonment for three months. Additional detailed regulations relating to liquor on Aboriginal institutions, and providing maximum penalties of $200 or imprisonment for six months, were promulgated in April 1965.[10]

It can be seen that these regulations made Aborigines liable to be punished for many offences which are not offences at all under the general criminal law. Although Regulation 10 referred to 'any person, being or residing within any Aboriginal Institution' and thus contemplated that whites might be guilty of these offences, it is obvious that its impact would be felt more frequently by Aborigines.

WESTERN AUSTRALIA

The legislative scheme for the control of institutions in Western Australia was somewhat similar to that in South Australia. One difference was that 'institutions' and 'reserves' were required to be separately proclaimed.

Section 4 of the Native Welfare Act, 1963[11] included within the definition of 'native institution' a 'reserve, mission, or other institution for the benefit or care of the native inhabitants of the State, declared by proclamation to be a native institution for the purposes of this Act'. Section 4 defined 'reserve' as 'a reserve for natives proclaimed under this Act' and section 18 conferred the power of proclamation of reserves on the Governor. Thus, unlike the position in South Australia, a reserve under the Western Australian legislation was not necessarily also an institution.

The legislation and regulations made under it provided for control of both reserves and institutions. It was made an offence by section 20 'for any person other than a native to enter or remain or be within the boundaries of a reserve for any purpose whatsoever, unless he is . . . an

[9] Amended 22 April 1965.

[10] *Government Gazette* (S.A.), 1/4/65, p. 749.

[11] Act No. 79 of 1963 (W.A.).

officer of the Department . . . or a person authorised in that behalf under the regulations'.

A 'native' could be guilty of an offence under this section. 'Native' meant any full-blood and any part-Aboriginal who was more than a quarter-caste (section 4). The definition excluded a person 'who is only one-fourth or less than one-fourth of the original full blood'. The definition rested on unscientific notions of the nature of inheritance. It also led to the ridiculous situation where the Native Welfare Department recorded part-Aborigines in its files as being, for example, 29/64 caste.

The legislation in section 37(2) (a), (e), (i), (j) and (k) authorised the making of regulations relating to reserves, institutions and missions. Regulation 20 gave authority to certain categories of persons, including police, to enter reserves.[12] Regulation 21 provided for the issue of permits to other persons wishing to enter reserves. It was provided in Regulation 22(4) that 'every native while upon a reserve or within a native institution shall be deemed to be an inmate thereof and shall obey all reasonable instructions and commands of the manager'. Thus the manager had more power over an Aboriginal visitor than over a white visitor.

Regulation 23 was also primarily directed at Aborigines. It specified the procedure to be followed by any Aboriginal who wished to enter an institution. It also provided that 'any native who is found entering or remaining in any native institution without the permission of the manager commits a breach of these regulations'. A 'native' could not be guilty of an offence of entering a reserve under section 20 of the Act, but if the reserve had also been proclaimed a 'native institution' he could be guilty of a breach of the regulations if he entered without permission.

Conduct (or rather misconduct) on reserves and native institutions was dealt with in Regulations 24-8, which created offences that could be committed by any person, whether Aboriginal or not. For example, Regulation 25 provided: 'A person who is charged with insubordination, indecent or unseemly behaviour, disorderly or immoral conduct, or the use of abusive, threatening or obscene language within a reserve or native institution is liable upon conviction to a penalty in accordance with these regulations.' It is clear that Aborigines would run the risk of being charged with such offences more often than whites and that behaviour that is not criminal in the outside community might here constitute an offence. Lest it be thought

[12] Native Welfare Act Regulations, 1964 (W.A.) (*Government Gazette* (W.A.), 25/6/64).

that the penalties provided for such trivial offences as 'unseemly behaviour' must themselves be trivial, it should be mentioned that the penalty for a first offence was a maximum fine of $40 or imprisonment for three months or both (Regulation 54). Penalties for subsequent offences were correspondingly high.

Regulations 29-37 inclusive were headed 'Care of Inmates of Native Institutions' and some of them (for example Regulation 29) were amongst the few legislative provisions that imposed an obligation on those who controlled the institutions instead of on the inmates. But even here the question of discipline creeps in. To quote Regulation 34:

> (1) The discipline enforced in a reserve or native institution shall be mild and firm, and all degrading and injurious punishments shall be avoided.
> (2) Every case of punishment shall be recorded in a punishment book immediately after the infliction thereof, and in respect of such punishment there shall be entered in that book the details of the offence, the date of the infliction, and the form of punishment inflicted.

One missionary expressed the view that this regulation was primarily intended to deal with punishment inflicted on Aboriginal children. There is nothing on the face of the regulation to indicate that it was confined to children. It may be argued that the only power which a manager or staff member had to punish Aborigines was that arising from his status *in loco parentis* to children and that he had no legal right to impose any punishment on adults. It would then follow that Regulation 34 applied only to the punishment of children. If this is a correct analysis of the situation it seems unfortunate that it was not spelt out more clearly in the regulations, since these had to be interpreted in practice by managers, not lawyers. The extent to which the requirements of Regulation 34 were observed in practice even in the case of children will be discussed more fully later in this chapter.

The Regulations dealing with 'Subsidised Native Institutions and Missions' (38-46) appear to have been mainly designed to enable the Minister and the Department of Native Welfare to exercise some control over these institutions, which were not directly operated by the government.

The legislative framework in both South Australia and Western Australia thus provided ample scope for those in charge of institutions to exercise detailed control over the lives of the Aboriginal inmates, if they chose to take advantage of all the powers legally available (for a comparison with the situation in Queensland see Tatz 1963). It is necessary to examine the extent to which these powers were actually invoked.

RESERVE OFFENCES

ILLEGAL ENTRY ON RESERVES

'Permit system attacked' was the heading of an article in the *Aboriginal Quarterly*.[13] It reported that the Federal Council for the Advancement of Aborigines and Torres Strait Islanders had strongly attacked the administration of the permit system in North Australia. The article referred to the exclusion of several distinguished academics and native leaders from Aboriginal reserves by the refusal of permits. The article did not mention a facet of the permit system which is of even greater importance, that is, the refusal of permits to ordinary Aborigines who have relatives on reserves and the prosecution of those who venture onto reserves without permits. It also concentrated on North Australia, whereas the permit system has also been a source of contention in southern Australia for some years. No doubt it is important that academics should have access to reserves for the purposes of research, and the permit system can constitute quite a serious restriction on their freedom of movement and also indirectly on free speech (Barnes 1969). But the rights of Aborigines wishing to visit relatives and friends are even more important.[14]

The history of prosecutions for the offence of unlawfully entering one South Australian Aboriginal reserve illustrates the operation in practice of restrictions on entry to reserves. This reserve is not typical of all South Australian reserves in all respects, since it has a large population of part-Aborigines with a long history of contact with whites. But it is probably reasonably representative of the southern reserves in South Australia.

A list of prosecutions for illegal entry gives no information on the numbers of people who applied for permits, were refused and did not pursue the matter further. Nor does it show how many visitors were granted permits and entered legally. On the other hand, there is no definite record of how many people entered illegally but were not prosecuted, either because they were not discovered or because the superinten-

13 *Aboriginal Quarterly* **1** (July-September 1968).

14 Many Aboriginal Councils now have the right to issue permits. They have shown that they share this view by refusing permits to some academics.

dent of the reserve decided not to initiate legal action against them. The superintendent had a discretion granted by a proviso to section 23 of the Aboriginal Affairs Act, 1962 (S.A.) to decide whether individuals should be permitted to enter reserves or not. In addition, he clearly had a discretion, in practice, about who was reported to the police for being on the reserve without a permit.[15]

The numbers of charges laid in the Port Victoria court for being unlawfully on Point Pearce reserve were: 1964 two charges (both white defendants); 1965 twenty charges (all Aboriginal defendants); 1966 (January to June) eight charges (seven Aborigines, one white). All these charges resulted in convictions, with the exception of one in 1965, which was withdrawn before hearing.

The 1964 charges represented the initiation by the superintendent of this reserve of a new policy of prosecuting persons found on the reserve without a permit; it followed a considerable period of non-enforcement. He addressed a written request to the local police for the prosecution of the two white defendants and also of an Aboriginal woman. She was not prosecuted.

The two defendants were involved in a disturbance on the reserve when an Aboriginal woman hit one of them because she blamed him for making her daughter drunk. She reported the incident to the superintendent. The first defendant was fined $18 with costs of $2; the other was fined $16 with $4 costs on the charge of being unlawfully on the reserve.

The element of harassment in charges for this offence is shown by the policeman's account of his conversation with the Aboriginal woman against whom the superintendent had also requested prosecution. She said (as transcribed in the police report): '. . . but listen my husbands grave is on this place and I am going to come and visit it. You can arrest me and do what you like but you wont stop me. It is fathers day on Sunday and Ill tell you now I am coming with my children to there fathers grave.'

Of the nineteen Aboriginal defendants convicted of this charge in 1965, one (a juvenile) was convicted without penalty; one was committed to a juvenile institution; eleven were fined from $10 to $30; six were imprisoned for periods between one and two months. Of those fined, seven paid the fine in full; two were imprisoned in default of payment of

[15] From reserve records available it appears that all offences of this kind came to the notice of the police through a report from the superintendent. In fact, at one period, the police would not proceed without a written request from the superintendent.

the fine; one served part of the default sentence and there is no record of payment in the remaining case.

Four defendants charged together pleaded not guilty. They were unrepresented. One applied for an adjournment at the close of the case for the prosecution in order to seek legal advice. This was refused. The chief witnesses for the prosecution were the superintendent of the reserve and another departmental officer, a former superintendent of the same reserve. Both gave opinion evidence that these men were not full-bloods and therefore not 'Aboriginals' within section 4(1) who would be entitled to be on the reserve without a permit.[16]

It appeared that a senior departmental officer had previously gone to the reserve to offer employment and an opportunity to leave the reserve without a prosecution being instituted. One defendant claimed he could not accept the employment because he had had an operation on his arm. His wife, who gave evidence for him, gave an additional reason: that the job was at Point McLeay reserve and the people of the two reserves 'never got on'. Another defendant claimed that he had a moral right to be on the reserve.

Of the seven Aboriginal defendants convicted of this offence in January to June 1966 one was convicted without penalty; two were fined from $10 to $12; four were imprisoned for periods between fourteen days and two months. One defendant served ten days in default of payment of a fine of $10; the other fine was paid. The one white defendant convicted of being unlawfully on the reserve in June 1966 was sentenced to ten days' imprisonment.

The most interesting case in this series is that of an Aboriginal woman who was convicted and discharged without penalty. The two justices who heard the case made a recommendation that the police contact the Department of Aboriginal Affairs with a view to having a permit granted for the following three days so that her case could be put to the Aboriginal Affairs Board.

Her case became virtually a test case between the Department of Aboriginal Affairs and the recently elected Reserve Council, consisting of Aborigines. The prosecution was initiated on instructions from the Head Office of the Department. The Reserve Council believed she should be permitted to stay with her parents on the reserve. She was a young woman,

[16] Section 35 of the Aboriginal Affairs Act, 1962 (S.A.) made such opinion evidence *prima facie* evidence that the person was not an Aboriginal.

separated from her husband, with four children. Over a period of some months, she was told several times to leave but was prosecuted only once. At several meetings the Council protested about the action taken in this case and their protests were forwarded to the Minister. The ultimate outcome of her application for a permit is unknown but the case has a wider significance than the treatment of one individual, important though that is.

The history of the permit system on this one reserve demonstrates a swing from the prosecution mainly of whites, from whom the residents were considered to need protection, to the prosecution mainly of Aborigines who, in most cases, were relatives of residents and for whom the reserve was 'home'.

The Aboriginal woman had no previous convictions before she was prosecuted for this offence in 1966. Her case may be contrasted with that of the truck drivers who illegally entered the Central Reserve. They were subcontractors for a well known commercial airline and transport company, moving ore for a mining company from a lease in Western Australia. Some did not have permits and were stopped temporarily by the superintendent of the Central Reserve but were not prosecuted. Mining development cannot be hindered by prosecutions for the illegal actions of those involved. On the other hand, in the case of the Aboriginal woman: 'There should be no confusion of the basic principle involved in this case. The due process of upholding the law must not be withheld because the offender indicates helplessness.'[17]

The permit system raises two basic issues of policy. First: are permits necessary? Secondly: if they are necessary, who should control their issue, renewal and withdrawal? The original purpose of the permit system appears to have been to segregate Aborigines on the reserves and protect them from exploitation and corruption by unscrupulous whites. The philosophy behind the later policy of enforcement mainly against Aborigines appears to be that it would enable reserves to be run more efficiently as training establishments and prevent the houses from becoming overcrowded. To some extent this view may be justified. The accommodation on reserves is limited and it undoubtedly does make it easier for staff to control employees and householders if they control all movement of people on and off the reserves. But the plight of those Aborigines with nowhere to go is certainly not alleviated by prosecuting them for being illegally on a reserve. The provision of more housing for Aborigines both

[17] Extract from Department of Aboriginal Affairs File (fieldwork notes).

on and off reserves would be a better approach to the problem of overcrowding. Ultimately the question is whether reserves are to remain primarily 'institutions' to which only 'inmates' have right of entry or whether they are to become open townships where freedom of movement applies as in the ordinary community.

To a certain extent, then, the enforcement of the permit system rested on a genuine concern over Aboriginal reserve residents. But it also reflected authoritarian elements in some official thinking, even though often disguised by references to requiring Aborigines to shoulder their responsibilities. The underlying motivation appears to have been to assert the authority of the Department of Aboriginal Affairs over persons who dared to disregard the rules.

The Point Pearce Reserve Council went further than merely protesting over an individual case; it suggested that the Council should have power to make decisions on permits. At this time the members accepted the framework of the permit system but purported to make decisions about individual applications. Its recommendation about the refusal of a permit to a white fisherman was accepted by the Department but the Aboriginal woman's case showed how little real power the Council had at that time.

The Reserve Council then was not established under legislative authority, although it had been set up with the active encouragement of the superintendent. The 1967 amendment to the Aboriginal Affairs Act later provided that:[18]

> The Governor may make regulations for the following purposes:—
>
> 1. Providing for the establishment and constitution of Aboriginal Reserve Councils . . . and defining the rights, duties, powers and functions of such Councils, but without limiting the generality of the foregoing for empowering any such Reserve Council notwithstanding the powers of the Aboriginal Affairs Board to grant with or without conditions or refuse permission for any person or classes of persons to enter, or be in, or remain upon, an Aboriginal institution for and in respect of which such Council is constituted and providing that entry into and remaining upon any such institution without the permission . . . of such Council shall be an offence . . .

This provision recognised that the power to issue permits was one that might be considered particularly appropriate to confer on Reserve Councils consisting of Aboriginal members.

[18] Aboriginal Affairs Act Amendment Act, 1966-1967 (S.A.) (No. 11 of 1967). New section 41 inserted.

It became general policy in South Australia that on all southern reserves the Aboriginal Reserve Council had authority to issue permits to visitors and make a recommendation on an applicant for a residence permit. The superintendent of the reserve also made a recommendation and the Director of Aboriginal Affairs then approved or declined the application.[19]

In my view, if permits are to continue, it is desirable that the Reserve Councils be vested with complete power over them. The main objection that has been raised is that councillors would find it difficult to be impartial when members of their own families are the applicants for permits. This objection would apply equally to many other issues which may confront Reserve Councils. If the Councils are to exercise any real power, then 'permit power' should be granted to them.[20] If they are not to exercise real power, it is difficult to see why they are appointed, except possibly as a public relations exercise.

The more radical reform, that permits should be abolished and reserves converted into open towns, seems preferable.[21] Goffman (1968) has shown the adverse effects total institutions have on inmates. Prisons have already been considered as total institutions in Chapter 6. If it is desirable to mitigate the effects of institutionalisation on prisoners, how much more so in the case of Aboriginal residents on reserves, who are in 'institutions' not because they have committed any offence, but simply because they belong to a vulnerable segment of society and are considered to need special assistance.

Preliminary discussions took place with the residents of another South Australian reserve but the Aboriginal people later presented a petition to

[19] Personal communication from Department of Aboriginal Affairs, 3 July 1970.

[20] To bring history up to date, it appears that this view has now been substantially accepted in South Australia. Reg. 50 of the Community Welfare Regulations, 1972 provides: 'A council may apply in writing to the Minister to delegate his authority to the council to grant permission to any person or class of persons to be within the boundaries of an Aboriginal Reserve . . . ' The Point Pearce Community Council considered (in the year reported on) sixty-three permit applications for people to reside on Point Pearce. See Point Pearce Community Council First Annual Report 1972/73, March 1973, p. 8.

[21] An opinion poll conducted at Point Pearce 'showed that 67% of the people did not like permits, but there was a 50% vote for keeping them to avoid overcrowding. The majority of people felt that eventually overcrowding should be a matter for the householder.' See Point Pearce Community Council First Annual Report 1972/73, March 1973, p. 17.

the Minister asking for it not to be declared an open village.[22] One of the goals of Aboriginal policy and one of the reasons for suggesting the conversion of reserves into open towns is that of self-determination for Aborigines. If this petition represents the true feelings of the people concerned, the paradoxical situation arises that in the exercise of the right of self-determination this group chose to remain under the control of the Department of Aboriginal Affairs. The petition may represent a fear of freedom or it may demonstrate a misunderstanding of what is or could be involved in the proposal for an open village.

Such a proposal does not necessarily mean the withdrawal of all financial and expert technical assistance by the government. The removal of barriers on freedom of movement could leave the existing administrative structure on a reserve intact (assuming it has resident white staff) or it could lead to an autonomous community led by Aborigines like that at Cummeragunja in New South Wales. Residents there run a co-operative farm with financial assistance from the State government. The Commonwealth government has also made a grant to the project and government officers are assisting with expert advice on farm management.[23]

EXPELLED ABORIGINES

Legal power to expel Aborigines was conferred by Regulation 9 of the Aboriginal Affairs Regulations, 1963 (S.A.) and by Regulation 28 of the Native Welfare Act Regulations, 1964 (W.A.).

South Australia. In South Australia the number of prosecutions for offences against Regulation 9 does not appear to have been high, at least in recent years. But again it must be pointed out that court actions deal only with Aborigines who have entered reserves after having had a notice served on them by the Minister. They do not give any indication of the number of these notices which have been served and the number of Aborigines who had their freedom of movement thus curtailed.

The power given to the Minister to serve such notices was extremely wide. For example, if it was his opinion 'that the presence of any person within an Aboriginal Institution is inimical to the maintenance of discipline or good order in an Aboriginal Institution; . . . he may cause to

[22] Fieldwork notes. Also *Report of the Aboriginal Affairs Board for the year ended 30th June, 1966* (1967), p. 11. Adelaide: Government Printer.

[23] *Australian* 14/2/70, p. 3 and personal knowledge.

be delivered to the person a notice in writing . . . forbidding the person to be within any Aboriginal Institution . . .'[24]

The validity of the regulation under earlier legislation which conferred a similar power on the Chief Protector was upheld by the South Australian Supreme Court in *Bray* v. *Milera*.[25] The complainant appealed against the dismissal of a complaint against an Aboriginal by two lay justices of the peace. The justices held (p. 212) that 'the regulations are *ultra vires* and inconsistent with the Act and is offending under natural justice and are altogether too drastic.' Counsel for the Aboriginal argued on appeal that the regulation was invalid, as being, first, inconsistent with the Act; second, in excess of the regulation making power; and third, so unreasonable and oppressive that power to make it cannot have been intended. The court rejected all these arguments. In upholding the regulation Richards J. stated (p. 215):

> In order to control effectively the aborigines and half-castes residing in an institution, he must surely have power to exclude any disturbing element . . . And if he can be given power to exclude from one institution he should have power to exclude from all; for if the presence of a particular aboriginal or half-caste in one institution is calculated to interfere with the effective control of the others within it, that may well be the position in other institutions if he is permitted to be in them.

This conclusion does not square well with the following paragraph of the judgment which is in these terms (p. 215):

> If the regulation purported to authorize the exercise of the power without good cause, merely in accordance with the protector's whim or prejudice, it would be different. But he can act only on his opinion, and that must . . . imply an opinion arrived at reasonably and fairly, and, at the least, with full knowledge of the circumstances of the individual cases.

Bearing in mind the vast differences between the different Aboriginal institutions, it is difficult to see how the protector (or Minister) could decide, in accordance with this requirement, that a particular Aboriginal was a menace to discipline on all reserves merely because he had been a nuisance on one.

Putting that objection aside, and accepting the law as enunciated in *Bray* v. *Milera*, the policy of the legislature in permitting a blanket exclu-

24 Aboriginal Affairs Regulations, 1963 (S.A.) Reg. 9.

25 [1935] S.A.S.R. 210.

sion order may still be queried. For Aborigines who find it difficult to obtain accommodation in the outside community and have an emotional attachment to a particular reserve, the exclusion from reserves is a very severe punishment. Another aspect of expulsion orders gives further grounds for disquiet. This is that they seem to be unlimited in duration.

In 1959 the superintendent of one reserve recommended the expulsion of an Aboriginal because of his conduct and idleness on the reserve and because he had taken away an eighteen year old girl, against the instructions of her parents and 'flouting my directions'. It appears that the recommendation was accepted, because in 1962 there is a record of a meeting of the Aborigines Protection Board at which permission was given to this Aboriginal, 'an expelled native', to visit the reserve with his wife.

In a more recent case, an expulsion order was served on an Aboriginal on 8 June 1965. In January 1966 he was convicted of an offence under Regulation 9(2) of the 1963 Regulations and sentenced to two months' imprisonment. The maximum penalty which can be imposed is three months' imprisonment. He was again convicted of the same offence in May 1966 and sentenced to a further two months' imprisonment. The police gave evidence that the expulsion order was still in force. Not only was it still in force eleven months after it was originally served on the Aboriginal, but there was no indication of any time limit being imposed on its continuation. No such time limit is required by the regulation but the fact that an expulsion order can relate to all institutions in the State and last for an indefinite period greatly increases the severity of the punishment that can thus be imposed by administrative action.

This case illustrates the relative infrequency of charges for offences under Regulation 9. The two charges against this defendant were the only ones laid in the first six months of 1966 in respect of this reserve and there had been none in the previous two years.

Western Australia. Prosecutions for the similar offence in Western Australia have also been infrequent. In one of these cases the defendant was represented by a solicitor who submitted that Regulation 28 was *ultra vires* the Act.[26] The magistrate's decision was that: 'Regulation 28 purports to be made under the power conferred by Section 37(2)(i) and I am satisfied that it is a valid exercise of that power. I am not prepared to declare that it is ultra-vires the Act.' The defendant was convicted and fined $4

[26] Native Welfare Act, 1963 (W.A.).

with $21 costs. He paid part of the amount due and served two days' imprisonment in default of payment of the balance. He had intended to appeal but did not do so, probably because he could not afford the legal costs.

Regulation 28 empowered the manager to order an Aboriginal to leave a reserve only after the latter had been convicted of an offence against Regulations 22 to 27. In this case, the defendant had, some two months previously, been convicted of four offences under these Regulations. On 10 May 1965 he was convicted under Regulation 24 of being under the influence of liquor on a reserve. On 31 May 1965 he was convicted again of being under the influence of liquor on the reserve and also under Regulation 27 of wilful damage. Although it may seem harsh that he should be turned out of his home on the reserve for such relatively petty offences, the Western Australian regulation at least requires the satisfaction of an objective standard (conviction in a court) before expulsion. Under the corresponding South Australian regulation, there is a grave risk that an Aboriginal will be expelled simply for being 'cheeky'. But it should be noted that in Western Australia wider powers are given to managers of institutions than of reserves.

INSUBORDINATION

The essentially authoritarian nature of supervised Aboriginal reserves in South Australia is shown by the creation of at least two offences enabling Aborigines to be punished for insubordination. Regulation 10 of the Aboriginal Affairs Regulations, 1963 provided:

> If any person, being or residing within any Aboriginal Institution—
>
> (a) fails to obey the orders of the superintendent; . . .
>
> (h) . . . being employed within . . . the Institution, and occupying a house or other building therein, absents himself from . . . work . . . without the written permission of the superintendent thereof; . . .
>
> he shall be guilty of an offence . . .

Prima facie, these offences could be committed by whites, but, in practice, the provisions were enforced only against Aborigines. It might be thought that a wise superintendent would regard such punitive measures as obsolete and unworkable. An examination of the records of the court nearest to Point Pearce reserve shows, on the contrary, that a number of prosecutions for these offences have been initiated by superintendents, as shown in the following table:

	1964	1965	1966 (Jan-July inclusive)
Failed to obey orders (offence against Reg. 10(a))	3	3	2
Absent from work (offence against Reg. 10(h))	5	Nil	Nil

One horrifying feature of these prosecutions is that, of the thirteen defendants, four were juveniles. The charge against one was withdrawn because at the time of hearing he was already in a juvenile institution on a more serious charge. Two juveniles were convicted without penalty on the charge of failing to obey the superintendent. But one of these was ordered to pay costs of $4 and was later imprisoned for non-payment of the costs. He was released the same day after payment.

In the last case in this series, a fifteen year old boy was convicted of failing to obey the order of the superintendent. He paid the fine of $2 and costs of $3. The charge was based on the defendant's having driven a tractor on the reserve after having been told not to do so. The defendant was unrepresented and pleaded guilty. It appears that counsel, if one had appeared, might have been able to raise a defence that no specific order had been given by the superintendent on the day in question. It is disquieting that so young a boy was arrested rather than being summonsed and was held overnight before hearing.

The corresponding regulation in the Native Welfare Act Regulations, 1964 of Western Australia, Regulation 25, provided: 'A person who is charged with insubordination, indecent or unseemly behaviour, disorderly or immoral conduct, or the use of abusive, threatening or obscene language within a reserve or native institution is liable upon conviction to a penalty in accordance with these regulations.' Thus it was possible to be convicted of an offence against this regulation for conduct that would never be considered criminal in the wider community.

Regulation 16 could also be used as a potent weapon to control troublesome Aborigines. It was in these terms: 'A Person who hinders, delays or obstructs a representative or an officer of the Department in the exercise of his powers and duties under these regulations commits a breach of these regulations.' That may seem sufficiently precise but such a regulation may become an instrument of oppression when a prosecution under it is heard by lay justices who do not insist on rigorous proof of the commission of the offence.

LIQUOR OFFENCES ON RESERVES

Regulations also created offences relating to drinking and bringing liquor on reserves. If reserves were made 'open towns' there should be no real problem about applying the general law relating to disorderly or intoxicated behaviour, in place of the present regulations.[27] The fact that the former is narrower in scope than the latter, for example, in not punishing mere possession of liquor, would produce an improvement on the present situation. The general law is quite wide enough to deal with any socially harmful behaviour.

In South Australia the Department of Aboriginal Affairs considered the possibility of using the Police Offences Act on reserves instead of the regulations. One senior officer considered that a charge of 'Drunk and Disorderly' would be a much more suitable charge than the charge of 'Consumed liquor on an Aboriginal Reserve'. In his view, the latter charge 'bears more of an aura of persecution and discrimination'.

Another possible approach to the question of liquor on reserves is the establishment of 'wet canteens' to permit controlled consumption of alcohol. In South Australia legislative changes since the fieldwork period now enable the Licensing Court to grant a publican's licence for premises on an Aboriginal institution. One such licence has been granted to the Lutheran Church for the Yalata mission.[28] This solution might be preferable to making liquor on reserves completely uncontrolled, particularly if it rests on a system of local option. A referendum should be held on each Aboriginal institution to see whether the resident Aborigines want the continuation of a 'dry' reserve, or the establishment of a 'wet canteen' or the abandonment of all controls on the entry of liquor.

THE INITIATION OF CRIMINAL PROSECUTIONS

The most serious offences committed by Aborigines on missions and reserves are assaults (both on the staff and on other Aborigines) and storebreakings. Since these are offences under the ordinary criminal law, the law which applies is the same as in the general community. But there are special problems arising from the institutional situation, which mean

[27] Native Welfare Act Regulations, 1964 (W.A.) Reg. 24; Aboriginal Affairs Regulations, 1963 (S.A.) Reg. 10; see also Regulations made 1/4/65 and 22/4/65 (S.A.). See Chapter 7 on status offences. The same arguments against making drunkenness a criminal offence apply to reserve liquor offences.

[28] Licensing Act, 1967-1973 (S.A.) section 17; *Australian* 7/12/68, p. 12.

that the way the law actually functions is somewhat different from its operation in the wider society. The first difference to be discussed is that of how offences come to the notice of the police.

REPORTS TO THE POLICE

In Chapter 2 the way in which the police exercise their discretion and the oversubjection of Aborigines to the criminal process were observed. On some remote missions and reserves the situation is the reverse. The police are not called in unless the matter is considered serious. In these cases the decision about whether legal action will be taken or not usually falls to the missionary or superintendent in charge of the institution.

The special problems arising from remoteness from the nearest police station were well recognised on one South Australian mission; and an informal conference was held in 1955 between representatives of the police and the superintendent of the mission. An agreed policy about police action was drawn up. It was agreed that the local constable (some hundreds of miles away) would come out readily and willingly when called, when possible and when the nature of the case warranted it; and the mission gave an undertaking that the police would not be called unless the mission considered it was necessary. This led to the drawing up of a short list of possible offences which might occur at the mission and which would warrant the immediate calling of the police. The list was as follows:

Assault—actual or threatened violence—with intent to do bodily harm. The exceptions to this, it was mutually understood, were ordinary tribal 'disciplinary' fights, where no serious harm is done.
Attempted murder.
Murder.
Serious wife-beating.
Stock-killing—goats, sheep, horses, etc.
Serious house-breaking or stealing.
Arson.
Supply of liquor to Aborigines or possession of same by them.

During the fieldwork period there was a different superintendent of this mission, but he adhered to the policy of calling the police only for the most serious offences. In fact, any other policy would not be feasible. A search of the records of the court in which most of the offences occurring on the mission were tried, reveals that in an eleven year period (1955-65 inclusive) there were only nineteen cases: assault (ten charges); attempted murder (one charge); storebreaking and housebreaking (four charges);

escaping legal custody (two charges); expelled Aboriginal remaining on institution (two charges).

There was a tendency to report all assaults on members of staff (including those where no injury resulted), but only the most serious assaults occurring in fights between Aborigines. The statement of policy referred to above specifically recognised the different approach to reporting assaults, differentiating between ordinary tribal disciplinary fights and others. The superintendent informed me that one prosecution was launched, at the insistence of the police, against an Aboriginal who had threatened but not injured him. He reported it to the police because he wanted an expulsion order against the Aboriginal, but did not consider a charge of assault was necessary.

The non-reporting of minor assaults occurring between Aborigines may be justified on the ground that they prefer to deal with internal disputes themselves. There is much to be said for leaving decision making powers with the tribal authorities in such cases. But the contrast with the response to assaults on staff did have the unfortunate effect of emphasising the social distance between the staff (the rulers) and the Aboriginal inmates (the ruled). The legal structure of the dominant society was used to uphold the authority of those in charge of the institution. Reading the records of many of these institutions and the types of cases taken to court, the abiding impression is that a major concern of the staff is to uphold their own authority and maintain discipline rather than to ensure that more constructive purposes of the institution are fulfilled.

Even on reserves close to country towns there may be no facilities for Aboriginal victims of offences themselves to call in the police. The only phone available may be in a staff house or office. Even if a public phone is available, the local police may refuse to come out on an Aboriginal complaint and insist on a complaint from a staff member. The problem here is not that the distances are too great for the police to attend to the calls but that they refuse to treat a complaint from an Aboriginal as seriously as one from a white. Again it means that the person with the effective choice as to whether the police are called is a staff member. It need not follow that staff misuse their discretion, although it has been shown that on one southern reserve in South Australia Aborigines were reported to the police for insubordination. In any event it does mean that the Aboriginal inmates are not treated like ordinary members of the community and they are deprived of a power of decision making they should have.

'ARRESTS' BY WELFARE OFFICERS AND OTHER STAFF MEMBERS

Private citizens have certain limited powers of arrest at common law and by statute. But the experience of controlling an Aboriginal institution seems to encourage some officials to believe that their powers to arrest Aborigines are more extensive than those of the ordinary citizen in the general community. Welfare officers purport to 'arrest' or otherwise deal with suspected offenders in cases where often it seems they exceed legal powers.

An incident which occurred in the Northern Territory illustrates the extent to which superintendents are sometimes prepared to go in dealing with Aboriginal suspects. The superintendent of an Aboriginal reserve in South Australia was advised that Aborigines had stolen goods to the value of about $60 from a party of geologists. Four Aborigines admitted that they had stolen clothing and produced some of it. They claimed they had committed the larceny on the instructions of another Aboriginal. On a visit to a pastoral property across the Northern Territory border the superintendent saw the suspect, who denied any connection with the offence. Nevertheless, the superintendent started to search the wiltjas (Aboriginal dwellings) in the camp. These wiltjas were the homes of other Aborigines. Later the suspect produced a bag, which the superintendent attempted to grasp. The Aboriginal struck the back of his hand with a machete causing a slight abrasion. Two months later the Aboriginal was arrested by the police and charged with unlawful possession of one singlet (found by the superintendent in the bag) and also with unlawful assault on the superintendent.

He pleaded not guilty and was defended by a welfare officer (of the Northern Territory Administration). He was convicted and sentenced to imprisonment for one month on each charge, the sentences to run concurrently. In cross-examination the superintendent stated that he believed he had authority to search a camp on the reserve he controlled but admitted that his authority did not extend to the Northern Territory.

It is unfortunate that the Aboriginal defendant was not legally represented, because he gave evidence that the superintendent had also struck him and with skilled representation it might have been possible for him to make out a successful plea of self-defence. Even on the assumption that the Aboriginal was properly convicted of the two charges, it is clear that the whole incident was triggered off by the high-handed way in which the superintendent conducted the illegal search and asserted his authority over the Aboriginal suspect.

Unfortunately a tradition of authoritarianism appears to have been established on this reserve. In 1968 the press reported that officers of the reserve fired shots during a dispute with Aboriginal boys.[29] There is a conflict of evidence whether the shots were fired before or after the Aborigines had started throwing stones and also whether the officers fired into the air or near the boys. Even accepting the view most favourable to the officers, it appears quite unnecessary to resort to such measures when dealing with young Aborigines. In the general community such action is permitted to private citizens only in limited circumstances. As a means of winning the confidence of the Aboriginal people it is obviously completely useless and quite inappropriate for the officers of a department set up to look after their welfare.

LEGAL REPRESENTATION IN INSTITUTIONAL CASES

It is in assaults on staff members, storebreakings and other cases where the interests of the staff are directly opposed to those of the Aboriginal defendant that he most needs legal representation and is least likely to have it. This point has already been made but its importance bears repetition. It seems to me imperative that departments dealing with Aborigines should take action to remedy this situation. It may be that Aborigines would continue to be convicted in all such cases, although this is unlikely, but at least justice would be seen to be done if they all had the benefit of independent legal advice and representation.

The case of the tribal Aboriginal boys charged with storebreaking and provided with an interpreter but not with a lawyer (see Chapter 4) is a good illustration of the need for legal representation but it is not an isolated instance. In a Western Australian case the local welfare officer gave evidence as complainant on a charge of wilful damage to Department of Native Welfare property. He said that although the Aboriginal defendant had caused a small amount of damage the Department viewed it seriously.

EXTRA-LEGAL ACTION

If an offence is not reported to the police, what action is taken instead? Sometimes the staff try to settle the matter. For example, they may

[29] *Australian* 4/4/68, p. 3 and fieldwork notes.

successfully stop a fight between Aborigines. They do not necessarily then impose any punishment; they may be satisfied that the disturbance is over. But sometimes the staff go further and impose extra-legal punishments, that is, punishments not specifically authorised by law. Sometimes these punishments are actually illegal.

The police sometimes assist institutional authorities with these extra-legal punishments. When four boys were arrested for storebreaking on one reserve, other boys who had admitted being involved in the thefts were driven to a distant area of the reserve and left to find their own way back to camp. (The authorities believed they would come to no harm since they should be able to live off the land. In fact, the boys were able to fend for themselves so well that the authorities were disappointed to find them back in camp after only a few days.) Although this punishment of temporary banishment might not be considered very severe, it was entirely without legal warrant since the boys concerned had not been tried in court for any offence.

A more serious example of illegal punishment was the brutal caning of Aboriginal children on a remote Western Australian mission. This incident came to light only because a mission teacher reported it. The staff member who inflicted the caning left the mission but no action for assault was taken against him. This is another example of the double standard applied to Aborigines. If an Aboriginal even threatens a staff member he is taken to court, but when there is substantial proof of assault on Aboriginal children by a person entrusted with their care no legal action is taken against him. A welfare officer told me that he had not himself hit any Aborigines but that he had asked one Aboriginal to beat up a young boy for him, because the younger Aboriginal was causing trouble.

Regulation 34 of the Native Welfare Act Regulations, 1964 (W.A.) required a punishment book to be kept but this regulation appeared to be honoured more in the breach than in the observance. One missionary stated that he did not keep a punishment book and that he thought it would be unfair to children to record all their minor peccadilloes. The punishments he imposed on children were keeping them away from sport or entertainment and in some cases corporal punishment. The point about the punishment book constituting a record of childish mischief as well as of punishment is well taken. The purpose of requiring a punishment book to be kept is clearly to provide some control on the more severe punishments, including corporal punishment. The Department of Native Welfare endeavoured to tighten its control of missions after the caning incident was revealed. It also needed to improve control of its own staff. It tried to enforce the regulation about punishment books.

It should not really be necessary to use corporal punishment on Aboriginal children at all. But if it is still considered necessary by those making Aboriginal policy, then it should be regulated along lines applying to ordinary schools in the state education system. All such punishments must be recorded. Any punishment involving the imprisonment of children should be prohibited. The regulation should provide that any punishment consisting merely of depriving children of entertainment need not be recorded. Alternatively, such punishments could be recorded but the records destroyed after a specified period so that they could not constitute a history of 'offences' against an Aboriginal child.

Of course, the complete enforcement of any such regulation is impossible. Anyone who can brutally cane a small Aboriginal girl is not likely to be deterred by the rule requiring him to enter every punishment in a book. Nevertheless the regulation would be of some value in setting a standard and providing a weapon for another staff member or a teacher to use in argument against the use of such punishment. The protection of Aborigines in institutions may sometimes depend on divided authority on the reserve, for example, the teacher acting as a shield for the Aborigines against the missionary or vice versa. But in other institutions Aborigines are subjected to dual authority. Their protection would be secured by better selection of personnel so that staff on all institutions are sympathetic and understanding to match the best of those already working in the field.

The missionary already quoted stated that the punishments he imposed on adult Aborigines were a fine on a working man; a direction to work if not already working; in certain cases, banishment from the mission. The missionary took this disciplinary action on his own responsibility and did not see any need to take action through the courts. In six years he had never had to call the police to the mission. On other missions the store was closed as a method of discipline.

One can feel a certain degree of sympathy with the desire of institutional staff to settle matters internally without involving more formal legal institutions. After all, the staff were responsible for the welfare, administration and control of Aboriginal institutions (Regulation 22(1) of the Native Welfare Act Regulations, 1964 (W.A.) imposed this duty on the manager). In remote areas, the practical difficulties of calling the police or otherwise initiating court action may be great. Further, the absence of court action may operate to the advantage of an Aboriginal in that it avoids an official record of conviction. It could also be argued in favour of the mission approach that there is nothing illegal in the imposition of such punishments as banishment from the mission. If the mission owns or leases the land and voluntarily organises a community of Aborigines, it can be argued that it can impose rules on all who choose to live there and insist that they leave the community if they fail to conform to the rules.

Tatz (1964a: 251) concluded that banishment from missions or settlements was an illegal punishment in the Northern Territory. Whether this argument is valid for Western Australia and South Australia depends on the relevant legislation, since it differed from that in the Northern Territory. In Western Australia, Regulation 29 imposed an obligation on a Native institution to supply inmates daily with food and drink. If the institution supplies communal meals and the store only supplied extra goods for the Aborigines, then the closing of the store would not involve the institution in a breach of the regulation. It would be otherwise if the Aborigines were expected to buy their own food and if the store were the only source of supply.

What about the Aboriginal who is banished? Tatz argued that the geographical location of many of the Northern Territory settlements meant that an order of banishment in practice amounted to a deprivation of the Aboriginal's legal right to be supplied with food because the only place he could go away from the settlement was into the bush. In Western Australia, Regulation 23 purported to give the manager of an institution complete control over the question of who could be an inmate in these terms: '(2) The manager . . . may admit natives thereto and discharge them therefrom upon his own authority.' Another power of the manager to order an Aboriginal to leave the institution was that conferred by Regulation 28. This applied to both reserves and institutions and required a previous conviction of an offence under Regulations 22 to 27.

Thus banishment was not illegal, though, of course, it was a power which should have been exercised with restraint. I found no cases in Western Australia where an Aboriginal on a remote reserve was banished. The mission where this punishment was used was sufficiently close to a town for any Aboriginal discharged not to be forced to take to the bush.

The position in South Australia was different. There was no legislative provision requiring Aboriginal inmates to be supplied with food. Further, the superintendent was not given the power to discharge inmates on his own authority. The only circumstances in which an Aboriginal who had originally legally entered an institution could legally be required to leave were those specified in Regulations 7 and 9. The former regulation provided: 'When a permit issued to any person expires, is cancelled, or becomes void the person to whom such permit was issued shall leave the Institution immediately. Every such person who fails to leave the Institution immediately may be removed by a member of the Police Force.' Regulation 9 provided that the Minister might in certain circumstances deliver a notice to an inmate forbidding him from being within any Aboriginal institution. Any purported banishment of an Aboriginal otherwise than under these regulations could not be legally enforced.

These provisions were in some respects preferable to those in Western Australia. First, the decision to exclude an individual had to be taken by a responsible Minister and not just by the manager of the institution concerned. Moreover, the decision had to be based on certain specified grounds, although admittedly these were fairly widely framed. Finally, the fact that it was made an offence to remain on an institution after service of a notice under Regulation 9 meant that the validity of the notice could be tested in a court of law. Regulation 7 was deficient in this respect. Under it an Aboriginal issued with a permit for twelve months, for example, could be removed by the police the minute the period expired, even if he had forgotten the relevant date.[30] Some legal process should have been interposed between the expiry of the permit and the removal power of the police, even if it was only the requirement of a warrant from a justice.

In summary, the position of Aborigines on South Australian reserves was more protected than in Western Australian 'institutions', but less protected than on those Western Australian 'reserves' which were not also 'institutions'. In no case was an Aboriginal absolutely immune from banishment.

Banishment could be a very severe sanction for an Aboriginal, particularly for one who was still traditionally oriented. Meggitt (1962: 258) found amongst the Walbiri that: 'The notion of enforced, permanent exile is repugnant to the people. Exile would sever a man from his dreamings . . . and without his dreamings he would no longer be human'.

ABORIGINAL CONTROL OVER DISCIPLINE

Other cases which are not reported to the police are left entirely for the Aborigines themselves to settle. Many fights between Aborigines are not

[30] One Aboriginal woman given permission to stay on a reserve for half an hour was removed by police less than two hours later. Fieldwork notes.

dealt with by institutional staff in any way. This non-interference is particularly strong where tribal Aborigines are involved.

There are advantages in leaving such matters for the Aborigines to settle. But if this is given by staff as the reason for not reporting to the police, then there should be complete non-involvement by staff, not attempts by staff to settle matters by imposing extra-legal punishments of the type described in the preceding section.

At present, Aboriginal control over discipline is mainly exercised informally or through traditional channels rather than through formal structures established by Australian law. Aboriginal Councils now exist on some reserves. It is hoped they will take on increasing responsibility for discipline. Future prospects will be discussed more fully later.

MISSIONS AND RESERVES AS 'TOTAL INSTITUTIONS'

Goffman (1968: 11) defines a 'total institution' as 'a place of residence and work where a large number of like-situated individuals, cut off from the wider society for an appreciable period of time, together lead an enclosed, formally administered round of life.' His work deals primarily with mental hospitals, but he also uses illustrations from prisons, monasteries and military camps. To what extent are Aboriginal missions and reserves 'total institutions' within this definition? To what extent do they share the characteristic features of total institutions, so interestingly described by Goffman; features which, unfortunately, often degrade the inmates and reduce their dignity as human beings?

Rowley (1966: 348) considers that Aboriginal institutions 'have tended to become "total institutions"; even in the last decade in the Northern Territory and Queensland this has been the case.' It seems fair to reach the same conclusion about many missions and reserves in South Australia and Western Australia, and Lake Tyers in Victoria,[31] at least until very recently.

A comparison between specific features of these institutions and those in Queensland described by Tatz (1963) may help to substantiate this point. Tatz criticizes (p. 37) the Aboriginal Courts on Queensland reserves on the grounds that these are constituted by the superintendents and an official thus acts as a judge in his own cause. There are no Aboriginal Courts in

[31] On Lake Tyers, see *Report of the Lake Tyers Planning and Action Committee on Rehabilitation and Training for Aborigines at Lake Tyers Reserve* (mimeographed).

Victoria, South Australia or Western Australia. Any legal action initiated by a reserve superintendent must be in the ordinary courts. This is preferable to the Queensland system because an external check is imposed on the otherwise arbitrary power of superintendents. In South Australia, for example, the advantage to Aborigines of proceedings in the ordinary courts is demonstrated by the cases in which defendants convicted of failing to obey the superintendent were released without penalty (see earlier in this chapter). There is little doubt that in Queensland they would have been subjected to some penalty. There, 'imprisonment is almost always imposed' (Tatz 1963: 45-6). There have also been occasions in South Australia when the police have refused to charge an Aboriginal with an offence even though the superintendent has requested them to do so. This safeguard, of a third party having to decide to prosecute, does not exist in Queensland.

On the other hand, the lack of any readily accessible court on remote missions and reserves in South Australia and Western Australia leads to the temptation to take extra-legal action. Even the arbitrary Aboriginal Courts in Queensland may be preferable to this situation. At least there is some record of proceedings that may be examined and criticised by researchers. Review by senior officials would be possible if they cared to oversee the operation of the courts. It is not suggested, however, that Aboriginal Courts on the Queensland model should be set up in other States. A better solution would be to provide ordinary police and courts in remote areas. Alternatively, provision should be made for 'Aboriginal Courts' in the sense of courts staffed by Aborigines, or recognition of existing methods of indigenous social control. These suggestions will be examined in Chapters 9 and 10.

Tatz's second major criticism (p. 46) of the Queensland system is that 'Aborigines are being punished for "offences" which are not criminal in the outside community, for example, intercourse and adultery, although by virtue of their broad powers superintendents are punishing these "offences" legally.' The extent to which Aborigines in South Australia and Western Australia were subjected to punishment for behaviour which is not criminal outside reserves has been shown (earlier in this chapter). It is rare for any white worker to be subjected to criminal sanctions for being absent from work, yet Aborigines were punished for this offence.

The third main defect of the Queensland system is the width of the removal power. The Director may cause any Aboriginal to be removed from any district or from a reserve *to* any reserve and kept there 'for such time as may be ordered by the Director'.[32] By contrast, legislation in South Australia and Western Australia provided for expulsion *from* reserves. The permit system in South Australia also operates to exclude a number of Aborigines from reserves. It is arguable which restriction on freedom of movement is more irksome: the Queensland confinement to a particular reserve or the South Australian and Western Australian exclusion from reserves. The former means that some Aboriginal reserves are virtually prisons; the latter deprives some Aborigines of the right to visit the place they regard as 'home'. Under both systems the period of operation of the restriction may be unlimited.

The Queensland legislation formerly made no provision for a court hearing or appeal in removal cases.[33] Expulsion orders in South Australia and Western Australia were likewise administrative actions. It would require a very knowledgable Aboriginal to think of testing the validity of an expulsion order in the courts.

These considerations suggest that Aboriginal reserves are 'total institutions' in Goffman's (1968: 11) sense that the inmates 'together lead an enclosed formally administered round of life'. The restrictions on freedom of movement onto South Australian and Western Australian Aboriginal reserves mean that the residents are 'cut off from the wider society for an appreciable period of time' within Goffman's definition. Even the most restricted reserves are less 'total' institutions than prisons. In South Australia an Aboriginal with a permit to reside may move freely on and off the reserve, at least outside working hours. He is subject to considerable supervision and control while on the reserve but he is not confined within its boundaries. There is some interaction with the wider society. Residents on southern South Australian reserves visit local towns for shopping. Nevertheless, most social interaction occurs within the boundaries of the reserve, and thus within an authoritarian framework.

PROBLEMS OF 'INSTITUTIONALISATION'

The difficulties of using institutions as means by which individuals may be changed have already been adverted to (Chapter 6) in relation to prisons.

[32] Aboriginals' Preservation and Protection Acts, 1939-1946 (Qld) cited by Tatz 1963: 46.

[33] Tatz 1963: 48. For later Queensland amendments on appeals see Tatz 1966: 87-8.

They are hardly less serious in the case of reserves, even though they are less 'total' institutions than prisons.

On supervised reserves, the objectives of the staff include changing Aborigines so that they may be assimilated into the wider society. They are to be 'trained' for employment rather than 'reformed' or 'rehabilitated' as in prison. Section 3 of the South Australian Aboriginal Affairs Act, 1962 defined 'Aboriginal institution' to mean an 'institution for the benefit, care, or promotion of the welfare of the Aboriginal inhabitants of the State'. Regulation 8(5) of the Aboriginal Affairs Regulations, 1963 provided that the superintendent shall: '(a) provide, as far as may be practicable, within the Aboriginal Institution employment and courses of training for Aborigines and persons of Aboriginal blood.' In Western Australia section 4 of the Native Welfare Act, 1963 similarly provided that 'native institution' meant an 'institution for the benefit or care of the native inhabitants of the State . . . ' But the concept of reserves and missions as training institutions was not as strong in Western Australia as in South Australia.

> In mental hospitals there are what are officially known as 'industrial therapy' and 'work therapy'; patients are put to tasks, typically mean ones, such as raking leaves, waiting on table, working in the laundry and washing floors. Although the nature of these tasks derives from the working needs of the establishment, the claim presented to the patient is that these tasks will help him to relearn to live in society and that his capacity and willingness to handle them will be taken as diagnostic evidence of improvement. (Goffman 1968: 86)

With minor modifications this statement could be applied to the work programs on Aboriginal reserves. From my observations there was a limited but genuine attempt to provide training in employment on the South Australian reserves. But the employment situation created was artificial and not like that in outside employment where employer and employee are interested in creating or maintaining an economically viable enterprise.

The training programs on reserves do not appear to have been very successful, either in terms of providing Aborigines with saleable employment skills or of enabling their successful integration in the wider community. Fay Gale (personal communication and 1972: 236-7) found that Aborigines brought up on the segregated reserves and missions have a very high crime rate.

The conditions of reserve life lead to the expectation that residents will experience difficulty in adjusting to life outside and will be 'deviant' in terms of the wider society. The inevitable authoritarianism and ascription of inferior status to Aborigines imposed by the very structure of the institution must discourage the development of independence and initiative in the residents.

Goffman argues (1968: 115) for a functional explanation of total institutions and believes that when we understand the underlying structural design common to all total institutions we will give less praise and blame to particular superintendents. My view is that this somewhat understates the difference between the most authoritarian superintendent and the most permissive. But it is true that even the least authoritarian superintendent finds himself limited by the structure of the institution. This has been recognised by one missionary: 'Permanent confinement to large settlements with their discipline, tensions, etc. may well have an adverse effect on the psychology of these people.'

Supporters of the Aboriginal reserve system may claim that the treatment of Aboriginal residents is the same as that accorded to the inmates of any institution, for example, an army camp or a hospital. Discipline must be maintained to enable the efficient management of any institution; therefore, the criticisms of reserves for discriminatory treatment of Aborigines are misplaced. It may be true that Aborigines are no worse off than inmates of other institutions.

But a further question then arises: what is the justification for keeping people in total institutions and, specifically, what is the reason for making reserves into total institutions? In any institution, a balance of conflicting interests is necessary. On one hand are the objectives sought to be achieved by compulsion, by the exercise of authority; on the other, the interest of the individual inmate in his autonomy and self-respect. In an army camp, for example, the overriding objective of national defence may be felt to justify a considerable degree of loss of individual freedom. The objectives of Aboriginal administration should not operate in the same way to justify the subjection of reserve residents to authoritarian control.

In fact, an authoritarian structure is a positive hindrance to achievement of any rational policy objectives in Aboriginal affairs. Most Aborigines are voluntary inmates of reserves in the sense that they have made the choice to live there rather than in the outside community. But that is not to say that they prefer the reserves to be run on authoritarian lines, as total institutions.

If given the choice, the majority might well prefer to administer the reserves themselves. Their emotional attachments to the reserves persuade them to live there but their resentment at white control makes them, I believe, no more than semi-voluntary inmates of the reserves as 'institutions'.

SUGGESTIONS FOR REFORM

Accordingly, the reform proposed in connection with reserves is not any piecemeal tinkering to make discipline less harsh, but a complete transformation of reserves from 'institutions' into 'open towns' or Aboriginal communities. Even a semantic change would have some value. One of the grounds for upholding the regulation in *Bray* v. *Milera*[34] was the definition of 'institution'. 'Having regard to the nature of the places coming within the definition of "aboriginal institution", and to the term "institution" itself, it does not seem likely that the aboriginals and half-castes in them would, as such, be more than bare licensees.' (p. 216).

The trend is now towards Aboriginal management of reserves and ownership of reserve land. Mrs Natasha McNamara, a member of the South Australian Aboriginal Lands Trust, is reported to have said: 'The whole concept of reserves will change with land owned by the trust, and instead of having what are now virtually training centres, it will be possible for them to become communities in the accepted sense.'[35]

The creation of Community Councils in South Australia is a step towards self-government by Aborigines in 'open towns'. The sooner this role is assumed by Aboriginal Councils the better. There is a risk that as long as superintendents and white staff remain on reserves they will be slow to hand over responsibility to Aboriginal residents on the ground that they are 'not ready for it yet'. As one Aboriginal councillor said: 'They want us to stand on our own two feet, but as soon as we really want power, they don't want to give it to us.'

The dilemma of administrative self-sufficiency and economic dependency has already been mentioned. If governments simply hand over control of reserves to Aborigines and cease to provide financial assistance, Aborigines will have freed themselves of authoritarianism at the price of continuing poverty. Governments have acknowledged a duty to assist Aborigines to

[34] [1935] S.A.S.R. 210.

[35] *Australian* 22/11/69, p. 16. Mrs McNamara is no longer a member of the Trust, having resigned in May 1970.

escape from poverty and attain equality with other Australians. This duty continues even after Aborigines are granted self-government on reserves. It can be met by giving Aborigines access to financial resources, as has been successfully done at Cummeragunja in New South Wales.

9 RECOGNITION OF TRIBAL LAW

The Australian legal system has generally assumed that Aborigines are subject to the ordinary Australian law, including legislation specifically applying to them, and has ignored the existence of tribal law. As with other culture-contact situations, European settlement here produced a 'conflict of laws' problem, whether or not this was officially acknowledged. Many former African colonies were faced with the conflict problem and dealt with it in ways different from Australia.

Australian lawyers generally think of 'conflict of laws' in an international context, rather than as embracing the conflict between Australian and Aboriginal legal systems. The main difference between the international 'conflict of laws' and the Aboriginal problem is that in the former two legal systems operate within clearly defined and mutually exclusive territorial boundaries. On the other hand, the tribal Aboriginal situation arises in an area over which the Australian governments and their legal institutions assert full jurisdiction and sovereignty.

The similarity between the two types of 'conflict of laws' is also important. The essence of the problem in both cases is the same, namely, the conflict arising between the rules of law and legal institutions of two different societies or groups of people. In the culture-contact situation the conflict arises when at least some members of each group come into contact with each other and disputes occur which are capable of being brought before the law courts of the dominant group.[1]

[1] Several students of African law have categorised this problem in the culture-contact situation as 'inter-personal conflict of laws' thus helping to elucidate the

LAW IN ABORIGINAL TRIBAL SOCIETY

To understand the kinds of conflict that might be expected to arise between Australian law and tribal law, some picture of how the latter operated in pre-conquest days, and to what extent it still functions today, is needed. The following account is drawn mainly from anthropological sources and should be read bearing in mind that a generalised picture is likely to be inaccurate if applied to any specific tribe, since the tribes varied considerably.

Some difficulty is experienced in identifying what should be regarded as 'law' in tribal society because the Aborigines did not regard 'law' as a separate system as it is perceived in our society (Wilson 1961: 174-5) and there were in most tribes no clearly separated legislative and judicial institutions nor indeed formal institutions of any kind. Law and religion were intimately bound up in Aboriginal society (R.M. Berndt 1965: 201) and any attempt to identify certain segments of Aboriginal life as 'legal' involves the imposition of alien categories of thought on the tribal society. Some modern Aborigines have made comparisons between their law and the Australian legal system on the basis of common notions of rules and sanctions for their breach but they have also interpreted the word 'law' to mean 'way of life' and 'religion' (Wilson 1961: 58, 71; R.M. Berndt 1965: 174).

This is not to deny that there was a system of 'law' in traditional Aboriginal society. I am using a functional definition of 'law'; one which places primary emphasis on law as a means of social control. I adopt Hoebel's working definition of law (1964: 28), which is in these terms: 'A social norm is legal if its neglect or infraction is regularly met, in threat or in fact, by the application of physical force by an individual or group possessing the socially recognized privilege of so acting.'

The use of the word 'law' to describe measures of social control in Aboriginal society is justified, in my view, by the belief that every society must have means for settling disputes, and must have law in this sense, no matter how difficult it might be to identify binding rules or institutions corresponding to the legal system in our own society.

The following features appear to have been common to Aboriginal tribal society and have some relevance to what we classify as 'legal' problems.

---

essential core of the problem. See, for example, Cowen 1963: 18 and Lewin 1941: 365.

The features selected for inclusion are those which have the potential for conflict with Australian law. It is not intended to provide a complete description of tribal law.

SUBSTANTIVE RULES

Certain norms of conduct were regarded as binding in traditional society. Many of these rules differ from Australian norms and so could produce conflict in the current situation.

Marriage rules permitted or encouraged marriage with certain relatives and prohibited marriage with others. 'Wrong' marriages had certain consequences, which, since European settlement, could bring Aborigines into conflict with the general law. The child of a 'wrong' marriage was sometimes killed and the persons responsible for the killing could be charged with infanticide or murder under Australian law.[2] Polygamous marriages were sometimes recognised by traditional society as being proper but are not accepted by Australian law.

The process of becoming a full member of the traditional society included initiation ceremonies which young men were required to attend. Some ceremonies involve technical 'assaults' on initiates by older men which could bring the latter into conflict with the Australian criminal law.

Tribal law recognised offences which are not regarded by Australian law as constituting offences. Offences against sacred laws were the most serious. The viewing of secret objects or the crossing of a sacred area by women (even if inadvertent) were serious offences (R.M. Berndt 1965: 191, 193). Similarly it was an act deserving severe punishment for an initiated man to reveal sacred knowledge to an uninitiated person. The punishment for such transgressions was often death and, when carried out by members of the tribe in the approved way, their action as tribal law enforcement officers or executioners could in itself make them 'criminals' under Australian law.

The action concerned in any individual case may be considered by the Aboriginal community to be justified, obligatory, or unjustified. The first class of actions are justified or legitimate, in the sense that no further action would be taken against the actor. Although a defendant in an Australian court, he would not be considered an offender in Aboriginal

[2] A case of this kind occurred in 1965 in South Australia. The defendants were committed for trial on charges of murder but later the charges were reduced to assault.

eyes. He was not obliged to take the action, but having taken it, he would not be subject to any punishment.

The second type of action is obligatory, that is, a positive duty is laid on the person concerned to perform the action. For example, certain kin are obliged to defend each other in fights. If they do not do so, they are considered guilty of an offence which must be expiated in some way. So if they do fulfil their obligations by joining in the fight they may be considered to be acting under compulsion.

The action of a tribal law enforcement officer may occur either voluntarily or under compulsion. Berndt gives an example of a man who intervened in a fight. Although he was not obliged to intervene in this way, it was apparently accepted by the rest of the Aboriginal group that he was here acting as a policeman (R.M. Berndt 1965: 170). Younger men are sometimes ordered by elders to go on revenge expeditions. The young men then have no choice, they act under compulsion as tribal executioners.

Finally, there is a class of unjustified actions. The action may represent truly deviant behaviour in the sense that no warrant in tribal custom can be found for it or it may be unwarranted in the sense that the individual went too far. For example, although entitled to throw spears, he was not allowed to use a club (R.M. Berndt 1965: 196). In such cases, the tribe will probably punish the offender even though he serves a term of imprisonment. He is an offender in their eyes as well as ours and they may not consider that the European punishment provides any satisfaction for the offence to the aggrieved party.

ABORIGINAL LEGAL INSTITUTIONS AND PROCEDURES FOR SETTLING DISPUTES

There has been some disagreement amongst anthropologists as to the way disputes were settled in traditional Aboriginal society. Berndt and Elkin consider that there were definite legal institutions, composed of the elders, and accepted procedures by which they settled disputes (R.M. Berndt 1965: 167, 177; Elkin 1964: 114). Hiatt and others do not agree that there were elders who exercised authority over an entire group (Hiatt 1965: 141-7; Meggitt 1962: 248-50; Wilson 1961: 12). They view the procedures as more flexible and dependent largely on how many kin happen to be at hand to support each party in the dispute. But they also acknowledge that behaviour is governed by rules in each situation. Kinship responsibilities and expected behaviour in supporting a party to a dispute are prescribed by 'legal' rules.

Whichever view is correct, there is a potential source of conflict with the ordinary legal system in that Aborigines are purporting to settle disputes by methods which often include physical violence, for example, token spearing and revenge expeditions which constitute 'criminal' actions under the general law. Other methods not involving physical force are also used but these do not produce a 'conflict of laws' problem.

The difference in views might have some significance for an Aboriginal trying to raise a defence to a criminal charge. If Hiatt (1965: 141-7) is right, it seems to make it more difficult for an Aboriginal to make out a defence under some category intelligible to Australian law. He cannot rely on his membership of any formalised legal institution as justification for his actions. He could set up a rule of tribal law that he was bound to act in a certain way by kinship obligations but in many situations there is an area of choice available to him—to intervene or remain on the sidelines. If he intervenes, he may have a choice of supporting one side or the other because he may have kinship ties with both. The only other claim he could make in his defence is that Aborigines should be left alone to settle internal disputes in any way they please.

But if Berndt's view (1965: 167, 177) is accepted, the Aboriginal seems to be in a stronger position to raise a defence. In appropriate cases he could say that he was acting in accordance with the rules of an alternative system of law and was a 'law man' of the tribe. Such a defence is not at present available to him but may become so if reforms suggested later in this chapter are adopted.

The kinship system is a fundamental aspect of Aboriginal society. The Aboriginal collective outlook is often contrasted with European individualism. Apart from kinship support in fights, there is another aspect of kinship that may be significant in the 'conflict of laws'. This is that if the actual offender cannot be found tribal law permits one of his kin to be punished instead. Again, if the punishment takes a physical form it may bring the person who executes the punishment into conflict with the criminal law.[3]

It can be seen from the above outline that the main areas of Australian

[3] Three Aborigines were charged with assault in this type of case in South Australia in 1953. One was the uncle of a boy who had died of tetanus. Believing that human agency must be responsible for the death, he and the other two defendants set out to revenge the death on the men they believed responsible. When they could not find them they threw spears at the nearest relative instead. They were sentenced to fourteen days' imprisonment (fieldwork notes).

law which are likely to involve conflict with Aboriginal customary law are the criminal law and the validity of marriage. Only the criminal law will be considered here, but first some indication is needed of the extent of the problem in terms of the numbers of people affected and the number of cases brought before the courts.

TRIBAL LAW TODAY

There are very few Aborigines living a completely traditional life today without any contact with whites and the extent of 'pure' tribal law is thus very limited. In 1961, Berndt estimated the number of nomadic Aborigines who had not had any contact with Europeans as only a few hundred and the number would be even smaller today as desert people have continued to come in to settle on missions, reserves and pastoral properties. However, there is a larger group of 'traditionally-oriented' Aborigines, defined by Berndt as 'those people whose life is still meaningful in traditional Aboriginal terms'. These were estimated to total 7500 in 1961 (R.M. Berndt 1963: 385-7, 389).

There is a third group of largely detribalised people who live on the edges of towns or on reserves and may be said to have a 'reservation culture'. Although they have largely lost the traditional culture they have not fully accepted the wider Australian culture. There are comparatively few Aborigines who may be said to fall into a fourth category, those fully integrated into the wider society. This chapter is concerned mainly with the first two groups.

I agree with Mr Justice Kriewaldt's view (1960: 16) that the assumption 'that every crime with which an Aborigine is charged arises from acts done by him either in accordance with or under the compulsion of tribal customs' is disproved by an examination of a large number of cases brought before the courts. Although the absolute number of such cases may be small and may form only a small proportion of all criminal charges against Aborigines, the tribal law problem is still important and has exercised the minds of a number of judges and magistrates. The problems raised by the modified tribal law of the second and third groups of Aborigines referred to above are perhaps even more difficult than those involving 'pure' tribal law, that is, tribal law unchanged by any contact with European ideas. Another factor that makes the actual size of the problem greater than it appears on the face of the court records is that the true reason behind Aboriginal behaviour does not always come out at trial.[4] It is difficult for anyone but an anthropologist to discover and assess the extent to which tribal law survives and is influential amongst traditionally oriented Aborigines living on reserves and missions and amongst largely detribalised Aborigines, because it is necessary to know enough about the traditional system to know the right questions to ask and also because much of the information is secret and will not be divulged to a casual inquirer.

CONFLICT BETWEEN TRIBAL LAW AND AUSTRALIAN LAW

The chief area in which conflict arises between the two legal systems is in the field of Australian criminal law. It arises because Australian law enforcement agencies (police and courts) assert jurisdiction over actions by Aborigines which constitute crimes under Australian law but which are not considered as such by tribal law, in fact, they may even be the legitimate actions of Aboriginal law enforcement agencies.

The actions by Aborigines that, if they come to the attention of the police, may set the processes of Australian law in motion and bring them before a court, usually constitute crimes of violence in terms of the general law, for example, rape, assault or murder. Some cases of direct conflict in which Aboriginal law categorised such actions as lawful or justified are discussed in the next section. There may also be a more subtle kind of conflict arising out of the fact that the two legal systems are completely different in concepts, in complexity and in the institutions used to enforce the law. This conflict may arise in cases in which it is difficult to point to any direct clash of rules.

RECOGNITION OF TRIBAL LAW AND CUSTOM IN CRIMINAL ACTIONS

The general policy of Australian law has been to grant no formal recognition to Aboriginal law. An exception was Western Australian law, which at one period provided for special Courts of Native Affairs, which were authorised to take tribal custom into account. In addition, tribal law has

[4] A press report on four Aborigines charged with having been disorderly by fighting appeared under the headline 'Gaol over cup of tea' and the report stated that an argument had arisen about a cup of tea. The true reason was apparently a matter of tribal law (Melbourne *Herald* 3/3/66 and fieldwork notes).

been taken into account unofficially in various ways in South Australia and Western Australia.[5]

LEGISLATIVE RECOGNITION: NATIVE COURTS IN WESTERN AUSTRALIA

Legislation in Western Australia providing for the establishment of Courts of Native Affairs was operative between 1936 and 1954.[6] It provided that a Court of Native Affairs could be established by proclamation for the trial of any offence committed by a Native against another Native. The legislation made no provision for offences involving white persons, either as offenders against Aborigines or as their victims. Each such court was to be constituted by a special magistrate and a protector nominated by the Commissioner of Native Affairs.

Section 59D(3) of the Aborigines Act Amendment Act, 1936 provided that the court 'may . . . take into account in mitigation of punishment any tribal custom which may be set up and proved as the reason for the commission of the offence'. Section 59D(4) made special provision for lesser sentences for Natives who committed offences 'in pursuance of any tribal custom' which, under the Criminal Code, would ordinarily have involved punishments of death or imprisonment for more than ten years. Thus the legislation provided that tribal custom could be taken into account in mitigation of sentence but not as a complete defence to a charge.

An examination of the Native Court Evidence Book covering the period 1947 to 1952 held at Broome courthouse gives some insight into the working of this legislation in practice. In this period six cases were heard by the court, sitting at Broome, Derby and Hall's Creek. On each occasion the court was constituted by the resident magistrate (who was not necessarily legally trained) and another member, who in some cases was a justice of the peace.

The offence with which each Aboriginal defendant was charged, the finding of the court and the sentence imposed are set out in the following table.

[5] For the position in the Northern Territory, see Criminal Law Amendment Ordinance, 1939 (N.T.) section 8.

[6] Kriewaldt 1960: 45. The legislation providing for these courts was the Aborigines Act Amendment Act, 1936 (W.A.) (No. 43 of 1936). It inserted new section 59D in the Native Administration Act. It was repealed by Native Welfare Act, 1954 (W.A.) (No. 64 of 1954).

Charge	Finding	Sentence	Whether tribal law treated as mitigation
Manslaughter	Guilty	12 months	Yes
Wilful murder (3 defendants)	Guilty	Defendant 1—death; 2 and 3—death but recommendation for mercy	No
Grievous bodily harm	Guilty	6 months	Yes
Wilful murder	Guilty	Death	No
Wilful murder	Guilty	5 years	Yes
Wilful murder	Guilty	Death	No

The information in the last column is in most cases my inference from the sentence imposed combined with the terms of the legislation. Unfortunately the court records are brief, even in relation to the decision of the court. In some cases reasons for the decisions are not given. All these cases appear to involve the question of whether the accused's act was in accordance with tribal law or not, although the tribal law argument for the defence is not always made very clear. In some cases it is difficult to tell why the court rejected the tribal law argument or even how it dealt with this question.

Section 59D(2)(c) provided: 'The court shall if practicable call to its assistance a headman of the tribe to which the accused person belongs.' In three of the cases listed above the court took evidence from an elder or head man. In the case involving three defendants the evidence of the elder was taken *after* the court had found the defendants guilty. In two other cases a head man appeared as a witness for the defence in the ordinary way. Elkin (1947: 207) congratulated Western Australia on authorising consultation with a tribal head man. However, if similar legislation is ever contemplated again it is suggested that the following points should be considered. First, the legislation did not make clear in what capacity the head man was to act, whether as an assessor, a witness for the defence or in some other way. In one of the cases where a head man was called as a witness for the defence, a witness for the prosecution gave different evidence about tribal law. It seems preferable for the legislation to be given greater clarity by providing either that the head man should sit with the court as an assessor, joining in the decision, or that he should be called by the court as an expert witness to supply evidence as to the tribal law applying in the particular case, or that it should be open to the prosecution and defence to call head men as expert witnesses. Secondly, the disagreement between Berndt and Elkin on the one hand and Hiatt on the other (discussed earlier in this chapter) again seems relevant here. If the latter is correct in his view that everything depends on kinship there may be real dangers in relying on the version of tribal law put forward by one Aboriginal calling himself a 'head man'. He may call himself this because he is one of the older men of the tribe and an initiated man but if he has no authority over the tribe in general his version of 'tribal law' may be the partisan version of one group of kin. Unless the version of other kin groups is also put before the court serious injustice may result.

One magistrate interviewed claimed that magistrates today carry on the traditions of the Native Courts by taking tribal law and custom into account in mitigation of sentence. This may be true of the current situation but on the basis of the above table the Native Court could not be said to have built up a tradition of lenient sentencing. Out of eight defendants tried in this court, five were sentenced to death. Of the two cases in 1943 referred to by Elkin[7] one resulted in a death sentence.

Elkin (1947: 207) seems to have misread section 59D in making the criticism that 'the court seems to have exceeded its powers in bringing in the death sentence'. Section 59D provides for a reduction of sentence where a Native has acted 'in pursuance of any tribal custom' but it does not rule out the possibility of a death sentence where the court finds that the Native was not acting according to tribal custom and it does not deprive the court of jurisdiction in such a case.

Elkin's other objections (1947: 208) to the Court of Native Affairs are well founded; in fact his objections gain added force when it is realised that the court had not only the wide powers which he thought a stipendiary magistrate and a justice of the peace should not possess but also the power to pass a death sentence. Section 59D(4) removes the right of appeal but the whole section is badly drafted and it is not clear whether this restriction on the right of appeal applies only where the defendant has received a reduced sentence under section 59D(4) or whether it applies to all cases heard by the court. Whatever the correct interpretation of the section, it appears that no appeal was taken in any of the cases in

[7] 1947: 206-7. I do not have any information on Native Court cases for the remainder of the period during which the relevant legislation was operative.

the table above, although in all cases the death sentence was commuted by executive action.[8]

Elkin (1947: 207-8) was strongly in favour of special Native Courts, although he criticised the actual form adopted in Western Australia. None of my informants advocated the reintroduction of Native Courts. The main reasons given were that it would be contrary to the policy of assimilation and that there are not enough traditionally oriented Aborigines left to make it practicable.[9] Neither of these reasons seems sufficiently strong to warrant a final policy decision against Aboriginal courts. Assimilation has now been rejected as official policy. The emphasis today is on cultural pluralism and Aboriginal self-determination, which would seem to favour Aboriginal courts.

The small number of traditionally oriented Aborigines also need not be conclusive. The former Courts of Native Affairs were set up on an *ad hoc* basis as required and the same could be done again even if such a court were not required very often. Legislation could provide for them in much the same way as it does now for Children's Courts in country areas. It could provide that such courts should only be staffed by persons with certain qualifications and that procedure should be different from that of ordinary courts. There would be no practical difficulty about such requirements. Practical difficulties would arise only if the requirements were unreasonable, including matters like separate court buildings and special staff who had no other employment. Final consideration of the desirability of setting up a separate Aboriginal court system is deferred until after an examination of the other solutions which have been tried for the tribal law problem.

INFORMAL RECOGNITION

At present, no legislation provides specifically for recognition to be given to tribal law in criminal cases in Western Australia, Victoria and South Australia. This has always been the position in the two last-mentioned jurisdictions.

In spite of this, tribal law has in practice been recognised by informal means. First, the police have some discretion in regard to prosecution. Especially in the past it seems to have been quite common for the police

[8] Information from Crown Law Department, Perth. At least two of the defendants originally sentenced to death served fifteen years' imprisonment.

[9] Professor Berndt in an interview on 17/10/66 gave the second reason.

not to prosecute when they believed tribal law was involved. In part this policy may be due to difficulties of obtaining evidence of such offences but in part it stemmed from the police view that the law did not allow enough recognition to tribal law. For example, there seems never to have been a prosecution for an 'assault' committed in the course of an initiation ceremony. In one area the older men were warned that they would be prosecuted for assault if they continued to hold these ceremonies. The warning alone was sufficient to end the practice.

Similarly, missionaries and reserve superintendents have, in practice, considerable discretion as to whether to report offences to the police or not. They also have often decided that matters involving tribal law are not appropriately dealt with by the general law and have not reported them. The result of this attitude of the police and other authorities has been that in some remote areas the only offences by Aborigines against other Aborigines brought to court have been those amounting to homicide or serious assault. This situation is changing as communications improve and as Aborigines come increasingly into contact with white culture.

Even if an arrest is made, the prosecuting authority may take tribal law into account in decisions as to which offence to charge and whether to enter a *nolle prosequi.* A jury may take tribal law into account in reaching a verdict of acquittal even though they have been directed by the judge that the Aboriginal defendant must be treated strictly according to the general criminal law. Kriewaldt (1960: 17) mentions his emphatic lecture to the jury in *R.* v. *Willie* that 'the law requires you to judge this case as if the accused were a white person'. The jury found the defendant guilty but in a very similar case where the judge did not repeat the lecture the jury acquitted the defendant. One might suspect that the verdict in the latter case was reached on the ground that tribal law was involved or on the broader ground that whites should not concern themselves at all with offences committed by Aborigines on each other.

'The Australian courts have consistently held that the whole of the law at any given time applies to Aborigines and whites alike, except to the extent that the legislature had seen fit to make differences or to allow exceptions.' (Kriewaldt 1960: 17). In the absence of legislation authorising them to do so, individual judges and magistrates have nevertheless taken tribal law into account in specific cases, usually in mitigation of punishment rather than as constituting a defence. This does not seem to have been done pursuant to any clearly formulated principle but simply because they thought that justice required it in the individual case. These cases have generally occurred at first instance and have not been reported, so that they have not constituted precedents for the future.

A South Australian case, the Chimney Evans case, illustrates several of the points discussed above.

THE CHIMNEY EVANS CASE

Chimney Evans, an Aboriginal, was found dead at Coober Pedy on 3 March 1964.[10] One Aboriginal was charged with murder on the following day. As a result of further investigations by Department of Aboriginal Affairs officers and the police, five other Aborigines were arrested. The last arrest occurred on 4 May 1964.

The first defendant was a full-blood member of the Pitjantjatjara tribe. He had undergone some stages of initiation but was not fully initiated. He was tribally married. He wore his hair long after the custom of the Pitjantjatjara, but was completely European in dress. He supported himself as an opal miner. He was still traditionally oriented and spoke English with difficulty. The other defendants could all be regarded as traditionally oriented, with the possible exception of one who spoke good English and had lived most of his life with white men.

At the preliminary hearing, the magistrate committed the first defendant for trial on a charge of assault occasioning actual bodily harm and the other defendants on a charge of conspiracy to murder. Later the Attorney-General filed an information charging all six defendants with conspiracy to kill and murder Chimney Evans.[11]

All pleaded guilty to this charge in the Supreme Court on 6 July 1964. Officers of the Department of Aboriginal Affairs were called as character witnesses. Their evidence included statements about the tribal law basis for the actions of the defendants which resulted in the death. They stated that the deceased had been guilty of a serious tribal crime. He had stolen important corroboree stones and sold them to a white man in 1959 and had been a fugitive from tribal justice ever since. A meeting of the six defendants held on the night of 2 March 1964, sat solemnly in determination of a tribal crime and decided that the offender (Chimney Evans) should be killed. This sentence was then carried out by strangulation of the victim.

[10] The information on this case was obtained from the Crown Prosecutor's file, the police brief, Supreme Court file and Department of Aboriginal Affairs file and interviews.

[11] Criminal Law Consolidation Act, 1935 (S.A.) section 12.

One departmental officer expressed the opinion that the final decision of the meeting would be unanimous. It would have to be before it could be carried out. The other officer's view was that the two youngest men who were only 'partially initiated members of the tribe would be more under the influence of the older men than a fully initiated member of the tribe and would more or less do what the elder men told them to do.'

On the basis of these statements the arguments in mitigation of sentence put forward by defence counsel included a plea based on tribal law. Counsel for the first defendant argued:

> They are not charged with [the execution] but only the unlawful and criminal agreement. Now it was unlawful and criminal according to our law but it is perfectly clear . . . that according to tribal law they were doing only what they had to do. From time to time these sentences are carried out but generally speaking carried out beyond the purview of the white man . . . Now if Your Honour took too severe a view of their breach of our law, Your Honour would in effect be punishing them for adherence to their own code.

Counsel for the other defendants added the further plea in respect of the two youngest men that in their case the consideration of actual coercion would apply. He did not suggest that there was physical coercion but he said, 'being men proceeding to full tribal rights and a suggestion like this being made, it was more than their life was worth to pull out'.

Chamberlain J., in passing sentence, made the following remarks on the tribal law issue:

> It is accepted that some five years ago the deceased had stolen certain sacred relics of his tribe and sold them to a tourist. This was a serious offence for which under the tribal customary law the offender was liable to be put to death. The deceased appears to have been aware of this danger, and to have accordingly kept out of the reach of the tribal executioners by living under white protection at Coober Pedy . . . [T]he six defendants met and decided that Evans was to be put to death, and the sentence so imposed was carried out by strangling him with a rope as he lay in a drunken sleep in his car. The evidence does not reveal who actually applied the rope, but all six defendants had agreed to what was to be done and five of them were present . . .
> I have been urged to impose more or less nominal sentences for a number of reasons. . . . [T]he main contention is that they acted in accordance with tribal laws and that particularly the younger ones may have been in a serious position if they had refused to agree to a decision of the elders of the tribe. This may be true enough, but there is a limit to which this Court can accept it as an excuse for what is after all a very serious crime.

> No doubt tribal justice may be administered amongst the tribes in their native habits, in ways in which white authorities may be well advised not to interfere. But where the aborigine comes within white influence he must learn to obey white man's laws, and if tribal elders do not understand this they must be taught it in no uncertain terms. They must learn that whatever their own customs, they must obey, first and foremost, the law of the land . . . In accepting the contention that this was in effect nothing more than the carrying out of a sentence imposed in accordance with tribal law, I am giving the prisoners the benefit of the doubt rather than acting on what, with ordinary people, would be the commonsense inference. With ordinary people it would seem odd that the authorities of the tribe should have waited until the deceased had given serious personal affront to [one defendant] to do what they could have done equally well at any time within the last four or five years.
>
> This does not mean that I have not made allowance for the matters urged on the prisoners' behalf. Indeed if they were white men convicted of a similar crime they could expect sentences many times as severe as those I am about to impose. Moreover, I would have expected the charge to be murder and not merely conspiracy to commit it . . . I think I can properly make allowance for the youth of [two of] the prisoners . . . who are stated to be only partially initiated members of their tribe, and therefore likely to be very much under the dominion of their elders. It is of the first importance however that they and others in their position should understand that no orders from their own people can justify them in committing crime.

He sentenced the four older men to two years' imprisonment and the two younger men to one year, in each case dating from the date of arrest.

This case illustrates ways in which unofficial recognition may be given to tribal law even though strict legal theory would not permit recognition. First, the charge to which the defendants pleaded guilty was 'conspiracy to murder' and not 'murder' with which the police had originally charged them. This may be thought to be an example of a reduction in charge by the prosecution because of the influence of tribal law. The judge certainly thought so. However, the magistrate told me that he committed them for trial on lesser charges because he did not consider there was sufficient evidence of murder. Their statements did not amount to complete admissions and there was no other evidence to connect them with the death.

Secondly, it is clear that the judge took tribal law into account as a factor in mitigation of sentence, in spite of some wide remarks which could be interpreted to mean that it should be entirely excluded from consideration. It is noteworthy that no one connected with the case suggested that tribal law should be a complete defence to the charge. One of the departmental officers under cross-examination stated that he considered it important that the true facts of this killing should be brought to light and that the Aborigines must learn that white man's law is paramount over theirs. However, he expressed concern about the conflict these people go through in trying to learn that lesson.

It is of some interest that the Department of Aboriginal Affairs played a major role in uncovering the tribal law aspect to this case. Secrecy about tribal law inhibited the first defendant from speaking about it at first and it might never have come to light if one of the departmental officers had not been struck by some unusual features in the description of the crime. This reluctance to speak about secret tribal matters also made it difficult for defence counsel to obtain proper instructions.

Apart from scattered statements about tribal law made by the defendants during police interrogations and recorded in the depositions, much of the 'evidence' of tribal law was introduced in the course of the statements made by the character witnesses. Although sworn, they were not expert witnesses and many of their statements about tribal law were really hearsay or opinion evidence. It seems desirable that before such evidence is accepted the witness should be asked his qualifications and his sources of information. Qualified anthropologists could well be used as expert witnesses in such cases.

The view that tribal law was operating here was accepted by the judge, though with some scepticism. Doubt arose because of the possibility that the defendants were simply using tribal law as an excuse for disposing of the victim. In my view, sentimentality should not permit Aborigines to escape with overlenient sentences in such circumstances. Some features of the case raise doubt but there are the following points in favour of accepting the tribal law explanation. First, offences against the sacred life, such as the sale of churingas which occurred here, are the most serious in traditional Aboriginal life (R.M. Berndt 1965: 193). This may explain the tribal execution even after a long delay. Secondly, the fact that the defendants came from more than one tribe does not destroy the tribal law argument. Intertribal meetings occurred even in pre-conquest days and are more common in quasi-traditional society, that is, since culture contact.[12] The fact that it is modified tribal law which is operating rather than 'pure' tribal law does not mean it is not genuine. Finally, the fact that

12 Interview with W. Douglas, Kalgoorlie.

some of the defendants were still strongly traditionally oriented while at least one was apparently fairly detribalised makes it difficult to believe that they all felt equally bound by tribal law. But even apparently detribalised Aborigines may hold traditional beliefs quite strongly and sincerely.

INDIRECT RECOGNITION

In certain circumstances it might be possible for an Aboriginal to bring himself within one of the defences recognised in the general criminal law relying on evidence of his having acted in accordance with tribal law. This may be regarded as indirect recognition of tribal law since the ground of defence is not that he has acted in accordance with tribal law in itself but that his having so acted is sufficient to bring him within one of the accepted defences.

Provocation. The main defence under which a difference has been recognised between white and Aboriginal defendants is that of provocation. In spite of his view that the law 'applies to aborigines and whites alike' Kriewaldt J. (1960: 17) did instruct juries that the degree of provocation required was not necessarily the same for an Aboriginal as it was for a white man. His directions to juries in a series of cases are fully discussed by Morris and Howard (1964: 93-9; Howard 1961). His view that the standards of the reasonable Aboriginal need not be the same as the reasonable Englishman was also applied in relation to the questions of mere words as provocation and the cooling-down period after the provocation. In *Nelson* (quoted Morris and Howard 1964: 97) he said in the course of summing up: 'We all know that a white person cools down comparatively quickly . . . In the case of a native you may think it right to say that the effect of provocation lasts longer than in the case of a white person.' Morris and Howard (p. 94) approve this as 'a humane and sensible modification of the law to meet local conditions'. Brown (1964: 227) also approves the 'adoption of a more flexible attitude towards the assessment of [Aboriginal] criminal responsibility in provoked killings . . . '

The Privy Council in *Kwaku Mensah* v. *The King*,[13] an appeal from the West African Court of Appeal, said that the tests of provocation have to be applied to the ordinary West African villager. It was held (p. 93) that 'the question whether in the circumstances the provocation was such as to deprive an ordinary person of self-control, and whether sufficient time had elapsed to enable control to be regained, are questions for the jury . . .

[13] [1946] A.C. 83.

It is on just such questions as these that the knowledge and common sense of a local jury are invaluable.'

It seems to me that this wholesale approval of different standards for Aboriginal and white defendants is rather too facile and the reasons for permitting different standards to be applied have not been sufficiently thought out. If such different standards are justified it must be on the basis of a proper appreciation of the way the present provocation rules function and also some ideas on the nature of differences between races.

The writers referred to were not considering the question of provocation in the context of tribal law. Morris and Howard (1964: 97) believe 'this law provides adequately and justly for the situation where the defendant is an aborigine living in his native community and that it is immaterial from what race or community the deceased person comes'. They distinguish the case where members of one community voluntarily join another for some economic advantage from the case in the Northern Territory where there are two distinct and separate communities.

What are the differences between races which are thought to justify different standards in regard to provocation? There probably do exist some real differences between tribal Aborigines and other Australians which are relevant to this defence. These differences consist in the first place of different perceptions of facts. For example, to the average Australian a certain joke might be perfectly innocuous whereas to an Aboriginal the same joke might be a serious breach of tribal custom (on kinship avoidance including joking see Elkin 1964: 148). Thus the type of conduct which would in fact provoke the average member of the community may differ between different cultures. Secondly, the type and extent of retaliation socially sanctioned might differ between different communities. The average Australian might respond to provocation by abuse or an invitation to a fist fight, whereas an Aboriginal who was actually provoked to the same extent might throw a spear.

The differences so far referred to are culturally determined rather than racially, constitutionally or physiologically determined. The idea that there are inherent intellectual or emotional differences between races is somewhat out of fashion with modern students of race (UNESCO 1952: 15) yet some such notion seems to underlie the approach of Kriewaldt, for example.[14]

[14] As described in Morris and Howard 1964: 94; cf. O'Regan 1972c: 65-8. O'Regan approves the modifications of the doctrine of provocation applied in Papua New

Even if such differences exist, it is extremely difficult to say what are the characteristics of any national or racial group of people. Such generalisations are likely to be inaccurate and misleading. Each national or racial group is likely to contain a whole range of individuals when assessed on such factors as intelligence and susceptibility to provocation. In fact it is precisely because all individuals of one racial group do not possess exactly the same characteristics that it is possible to distinguish the result produced by the present objective test of provocation from that which would be produced in some cases by applying a subjective test.

It is difficult to reach a logical conclusion about the special problem of applying the law of provocation to Aboriginal and other indigenous races because the existing general tests of provocation themselves contain elements of illogicality. The rationale of a defence of provocation seems to be that it is unjust to treat a defendant who was provoked by the conduct of the deceased as severely as one who had no such excuse to offer for his crime. If that is so, it seems that a subjective test would be appropriate: was the defendant in fact deprived of self-control by the provocation offered? Brett and Waller (1971: 333) suggest that the adoption of a subjective test would be desirable.

But that is not yet the law. While the objective test remains the law there seems no reason for being more lenient to Aborigines on the basis of some presumed racial tendency to be provoked. Such a rule might well provide a defence for a calm Aboriginal in circumstances where an unusually excitable white would be denied it and would be unjust to the latter. Similarly, it seems unjust to the white defendant to permit an Aboriginal to raise a defence of provocation on the ground of a verbal insult when there is otherwise a rule of common law that mere words cannot constitute provocation.[15]

On the other hand, I do consider that an Aboriginal defendant should be permitted to introduce evidence showing that the type of provocation he received was perceived by him as more serious than it would be by a white person and that the way he responded to it was socially sanctioned, that is, that it was in accordance with tribal law. He should be permitted to

---

Guinea but shows more appreciation of the distinction between racial and cultural differences than other writers do.

[15] But this may not be an inflexible rule of common law. *Parker* v. *R.* [1963] A.L.R. 524, 552 *per* Windeyer J. Note that the Criminal Code (W.A.) does allow for an insult as provocation.

offer evidence of cultural differences but he should not be allowed to rely on some vague ideas of racial differences.

Of course, the whole question is complicated by the fact that juries are involved. If Aboriginal juries or courts were hearing cases involving Aboriginal defendants there would be less need to require evidence about cultural patterns of behaviour and tribal law because the jury or court would be expected to take judicial notice of these facts in their own community. That is why the decision in *Kwaku Mensah* seems sensible in spite of my criticism of what may seem to be a similar approach by Kriewaldt J. The difference is that Kriewaldt was sitting with juries entirely composed of whites.[16] Such juries would be likely to base their views on provocation not on any precise knowledge of Aboriginal custom and law but on folklore about how Aborigines behave.

Duress. The remarks of defence counsel in the *Chimney Evans* case (discussed earlier in this chapter) about coercion of the two younger defendants raise the possibility that they would have had available a defence of duress. At that time there was not much case authority on the subject of duress, but recent decisions throw some light on the matter.

One question is whether a court would permit the defence to be raised in a case of conspiracy to murder. In *R.* v. *Brown and Morley* the majority (Bright and Mitchell, JJ.) were 'not prepared to hold that duress can ever excuse a person who performs an act which he intends to be in furtherance of a proposed murder'.[17] They went on to distinguish the case where the defendant merely entered into an agreement about a killing, which was not manifested in any act. Since the defendants in the *Chimney Evans* case were charged only with conspiracy, that is the agreement to murder, it is possible that technically the younger men would have had available the defence of duress, even on the view adopted by Bright and Mitchell JJ. Bray C.J. delivered a separate judgment in which he took a broader view of the defence, namely that it is available to a defendant accused of complicity in an agreement to commit murder and even of minor participation in the killing itself. Commentators have favoured the Chief Justice's view (Brett and Waller 1971: 658; O'Regan 1972b).

Even if the court permitted evidence to be led on the issue of duress

[16] 'Only white persons have hitherto qualified for jury service' in the Northern Territory (Kriewaldt 1960: 40). For a fuller discussion of Aborigines on juries see Chapter 5.

[17] [1968] S.A.S.R. 467, 485.

in a case of conspiracy to murder, there is a further difficulty in the Chimney Evans situation. Earlier cases referred to 'threats of immediate death or serious personal violence' as constituting duress. In the *Chimney Evans* case it seems that the youngest men were not subject to 'threats of immediate death or serious personal violence'. It is more likely that they feared some ill defined retribution at some future date if they refused to join the conspiracy. The very vagueness of the future punishment might be thought to make it more terrifying and the lesson of the delayed retribution being inflicted on Chimney Evans would reinforce the lesson of obedience to tribal authorities. If the proper basis for the defence of duress is that the threats negative *mens rea* it is suggested that evidence should be permitted to be introduced of fear so strong that it takes away the defendant's free agency, even if that fear is induced by threats of something other than immediate death or serious personal violence.

This view now draws support from *R.* v. *Williamson*[18] which makes it clear that it is the threat which must be present and immediate, rather than the carrying out of the threatened action. Thus, the defence would be available if the defendants acted under the influence of the threat, even though the threat could not be implemented until some time in the future.

The *Barenblat* case (Brett and Waller 1971: 659) prompts the thought that there is a difference in principle between the case in which a man acts under the threat of a person or group who can clearly be seen to be criminal within the context of the community as a whole and the case in which the threat comes from someone who purports to have legal authority to compel obedience, for example, the German authorities in Poland in the *Barenblat* case or the tribal elders in an Aboriginal community. In the latter case the element of fear in the immediate situation is reinforced by the element of legitimacy and also there is more reason to believe that the threat will be a continuing one since the persons making the threats have access to powerful sanctions to back up their threats. In the Aboriginal case these include religious sanctions. In the latter case, a lesser degree of threat or fear might be sufficient to warrant the defence because of these additional factors. It is submitted that a defence should be available to traditionally oriented Aborigines provided they can introduce evidence of fear sufficient to overbear the will in all the circumstances, including their knowledge of how tribal punishments function and their belief in the

[18] [1972] 2 N.S.W.L.R. 281.

legitimacy of the authority of the person who is threatening them or ordering them to join in the commission of the offence.

Mistake. The defendants in the *Chimney Evans* case might also have had a defence of mistake. In *Washington Territory* v. *Fisk*[19] an American Indian was acquitted when the trial judge instructed the jury that he could rely on his belief that the victim had magical powers. The defendant claimed that he killed the victim to save his own wife from sorcery.[20]

In New Guinea, the defence of duress would be coupled with the defence of mistake of fact to seek acquittal when part of the duress was the defendant's mistaken belief that he would be a sorcery victim if he did not comply.[21]

DIFFICULTIES FACING COURTS IN TRIBAL LAW CASES

In the absence of legislative guidance, a court called on to decide a case involving traditionally oriented Aborigines faces many difficulties. It could take the easy way out and simply ignore the possibility that tribal law is involved, but most judges and magistrates believe this would be unjust to defendants. They then face the problem of determining whether tribal law or custom is in fact involved and, if so, what the tribal law is. This is a practical problem but one which is difficult to solve. There is no code of tribal law and no recognised method for the courts to obtain anthropological information from experts. There is a lack of qualified interpreters to assist where Aboriginal defendants or witnesses do not speak fluent English. There may be a desire for secrecy on the part of the Aborigines. Finally, there is the lack of official sanction for the search, which must limit the extent to which it can be pursued.

If the applicable tribal law is ascertained and is thought to have affected the circumstances of the case, the major problem then is faced: should this tribal law be legally recognised, and, if so, to what extent and in what way? The answer to this question involves broad considerations of policy and of the ends law is considered to be serving.

In the criminal law field there are two major considerations. The first is that of justice for the individual Aboriginal defendant. Since the result

19 (1874) 1 Bishop, Criminal Law 218, cited in Brett and Waller 1971: 618.

20 Contra, *R.* v. *Machekequonabe*, 28 Ont. 309 (1894) cited in Brett and Waller, 1971: 617.

21 Personal communication from Mr T.E. Barnett, formerly Senior Lecturer in Law, University of Papua New Guinea.

of not recognising tribal law or of limited recognition will probably be to subject him to some form of punishment, a question of civil liberties is involved here. The second consideration is the interests of the community as a whole, including the Aboriginal community. What is required is a balancing of the different purposes of the criminal law, which may be mutually conflicting.

Arguments can be raised in favour of recognising tribal law. It seems unjust to an Aboriginal defendant who is ignorant of white law and acts in accordance with tribal law to subject him to criminal punishment in the ordinary courts. It seems equally unjust to convict an Aboriginal who acts under the compulsion of tribal law, even though he knows that his action is contrary to white law. He may have no real choice but to act in accordance with tribal law.

In cases where the defendant's action is considered legitimate under tribal law but not compulsory, the considerations in his favour are perhaps not as strong from our conventional point of view. He knew it was wrong according to white law and he was under no compulsion, yet he chose to commit a 'crime'. But from the defendant's point of view, he has acted perfectly correctly in accordance with the functioning legal system of the society to which he owes allegiance. He is thus in a different position from the migrant who has voluntarily entered a society but who may not accept the rationale of all its laws. The traditionally oriented Aboriginal cannot be considered to have made the same free choice in placing himself within the jurisdiction of the Australian legal system.

Even where the defendant's action is considered wrong by the tribe and there is therefore no question of injustice in convicting him (since he *is* morally blameworthy), there might still be an argument against it if he will be punished again by the tribe. He would then be subject to a type of double jeopardy.

In 1967 there was an outcry in the press in Western Australia over the gaoling of an Aboriginal, Yadabuka, for killing a woman. He was a desert Aboriginal who was said to have had no contact with white people until he started living at Jigalong Mission in August 1966. The killing and his arrest took place in December 1966. It was assumed in many letters to newspapers protesting about his imprisonment that what he had done was justified by tribal law. Although there is no evidence to suggest that this was the case, there could still be considerations to be urged in his favour as a traditionally oriented Aboriginal. He was probably completely ignorant of white law and he had never enjoyed the privileges of white society and therefore owed it no allegiance. There was also the possibility that he would have to suffer tribal punishment after he was released from gaol.

Arguments against the recognition of tribal law based broadly on the interests of society rest on various specific bases. First, there is the desire to change Aboriginal customs; in other words, an emphasis on deterrence, both general (of the whole Aboriginal community) and special (of the individual defendant). Criminal law has an educative function. Aborigines, by being punished, learn that killing is disapproved and the incidence of killing decreases. Sometimes other methods of settlement of disputes are substituted, that is, non-violent methods or methods falling short of killing—for example, minor assaults. In other cases the whole custom changes and it is seen by the Aborigines that no action is necessary. The practice of infanticide has almost totally died out amongst the Pitjantjatjara. This seems to be due to the combined effect of criminal sanctions and the educational influence of Ernabella Mission (Edwards n.d.). There seems no doubt that penal sanctions, even if not the ideal method, do in fact change customs (R.M. Berndt 1965: 185, 193). They have been effective in New Guinea in reducing revenge killings and cannibalism.

Thus, even though it might be unjust to individual Aborigines to punish them for killings, especially in the early days of contact, the conviction may be justifiable on these grounds. The harshness and injustice can be modified by imposing lenient sentences. Today, when considerable modification of tribal custom has already occurred, it seems a retrograde step in most cases to make tribal law an absolute defence to a charge of murder, though it should mitigate punishment and could possibly be made the basis for reducing the charge to manslaughter.

Second, there is the belief that it would be divisive to recognise more than one legal system in our society. But other countries such as the United States have found it quite possible to recognise indigenous law without tearing society apart. Indian tribes on reservations have certain law making and law enforcement powers, including powers to deal with many crimes (Cohen 1960: 234, 253). Nowhere does the dominant system accord absolute freedom and complete recognition to the indigenous system, but many degrees of limited recognition are possible.

Third, there is the desire to protect the white community from crimes by Aborigines. Usually tribal law will be relevant only in internal Aboriginal matters but Berndt (1965: 191-2) mentions one case where it was used to sanction action against the white invaders. The protection of the white community is of course a legitimate aim of the criminal law but if the law is applied to tribal Aborigines for this purpose the interests of the defendant must also be kept to the forefront.

Kriewaldt (1960: 13) suggests two other reasons for subjecting tribal Aborigines to the criminal law. He maintains that it is the function of the criminal law to keep the peace by removing the temptation to private revenge. The following objections may be made to this contention. First, Aboriginal revenge is not private revenge; it is often socially sanctioned. Second, if Aborigines do not accept the white punishment as having any relevance to them, tribal revenge may still occur. In many cases they do not see the prison term as being in satisfaction of the rights of the injured Aboriginal or his kin.

Kriewaldt's second reason (p. 10) rests on the reciprocity of subjection to the criminal law and protection of the criminal law. If people are protected by the criminal law, they must accept that they are subject to it. His argument here would be valid if the Aborigines accepted and took advantage of the protection of the criminal law to the fullest extent, both against whites and against other Aborigines. So far, such acceptance is limited, though it differs among different Aboriginal groups. Kriewaldt also confines his attention to criminal law. It seems more important that people should be accorded the fullest protection of both the civil and criminal law before they are fully subjected to the criminal law. At present Aborigines are subjected to the criminal law and do obtain some protection from it but their enforcement of rights under civil law is very limited.

In the light of the material presented above it is submitted that the principle of recognition of tribal law should be adopted. This conclusion is based mainly on the injustice which is otherwise caused to Aboriginal defendants. It draws support from the fact that the police and courts have felt constrained to extend considerable unofficial recognition to tribal law. Because of the doubt and uncertainty at present existing it seems most desirable that this policy should be expressed in legislation.

The legislature would then have to consider another question of policy: should full recognition be accorded to tribal law or should it be recognised only to a limited extent? A limitation on policy grounds might be suggested, that tribal law should not be recognised if contrary to the 'general principles of civilisation'. This exception was inserted in legislation applying in various areas of Africa and caused trouble because different courts interpreted it in different ways and sometimes imposed considerable restrictions on the scope of tribal law. If it is desired to incorporate some such limitation here it would be desirable to spell out in some detail what is meant by this principle, for example, whether polygamy is or is not to be recognised. A limitation on practical grounds should also be considered. If an intertribal dispute or a dispute between Aboriginal and white is involved, it may not be possible to recognise tribal law because each party gives allegiance to a different legal system. Alternatively, a choice of law rule might be provided for this situation. This difficulty should be considered and a solution provided by the legislature.

Once it is decided that recognition should be given to tribal law and the degree of recognition which should be extended to it, the next problem is the practical one of providing facilities for its enforcement.

SUGGESTIONS FOR REFORM

In order to be able to apply tribal law, the tribunal has to know what rules of law exist in the Aboriginal system. This would not be difficult for a tribunal composed of Aborigines set up for a specific separate community but in every other situation it would be a problem. Alternative solutions are that the Aboriginal law should be codified or that it should be left to the tribunal to discover it in each individual case. Codification is unsatisfactory mainly because of the rigidity thereby perpetuated in the tribal law. It would not be a practical proposition in Australia.

A better approach would be to permit expert evidence in each individual case. Anthropologists should be encouraged to appear as expert witnesses. In addition, any works anthropologists write about tribal law, including works about specific tribes, general principles and the effect of culture contact, would be invaluable to courts deciding such cases. Such works, while not forming binding codes, would help to overcome the difficulty that evidence collected from Aborigines for a specific case could well be biased by the interests involved in that case (a difficulty experienced in South Africa—see Rogers 1949: 232).

The question of whether decisions and findings on Aboriginal law should form binding precedents for the future is a difficult one. Since tribal law is being rapidly modified under the impact of culture contact it seems undesirable to tie the definition of any particular tribal law to the finding of a court in a past case.

The next major matter concerns the tribunals which should be authorised to enforce tribal law. Should it be enforced in the existing courts or should special courts be set up? If special courts are set up, should they be staffed by whites or Aborigines and should they constitute a completely separate system of courts or should they be incorporated within the general system?

Many possible alternatives exist. Tribunals could be completely staffed by Aborigines. This would constitute complete non-interference by whites with existing tribal structures. Alternatively there could be non-interference except by way of appeal from these Aboriginal courts to existing courts. If it had been decided as a matter of policy that, for example, Aboriginal civil law would be recognised but not Aboriginal criminal law, then this would also involve some interference with existing tribal practices.

Alternatively, the existing tribunals completely staffed by whites could be continued with no Aboriginal participation at all. Or they could be permitted to relax the laws of evidence, for example the hearsay rule, to allow any Aboriginal to give his opinion on the matter before the court. Some experiments on these lines have already occurred at Hermannsburg in the Northern Territory and Amata in South Australia, with encouraging results.

The other possibility is to have mixed tribunals, for example, white magistrates sitting with Aboriginal assessors on tribal law cases. This might work well provided the assessors were selected so as to avoid kinship bias. Their functions would need to be carefully defined. It would have to be decided whether they were expected to advise their white colleagues on the relevant tribal law or whether they were really additional judicial officers, bound to decide in accordance with the evidence presented.

If it is decided to have tribunals staffed solely by Aborigines they would be to some extent separate from the ordinary hierarchy of courts. They could be set up on a permanent basis to deal with all cases involving members of a particular Aboriginal community, whether the case involved tribal law or not. Such courts could even function in urban areas, following the precedent of the Maori Committees in New Zealand.[22] The degree of control to be exercised by the ordinary courts by means of appellate review or other procedures would need to be carefully thought out and specified in the legislation.

If staffed by whites, the tribunals could be composed of magistrates or

[22] Maori Welfare Act, 1962 (N.Z.) section 35 and information from Professor C.M. Tatz.

justices who ordinarily exercise other jurisdiction. Theoretically, it would be possible to appoint magistrates or justices to sit exclusively on tribal law cases. This does not seem practicable in Australia because of the relatively small number of tribal law cases. Another alternative is to draw the tribunal from the pool of justices and magistrates available for ordinary cases but to provide that only certain members of the pool are eligible to sit on special Aboriginal cases. This is similar to some existing juvenile court provisions.

Another matter that should be considered is the desirability of providing an exemption clause for individual Aborigines who do not wish to be governed by tribal law.

I strongly believe that attempts should be made to pass over more responsibility to Aborigines in relation to the whole legal process, whether tribal law is involved or not. For this reason I favour the creation of special courts staffed by Aborigines. The United Nations study of Equality in the Administration of Justice of 10 June 1969 recognises (p. 42) that separate systems of courts for specific ethnic groups may be 'concessions to traditional tribal patterns or types of temporary legitimate protection of minorities' and thus need not necessarily be regarded as discriminatory (though others may be discriminatory in effect). This non-discriminatory ideal should be regarded as the policy underlying any creation of special courts for Aborigines and specific provisions should be tested by reference to it. Aboriginal communities should be consulted before detailed legislation is framed. Intensive study of overseas experience with plural systems of law is also needed, so that the best model may be adopted and the most serious problems be avoided.

A very difficult problem is that of providing protection for individual Aborigines from the tyranny or oppression of the group if Aboriginal communities are given more power in respect of self-government.[23] If individuals are allowed to exempt themselves from the jurisdiction of their own communities this might weaken the fabric of Aboriginal society. Yet many people are likely to feel concern about the position of certain individuals, if Aboriginal authorities are not subject to any control, for example, by way of appellate review. A similar problem has given rise to considerable debate in the United States. Concern for individual rights led to the passing of the 1968 Civil Rights Act (referred to as the Indian Bill of Rights). Yet many Indians are worried about its effect on tribal govern-

[23] Cf. 'Malawi—criminal jurisdiction', *I.C.J. Review* 5 (1970).

ments (Smith 1970). They see the Act as an infringement on tribal sovereignty, which may weaken the tribes in their relationship with the federal government. The debate rests to some extent on the conflict between Indian communal concepts and the European individualistic ethic.

Even if authority over law and order is transferred to Aboriginal communities it is probable that their powers would be limited. Their jurisdiction might only extend to minor crimes leaving homicides to be dealt with by the ordinary courts. The ordinary courts should then be encouraged to give more recognition to tribal law and better means of finding out the actual beliefs of the Aboriginal people than at present exist should be devised.

The official recognition of tribal law, as proposed, would not only solve some practical difficulties but would be tangible recognition by white society of the value of Aboriginal culture.

10 JUSTICE AND THE RULE OF LAW

In this world justice only comes into question between equals . . . the strong do what they can and the weak accept what they must.[1]

The Athenians' assertion to the Melians may be considered first as a statement of fact. Applied to the law, it implies that the legal system supports and reinforces the power structure of the social system. The crudest Marxist view is in accord: it sees law as a weapon by which the ruling class dominates and exploits the other classes (Sawer 1965: 177-8). The law expresses power, not justice.

Is this view justified by the findings of this study of the Aboriginal position before the law? It is clear that Aborigines do suffer discrimination in a number of ways when they come into contact with the law. There is discrimination in the administration of justice between two groups in the community, Aborigines and whites.

But this general statement makes insufficient allowance for the complexities of the situation. Preceding chapters have shown in detail the stages of the legal process at which discrimination does occur and, on the other hand, some aspects in which Aborigines find themselves in a favoured position. Though the discriminatory treatment outweighs the preferential treatment, it cannot be claimed that the law has been used solely as a weapon for maintaining the subordinate social and economic status of Aborigines.

Further, when viewed in historical perspective, there is ground for hope

[1] Thucydides' Melian Dialogues, translated by Dr John Bray. The translation forms part of a prologue written by Dr Bray for a production by the Adelaide University Theatre Guild of Euripides' *The Trojan Women.* I am grateful to Dr Bray and the Adelaide University Theatre Guild for giving permission to use this translation.

that discrimination will increasingly be replaced by equality or preferential treatment of Aborigines. Before considering future prospects, an attempt will be made to summarise the ways in which discrimination has occurred in the legal system because such knowledge should provide a firm foundation for planning.

The legal system here is considered to comprise substantive law (both legislation and case law), procedural law and the actual practice of persons administering the law (including police and judicial officers). Aborigines may suffer discrimination because legal rules, substantive or procedural, specifically provide that they are to be treated unequally. Alternatively, officials who administer the law may discriminate against them even though the law on its face applies equally to all citizens. Finally, some laws when applied equally, that is uniformly, do not produce equal results but actually reinforce inequality. Instances of each type of discrimination have been set out in earlier chapters.

The Athenian statement may also be interpreted as expressing a value judgment, a preference for power over justice. Australian society and the Australian legal system have adopted the contrary view, at least as a professed ideal. The ideal is that everyone is equal before the law; that no one is to be discriminated against in the administration of the law because of the colour of his skin or the racial group to which he belongs. This is expressed in the oath of office of police and judicial officers.

Why has this ideal not been achieved in practice? How has it been possible for this study to find considerable discrimination against Aborigines? Several factors are responsible, some of which are peculiar to Aborigines, while others are shared with some other members of the community.

First, the policy of equal treatment of Aborigines is relatively recent. There are still survivals of the past in the form of discriminatory legislation, not yet repealed. Other such legislation has been repealed but has contributed, with other historical factors, to produce the situation in which Aborigines are at the bottom of the socioeconomic scale (see Chapter 7 on discriminatory legislation).

Secondly, some people who administer the law are prejudiced against Aborigines and have the opportunity to translate their prejudiced attitudes into overt action, usually because the law allows them some discretion in the performance of their functions. Non-acceptance of the policy aim of equal treatment by persons who have to administer the law seriously militates against the successful translation of the ideal into the actual.

These two factors affect Aborigines uniquely, but other persons of low social and economic status (poor whites) also experience economic and social discrimination. Lawyers have been very slow to recognise the extent to which justice in an individual case depends on the financial resources of the litigant. The ideal has been expressed that persons should not be discriminated against on racial grounds, but the extent to which the law embodies economic discrimination has not been recognised. Probably this is because it operates indirectly and lies in the procedural field rather than in substantive law. The earlier description of the operation of the bail system and of imprisonment for non-payment of fines illustrates quite clearly that economic discrimination does operate. The abolition of discrimination based solely on race would not remove all discrimination against Aborigines so long as most of them remain poverty stricken.

Social discrimination may be said to operate whenever differential treatment is accorded to a person of low social status, because he is helpless to complain, having no powerful friends. Examples may be found in some exercises of the police discretion to arrest. Social status is not always directly correlated with wealth, though in Australia they tend to coincide. Aborigines as a group have the lowest social status in the community, partly as an accompaniment of low economic status and partly owing to racial prejudice.

Another factor in the discriminatory pattern is the geographical distribution of Aborigines. Their present-day concentration in outback areas results from the historical process of white invasion and culture conflict. They experience with other rural dwellers the disadvantages of remoteness from legal representation, of courts more often constituted by untrained justices, of harsher sentences. They experience these disadvantages to a greater extent than whites because so many of them are rural dwellers in a predominantly urban country and because they do not have access to the economic resources by which many whites overcome or mitigate rural isolation.

ABORIGINES AND JUSTICE: EQUALITY OR PREFERENCE?

So far discrimination, injustice and inequality have been used as if they were more or less synonymous terms. But this usage is clearly imprecise. In making an attempt to articulate the relationships between these words and the distinctions between them, I do not intend a full-scale philosophical investigation.

Most writers attempting to define justice have agreed that it carries some connotation of equality. It is also intimately associated with law. It is common to refer to the administration of justice rather than the administration of law: this usage suggests that the chief purpose of law is to achieve justice.

Sir Isaiah Berlin (1961: 132) points out: 'All rules, by definition, entail a measure of equality . . . This type of equality derives simply from the conception of rules as such—namely, that they allow of no exceptions.' So the person administering a law—the policeman initiating a prosecution or the judicial officer hearing a charge—should apply it equally to all persons who fall within its scope. The race of the suspect or defendant should be an irrelevant consideration in the performance of the official's duty. Provided the law on its face applies equally to all citizens, any decision which produces a more unfavourable consequence for an Aboriginal than for a white is discriminatory and unjust.

But if the law on its face does not apply to everyone equally, if it sets up a special class of people to whom the law applies, the policeman who simply enforces the law can hardly be accused of discriminatory treatment. In this case the law itself is at fault. Sir Isaiah Berlin's definition of formal equality says nothing about the inequality apparent only when one rule is compared with another or when the rule applying to one group is compared with the absence of law applying to another.

In Australia, at present, there is no procedure by which such discriminatory legislation can be challenged. All that an affected group, such as the Aboriginal community, can do is to lobby for legislative change. But if the proposed Human Rights and Racial Discrimination Bills are enacted, then it would become possible to challenge legislation on the ground of conflict with basic human rights. For this reason it is useful to look at the approach of courts in the United States to the problem of defining 'equal protection of the laws' and to the task of deciding when particular legislation should be held to be invalid as denying 'equal protection'. This examination may throw some light on what equality should mean for Aborigines.

'EQUAL PROTECTION' UNDER THE U.S. CONSTITUTION

In *Shapiro* v. *Thompson* Mr Justice Harlan spelt out the doctrine the Supreme Court has adopted in deciding equal protection cases: 'the rule that statutory classifications which either are based upon certain "suspect" criteria or affect "fundamental rights" will be held to deny equal protection unless justified by a "compelling" governmental interest'.[2] Where there is neither a suspect criterion nor a fundamental right at stake, the classification will be upheld if it bears a reasonable relationship to the purpose of the law. This is the well known two-tier test of judicial review under which the court scrutinises some laws much more strictly than others.

The prime example of a 'suspect' criterion is a racial classification. The court scrutinises very carefully any state law which imports a racial classification; it is difficult for any to be held justified by a countervailing compelling governmental interest. Amongst laws which have been struck down on this ground are the Virginia antimiscegenation statutes[3] and the Florida cohabitation statute.[4] In an early case a San Francisco law under which a Chinese man had been imprisoned for illegally conducting a laundry was held to have been administered in a discriminatory fashion, so that a denial of equal protection had occurred.[5] A long series of cases beginning with *Brown* v. *Board of Education*[6] has also held that segregation in public schools denies Negro children equal protection of the laws under the Fourteenth Amendment.

Though the Supreme Court now appears to be moving away from the two-tier test as set out above, it is improbable that there will be any change in its strict scrutiny of laws embodying a racial classification. 'Historically the Equal Protection Clause was largely a product of the desire to eradicate legal distinctions founded upon race.'[7] That is to say, it grew out of the American historical situation in response to the fact of slavery and its abolition. This may have some significance in suggesting a different interpretation for equality in the Indian and Aboriginal context.

Most of the American cases have been brought by blacks seeking to desegregate schools and other public facilities. They represent a demand

[2] 394 U.S. 618, 89 S. Ct. 1322, 22 L. Ed. 2d 600, 629 (1969). Although this is a dissenting judgment the passage quoted is a summary of the majority's view, of which Harlan J. disapproves.

[3] *Loving* v. *Virginia* 388 U.S. 1, 87 S. Ct. 1817, 18 L. Ed. 2d 1010 (1967).

[4] *McLaughlin* v. *Florida* 379 U.S. 184, 85 S. Ct. 283, 13 L. Ed. 2d 222 (1964).

[5] *Yick Wo* v. *Hopkins* 118 U.S. 356, 6 S. Ct. 1064, 30 L. Ed. 220 (1886).

[6] 347 U.S. 483, 74 S. Ct. 686, 98 L. Ed. 873 (1954).

[7] *Shapiro* v. *Thompson* 394 U.S. 618, 89 S. Ct. 1322, 22 L. Ed. 2d 600, 630 (1969) per Harlan J.

by members of the Negro community to be integrated into the general community. The Supreme Court has acceded to this demand, holding that to do otherwise would be to deny the black plaintiffs the equal protection of the laws.

The newer claims by the more militant blacks for recognition as a separate cultural group have hardly made an appearance in the courts. In the education cases, for example, the Supreme Court talked of the positive value of integration not only for black children but also for other children. The school authorities were under an affirmative duty to desegregate, to dismantle the dual system of schools previously existing.

In the past this was what the blacks were seeking. But in *Norwalk CORE* v. *Norwalk Board of Education*[8] black plaintiffs objected to plans for integration of schools and wished the neighbourhood schools with their preponderance of black and Puerto Rican pupils to remain. Timbers Chief Judge in the District Court for the District of Connecticut held otherwise, saying (p. 222) that the court should not interfere where a school board 'in good faith and without improper racial motivation or arbitrary disregard of the rights of a minority, concluded that educational facilities should not be maintained and constructed in plaintiffs' neighborhoods'. Thus the school board could adopt this policy even over the protests of the minority parents. Similarly in *Guey Heung Lee* v. *Johnson*[9] Americans of Chinese ancestry applied for a stay of a Federal District Court's school desegregation order. The District Court's order had reassigned Chinese-American pupils to certain elementary public schools in San Francisco in order to reduce racial imbalance. Douglas J. as circuit justice in denying the application for a stay clearly decided in favour of desegregation, even though it was members of the minority race who wanted to remain segregated.

These and other cases suggest that the courts see integration of the races as the value to be implemented under the equal protection clause. Self-determination and the right of the minority group to choose the form in which public facilities are to be made available to it may be denied. This looks as if equality is being interpreted as uniformity of treatment rather than respect for different points of view.

Susan Appleton (1973) makes a convincing case for the constitutional validity of Black House and Casa de la Raza, racially exclusive schools

[8] 298 F. Supp. 213 (1969), affirmed 423 F. 2d 121 (1970).

[9] 404 U.S. 1215, 92 S. Ct. 14, 30 L. Ed. 2d 19 (1971).

run for blacks and Chicanos respectively in Berkeley, California. However, she stresses that the Berkeley situation is unique. All other schools in the school district are racially integrated so that the existence of these two separate schools does not remove the chance for any child to obtain an integrated education, if that is what he and his parents want. The overall commitment of the system is to integration and even the two minority group schools are seen as temporary only and furthering the aim of ultimate integration by enhancing the self-confidence of their students.

The full Supreme Court has yet to rule on the specific question of separate schools set up by minority racial groups but the general point at issue here is likely to prove increasingly troublesome in the future. Many blacks are espousing a separatist position as they become disillusioned with what they see as the failure of the traditional civil rights movement. American Indian claims to equality are also likely to be couched in the language of cultural pluralism and the right to be Indian.

Few Indians have relied on equal protection arguments, at least compared with the flood of civil rights litigation on behalf of blacks. Some exceptions are to be found in the criminal field. The Indian defendant in *State of South Dakota* v. *Adolph Plentyhorse*[10] succeeded in his equal protection attack on a racially discriminatory jury. This case followed precedents established in trials involving Negro defendants. In such cases, the courts have held that the defendant is entitled to a jury selected on criteria other than race. But he is not entitled to a jury of his peers, in the sense that members of his own racial group *must* be on the jury.

Another criminal case involving American Indian defendants exposed the potential conflict between integration and separation policies. In *Gray* v. *United States*[11] the Indian defendants attacked the validity of legislation which included capital punishment as a penalty for rape by an Indian of a non-Indian woman, while permitting only imprisonment where the victim was an Indian woman. This federal legislation applied only to 'Indian country', that is, reservations and other Indian land. (State legislation generally applies to off-reservation crimes.) The defendants' argument was framed in terms of the due process clause of the Bill of Rights, since the equal protection clause does not apply to the federal government. But if a similar result had been produced under State legislation, the challenge would probably have been framed in equal protection terms. Legislation

10 184 N.W. 2d 654 (1971).
11 394 F. 2d 96 (9th Cir. 1968).

which discriminates on the basis of arbitrary criminal law classifications is usually seen as a denial of equal protection.

The circuit court in *Gray* upheld the validity of the challenged legislation (pp. 98-9).

> It has long been acknowledged that Congress . . . has recognized and established for the Indian people a peculiar and protected status as wards of the Federal government . . . Congress has seen fit to diminish the penalty to be imposed upon an Indian who is convicted of rape upon another Indian in Indian Country . . . Appellants here seek to challenge as unconstitutional this statute . . . which is of benefit to them. We cannot say that such a statute denies its beneficiaries due process of law.

It may seem strange to refer to Indian defendants as beneficiaries of this law. These particular defendants had raped a non-Indian woman so were liable to the harsher penalty provided in the legislation. It is true, though, that the lesser penalty for the rape of an Indian woman could be considered as preferential legislation for Indian defendants in general. Non-Indian defendants were liable to be executed for rape whatever the race of their victim.

In a perceptive Note in the *Stanford Law Review* McMeekin (1969) accepts the circuit court's view of the protected status of the Indian. He analyses the case in terms of the tension between what he calls the 'assimilative' premise and the 'separative' premise. 'Even assuming that such treatment of Negroes and whites would be an unacceptable manifestation of the separative premise, a similar assumption may not be indulged when some separation is traditionally accepted.' (p. 1245). Here he draws a valid distinction between members of the two minority races in terms of their different history: the Negroes living close to whites but with access only to segregated facilities; the Indians living in isolation on reservations, not solely under compulsion but largely by choice, and in a position to retain more of their original culture. Nevertheless he considers (p. 1245) 'the likelihood of invidious discrimination is so great that there should be close judicial scrutiny of any separatist statute.' He concludes that this statute showed a legislative purpose to discriminate against perpetrators of interracial rape (specifically the Indian rape of a non-Indian woman) and was not a valid attempt to make allowance for different cultural values.

Though they reach different conclusions on the specific facts of the case both the circuit court and the commentator provide a rationale for upholding legislation that does accord different treatment to a minority race. Such legislation need not be invalidated under the equal protection clause if it confers a benefit on minority group members and rests on an appreciation of real cultural differences.

It may be forecast, as suggested earlier, that the Supreme Court will have to face this issue more often in the future and may have to abandon its simple integrationist position. Time may remove the historical distinctions between the black and Indian races as blacks more and more seek a separate identity by reviving black culture.

If the Supreme Court does accept arguments based on the importance of retaining cultural identity this appears to be a move away from the 'colourblindness' which early cases held was mandated by the equal protection clause. It is worth noting that the Supreme Court has not regarded 'colourblindness' as requiring that the judges completely ignore the race of the persons involved. As the court said, in striking down the North Carolina Anti-Busing Law:

> But more important the statute exploits an apparently neutral form to control school assignment plans by directing that they be "color blind"; that requirement, against the background of segregation, would render illusory the promise of *Brown* v. *Board of Education*, 347 U.S. 483, 74 S. Ct. 686, 98 L. Ed. 873 (1954). Just as the race of students must be considered in determining whether a constitutional violation has occurred, so also must race be considered in formulating a remedy.[12]

American courts' willingness to go behind the face of the statute or other state action and get at the real situation is also demonstrated in the jury cases. The court does not simply accept an official's assertion that he acted without racial bias; it looks at the pattern of jury selection and regards the absence of minority jurors as raising a *prima facie* case of discrimination. In the field of employment, the Supreme Court has held that an employer is not permitted to use aptitude tests which have the effect of discriminating against minority groups unless they can be shown to measure job capability.[13] It so held even though there was no evidence of discriminatory intent; the tests had been applied fairly to whites and Negroes alike.

The aim of the Supreme Court to date has been to produce substantive equality, that is, the same treatment for everyone. In this sense it has

[12] *North Carolina State Board of Education* v. *Swann* 91 S. Ct. 1284, 1286; 402 U.S. 43, 45-46 (1971).

[13] *Griggs* v. *Duke Power Coy* 91 S. Ct. 849, 401 U.S. 424, 28 L. Ed. 2d 158 (1971).

adhered to colourblindness as an ideal. It has regarded state action as improper when it denies benefits or imposes burdens on members of the coloured races in the United States. The new challenge will be to work out a rationale for upholding state action which recognises legitimate cultural differences, even though these follow racial lines. Similarly there is the question of preferential legislation, conferring benefits on historically disadvantaged groups.

The Supreme Court has recently upheld the Indian employment preference policy in the Bureau of Indian Affairs in the face of an attack launched by non-Indian BIA employees.[14] The plaintiffs alleged that the preference provisions of the Indian Reorganization Act of 1934 violated the Due Process Clause of the Fifth Amendment. The Supreme Court unanimously held that the preference policy does not constitute invidious racial discrimination and thus does not violate the Due Process Clause. Rather it is reasonable and rationally designed to further Indian self-government.

In reaching this conclusion the court relied on the special relationship between Congress and federally recognised Indian tribes. Congress has plenary power under the Constitution to deal with the special problems of Indians. The court said: 'The preference, as applied, is granted to Indians not as a discrete racial group, but, rather, as members of quasi-sovereign tribal entities whose lives and activities are governed by the BIA in a unique fashion . . . [T]he preference is reasonably and directly related to a legitimate, nonracially based goal.'[15]

Since the decision is based on the special history of Indian/federal government relations and the unique legal status of the Indian, it says nothing about the position of blacks who wish to support preferential legislation for their racial group.

Its rationale may perhaps be more directly transferred for the benefit of Australian Aborigines. The United States Supreme Court has described the origin and nature of the special relationship between Indians and the federal government:

> In the exercise of the war and treaty powers, the United States overcame the Indians and took possession of their lands, sometimes by force, leaving them an uneducated, helpless and dependent people needing protection against the selfishness of others and their own improvidence. Of necessity the United States assumed the duty of furnishing that

[14] *Morton* v. *Mancari* 42 United States Law Week 4933 (1974).

[15] 42 U.S. Law Week 4933, 4939 (1974).

> protection and with it the authority to do all that was required to perform that obligation and to prepare the Indians to take their place as independent, qualified members of the modern body politic.[16]

Though the federal government's power to legislate for Aborigines was inserted in the Australian Constitution only within the last decade, it does appear that the community, in voting in favour of the 1967 referendum, was expressing its sense that the federal government did owe a special obligation to Aborigines similar to that recognised towards Indians in the passage cited. This would then justify preferential treatment of Aborigines in relation to employment, education, the provision of public facilities and other special services.

Rather than relying solely on a history of recognition of the special status of a particular racial group, it would seem to be preferable to adopt general principles recognising the special needs of minority groups and their desire to retain their culture and a separate identity. Aborigines cannot rely on a history of treaty making and a long-standing recognition of their special federal status, as Indians can. Yet the justice of their claim to special treatment now, in recognition of the past dispossession of the continent and the discrimination they have suffered, is equally as strong as the Indian case.

Summarising the value of the United States experience Gareth Evans (1973) says:

> At the heart of the American equal protection doctrine . . . there has always been a recognition of the simple truths that numerical equality is usually impossible and often undesirable, that laws must accordingly differentiate and classify, and that the central question in evaluating them is always whether the classifications are reasonable.

He concedes that the United States Supreme Court by insisting that race is always a suspect classification demanding active review has painted itself into a corner and may find it difficult to deal satisfactorily with the question of benign racial discrimination.

The recognition of the special status of Indians will help members of that racial group who are also members of federally recognised tribes. It remains to be seen whether the Supreme Court can develop a general rationale for benign racial discrimination (where the aim is to integrate the minority into the wider society) and for the concession of legitimate cultural separation, if that is what the minority group prefers.

[16] *Board of County Commissioners* v. *Seber* 318 U.S. 705, 715 (1942).

EQUALITY FOR ABORIGINES

This brief examination of the American cases suggests that mere formal equality is not enough to satisfy the legitimate demands of a minority that asks for recognition of its different culture. Spokesmen for Aborigines criticise discriminatory legislation and call for its repeal. At the same time they demand preferential legislation; thus they are not asking for absolute equality or uniformity of treatment.

A policy statement of the Victorian Aborigines Welfare Board justified preferential legislation on the ground that: 'It is as unjust to treat unequals equally as it is to treat equals unequally.'[17] This sentiment dates back to Aristotle, and no thoroughgoing egalitarian can be found prepared to assert that the ideal society is one in which all citizens are treated absolutely equally. The notion of desert enters at some stage into every concept of justice; as soon as it does, absolute equality disappears as an ideal. Justice still demands equality of treatment for those considered to belong to the same class; but it is recognised that there may be different groups of people for whom different treatment is appropriate. Some may attempt to justify different treatment on the grounds of merit; others will see need as a more appropriate criterion (see Ginsberg 1965).

Once the possibility of differentiating between groups is recognised, difficult problems arise as to how the groups should be defined and what differences of treatment may justly be applied to them. The Aborigines Welfare Board policy statement rejected differential practices based on race alone. 'Justification is not valid on the basis of race or colour, but on relevant differences in needs, capacities, interests, incentives and the weight of responsibility that can be borne.'[18] Aborigines as a group are seen as having different needs, capacities and interests from other members of Australian society and therefore legislation favouring them as a group is considered to be justified.

The individual's reaction to this proposition and to detailed proposals for preferential legislation depends ultimately on his vision of the ideal society. In my view the ideal society is one in which everyone is regarded as of equal worth, despite differences of temperament and talent. Further, as far as possible, there is an equal distribution of wealth.

[17] 'Aboriginal Policies of the Aborigines Welfare Board' in *Report of the Aborigines Welfare Board for the Year Ended 30th June, 1967* (1967), p. 12. Melbourne: Government Printer.

[18] Ibid.

A similar view has been accepted by the Australian community to the extent that a welfare state philosophy has been adopted. It cannot be claimed that measures like social services legislation and flood relief aim at a completely equal distribution of wealth but at least they express the view that there should not be vast inequalities and that everyone is entitled to a minimum standard of living.

Since Aborigines are clearly the most disadvantaged group in the community there can be no quarrel with special legislation passed on their behalf. Such legislation can justifiably be regarded as redressing inequality, largely produced by historical factors, rather than as producing inequality.

The laissez faire philosophy of last century believed that equality before the law was enough. As Anatole France wryly commented: 'the law, in its majestic equality, forbids the rich as well as the poor to sleep under bridges, to beg in the streets, and to steal bread' (quoted Fortas 1967: 402). In order to make justice and equality a reality for all, it is clear that laissez faire or merely formal equality is not enough. Fortas claims (p. 402) that 'it is the mark of greatness of this age' to have recognised this and to have decided that 'rights must be made realities, that equality in theory is not enough'.

But the most difficult problems arise when the specific question is faced: what changes in law and procedure are needed to produce real justice for Aborigines? The following is an attempt to sketch an approach to answering the question. Some specific suggestions for reform have already been made but there is no attempt to formulate an integrated plan. That is a task for politicians and administrators. However, in performing that task certain matters deserve consideration.

First, research in depth is necessary to find out which parts of the law and its administration operate unfairly and produce inequality. This book is a first step in this direction, but there certainly remain profitable avenues for future research. But I do not consider that reform should be postponed until all the research is complete. Since any change is likely to produce effects at various points of the legal system, perhaps the greatest need is not so much for a complete plan as for ongoing research to assess the impact and value of any reforms introduced.

A major problem is to decide in what areas uniform law and equal administration are desirable and in what respects unequal law is necessary to compensate for disabilities. Even where a case can be made out for special treatment of Aborigines, I consider that it may often be desirable to widen the class of persons benefited. For example, if it is intended to benefit Aborigines by an own-recognizance program in substitution for existing bail requirements it might be desirable to make eligibility depend on financial need and lack of education, rather than to make the criterion the race of the applicant.

There will be hard questions to be answered and dilemmas to be resolved in deciding whether any particular legislation intended to benefit Aborigines will actually have that effect. In solving these it is suggested that as far as possible there should be consultation with Aborigines, participation by them and the opportunity for them to make a free choice. The subjective reactions of the intended beneficiaries are immensely useful to policymakers. This topic is so important that it deserves extended treatment.

ABORIGINAL DECISION MAKING

Governments and administrators have accepted the ideal of consultation with Aborigines and it has become a fashionable catchcry in Aboriginal affairs. But to make it meaningful, attention to detailed structures and procedures is necessary. Participation by Aborigines in decision making is even more important than consultation by whites with Aborigines.

There are at least two levels on which such participation could occur: the judicial process and the process of legislation. Some developments in the direction of an integration between elements of Aboriginal and white culture, of mingling of elements of the two legal systems, have already taken place. Discussion of this topic was foreshadowed in the chapter on traditionally oriented Aborigines but the need for participation is not confined to them.

Two magistrates have experimented with holding courts on Aboriginal reserves in outback areas. Mr Grubb S.M. held a juvenile court at Amata in South Australia and asked the tribal elders to help him fix penalties.[19] Mr Hall S.M. adopted a practice of holding court at Hermannsburg Mission in the Northern Territory at the request of the Aboriginal village council.[20] Rules of evidence have been relaxed to the extent of allowing any Aboriginal to say anything he wants to about the case before the court. Both experiments appear to have had some success in encouraging Aborigines to believe that the law is not only an instrument of white oppression.

The Hermannsburg experiment was encouraged by Pastor Paul Albrecht,

[19] Melbourne *Herald* 26/9/67.

[20] Interview with Mr Hall, 4/7/66, and Melbourne *Herald* 18/11/68.

who has written a thoughtful paper on authority in the Aboriginal community.[21] He traces the breakdown of tribal authority as a result of white settlement and claims there is now an authority vacuum since white authority has not taken its place. (White police and courts do assert power over Aboriginal communities, of course, but Aborigines have not accepted the validity of this exercise of authority.) Albrecht suggests that the only answer is 'to give authority back to the Aboriginal people to deal with their own social problems . . . Legislation could be brought down to give authority to Aboriginal communities, to elect their own councils, and to give these councils the right to deal with their social problems as they think best.'

I support this suggestion because I believe that every effort should be made to extend and improve Aboriginal control over their own affairs and particularly in relation to involvement with legal matters. Aboriginal Councils have now been established with official blessing on many Western Australian and South Australian reserves and at Lake Tyers in Victoria. Their functions and powers in practice differ widely. They should be encouraged to exercise disciplinary powers over incidents occurring on the reserves. There are dangers in such a course; chiefly that family feuds will mitigate against just decisions. But the dangers of white staff exercising sole authority have been illustrated. Maori Committees in New Zealand and tribal government in the United States[22] appear to have worked well and there is no obvious reason why the same experiment should not work with Aborigines.

As well as participation in the maintenance of law and order, Aborigines should be encouraged to take part in the formulation of legislative policies. Aboriginal choice should be provided for both by allowing individuals to express their views before legislation is enacted and then by permitting each one to decide whether or not to bring himself under special legislation purporting to be for his benefit.

At the first stage adequate consultative machinery is essential. Rowley (1969: 236) stresses the powerlessness of individual Aborigines and the need for incorporation of Aboriginal rights to give them greater effectiveness in negotiations with whites. This does not necessarily mean that they must form companies under existing company law. Some other form of

21 (1965). Compare his later paper (1975) reporting that this experiment has not been a success because it was not based on Aboriginal lines of authority.

22 Personal communication from Professor Colin Tatz on his observation of Maori Committees in New Zealand; Cohen 1960: 234.

legal personality may be desirable; it may even be necessary to invent a new form and ensure the passage of new laws to protect it.[23] Ways in which an Aboriginal group with recognised legal personality could be effective would be as a pressure group seeking legislation or as a body which policy makers would find it convenient to consult.

ABORIGINAL STATUS

Aboriginal difficulties with the legal process (with which this book has mainly been concerned) are only part of a wider problem, that of the status of Aborigines as a group in the community. It has been shown that many legal disabilities are shared with other depressed groups. The significant fact is that so many Aborigines belong to the most deprived socioeconomic group and that their status will be improved only by considerable effort on the part of the rest of the community. In my view the aim should be improved social and economic standing for the whole Aboriginal group rather than increased social mobility for individuals. Lorna Lippmann (1973: 188) observes that administrative agencies often find it easier to deal with Aborigines who are ambitious to improve their position. But the apathetic and 'trouble-makers' are also entitled to a minimum standard of living considerably better than that most Aborigines currently enjoy.

The lawyer's concern for such matters as part of his effort to establish the Rule of Law has been recognised by the International Commission of Jurists.[24] The lawyer's involvement in this field stems mainly from his position as a citizen, but his expertise in relation to legislation casts on him a special responsibility to act.

Only when the social and economic status of Aborigines has been raised to a level comparable with that of the majority of the community will it be possible to abolish all preferential legislation conferring on them a special legal status. Only then will it be possible to say that those who presently suffer inequality have achieved justice.

[23] Cf. Tatz 1972: 103: 'Our notion of committees, councils, chairmen, treasurers, secretaries, agendas and rules of procedure have been foisted upon Aborigines—as if they were the only valid forms or vehicles for decision-making and spokesmanship.'

[24] See *The Dynamic Aspects of the Rule of Law in the Modern Age* (Geneva: International Commission of Jurists) 1965: 72: 'Lawyers should be anxiously concerned with the prevalence of poverty, ignorance and inequality in human society . . . '

APPENDIXES

APPENDIX 1

CODING OF THE TEN TOWNS SAMPLE

For ease and speed of manipulation, the raw data relating to the cases in the sample were transferred to punched cards and the statistical tables were produced by computer. A detailed code was drawn up for use on the punched cards and also full instructions for people who assisted with the coding. The code is too long to set out in full here so an illustration must suffice. For example, column 17—'Offence charged' was coded as follows:

Drunkenness	0
Traffic Act	1
Disorderliness and vagrancy	2
Stealing	3
Native Welfare offences	4
Assault	5
Offences against the police	6
Unlawfully using motor vehicles	7
All other major offences	8
All other minor offences	9

The following specific offences were included under each of the above offence categories:

'Drunkenness': drunk in a public place.

'Traffic Act': any offence under the Traffic Act or the Transport Co-ordination Act. Offences under the Traffic Act include driving without a licence, driving while disqualified, failing to stop after an accident, reckless driving, dangerous driving, careless driving, driving under the influence of liquor, unlighted headlamp.

'Disorderliness and vagrancy': disorderly conduct, obscene language, disorderly by fighting, any other offence under section 54 Police Act (W.A.), idle and disorderly, insufficient means, not being an Aboriginal Native, lodging with Aboriginal Natives, any other offence under section 65 Police Act (W.A.), causing a disturbance.

'Stealing': stealing, receiving.

'Native Welfare offences': any offence under the Native Welfare Act, 1963 (W.A.) and Native Welfare Act Regulations, 1964 (W.A.) and under sections of the Licensing Act, 1911 (W.A.) relating to 'Natives'. These include: Native receiving liquor, supplying liquor to Native, disorderly behaviour on a Reserve.

'Assault': any type of assault.

'Offences against the police': resisting police, hindering police, impersonating police, false name and address, escaping legal custody, false representation to police. Assaults on the police are not included in this offence category.

'Unlawfully using motor vehicles': unlawful use of any kind of vehicle.

'All other major offences': murder, manslaughter, sexual offences, breaking and entering, robbery, unlawfully on premises, negligent driving causing death, false pretences.

'All other minor offences': wilful damage, habitual drunkenness, unlawful possession.

APPENDIX 2

TEN TOWNS SAMPLE TABLES

Notes on the Tables in Appendix 2

1. Layout of the tables. For the more detailed tables (for example, Table 2.1), the number on the first line of each cell = observed frequency; the number on the second line of each cell = percentage of total reading down; the number on the third line of each cell = percentage of total reading across.

2. The computer program used excluded 'no record' cases from the sample. This explains the differences between the totals of different tables; if there was no record on the punched card of the particular variables being considered, then that card was not included in that table. Sometimes this was because the data was not collected or was unavailable; sometimes because the particular variables were not applicable.

3. Each 'case' in the sample represents one charge rather than one defendant. If a defendant is charged with a number of offences at one time, each is treated as a separate 'case' in the sample.

Table 2.1: *Offence charged*

	Drunkenness	Traffic	Disorderly conduct	Stealing	Native Welfare	Assault	Offences against police	Unlawful use motor vehicle	Major offences	Minor offences	Total
Aborigines	630	143	265	40	500	89	69	17	27	133	1913
	64·9	12·5	57·4	29·2	90·4	70·6	58·5	68·0	34·2	38·6	
	32·9	7·5	13·9	2·1	26·1	4·7	3·6	0·9	1·4	7·0	
Whites	341	1001	197	97	53	37	49	8	52	212	2047
	35·1	87·5	42·6	70·8	9·6	29·4	41·5	32·0	65·8	61·4	
	16·7	48·9	9·6	4·7	2·6	1·8	2·4	0·4	2·5	10·4	
Total	971	1144	462	137	553	126	118	25	79	345	3960
per 100	24·5	28·9	11·7	3·5	14·0	3·2	3·0	0·6	2·0	8·7	

Table 2.2: *Victims of assaults*

Defendants	Victims			
	Police	Other whites	Aborigines	Total
Aborigines	15	5	45	65
Whites	4	7	1	12
Total	19	12	46	77

Table 2.3: *Single and multiple counts*

	Total number of charges heard at same time								
	1	2	3	4	5	6	7	8	9
Aborigines	1307	212	42	12	4	2	1	2	1
Whites	1010	115	22	6	5	1	0	0	0

Note: This table shows individual defendants, whereas the other tables in this Appendix treat each charge separately. For example, 212 Aboriginal defendants were on two charges at once (total 414 charges). Thus this table demonstrates that 276 Aboriginal defendants were on multiple charges; 149 white defendants were on multiple charges.

Table 2.4: *Initiation of prosecutions—arrest and summons*

	Summons	Arrest	Total
Aborigines	158	1425	1583
	13·8	62·9	
	10·0	90·0	
Whites	985	840	1825
	86·2	37·1	
	54·0	46·0	
Total	1143	2265	3408
per 100	33·5	66·5	

Table 2.5: *Initiation of prosecutions—arrest and summons—by offence*

	Drunkenness	Traffic	Disorderly conduct	Stealing	Native Welfare	Assault	Offences against police	Unlawful use motor vehicle	Major offences	Minor offences	Total
Summons	0	950	21	1	14	24	3	0	2	131	1146
	0·0	86·7	5·2	0·9	2·8	21·2	2·7	0·0	3·0	48·7	
	0·0	82·9	1·8	0·1	1·2	2·1	0·3	0·0	0·2	11·4	
Arrest	731	146	380	110	484	89	108	20	64	138	2270
	100	13·3	94·8	99·1	97·2	78·8	97·3	100	97·0	51·3	
	32·2	6·4	16·7	4·8	21·3	3·9	4·8	0·9	2·8	6·1	
Total	731	1096	401	111	498	113	111	20	66	269	3416

Table 2.6: *Grant of police bail*

	Not granted	Granted	Total
Aborigines	1047	175	1222
	69·4	42·9	
	85·7	14·3	
Whites	461	233	694
	30·6	57·1	
	66·4	33·6	
Total	1508	408	1916
per 100	78·7	21·3	

Table 2.7: *Period in custody before first court appearance*

	Up to 24 hours	More than 24 hours	Total
Aborigines	638	205	843
	76·6	91·9	
	75·7	24·3	
Whites	195	18	213
	23·4	8·1	
	91·5	8·5	
Total	833	223	1056
per 100	78·9	21·1	

Table 2.8: *Amount of cash on arrest*

	Nil	Up to $3	Over $3	Total
Aborigines	322	305	100	727
	86·6	80·5	41·7	
	44·3	42·0	13·8	
Whites	50	74	140	264
	13·4	19·5	58·3	
	18·9	28·0	53·0	
Total	372	379	240	991
per 100	37·5	38·2	24·2	

Table 2.9: *Grant of court bail*

	Not granted	Granted	Total
Aborigines	50	65	115
	50·0	41·4	
	43·5	56·5	
Whites	50	92	142
	50·0	58·6	
	35·2	64·8	
Total	100	157	257
per 100	38·9	61·1	

Table 2.10: *Entry of bail bond (court bail)*

	Not entered	Entered	Total
Aborigines	7	47	54
	77·8	38·8	
	13·0	87·0	
Whites	2	74	76
	22·2	61·2	
	2·6	97·4	
Total	9	121	130
per 100	6·9	93·1	

Table 2.11: *Amount of police bail*

	Up to $3	$3.01–6	$6.01–9	$9.01–12	$12.01–15	$15.01–18	$18.01–21	Over $21	Total
Aborigines	13	42	3	70	0	0	4	4	136
Whites	21	62	0	58	1	0	13	13	168
Total	34	104	3	128	1	0	17	17	304

Table 2.12: *Amount of police bail—by offence*

	Up to $3	$3.01–6	$6.01–9	$9.01–12	$12.01–15	$15.01–18	$18.01–21	Over $21	Total
Drunkenness	28	99	3	63	0	0	0	0	193
Traffic	0	0	0	0	0	0	2	9	11
Disorderly conduct	0	2	0	39	0	0	8	3	52
Stealing	0	0	0	1	0	0	1	1	3
Native Welfare	4	1	0	14	0	0	0	1	20
Assault	0	0	0	0	0	0	4	0	4
Offences against Police	0	2	0	6	0	0	0	0	8
Unlawful use motor vehicle	0	0	0	0	0	0	0	0	0
Major offences	0	0	0	0	0	0	0	1	1
Minor Offences	1	0	0	5	0	0	2	2	10
Total	33	104	3	128	0	0	17	17	302

Table 2.13: *Amount of court bail*

	Up to $20	Over $20	Total
Aborigines	45	18	63
	55·6	25·4	
	71·4	28·6	
Whites	36	53	89
	44·4	74·6	
	40·4	59·6	
Total	81	71	152
per 100	53·3	46·7	

Table 2.14: *Amount of court bail—by offence*

	Up to $20	Over $20	Total
Drunkenness	14	0	14
Traffic	9	27	36
Disorderly conduct	19	3	22
Stealing	1	14	15
Native Welfare	10	4	14
Assault	7	5	12
Offences against police	6	1	7
Unlawful use motor vehicle	0	3	3
Major offences	3	12	15
Minor offences	11	4	15
Total	80	73	153

Table 2.15: *Form of court bail granted*

	No surety no cash required	1 surety no cash required	No surety but cash required	1 surety cash required	2 sureties no cash required	2 sureties cash required	No surety no record whether cash required	Sureties required no record whether cash required	Total
Aborigines	20	6	15	4	0	0	17	3	65
Whites	19	14	32	6	0	1	12	8	92
Total	39	20	47	10	0	1	29	11	157

Table 2.16: *Entry of bail bond (court bail)—by amount*

	Up to $20	Over $20	Total
Not entered	4 5·9 44·4	5 8·3 55·6	9
Entered	64 94·1 53·8	55 91·7 46·2	119
Total	68	60	128

Table 2.17: *Estreatment of bail*

	Aborigines	Whites	Total
Bail not estreated—			
defendant appeared	109	137	246
Bail estreated—			
warrant issued—defendant later appeared	2	5	7
warrant issued—defendant never appeared	0	0	0
no record of subsequent action	109	138	247
warrant issued—no record of defendant's appearance	0	3	3
warrant issued later withdrawn	1	0	1
no warrant issued	0	2	2
Total estreated	112	148	260
Total	221	285	506

Table 2.18: *Period in custody for 'bail' and 'gaol' defendants*

	Up to 2 days	3–8 days	9–16 days	17–24 days	25–32 days	33–40 days	41–8 days	49–64 days	Over 64 days	Total
'Bail' defendants (granted bail by court)	92	11	8	1	2	0	0	0	0	114
'Gaol' defendants (remanded in custody by court)	16	48	9	2	1	4	2	0	6	88
Total	108	59	17	3	3	4	2	0	6	202

Table 2.19: *Period in custody before final hearing*

	Never in custody (Summons cases)	Up to 2 days	3–8 days	9–16 days	17–24 days	25–32 days	33–40 days	41–8 days	49–56 days	57–64 days	Over 64 days	Total
Aborigines	158	1251	30	10	0	1	3	0	0	0	4	1457
Whites	985	339	42	7	3	2	1	2	0	0	2	1383
Total	1143	1590	72	17	3	3	4	2	0	0	6	2840

Table 2.20: *Plea for 'bail' and 'gaol' defendants*

	Guilty	Not guilty	Total
'Bail' defendants	180	72	252
(granted bail by	11·7	49·3	
police and/or court)	71·4	28·6	
'Gaol' defendants	1359	74	1433
(granted bail by	88·3	50·7	
neither police nor court)	94·8	5·2	
Total	1539	146	1685
per 100	91·3	8·7	

Table 2.21: *Outcome of hearing for 'bail' and 'gaol' defendants*

	Convicted	Cautioned	Withdrawn	Dismissed	Adjourned *sine die*	Acquitted	*Nolle prosequi*	Bail estreated—no further action	Total
'Bail' defendants (granted bail by police and/or court)	242	12	9	7	0	3	0	247	520
'Gaol' defendants (granted bail by neither police nor court)	1418	30	22	8	0	0	1	0	1479
Summons cases	1085	6	12	17	6	0	0	0	1126
Total	2745	48	43	32	6	3	1	247	3125

Table 2.22: *Outcome of hearing*

	Convicted	Cautioned	Withdrawn	Dismissed	Adjourned *sine die*	Acquitted	*Nolle prosequi*	Bail estreated—no further action	Total
Aborigines	1739	41	19	6	3	0	1	108	1917
Whites	1800	13	32	31	3	3	0	139	2021
Total	3539	54	51	37	6	3	1	247	3938

Note: For Aborigines, convictions = 90 per cent of total Aboriginal cases; dismissals and acquittals = 0·3 per cent of total. For whites, convictions = 89 per cent of total white cases; dismissals and acquittals = 1·6 per cent of total.

Table 2.23: *Sentence for 'bail' and 'gaol' defendants*

	Fine	Imprisonment	Total
'Bail' defendants	169	55	224
(granted bail by police	21·8	9·0	
and/or court)	75·4	24·6	
'Gaol' defendants	606	558	1164
(granted bail by	78·2	91·0	
neither police nor court)	52·1	47·9	
Total	775	613	1388
per 100	55·8	44·2	

Table 2.24: *Sentence imposed*

	Fine	Imprisonment	Total
Aborigines	964	716	1680
	58·2	81·0	
	57·4	42·6	
Whites	691	168	859
	41·8	19·0	
	80·4	19·6	
Total	1655	884	2539
per 100	65·2	34·8	

Table 2.25: *Payment of fine by 'bail' and 'gaol' defendants*

	Paid	Imprisoned in default	Total
'Bail' defendants	173	4	177
(granted bail by police	25·0	3·1	
and/or court)	97·7	2·3	
'Gaol' defendants	520	125	645
(granted bail by neither	75·0	96·9	
police nor court)	80·6	19·4	
Total	693	129	822
per 100	84·3	15·7	

Table 2.26: *Legal representation*

	Private lawyer	Legal aid	Lawyer (private or legal aid?)	Welfare officer	Not represented	No appearance (but case heard)	Total
Aborigines	25	3	11	237	1402	112	1790
Whites	102	0	0	0	1731	116	1949
Total	127	3	11	237	3133	228	3739

Table 2.27: *Constitution of tribunal*

	1 justice	2 justices	Magistrate	Superior court—judge and jury	Superior court—judge alone	Total
Aborigines	42	718	585	1	9	1355
Whites	8	188	735	8	0	939
Total	50	906	1320	9	9	2294

Table 2.28: *Constitution of tribunal imposing sentence*

	Fine	Imprisonment	Total
Justices	427	440	867
	48·0	60·6	
	49·3	50·7	
Magistrates	462	276	738
	52·0	38·0	
	62·6	37·4	
Superior court	0	10	10
	0·0	1·4	
	0·0	100·0	
Total	889	726	1615
per 100	55·0	45·0	

Table 2.29: *Constitution of tribunal—by offence*

	Drunkenness	Traffic	Disorderly conduct	Stealing	Native Welfare	Assault	Offences against police	Unlawful use motor vehicle	Major offences	Minor offences	Total
Justices	241	70	152	32	257	53	43	12	16	83	959
	51·4	11·2	56·1	36·8	66·1	53·0	50·6	66·7	32·0	40·1	
	25·1	7·3	15·8	3·3	26·8	5·5	4·5	1·3	1·7	8·7	
Magistrates	228	554	119	53	132	45	42	6	20	124	1323
	48·6	88·8	43·9	60·9	33·9	45·0	49·4	33·3	40·0	59·9	
	17·2	41·9	9·0	4·0	10·0	3·4	3·2	0·5	1·5	9·4	
Superior court	0	0	0	2	0	2	0	0	14	0	18
	0·0	0·0	0·0	2·3	0·0	2·0	0·0	0·0	28·0	0·0	
	0·0	0·0	0·0	11·1	0·0	11·1	0·0	0·0	77·8	0·0	
Total	469	624	271	87	389	100	85	18	50	207	2300
per 100	20·4	27·1	11·8	3·8	16·9	4·3	3·7	0·8	2·2	9·0	

Table 2.30: *Plea (including changes of plea)*

	Guilty	Not guilty	Change from guilty to not guilty	Change from not guilty to guilty	Total
Aborigines	1526	90	2	39	1657
Whites	1544	167	2	22	1735
Total	3070	257	4	61	3392

Table 2.31: *Plea*

	Guilty	Not guilty	Total
Aborigines	1565	92	1657
	50·0	35·2	
	94·4	5·6	
Whites	1566	169	1735
	50·0	64·8	
	90·3	9·7	
Total	3131	261	3392
per 100	92·3	7·7	

Table 2.32: *Victims of offences*

	Police	Welfare officer or department	Missionary or mission	Other white	Aboriginal relative	Other Aboriginal	Total
Aboriginal defendants	91	11	2	22	22	45	193
White defendants	43	4	0	15	0	2	64
Total	134	15	2	37	22	47	257

Table 2.33: *Outcome of hearing—by offence*

	Drunkenness	Traffic	Disorderly conduct	Stealing	Native Welfare	Assault	Offences against police	Unlawful use motor vehicle	Major offences	Minor offences	Total
Convicted	769	1100	411	129	519	112	111	24	69	308	3552
Cautioned	20	2	9	1	16	1	1	0	0	6	56
Withdrawn	2	22	3	0	5	3	1	0	4	11	51
Dismissed	1	15	2	5	1	6	2	1	2	3	38
Adjourned *sine die*	0	0	0	0	0	4	0	0	0	1	5
Acquitted	0	0	0	2	0	0	0	0	1	0	3
Nolle prosequi	0	0	0	0	0	0	0	0	1	0	1
Bail estreated — no further action	181	0	39	0	14	0	4	0	0	8	246
Total	973	1139	464	137	555	126	119	25	77	337	3952

Table 2.34: *Period of imprisonment*

	Up to 9 weeks	Over 9 weeks	Total
Aborigines	558	157	715
	84·9	68·6	
	78·0	22·0	
Whites	99	72	171
	15·1	31·4	
	57·9	42·1	
Total	657	229	886
per 100	74·2	25·8	

Table 2.35: *Amount of fine*

	Up to $5	Over $5	Total
Aborigines	313	642	955
	72·3	57·4	
	32·8	67·2	
Whites	120	477	597
	27·7	42·6	
	20·1	79·9	
Total	433	1119	1552
per 100	27·9	72·1	

Table 2.36: *Time to pay fine*

	Not granted	Granted—up to 48 hours	Granted—over 48 hours	Total
Aborigines	165	158	242	565
	78·6	92·4	81·2	
	29·2	28·0	42·8	
Whites	45	13	56	114
	21·4	7·6	18·8	
	39·5	11·4	49·1	
Total	210	171	298	679
per 100	30·9	25·2	43·9	

Table 2.37: *Payment of fine*

	Paid	Not paid	Total
Aborigines	792	214	1006
	57·5	84·9	
	78·7	21·3	
Whites	586	38	624
	42·5	15·1	
	93·9	6·1	
Total	1378	252	1630
per 100	84·5	15·5	

Table 2.38: *Sentence imposed—by offence*

	Drunkenness	Traffic	Disorderly conduct	Stealing	Native Welfare	Assault	Offences against police	Unlawful use motor vehicle	Major offences	Minor Offences	Total
Fine	451	491	187	39	304	32	35	3	4	119	1665
	67·9	95·7	56·5	44·8	59·8	32·0	36·5	14·3	9·1	63·6	
	27·1	29·5	11·2	2·3	18·3	1·9	2·1	0·2	0·2	7·1	
Imprisonment	213	22	144	48	204	68	61	18	40	68	886
	32·1	4·3	43·5	55·2	40·2	68·0	63·5	85·7	90·9	36·4	
	24·0	2·5	16·3	5·4	23·0	7·7	6·9	2·0	4·5	7·7	
Total	664	513	331	87	508	100	96	21	44	187	2551

Table 2.39: *Sentence imposed—by offence and race of defendant*

		Bond	Fine	Imprisonment
Drunkenness	Aborigines	0	342	190
		0·0	64·2	35·8
	Whites	0	108	22
		0·0	83·1	16·9
Traffic	Aborigines	0	126	13
		0·0	90·6	9·4
	Whites	0	355	9
		0·0	97·5	2·5
Disorderly conduct	Aborigines	10	116	115
		4·1	48·1	47·7
	Whites	1	70	27
		1·0	71·4	27·6
Stealing	Aborigines	2	16	21
		5·1	41·0	53·9
	Whites	5	22	27
		9·3	40·7	50·0
Native Welfare	Aborigines	2	280	182
		0·4	60·3	39·3
	Whites	0	23	22
		0·0	51·1	48·9
Assault	Aborigines	4	23	56
		4·8	27·7	67·5
	Whites	0	9	11
		0·0	45·0	55·0
Offences against police	Aborigines	1	20	44
		1·5	30·8	67·7
	Whites	0	14	17
		0·0	45·2	54·8
Unlawful use motor vehicle	Aborigines	0	2	15
		0·0	11·8	88·2
	Whites	0	1	3
		0·0	25·0	75·0
Major offences	Aborigines	1	0	23
		4·2	0·0	95·8
	Whites	7	4	17
		25·0	14·3	60·7
Minor offences	Aborigines	2	34	56
		2·2	37·0	60·8
	Whites	3	84	12
		3·0	84·8	12·2

Note: In this table, the first line in each cell represents the observed frequency; the second line represents the percentage in each racial category sentenced to bond, fine or imprisonment.

Table 2.40: *Sentence imposed—by prior convictions*

Prior convictions	Fine	Imprisonment	Total
None	34	9	43
1	21	9	30
2–6	41	37	78
7–12	45	52	97
13–18	19	24	43
19–24	3	11	14
25–30	9	16	25
31–6	6	10	16
Over 36	14	14	28
Not known	395	394	789
Total	587	576	1163

Table 2.41: *Prior convictions*

	First offender	Recidivist	Total
Aborigines	25	1021	1046
	42–4	79·9	
	2·4	97·6	
Whites	34	257	291
	57·6	20·1	
	11·7	88·3	
Total	59	1278	1337
per 100	4·4	95·6	

Table 2.42: *Sentence imposed—by legal representation*

	Fine	Imprisonment	Total
Represented	83	21	104
	5·3	2·5	
	79·8	20·2	
Not represented	1489	816	2305
	94·7	97·5	
	64·6	35·4	
Total	1572	837	2409
per 100	65·3	34·7	

Table 2.43: *Place of offence—Native Welfare offences*

	Reserve	Mission	Public place	Private place	No record of place	Total
Aborigines	266	11	3	2	218	500
Whites	6	0	0	0	47	53
Total						553

Note: Many of the 'no record' cases probably occurred away from reserves and missions.

Table 2.44: *Plea—drunkenness offences*

Guilty	675
	97·8
Not guilty	15
	2·2
Total	690

Table 2.45: *Representation—drunkenness offences*

Represented	4
	0·4
Not represented	916
	99·6
Total	920

Table 2.46: *Grant of police bail—drunkenness offences*

	Not granted	Granted	Total
Aborigines	279 69·9 74.2	97 45·8 25·8	376
Whites	120 30·1 51·1	115 54·2 48·9	235
Total	399 65·3	212 34·7	611

Table 2.47: *Prior convictions for same offence—drunkenness offences*

No prior convictions	19 16·2
1–2 prior convictions	25 21·4
3–12 prior convictions	48 41·0
Over 12 prior convictions	25 21·4
Total	117

APPENDIX 3

ABORIGINAL POPULATIONS

Table 3.1: *Western Australian Aboriginal population as at 30 June 1966*

Division and District	Full-blood Aborigines	Part-Aborigines	Total
Northern			
Wyndham	927	180	1107
Hall's Creek	1124	150	1274
Derby	2376	320	2696
Broome	844	402	1246
Total	5271	1052	6323
North-West			
Port Hedland	319	234	553
Marble Bar	627	158	785
Roebourne	445	404	849
Carnarvon	462	522	984
Total	1853	1318	3171
North Central			
Meekatharra	433	306	739
Mt Magnet	162	630	792
Mullewa	161	614	775
Geraldton	5	649	654
Total	761	2199	2960
Eastern			
Warburton	377	1	378
Laverton	371	22	393
Leonora	470	197	667
Kalgoorlie (incl. Esperance District	579	703	1282
Total	1797	923	2720
Central			
Moora	10	831	841
Perth	9	1376	1385
Kellerberrin	6	953	959
Total	25	3160	3185

Division and District	Full-blood Aborigines	Part-Aborigines	Total
Southern			
Narrogin	18	1372	1390
Gnowangerup	172	1285	1457
Collie	8	676	684
Total	198	3333	3531
Overall Total	9905	11985	21890

Note: These figures are based on all records and information available but are still, of necessity, near approximations only of those persons in Western Australia who possess more than one quarter Aboriginal blood.

Source: *Annual Report for Year Ended 30th June, 1966. Commissioner of Native Welfare* (1966), p. 62. Perth: Government Printer.

Table 3.2: *South Australian Aboriginal population (estimated) as at 30 June 1966*

Far Northern District	
North-west Aboriginal Reserve	365
Ernabella Mission	400
Indulkana Aboriginal Reserve	100
Oodnadatta	68
Coober Pedy	140
Coober Pedy Aboriginal Reserve	54
On Pastoral Properties	428
Total	1555
West Coast District	
Yalata Mission	332
Koonibba Aboriginal Reserve	159
Ceduna	52
Port Lincoln	163
Small towns, pastoral properties, Railway sidings	296
Total	1002
Flinders Ranges District	
Port Augusta	175
Davenport Aboriginal Reserve	282
Marree	158
Leigh Creek–Copley	63
Whyalla	75
Andamooka	79
Nepabunna Mission	78
Small towns, pastoral properties, Railway sidings	539
Total	1449
South East and Murray Mallee District	
Gerard Aboriginal Reserve	112
Point McLeay Aboriginal Reserve	121
River Murray Towns	110
South East Towns	510
Mallee District	63
Total	916
Central–Mid North District	
Towns, Railway sidings	243
Point Pearce Aboriginal Reserve	350
Total	593
Larger Metropolitan Area	
(Within a radius of 30–5 miles of Adelaide)	2500
Total	8015

Source: Information supplied by Department of Aboriginal Affairs, South Australia.

APPENDIX 4

OFFENCES CHARGED, WESTERN AUSTRALIA 1965

Table 4.1: *Offences charged*

Offence	Aborigines					Whites				
	Summary Courts		Higher Courts		Total charges	Summary Courts		Higher Courts		Total charges
	Convictions	Dismissals	Convictions	Dismissals		Convictions	Dismissals	Convictions	Dismissals	
I *Offences against the person*										
Murder	—	—	1	2	3	—	—	2	1	3
Attempted murder	—	—	—	—	—	—	—	1	—	1
Manslaughter	—	—	1	1	2	—	—	7	14	21
Negligent driving causing death	—	—	2	1	3	—	—	6	1	7
Attempted suicide	1	—	—	—	1	—	1	—	—	1
Rape	—	—	2	—	2	—	1	9	1	11
Incest	—	—	—	—	—	1	1	6	1	9
Carnal knowledge	8	9	1	—	18	70	6	3	—	79
Indecent assault	—	—	—	—	—	3	1	4	—	8
Indecent dealing	2	—	—	—	2	22	4	5	—	31
Gross indecency	2	—	1	—	3	2	—	7	—	9
Abortion	—	—	—	—	—	—	—	7	—	7
Bigamy	—	—	—	—	—	—	—	1	—	1
Assault	237	29	4	—	270	437	101	13	5	556
Other offences against the person	1	—	—	—	1	—	—	—	—	—

Table 4.1: *Continued*

Offence	Aborigines					Whites				
	Summary Courts		Higher Courts		Total charges	Summary Courts		Higher Courts		Total charges
	Convictions	Dismissals	Convictions	Dismissals		Convictions	Dismissals	Convictions	Dismissals	
II *Offences against property*										
Robbery	—	—	1	—	1	—	2	13	—	15
Breaking and entering	97	3	10	1	111	692	27	248	2	969
Unlawfully on premises	63	2	—	—	65	306	16	—	—	322
Stealing	442	18	—	—	460	4345	179	55	9	4588
Unlawfully using motor vehicles	113	3	—	—	116	604	21	1	—	626
Unlawfully using other vehicles	—	—	—	—	—	30	—	—	—	30
Arson	—	—	—	—	—	—	—	1	1	2
Wilful damage	97	3	—	—	100	394	25	—	1	420
Other offences against property	1	—	—	—	1	8	3	—	—	11
III *Forgery and Uttering*										
Forgery	—	—	—	—	—	11	—	51	—	62
Uttering	—	—	—	—	—	—	—	2	—	2

IV *Offences against good order*										
Drunkenness	3635	10	—	—	3645	4561	44	—	—	4605
Habitual drunkenness	107	—	—	—	107	92	2	—	—	94
Disorderly conduct	938	17	—	—	955	1329	52	—	—	1381
Vagrancy	165	8	—	—	173	337	37	2	—	376
Uncontrollable child	13	—	—	—	13	5	1	—	—	6
Indecent behaviour	3	—	—	—	3	80	2	—	—	82
Escaping legal custody	39	—	—	—	39	82	4	2	—	88
Offences against police	164	2	—	—	166	508	20	—	—	528
Other offences against good order	—	—	—	—	—	3	1	—	—	4
V *Other offences*										
Traffic	537	15	—	—	552	33362	957	—	—	34319
Licensing Act	91	1	—	—	92	1491	55	—	—	1546
Health	—	—	—	—	—	251	26	—	—	277
Gaming	16	—	—	—	16	235	3	—	—	238
Industrial	1	—	—	—	1	146	49	—	—	195
Maintenance	27	2	—	—	29	669	455	—	—	1124
Taxation	—	—	—	—	—	684	112	—	—	796
Native Welfare (receiving and supplying liquor)	420	5	—	—	425	119	3	—	—	122
Offences against other Acts	114	2	—	—	116	5799	377	4	1	6181
Total	7334	129	23	5	7491	56678	2588	450	37	59753
		Total convictions = 7357 Total dismissals = 134					Total convictions = 57128 Total dismissals = 2625			

Source: Compiled from information supplied by Deputy Commonwealth Statistician, Perth, W.A. Compare *Statistical Register of Western Australia for 1965–66. Part VIII—Law and Crime.*

Table 4.2: *Summary of offences charged*

Offence Class	Aborigines	Whites
I Offences against the person	305	744
	30	70
	4	1
II Offences against property	854	6983
	10	90
	12	12
III Forgery and uttering	0	64
		100
		0·1
IV Offences against good order	5101	7164
	42	58
	68	12
V Other offences	1231	44798
	3	97
	16	74·9
Total	7491	59753

Note: For each offence class, the following information is shown: number of charges against Aborigines and whites respectively; percentage that number represents of total charges in that offence class; percentage that number represents of total Aboriginal or white offences respectively.

Source: Computed from Table 4.1.

APPENDIX 5

RACIAL COMPOSITION OF FIELDWORK AREAS (WESTERN AUSTRALIA)

	Population at 30 June 1966		Aboriginal population at 30 June 1966
	Census (excluding Aboriginal)	Aboriginal	Department of Native Welfare Districts
Broome Shire	1923	1197	1246
Carnarvon Shire	4646	648	984
Geraldton Town	12125	229	654
Gnowangerup Shire	3815	399	1457
Katanning Shire	4488	133	—
Narrogin Town	4861	153	1390
Port Hedland Shire	3008	383	553
Roebourne Shire	1782	458	849
Wagin Shire	2774	87	—
West Kimberley Shire	2695	2302	2696

Note: 1. 'Aboriginal population' means those persons who described themselves at the Census as being 50 per cent or more Aboriginal, or simply as 'Aboriginal'.

2. Department of Native Welfare figures are based on the legal definition of 'Native', which meant persons of more than one quarter Aboriginal blood; also based on departmental administrative areas which may not entirely coincide with Census boundaries. The departmental figures for Gnowangerup and Narrogin districts probably cover Katanning and Wagin Census areas as well.

3. The towns in the Ten Towns Sample are included in the above table but the Census areas are larger than the town areas.

APPENDIX 6

RATES OF CLEARANCE OF OFFENCES

Table 6.1: *Rates of clearance of selected offences—Victoria 1965*

	Reported	Cleared	Clearance Rate (per cent)
Beg alms	55	55	100
Drink methylated spirits	210	210	100
Drunk and disorderly	24275	24275	100

Source: Victoria Police, Statistical Review of Crime.

Table 6.2: *Rates of clearance of offence categories—South Australia 1965*

	Clearance Rate (per cent)
Offences against the person	64·7
Offences against property	33·7
Offences against morality	62·03
Offences against good order	92·3
Other offences	99·4
(including Aboriginal Affairs Act	100)

Source: *Report of the Commissioner of Police for the year ended 30th June, 1965* (1966). Adelaide: Government Printer.

APPENDIX 7

AMOUNTS OF COURT BAIL SET IN ONE WESTERN AUSTRALIAN TOWN BY RACE AND OFFENCE

Aborigines	Whites
$ 2—drunk	$ 10—s. 160(4) Licensing Act
$10—under influence on Native Reserve	$ 10—obscene language
$20—assault (s. 313 Code)	$200—breaking and entering
$40—supply liquor to Native	$100—dangerous driving
$60—driving under the influence	$ 60—driving under the influence
$20—dangerous driving	$ 20—fail to stop when called on by police
$40—supply liquor to Native	$ 60—driving under the influence
	$ 60—driving under the influence
	$ 10—wilful damage
	$ 50—fraudulent trick
	$ 20—fraudulent trick
	$ 20—fraudulent trick
	$ 40—stealing
	$ 40—stealing
	$200—assault (s. 313 Code)
	$100—exhibit obscene photos
	$100—stealing
	$100—unlawfully on premises
	$ 20—create disturbance
	$ 10—fighting
	$200—stealing
	$ 20—unlawful possession
	$200—stealing (young of ewe) (s. 378(3) Code)

Note: The table shows the amount of bail set for each offence charged, rather than against each defendant. Some defendants were charged on multiple counts.

APPENDIX 8

RESULT OF CHARGES, WESTERN AUSTRALIA 1961

	Number	Per cent
Aborigines		
Summary convictions	4347	97·53
Discharged, withdrawn, etc.	91	2·01
Committed for trial, etc.	19	0·42
Total	4457	
Whites		
Summary convictions	45773	92·85
Discharged, withdrawn, etc.	2149	4·47
Committed for trial	278	0·57
Committed for sentence	20	0·04
Total	48220	

Source: *Annual Report. Commissioner of Police for Western Australia for the Year Ended 30th June 1962* (1963). Perth: Government Printer. Appendices B and I. (Criminal statistics for the year ended 31st December 1961.)

APPENDIX 9

REPRESENTATION BY ABORIGINES ADVANCEMENT LEAGUE SOLICITOR, VICTORIA

Date	Offence charged	Original sentence	Whether legally represented at original hearing	Represented by A.A.L. solicitor at:	Result (when represented by A.A.L. solicitor)	Arrangements for Representation	Legal costs paid by
1964	Gross indecency with male (two defendants)	see Result column	Yes (by A.A.L. solicitor)	General Sessions trial Also on committal proceedings	Probation	A.A.L.	No charge made by solicitor
1965	1. Driving under the influence 2. Driving dangerously	see Result column	Yes	Fitzroy Court of Petty Sessions	1. Fine $200 ($30 per month) Licence cancelled for 3 years 2. Withdrawn	A.A.L.	No record

Appendix 9: *Continued*

Date	Offence charged	Original sentence	Whether legally represented at original hearing	Represented by A.A.L. solicitor at:	Result (when represented by A.A.L. solicitor)	Arrangements for Representation	Legal costs paid by
1965*	1. Rape 2. Assault occasioning actual bodily harm	1. 10 years 2. 2 years' cumulative imprisonment (Minimum period 10 years) On first appeal minimum period reduced to 8 years	Yes (by Public Solicitor) No (on first appeal)	Petition for mercy (counsel also briefed)	Appeal allowed. Sentences varied 1. 8 years 2. 2 years Minimum period 6 years	A.A.L. and Monash University staff in private capacity	Legal Aid Committee
1965	1. Unlicensed driving 2. Exceeding 35 m.p.h. 3. False name 4. Insufficient means	see Result column	Yes (by A.A.L. solicitor)	Fitzroy Court of Petty Sessions	1. Fine $50 2. Fine $10 3. Convicted and discharged without penalty 4. Withdrawn	A.A.L.	No record
1965	Malicious wounding	Not applicable	Yes (by A.A.L. solicitor)	St Kilda Court of Petty Sessions	Charge dismissed	A.A.L.	No record

1966	House breaking	3 years' imprisonment (minimum 12 months)	No	General Sessions appeal against conviction and sentence	Appeals dismissed		
1967	Insufficient means (2 defendants)	12 months' imprisonment each	No (pleaded guilty)	General Sessions appeal	Sentences quashed. Substituted good behaviour bonds ($20 for 3 years)	A.A.L. and Legal Aid Committee	Legal Aid Committee
1967–8	Breaking and entering (3 counts); stealing (2 counts); unlawfully injuring property (1 count)	4 years' imprisonment	No	Appeal and retrial (through agents in Tasmania)	Appeal allowed. New trial ordered. On the retrial, he was again convicted but the sentence was reduced	Superintendent of Aborigines Welfare Board	No record
July 1968	Illegal use of motor vehicle (2 charges)	see Result column	Yes (by A.A.L. solicitor)	Warragul Court of Petty Sessions	Probation for 2 years	Ministry of Aboriginal Affairs	No record

Appendix 9: *Continued*

Date	Offence charged	Original sentence	Whether legally represented at original hearing	Represented by A.A.L. solicitor at:	Result (when represented by A.A.L. solicitor)	Arrangements for Representation	Legal costs paid by
August 1968†	Insufficient means	6 months' imprisonment	No	General Sessions Appeal against conviction and sentence	Conviction affirmed. Substituted good behaviour bond	A.A.L.	No record
August 1968‡	Illegal use of motor vehicle	3 months' imprisonment	No (pleaded guilty)	General Sessions appeal	Conviction quashed	Director of Aboriginal Affairs	No record
1968–9	Manslaughter (grandchild)	Not applicable	Yes (at inquest)	Inquest and at trial	Not guilty	A.A.L. and Legal Aid Committee	No record
1968	1. Insufficient means 2. Failure to provide for children (s. 71 Children's Welfare Act 1958 (Vic.))	1. 1 month 2. 6 months' imprisonment	No	General Sessions appeal	Appeal allowed. Sentences varied to probation	A.A.L.	Legal Aid Committee

1968§	Attempted buggery with assault	see Result column	No (at committal proceedings) Pleaded guilty	General Sessions on plea re sentence	Good behaviour bond ($100 for 3 years with conditions)	A.A.L. and Ministry of Aboriginal Affairs	No record

* This case is the same as that asterisked in Appendix 13.
† Section 37 of Aboriginal Affairs Act, 1967 (Vic.) not complied with. Pregnant when originally sentenced.
‡ Section 37 of Aboriginal Affairs Act, 1967 (Vic.) not complied with. No prior convictions.
§ Lenient sentence.

APPENDIX 10

LEGAL AID CASES REFERRED THROUGH NATIVE WELFARE DEPARTMENT TO LAW SOCIETY, WESTERN AUSTRALIA

Date	Offence Charged	Result	Sentence
1957	Grievous bodily harm	Acquitted	
1957	Assault causing bodily harm (s. 317 Code)	Convicted	Indeterminate
1957	No record	Convicted	
1958	Wilful murder	Pleaded guilty to manslaughter	2 years, then indeterminate
1958	Breaking and entering	Convicted	12 months
1959	1. Wilful murder	Convicted	2 years
	2. Breaking and entering	*Nolle*	
1959	Wilful murder	Convicted	9 months
	Appeal	Retrial	9 months
	2nd appeal	Dismissed	
1959	Unlawful wounding	Convicted	2½ years
1959	Robbery with violence	Legal aid application refused. Native Welfare Department arranged counsel privately.	
1960	(?) Rape	Convicted	7 years
1961	Manslaughter	Acquitted	
1961	Wilful murder	Convicted of manslaughter	2 years
1961	Wilful murder	Convicted (jury verdict)	Death—commuted to life imprisonment
1961	Unlawful killing	*Nolle*	
1961	Threat (s. 338 Code)	Acquitted	
1961	Stealing in house	Pleaded guilty	3 years
1961	Robbery with violence	Convicted	
1961	Gross indecency	Legal aid not approved. Pleaded guilty.	
1962	Unlawful wounding to cause grievous bodily harm	Convicted of unlawful wounding	8 months
1962	Wilful murder	Pleaded guilty to manslaughter	8 months

Date	Offence Charged	Result	Sentence
1962	Armed in public (s. 68 Code)	Case heard summarily before Law Society replied. Pleaded guilty to assault.	Bond 3 years
1962	Incest	Pleaded guilty	18 months
1963	Carnal knowledge	Convicted	Bond
1963	Murder	Application for legal aid withdrawn. Private representation. Convicted of manslaughter.	12 months, then bond for 5 years
1963	Murder	Acquitted	
	Then charged again: unlawful killing	Acquitted	
1963	Wilful murder	Convicted of manslaughter	
1963	Wilful murder	Acquitted	
1964	Murder	*Nolle*	
1964	1. Carnal knowledge	1. Withdrawn	
	2. Indecent dealing	2. Pleaded guilty	3 months
1964	Manslaughter	Acquitted	
1964	Indecent assault	Withdrawn	
1964	Assault	Withdrawn	
1964	1. Unlawful use of car	Acquitted	
	2. Unlawful killing	Convicted of negligent driving causing death	2 years
1964	Unlawful killing	Pleaded guilty	12 months
1964	Wilful murder	Pleaded guilty to manslaughter	12 years (min. 6 years)
	Appeal against sentence	Sentence reduced	5 years (min. 3 years)
1964	Unlawful killing	Pleaded guilty to reckless driving causing death	4 years (min. 2½ years)
	Appeal against sentence	Dismissed	
1964	Unlawful wounding	Acquitted	
1965	(i) Wilful murder	Acquitted	
1965	(ii) Wilful murder	Convicted of manslaughter	8 years
1965	(iii) Assault causing grievous bodily harm	Pleaded guilty to common assault	9 months
1965	(iv) Unlawful killing	Convicted of reckless driving causing death	10 months
1965	(v) Wilful murder	Pleaded guilty to manslaughter	14 years (min. 10 years)
1965	(vi) Carnal knowledge	Convicted of indecent assault	3 months
1965	(vii) Unlawful killing	Convicted of reckless driving causing death	2 years

Appendix 10: *Continued*

Date	Offence Charged	Result	Sentence
1965	(viii) Rape	Convicted	8 years
1965	(ix) Murder	Acquitted	
1965	(x) Rape	Convicted	6 years
1965	(xi) Wilful murder	Pleaded guilty to manslaughter	5 years (min. 18 months)
1965	(xii) Unnatural assault on child	Convicted	Probation
1965	(xiii) Unlawful killing	*Nolle*	
1966	Robbery with violence	Convicted	2½ years (no minimum)
1966	Robbery with violence	Convicted	2½ years (min. 2 years)
1966	Unlawful killing	Acquitted	
1966	Manslaughter (by motor vehicle)	*Nolle*	
1966	Robbery with violence	Convicted	12 years (min. 10 years)
1966	Robbery with violence	Convicted	6 years (min. 4 years)
1966	Wilful murder	Pleaded guilty to manslaughter	8 years, then indeterminate
1966	Rape	Acquitted	
1966	Rape	Acquitted	
1966	Wilful murder	Pleaded guilty to manslaughter	6 years (min. 3 years)
1966	Housebreaking	*Nolle*	
1966	No record	No record	
1966	Appeal against conviction for indecent language	Conviction quashed. Matter remitted to Police Court. Pleaded guilty.	Cautioned
1966	Rape	Acquitted	
1966	Appeal against conviction for street fighting	Application for legal aid not approved. (Conviction considered justified)	
1966	False pretences (2)	Convicted	9 months
1966	Housebreaking (2)	Application for legal aid not granted. Convicted	3 years (min. 2 years)
1966	Robbery with violence Appeal	No record	
1966	Assault causing bodily harm (s. 317 Code)	Pleaded guilty to common assault (s. 313 Code)	9 months

Note: 1965 cases have been numbered to enable ready reference to the same cases in Appendix 11.

APPENDIX 11

ABORIGINAL COMMITTALS TO SUPERIOR COURTS 1965—LEGAL REPRESENTATION, WESTERN AUSTRALIA

Case No.	Offence	Plea	Result	Legal Representation
(i)	Murder	Not guilty	Acquitted	Legal aid
(ii)	Manslaughter	Not guilty	8 years	Legal aid
(iii)	Assault	Guilty	9 months	Legal aid
(iv)	Negligent driving causing death		10 months	Legal aid
(v)	Murder	Guilty to manslaughter	14 years (min. 10 years)	Legal aid
(vi)	Carnal knowledge		3 months	Legal aid
(vii)	Negligent driving causing death (2)		2 years	Legal aid
(viii)	Rape		8 years	Legal aid
(ix)	Murder	Not guilty	Acquitted	Legal aid
(x)	Rape		6 years	Legal aid
(xiii)	Unlawful killing		*Nolle*	Legal aid
	Assault (2)	Not guilty	Probation	None
	Unnatural offence	Guilty	5 years (min. 3 years)	None
	Assault causing bodily harm	Guilty	6 months	Private
	Assault causing grievous bodily harm	Guilty	3 years (min. 2 years)	None
	Breaking and entering	Guilty	6 months	Private
	Breaking and entering	Guilty	18 months on each count (min. 3 years)	Private
	Breaking and entering		Imprisoned	No record (probably none)
	Breaking and entering	Guilty	18 months (min. 9 months)	None
	Breaking and entering	Guilty	3 years (min. 2 years)	None

Appendix 11: *Continued*

Case No.	Offence	Plea	Result	Legal Representation
	Breaking and entering	Guilty	2 years (min. 1 year)	None
	Breaking and entering	Guilty	2 years (min. 1 year)	None
	Breaking and entering	Guilty	12 months	None

Total legal aid: 11 defendants (on 12 charges)
Total private legal representation: 3 defendants (on 6 charges)
Total unrepresented: 9 defendants (on 10 charges)

Note: Case numbers of legal aid cases correspond with those in Appendix 10. In addition two other defendants were listed by the Department of Native Welfare as having been referred for legal aid in 1965. These were not included in the Commonwealth Statistician's list, possibly because they were not classified as Aborigines or because they were included in statistics for the next year.

Source: Commonwealth Statistician and Native Welfare Department.

APPENDIX 12

EXTRACT FROM INSTRUCTION FROM CHILD WELFARE DEPARTMENT DIRECTOR TO MAGISTRATES, WESTERN AUSTRALIA

Procedure on indictable offences committed by children and offences listed in s.20B of Child Welfare Act committed by persons over 18 years.

Persons over 18

Procedure to be adopted is as follows:—

1. Charge is read.
2. No plea is taken.
3. Statement of facts which constitutes charge is read by prosecution and copy supplied to Magistrate.
4. If accused shows any hesitancy in accepting prosecution's statement of circumstances, a remand will be granted where necessary, and prosecution will be required to bring their evidence.
5. Accused to be advised of his rights as to trial by jury.
6. If accused elects to trial by jury, hearing is to proceed in same manner as a preliminary hearing of an indictable offence before a Court of Petty Sessions.
7. If accused elects to submit to summary jurisdiction of Court, he should be warned of seriousness of charge, any defence available to him which is provided specifically by the Code and given an opportunity and adjournment if necessary, to consult a Solicitor. If he has a Solicitor, these stipulations may be relaxed.
8. If he submits to jurisdiction of Court he is then asked to plead.
9. If he submits to jurisdiction and pleads guilty Prosecutor passes to Magistrate the—

   (a) Character Report on accused
   (b) Character Report on girl complainant (when applicable)
   (c) Criminal history.

   and matter is then dealt with to conviction and penalty.
10. If he submits to jurisdiction and pleads Not Guilty matter is heard in ordinary way such as for a simple offence.
11. Magistrate has right to decide to send case on for trial or sentence, right up to stage where record, if any, of convictions is produced.

APPENDIX 13

COMPARATIVE SENTENCES FOR RAPE (VICTORIA)

Offences for which sentenced	Age of defendant	Age of victim	Minimum sentence	Maximum sentence (all offences)	Maximum sentence (for rape offence)	Previous convictions proved
Rape (mitigating circs.)	19	?	Probation	Probation	Probation	Nil
Rape (mitigating circs.) and abduction	19	17	½	3	3	Nil
Rape (mitigating circs.) and abduction	20	17	½	3	3	4: 1 assault; 1 dangerous driving; 1 unlicensed driving; 1 refusing name and address
Rape	19	?	½	3	3	Nil
Rape (mitigating circs.)	26	?	1½	3	3	14: 6 housebreaking and stealing; 2 stealing; 1 driving suspended licence; 1 assault; 1 illegal car use; 1 unlicensed driving; 1 unlawful piloting plane; 1 unlawful possession
Rape (mitigating circs.) and indecent assault	39	69	3	3	3	7: 1 carnal knowledge; 2 unlawful possession; 2 offensive behaviour; 1 assault; 1 indecent assault
Rape	18	17	1½	4	4	Nil
Rape	20	17	1½	4	4	2: 1 wilful damage; 1 threatening words

Offences for which sentenced	Age of defendant	Age of victim	Minimum sentence	Maximum sentence (all offences)	Maximum sentence (for rape offence)	Previous convictions proved
Rape	22	13	1	5	5	16: 7 larceny; 5 illegal car use; 3 breaking and stealing; 1 breach of bond
Rape	19	14	2½	5	5	10: 2 larceny; 3 housebreaking and stealing; 1 possessing stolen goods; 2 illegal car use; 1 trespassing; 1 possessing house-breaking tools; (plus 4 care and protection applications)
Rape	19	14	2½	5	5	26: 2 shopbreaking; 1 stealing; 4 larceny; 3 receiving; 1 firing rifle; 9 illegal car use; 2 unlicensed driving; 1 assault; 1 escape; 1 dangerous driving; 1 breach of probation
Rape	21	?	1	6	6	6: 2 illegal car use; 1 larceny; 1 vagrancy; 2 offensive behaviour
Rape and assault occasioning actual bodily harm	19	17	3½	6	5	4: 1 robbery with violence; 1 offensive behaviour; 1 larceny; 1 indecent language
Rape and abduction	?	?	5	7	7	14: 1 shopbreaking; 1 stealing; 1 house breaking and stealing; 1 vagrancy; 1 carnal knowledge; 2 indecent language; 6 assault; 1 resisting arrest
Rape and carnal knowledge	18	14	3	10	10	1: shopbreaking and stealing

Offences for which sentenced	Age of defendant	Age of victim	Minimum sentence	Maximum sentence (all offences)	Maximum sentence (for rape offence)	Previous convictions proved
Rape	25	18	5	10	10	11: 1 breaking and stealing; 2 offensive behaviour; 1 loitering; 1 carnal knowledge; 1 larceny; 3 assault; 1 resisting arrest; 1 breach of probation
Rape and other sex offences	30	10	6	10	7	13: 5 larceny; 1 assaulting police; 4 obscene exposure; 1 wounding with intent; 1 breaking and stealing; 1 breach of bond
Rape and robbery	25	21	6½	10	8	20: 2 shopbreaking and stealing; 8 larceny; 2 illegal car use; 1 breaking; 6 indecent assault; 1 breach of probation
Rape	22	16	8	10	10	8: 2 larceny; 1 house breaking and stealing; 1 carnal knowledge; 1 wilful damage; 2 vagrancy; 1 offensive behaviour
*Rape and assault occasioning actual bodily harm	20	22	8	12	10	Nil
Rape (2 counts)	24	16	9	12	12	5: 3 assault; 2 rape

Note: 1. The asterisked case is the Aboriginal defendant (and corresponds with that asterisked in Appendix 9).
2. Sentences are quoted in years.

APPENDIX 14

CASE HISTORY OF ONE WESTERN AUSTRALIAN ABORIGINAL ('N') (SUMMARISED FROM DEPARTMENT OF NATIVE WELFARE FILE)

Born 1920

1943 Warrant under section 12 of the Native Administration Act because N was not working. He was sent to Carrolup Reserve 'for corrective measures'.
Staff member at Carrolup requested relaxation of the warrant because N was going to work for a local farmer. The farmer said that N 'always works for him and that he simply could not get his crop in unless he could get hold of him'.

May
1943 Katanning Court. Charge: absconding from Carrolup. F$4. At this time N had no prior convictions.

1946 Perth Police Court. Charge: in prohibited area, namely the city of Perth. F$6 (committed to Perth Lockup). He had come to Perth because he required medical attention but had not obtained a permit.

1947 Guildford Police Court. Charge: Drunk. F$1.

1948 Perth Police Court. Charge: in prohibited area, namely the city of Perth. F$4. 'Continuance of central portion of Perth City block as prohibited area is considered necessary to effect control of unsatisfactory section of Native community who visit merely for the purpose of securing liquor'.

After 1948, N committed a number of other offences, culminating in 1965 in a charge of carnal knowledge. On this occasion he had legal aid.

APPENDIX 15

CRIMINAL HISTORY OF ONE WESTERN AUSTRALIAN ABORIGINAL (BORN 1930)

Date	Offence Charged	Result
1953	Drunk	Cautioned
27/6/55	Drunk	7 days' imprisonment
27/6/55	Native receive liquor	1 month's imprisonment
1957	Native receive liquor	Fine $2
1959	Drunk	Fine $2
1959	Drunk	$4 bail estreated
7/3/60	Drunk	Fine $6
4/3/61	Create disturbance	Fine $10
30/3/61	Native receive liquor	Fine $10
1961	Drunk	Fine $10
1961	Drunk	Fine $10
1962	Drunk	$2 bail estreated
1962	Drunk	Fine $4
1962	Drunk	Fine $10
1962	Drunk	21 days' imprisonment
1962	Drunk	14 days' imprisonment
1962	Habitual Drunkenness	3 months' imprisonment
1963	Drunk	Fine $2
16/4/63	Native receive liquor	1 month's imprisonment
16/4/63	Drunk	21 days' imprisonment (cumulative)
1963	Drunk	21 days' imprisonment
1963	Drunk	Fine $4
1963	Drunk	Fine $2
1963	Native receive liquor	7 days' imprisonment
1964	Drunk	2 days' imprisonment
1964	Drunk	Fine $2
12/4/65	Drunk	Cautioned
26/7/65	Drunk	$2 bail estreated
18/10/65	Drunk	Fine $4
6/11/65	Drunk	Fine $6
15/11/65	Drunk	7 days' imprisonment
26/11/65	Drunk	7 days' imprisonment
20/12/65	Drunk	Fine $4
23/12/65	Drunk	7 days' imprisonment

Date	Offence Charged	Result
29/1/66	Drunk	Fine $10
14/3/66	Drunk	Fine $10
21/11/66	Drunk	Fine $5
15/12/66	Drunk	Fine $4
14/1/67	Drunk	Fine $5

Note: It is not known how many of the fines imposed were paid or how many gaol terms were served in default of payment of fines.

REFERENCES *

'Aboriginal policies of the Aborigines Welfare Board' (1967). In *Report of the Aborigines Welfare Board for the year ended 30th June, 1967.* Melbourne: Government Printer.

ALBRECHT, PAUL G.E. (1965). The present problem of authority in the Aboriginal community. Unpublished paper.

—— (1975). 'Aborigines and alcohol'. *Newsletter on Aboriginal Affairs* no. 4.

APPLETON, SUSAN F. (1973). 'Alternative schools for minority students: the Constitution, the Civil Rights Act and the Berkeley experiment', *Calif. L. Rev.* **61**.

'Bail: an ancient practice reexamined' (1961). *Yale L.J.* **70**.

BARNES, J.A. (1969). 'Politics, permits and professional interests: the Rose Case', *Australian Quarterly* **41**.

BARRY, JOHN (1941). 'The ethics of advocacy', *A.L.J.* **15**.

BARRY, J.V., PATON, G.W. and SAWER, G. (1948). *An Introduction to the Criminal Law in Australia.* London: Macmillan.

BARTHOLOMEW, ALLEN A. (1967). 'Insufficient means': an offence? Unpublished paper.

BARTON, ROBERT W. (1971). 'Equal protection—an indigent cannot be imprisoned for his inability to pay a fine', *Dickinson L. Rev.* **75**.

BARWICK, DIANE E. (1963). A little more than kin: regional affiliation and group identity among Aboriginal migrants in Melbourne. Ph.D. thesis, A.N.U., Canberra.

BATEMAN, F.E.A. (1948). *Report on Survey of Native Affairs.* Perth: Government Printer.

BECKETT, J. (1964). 'Aborigines, alcohol and assimilation' in Marie Reay (ed.), *Aborigines Now.* Sydney: Angus and Robertson.

*A more detailed Bibliography on Australian Aborigines and the Law is available from the author. It was prepared for the research seminar on Aborigines and the Law held at Monash University in July 1974 and was adapted from the section on 'Australian Aborigines' in John Gilissen (ed.), *Bibliographical Introduction to Legal History and Ethnology*, Université de Bruxelles.

BERLIN, ISAIAH (1961). 'Equality as an ideal', in F.A. Olafson (ed.), *Justice and Social Policy.* New Jersey: Prentice-Hall.

BERNDT, CATHERINE H. (1970). 'Digging sticks and spears, or, the two-sex model', in Fay Gale (ed.), *Woman's Role in Aboriginal Society.* Canberra: A.I.A.S.

BERNDT, R.M. (1965). 'Native Welfare in Western Australia since the "Warburton Controversy" of 1957', *Australian Quarterly* **31.**

—— (1960–1). 'The status of Australian Aborigines', *Quadrant* **5.**

—— (1961). 'Tribal marriage in a changing social order', *U. Western Aust. L. Rev.* **5.**

—— (1963). 'Groups with minimal European associations', in W.E.H. Stanner and Helen Sheils (eds.), *Australian Aboriginal Studies*—a symposium of papers presented at the 1961 Research Conference. Melbourne: Oxford University Press.

—— (1965). 'Law and order in Aboriginal Australia', in R.M. and C.H. Berndt (eds.), *Aboriginal Man in Australia.* Sydney: Angus and Robertson.

—— and C.H. (1951). *From Black to White in South Australia.* Melbourne: Cheshire.

—— and C.H. (eds.) (1965). *Aboriginal Man in Australia.* Sydney: Angus and Robertson.

BISKUP, P. (1973). *Not Slaves Not Citizens: the Aboriginal problem in Western Australia 1898–1954.* St Lucia: University of Queensland Press.

BLOM-COOPER, L. (1963). *The A6 Murder.* Harmondsworth: Penguin.

BOTEIN, BERNARD and STURZ, HERBERT J. (1964). 'Report on pre-trial release practices in Sweden, Denmark, England and Italy to the National Conference on Bail and Criminal Justice', *Journal of the International Commission of Jurists* **5.**

BOULTON, W.W. (1971). *A Guide to Conduct and Etiquette at the Bar of England and Wales*, 5th ed. London: Butterworths.

BOWDEN, K.M. (1965). *Forensic Medicine.* Brisbane: Jacaranda.

BRAZIL, P. (1960). 'A matter of theology', *A.L.J.* **34.**

BRETT, P. and WALLER, P.L. (1971). *Cases and Materials in Criminal Law*, 3rd ed. Melbourne: Butterworths.

BROOM, LEONARD (1970). 'Educational status of Aborigines', *Aust. & N.Z. J. Sociology* **6.**

BROWN, B.J. (1964). 'The "ordinary man" in provocation: Anglo-Saxon attitudes and "unreasonable non-Englishmen" ', *Internat. & Comparative L.Q.* **13.**

—— (ed.) (1969). *Fashion of Law in New Guinea.* Sydney: Butterworths.

BURNS, PETER (1968). 'Status offences—some recent developments in New Zealand and South Australia', *A.L.J.* **42.**

CALVESBERT, A.R. (1974). Aboriginal/police relations in South Australia. Paper presented to research seminar on Aborigines and the Law, Monash University, 12–16 July.

CAMPBELL, E. and WHITMORE, H. (1966). *Freedom in Australia.* Sydney: Sydney University Press.

The Challenge of Crime in a Free Society, a Report by the President's Commission on Law Enforcement and Administration of Justice (1967). Washington, D.C.: Government Printing Office.

CLEAVER, ELDRIDGE (1969). *Soul on Ice.* London: Cape.

COHEN, LUCY KRAMER (ed.) (1960). *The Legal Conscience: selected papers of Felix S. Cohen.* New Haven: Yale University Press.

Commonwealth. Bureau of Census and Statistics (1968). *Official Year Book of the Commonwealth of Australia,* No. 54. Canberra.

——. Department of Territories (1967). *The Australian Aborigines.* Canberra: Government Printer.

COWEN, D.V. (1963). 'African Legal Studies—a survey of the field and the role of the United States', in H.W. Baade (ed.), *African Law, New Law for New Nations*. New York: Oceana.

CRANSTON, R. and ADAMS, B. (1972). 'Legal aid in Australia', *A.L.J.* **46**.

CROSS, RUPERT (1965). 'Paradoxes in prison sentences', *L.Q.R.* **81**.

DANDIE, JAMES N. (1966). 'Costs and legal aid' in R.A. Woodman (ed.), *Record of the Third Commonwealth and Empire Law Conference*. Sydney: Law Book Co.

DAUNTON-FEAR, MARY (1972). 'The fine as a criminal sanction', *Adel. L. Rev.* **4**.

DAVIS, ANTHONY (1971). 'Sentences for sale: a new look at plea bargaining in England and America', *Crim. L. R.*

DENNING, Lord (1967). 'Law and life in our time', *Tasmania U.L. Rev.* **2**.

DEXTER, BARRIE (1974). 'The Commonwealth Department of Aboriginal Affairs: its functions and underlying principles', in Lorna Lippmann (ed.), *Aborigines in the 70's: seminars 1972–73*. Melbourne: Centre for Research into Aboriginal Affairs, Monash University.

DICKINSON, G. (1958). 'The testimony of Aborigines in law courts in the N.T.', *South Pacific* **10**.

—— (1959). 'Kadaitcha', *South Pacific* **10**.

DOUGLAS, WILLIAM O. (1960). 'Vagrancy and arrest on suspicion', *Yale L.J.* **70**.

DUGUID, C. (1965). *No Dying Race*. Adelaide: Rigby.

DUNN, S.S. and TATZ, C.M. (eds.) (1969). *Aborigines and Education*. Melbourne: Sun Books.

The Dynamic Aspects of the Rule of Law in the Modern Age (1965). Geneva: International Commission of Jurists.

DUNSTAN, D.A. (1966). 'Aboriginal land title and employment in South Australia', in I.G. Sharp and C.M. Tatz (eds.), *Aborigines in the Economy*. Brisbane: Jacaranda.

EDWARDS, W.H. (1969). 'Experience in the use of the vernacular as an introductory medium of instruction' in S.S. Dunn and C.M. Tatz (eds.), *Aborigines and Education*. Melbourne: Sun Books.

—— (n.d.). Infanticide amongst the Pitjantjatjara. Unpublished paper.

EGGLESTON, ELIZABETH (1972). 'Alcoholism legislation in Victoria: a critical comment', *Aust. & N.Z. J. Criminology* **5**.

ELKIN, A.P. (1947). 'Aboriginal evidence and justice in North Australia', *Oceania* **17**.

—— (1951). 'Reaction and interaction: a food gathering people and European settlement in Australia', *American Anthropologist* **53**.

—— (1964). *The Australian Aborigines: how to understand them*, 4th ed. Sydney: Angus and Robertson.

EVANS, GARETH (1973). Benign discrimination and the right to equality. Paper presented to the Annual Conference of the Australasian Universities Law Schools Association, Port Moresby.

FITZPATRICK, BRIAN (1958). 'Lesser tribes without the law', *Meanjin* **17**.

FOOTE, CALEB (1958). 'Foreword: comment on the New York Bail Study', *U. Pa. L. Rev.* **106**.

FORTAS, ABE (1967). 'Equal rights—for whom?', *N.Y.U. L. Rev.* **42**.

GALE, FAY (1964). *A Study of Assimilation: part-Aborigines in South Australia*. Adelaide: Libraries Board of South Australia.

—— (1966). 'Patterns of post-European Aboriginal migration in South Australia', *Proceedings of the Royal Geographical Society of Australasia, South Australian Branch (Incorporated)* **67**.

—— (1972). *Urban Aborigines*. Canberra: Australian National University Press.

GINSBERG, MORRIS (1965). *On Justice in Society*. Harmondsworth: Penguin.
GLASBEEK, H.J. and PRENTICE, D.D. (1968). 'The criminal suspect's illusory right of silence in the British Commonwealth', *Cornell L. Rev.* **53**.
GOFFMAN, ERVING (1968). *Asylums*. Harmondsworth: Penguin.
GORTON, P. (1969). The Aboriginal child before the court. Paper presented to Justices' Conference, Port Hedland.
GRAVES, A.A. and COLLETT, A.C. (1972). A study of the nature and origin of Aboriginal petty crime in Port Augusta. Unpublished paper, Adelaide University.
GRAVESON, R.H. (1953). *Status in the Common Law*. London: Athlone Press.
GRIFFITHS, A.R.G. (1970). 'Capital punishment in South Australia, 1836–1964', *Aust. & N.Z. J. Criminology* **3**.
HASLUCK, PAUL (1970). *Black Australians: a survey of native policy in Western Australia, 1829–1897*, 2nd ed. Melbourne: Melbourne University Press.
HIATT, L.R. (1959). 'Social control in Central Arnhem Land', *South Pacific* **10**.
—— (1965). *Kinship and Conflict*. Canberra: Australian National University Press.
HILLIARD, W. (1968). *The People in Between*. London: Hodder and Stoughton.
HOEBEL, E. ADAMSON (1964). *The Law of Primitive Man: a study in comparative legal dynamics*. Cambridge: Harvard University Press.
HOWARD, C. (1961). 'What colour is the "Reasonable Man"?', *Crim. L. R.*
HUGHES, COLIN A. (1965). 'The marriage of Mick and Gladys: a discretion without an appeal' in B. B. Schaffer and D. C. Corbett (eds.), *Decisions: case studies in Australian administration*. Melbourne: Cheshire.
INGLIS, K.S. (1961). *The Stuart Case*. Melbourne: Melbourne University Press.
'Interrogations in New Haven: the impact of Miranda' (1967). *Yale L.J.* **76**.
JACKSON, R.M. (1964). *The Machinery of Justice in England,* 4th ed. Cambridge: Cambridge University Press.
JOHNSON, COLIN (1966). *Wild Cat Falling*. Harmondsworth: Penguin.
JOHNSTON, STANLEY W. and FOX, RICHARD G. (1965). *Correction Handbook of Victoria*. Melbourne: Criminology Department, University of Melbourne.
JONES, H. JULIE (1963). *The History and Training of Victorian Stipendiary Magistrates*. University of Melbourne: Criminology Department. Mimeographed.
JORDAN, A.K. (1966). Drunks, vagrants and prisons: homeless offenders in the State of Victoria. Unpublished paper.
—— (1968). Skid Row men: justice and welfare. Unpublished paper.
KALOKERINOS, A. (1969). 'Some aspects of Aboriginal infant mortality', *Medical Journal of Australia*, **1**.
KRIEWALDT, Mr Justice (1960). 'The application of the criminal law to the Aborigines of the Northern Territory of Australia', *U. Western Aust. L. Rev.* **5**. (Paper edited by G. Sawer).
LACEY, FORREST W. (1953). 'Vagrancy and other crimes of personal condition', *Harvard Law Review* **66**.
LEMAIRE, J.E. (1971). The application of some aspects of European law to Aboriginal natives of Central Australia. LL.M. thesis, University of Sydney.
LEWIN, JULIUS (1941). 'The conflict of native law and common law in South Africa', *S.Af.L.J.* **58**.
LIPPMANN, LORNA (1973). *Words or Blows: racial attitudes in Australia*. Harmondsworth: Penguin.
MCLEAN, CHARLES (1957). *Report upon the Operation of the Aborigines Act 1928 and the Regulations and Orders made thereunder*. Melbourne: Government Printer.

McMEEKIN, D.H. (1969). 'Red, white and *Gray*: equal protection and the American Indian', *Stanford L. Rev.* **21**.
MAITLAND, J. ANGUS (1966). *Law Society of South Australia Incorporated Legal Assistance Scheme.* Mimeographed.
MARCHANT, LESLIE R. (1954). Native administration in Western Australia 1886-1905. B.A. (Hons.) thesis, University of Western Australia, Perth.
MEGGITT, M.J. (1962). *Desert People.* Sydney: Angus and Robertson.
MILTE, K.L. (1968). 'Pre-trial detention', *Aust. & N.Z. J. Criminology* **1**.
MITCHELL, J.C. (1966). 'Theoretical orientations in African urban studies', in M. Banton (ed.), *The Social Anthropology of Complex Societies.* New York: Praeger.
MITCHELL, Justice (1969). *The Aboriginal and the Law.* Mimeographed.
MORRIS, NORVAL (1965). 'Prison in evolution' in Tadeusz Grygier, Howard Jones, John C. Spencer (eds.), *Criminology in Transition: essays in honour of Hermann Mannheim.* London: Tavistock.
—— and HOWARD, C. (1964). *Studies in Criminal Law.* Oxford: Oxford University Press.
MULVANEY, D.J. (1969). *The Prehistory of Australia.* London: Thames and Hudson.
MURRAY, B.L. (1965). Procedure on the interrogation of suspected persons by the police. Victorian Parliament, unpublished Parliamentary Paper.
MURTAGH, JOHN M. (1966). 'Arrests for public intoxication', *Fordham Law Review* **35**.
—— (1967). 'Status offences and due process of law', *Fordham Law Review* **36**.
MYRDAL, G. (1962). *An American Dilemma,* 20th ed. New York: Harper and Row.
NASH, G. (1965). *Paul's Justices of the Peace,* 2nd ed. Sydney: Law Book Co.
O'REGAN, R.S. (1972a). 'Aborigines, Melanesians and dying declarations', *Internat. & Comp. L.Q.* **21**.
—— (1972b). 'Duress and murder', *Mod. L. Rev.* **35**.
—— (1972c). 'Provocation and homicide in Papua and New Guinea', *Melanesian L. J.* **1**.
PARKER, DOROTHY (1974). Social agents as generators of crime. Case study: Aborigines in Western Australia. Paper presented to Australian Institute of Aboriginal Studies Conference, Canberra.
PATERSON, JENNIFER I. (1957). Native administration and welfare in Western Australia 1905-1936. B.A. (Hons.) thesis, University of Western Australia, Perth.
PERKINS, ROLLIN M. (1958). 'The vagrancy concept', *Hastings Law Journal* **9**.
RANKIN, ANNE (1964). 'The effect of pretrial detention', *N.Y.U.L. Rev.* **39**.
RANKIN, JAMES G. (1971). 'The size and nature of the misuse of alcohol and drugs in Australia', in L.G. Kiloh (ed.), *29th International Congress on Alcoholism and Drug Dependence.* Sydney: Butterworths.
REAY, MARIE (ed.) (1964). *Aborigines Now.* Sydney: Angus and Robertson.
'Report of Legal Aid Committee for the year ending 30th June, 1967' (1968). *L.I.J.* **42**.
'Responsibility of defending counsel' (1935). *A.L.J.* **9**.
ROBINSON, MICHAEL V. (1969). 'Imprisonment of Aborigines and Part-aborigines in Western Australia' in R.M. Berndt (ed.), *Thinking About Australian Aboriginal Welfare.* Perth: University of Western Australia Press.
ROGERS, H. (1949). *Native Administration in the Union of South Africa,* 2nd ed. Pretoria: Government Printer.

ROGERS, PETER H. (1973). *The Industrialists and the Aborigines.* Sydney: Angus and Robertson.
ROLLO, G.J. (n.d.). Notes on the Aboriginal problem. Unpublished paper.
ROWLEY, C.D. (1962). 'Aborigines and other Australians', *Oceania* **32**.
—— (1966). 'Some questions of causation in relation to Aboriginal affairs' in I.G. Sharp and C.M. Tatz (eds.), *Aborigines in the Economy.* Brisbane: Jacaranda.
—— (1967a). 'The Aboriginal householder', *Quadrant* **11**.
—— (1967b). 'The villager and the nomad: Aboriginals and New Guineans', *New Guinea* **2**.
—— (1970). *The Destruction of Aboriginal Society.* Canberra: Australian National University Press.
—— (1971). *Outcasts in White Australia.* Canberra: Australian National University Press.
RYAN, JOHN V. (1967). 'The last days of bail', *Journal of Criminal Law, Criminology and Police Science* **58**.
ST JOHN, R.J.B. (1968). 'Police in Court', *Quadrant* **12**.
SARGANT, W. (1959). *Battle for the Mind.* London: Pan.
SAWER, G. (1961). 'Judge Martin Kriewaldt: nine years of the Northern Territory Supreme Court', *Adelaide Law Review* **1**.
—— (1965). *Law in Society.* Oxford: Oxford University Press.
—— (1966). 'The Australian Constitution and the Australian Aborigine', *F.L. Rev.* **2**.
—— (1969). 'Comment', *Public Law.*
—— (1971). 'The guilty accused', *The Summons* (magazine of the University of Melbourne Law Students' Society).
SHARP, I.G. and TATZ, C.M. (eds.) (1966). *Aborigines in the Economy.* Brisbane: Jacaranda.
SHEARER, IVAN (n.d.). *Some recent legislation affecting rights of Aborigines in South Australia.* Mimeographed.
SILVERSTEIN, L. (1965). *Defense of the Poor in Criminal Cases in American State Courts.* Chicago: American Bar Foundation.
SIMONS, H.J. (1949). 'The law and its administration' in E. Hellman (ed.), *Handbook on Race Relations in South Africa.* Cape Town: Oxford University Press.
SIMPSON, G.E. and YINGER, J. MILTON (1965). *Racial and Cultural Minorities,* 3rd ed. New York: Harper and Row.
SMITH, MICHAEL (1970). 'Tribal sovereignty and the 1968 Indian Bill of Rights', *Civil Rights Digest.*
South Australia (1959). *Report of the Royal Commission in regard to Rupert Max Stuart.* Adelaide: Government Printer.
SPIGELMAN, JAMES J. (1969). 'Poverty and the law—the limitations of Australian legal aid', *Aust. & N.Z. J. Criminology* **2**.
STANNER, W.E.H. and SHEILS, HELEN (eds.) (1963). *Australian Aboriginal Studies: a symposium of papers presented at the 1961 Research Conference.* Melbourne: Oxford University Press.
STEPHEN, Sir JAMES FITZJAMES (1883). *A History of the Criminal Law of England,* vol. III. London: Macmillan.
STEVENS, FRANK (1969). 'Protection or persecution?: Aboriginal policy in North Australia', *Dissent,* Winter.
—— (1974). *Aborigines in the Northern Territory Cattle Industry.* Canberra: Australian National University Press.

STOLLER, ALAN (1969). 'Alcoholism: detection, diagnosis and assessment', in J.G. Rankin (ed.), *Alcoholism: problems in treatment.* Melbourne: Sandoz.

STREHLOW, T.G.H. (1936). 'Notes on native evidence and its value', *Oceania* **6**.

STUBBS, J. (1966). *The Hidden People: poverty in Australia.* Melbourne: Cheshire-Lansdowne.

Study of Equality in the Administration of Justice, Report Submitted by the Special Rapporteur Mr. Mohammed Ahmed Abu Rennat (1969). U.N. Economic and Social Council, E/CN. 4/Sub. 2/296, 10 June.

'A study of the administration of bail in New York City' (1958). *U. Pa. L. Rev.* **106**.

SYKES, GRESHAM (1962). 'The society of captives' in N. Johnston, L. Savitz and M.E. Wolfgang (eds.), *The Sociology of Punishment and Correction.* New York: Wiley.

TAFT, RONALD (1970). 'Attitudes of Western Australians towards Aborigines' in *Attitudes and Social Conditions.* Canberra: Australian National University Press.

TATZ, C.M. (1963). 'Queensland's Aborigines: natural justice and the rule of law', *Australian Quarterly* **35**.

—— (1964a). Aboriginal administration in the Northern Territory of Australia. Ph.D. thesis, Australian National University, Canberra.

—— (1964b). 'Commonwealth Aboriginal policy', *Australian Quarterly* **36**.

—— (1965). 'Some Aboriginal thoughts', *Dissent*, Spring.

—— (1966). 'Aborigines: equality or inequality', *Australian Quarterly* **38**.

—— (1967). 'The Centre for Research into Aboriginal Affairs', *A.I.A.S. Newsletter*, **2**.

—— (1972). 'Aborigines: law and political development', in F.S. Stevens (ed.), *Racism: the Australian Experience*, Vol. 2 *Black versus White.* Sydney: A.N.Z. Book Co.

TOBIN, P. (n.d.). *Fringe dwelling rural Aborigines and the law in New South Wales: preliminary investigation and report.* Mimeographed.

UNESCO (1952). *The Race Concept: results of an inquiry.* Paris.

WENTWORTH, W.C. (1967). 'A policy for Aboriginals', *New Guinea* **2**.

—— (1969). 'The position of the Aboriginals in law and society', *Justice* (Journal of the International Commission of Jurists. Australian Section), No. 2, June.

Western Australia (1905). *Report of the Royal Commission on the Condition of the Natives* (*W.E. Roth, Royal Commissioner*). Perth: Government Printer.

—— (1927). *Report of the Royal Commission of inquiry into alleged killing and burning of bodies of Aborigines in east Kimberley and into police methods when effecting arrests.* Perth: Government Printer.

—— (1935). *Report of the Royal Commissioner appointed to investigate, report, and advise upon matters in relation to the condition and treatment of Aborigines* (*H.D. Moseley, Royal Commissioner*). Perth: Government Printer.

WHITAKER, BEN (1964). *The Police.* London: Penguin.

WHITE, ISOBEL M. (1970). 'Aboriginal women's status: a paradox resolved', in Fay Gale (ed.), *Woman's Role in Aboriginal Society.* Canberra: A.I.A.S.

WILLIAMS, GLANVILLE (1963). *The Proof of Guilt.* London: Stevens.

WILLIAMS, MASLYN (1964). *Stone Age Island.* London: Collins.

WILLIS, J.E. (1973). 'Legal aid in criminal proceedings—the Public Solicitor's Office', *M.U.L.R.* **9**.

WILSON, J. (1961). Authority and leadership in a 'new-style' Australian Aboriginal community: Pindan, Western Australia. M.A. thesis, University of Western Australia, Perth.

WOODMAN, R.A. (ed.) (1966). *Record of the Third Commonwealth and Empire Law Conference.* Sydney: Law Book Company.
WOOTTON, BARBARA (1959). *Social Science and Social Pathology.* London: Allen and Unwin.
WURM, S.A. (1963a). 'Aboriginal languages and the law', *U. Western Aust. L. Rev.* **6**.
—— (1963b). *Some Remarks on the Role of Language in the Assimilation of Australian Aborigines.* Canberra: Linguistic Circle of Canberra Publications. Series A—Occasional Papers, No. 1.
ZELDITCH, MORRIS (1968). 'Social status', *International Encyclopedia of Social Sciences*, vol. 15. London and Glencoe: Macmillan Co. and Free Press.

INDEX

TABLE OF STATUTES

TABLE OF CASES

Elizabeth Eggleston was admitted as a barrister and solicitor of the Supreme Court of Victoria in 1957. During postgraduate study in Law at Berkeley, California, she visited the Navajo Indian Reservation and became interested in the legal problems of racial minorities. After some years' legal practice, she therefore began the research on which this book is based and for which she was awarded a Ph.D. by Monash University.

Dr Eggleston spent nearly a year in outback South and Western Australia collecting data for this study. She has, since then, maintained her interest in the comparative study of indigenous peoples and has spent nine months in the United States studying criminal justice as applied to the American Indians. She is at present a senior lecturer in law and Director of the Centre for Research into Aboriginal Affairs at Monash University. She is co-author of *Cases and Materials on Industrial Law in Australia* and co-editor of *Better Health for Aborigines?*

Designed by Philippa Walker
Text set in 10 point Linotype Garamond two point leaded and printed on 85 gsm Burnie English Finish at The Griffin Press, Adelaide, South Australia

/22/

ABORIGINAL POPUL

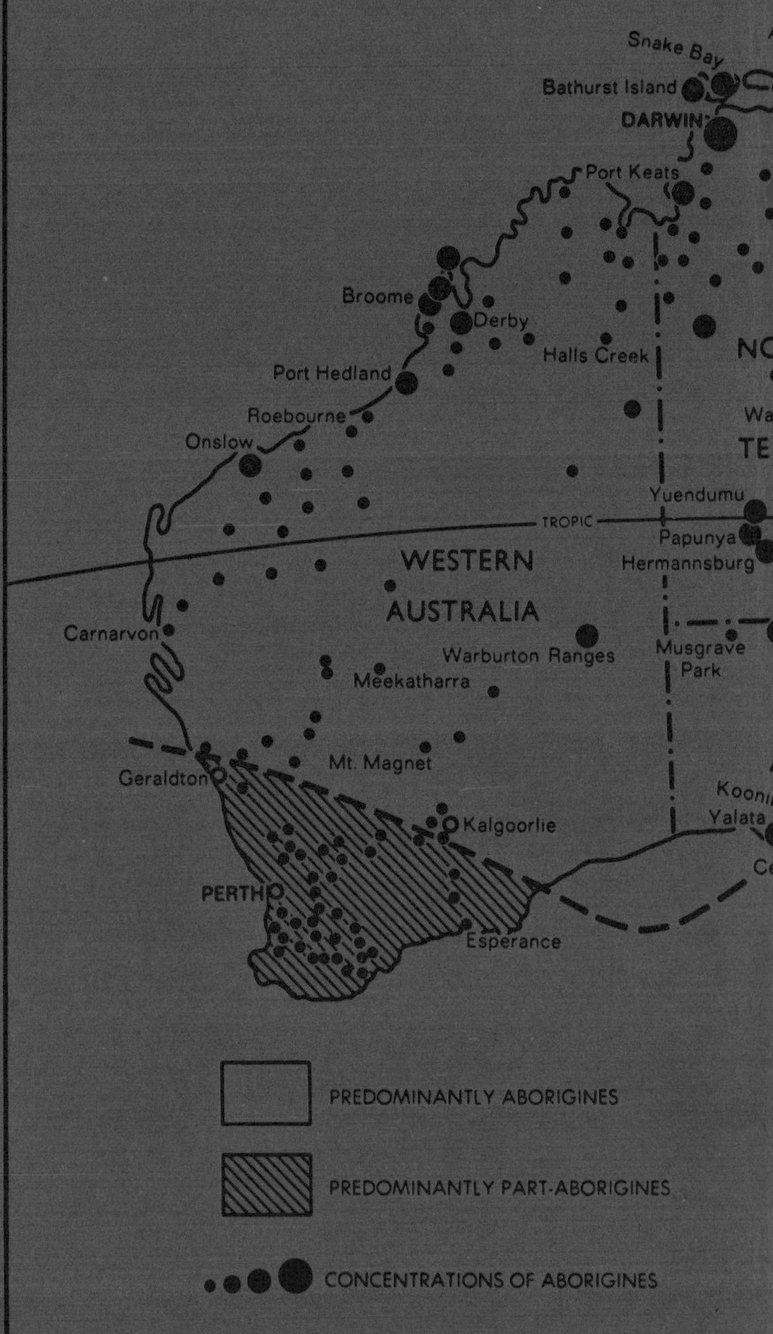